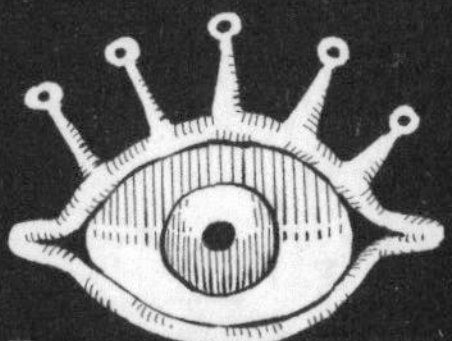

The Country Without Humans vol. 2

STORY & ART BY IWATOBINEKO

CONTENTS

Chapter 6

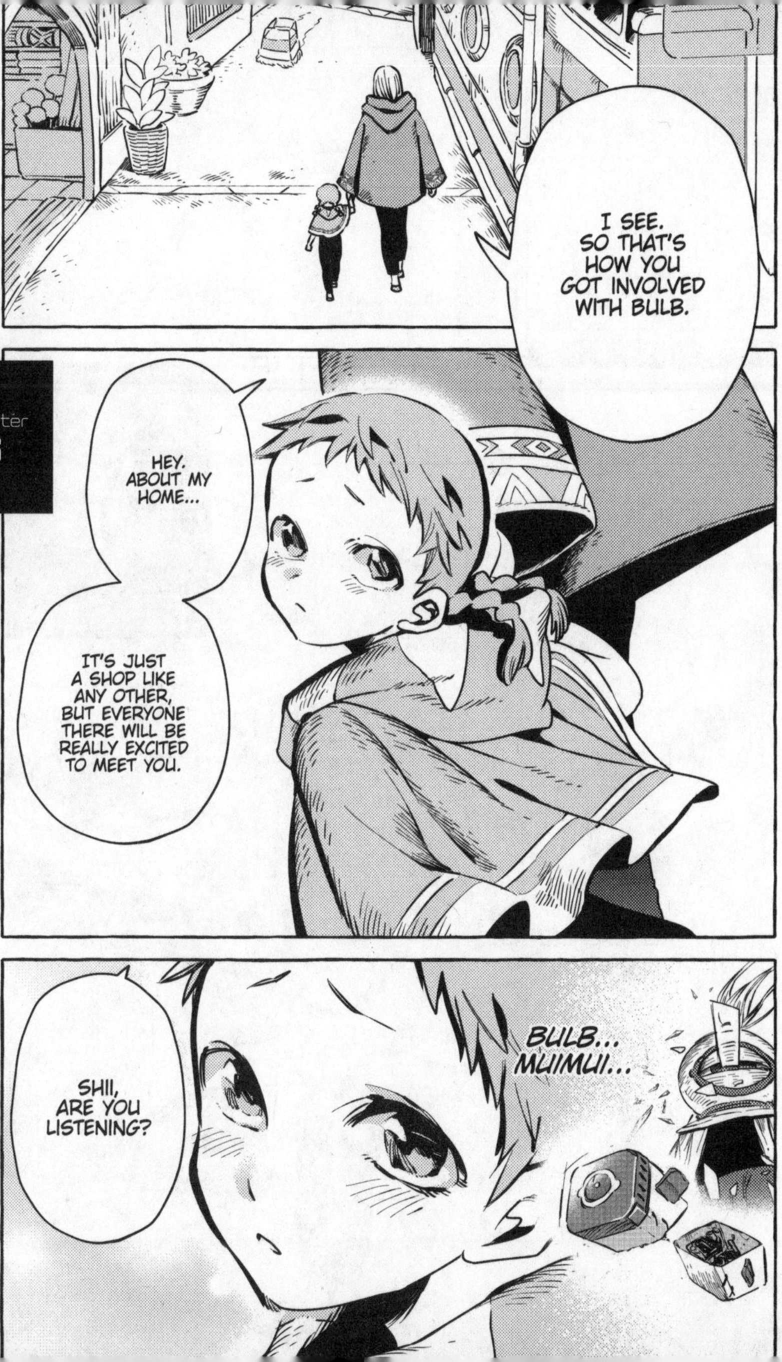
I SEE. SO THAT'S HOW YOU GOT INVOLVED WITH BULB.
HEY. ABOUT MY HOME...
IT'S JUST A SHOP LIKE ANY OTHER, BUT EVERYONE THERE WILL BE REALLY EXCITED TO MEET YOU.
BULB... MUIMUI...
SHII, ARE YOU LISTENING?

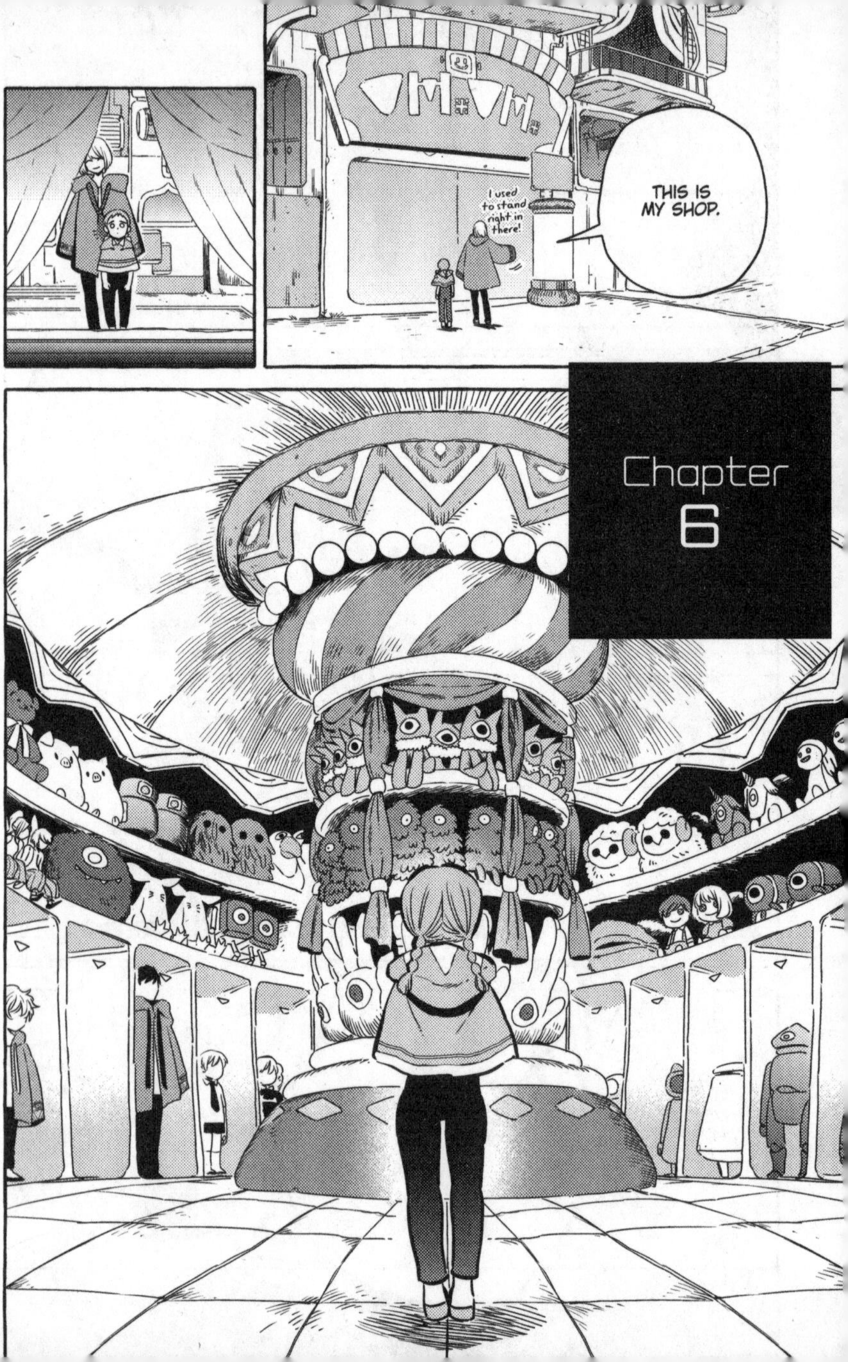
THIS IS MY SHOP.
I used to stand right in there!
Chapter 6

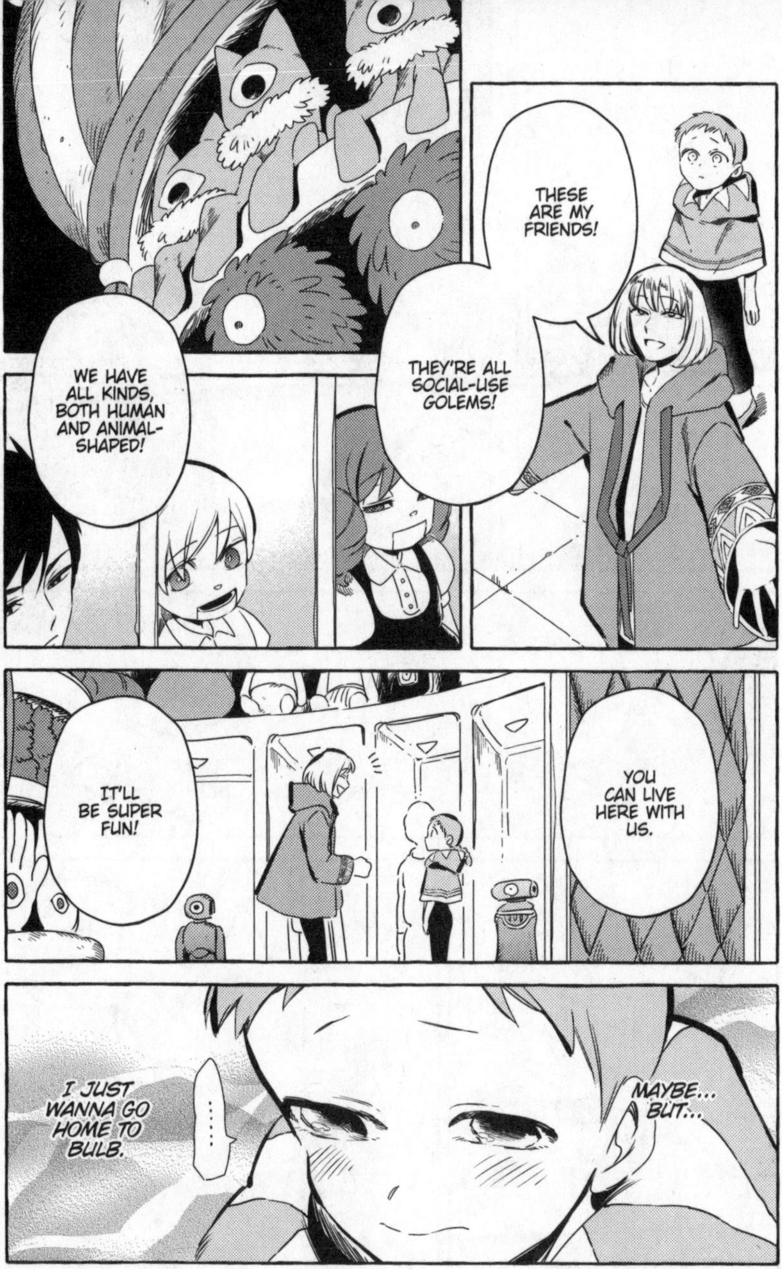
THESE ARE MY FRIENDS!
THEY'RE ALL SOCIAL-USE GOLEMS!
WE HAVE ALL KINDS, BOTH HUMAN AND ANIMAL-SHAPED!
YOU CAN LIVE HERE WITH US.
IT'LL BE SUPER FUN!
MAYBE... BUT...
......
I JUST WANNA GO HOME TO BULB.

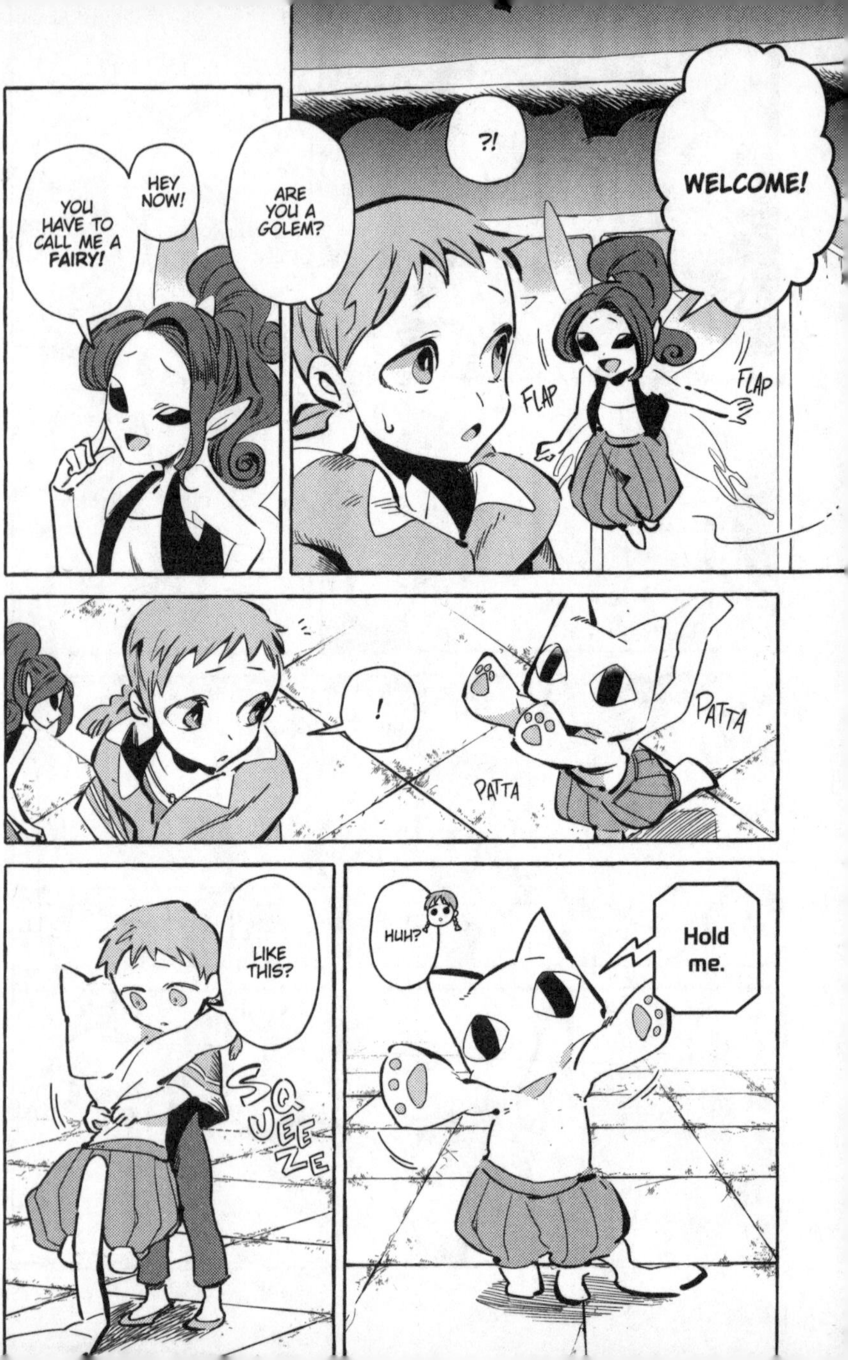
WELCOME!
?!
FLAP
FLAP
ARE YOU A GOLEM?
HEY NOW!
YOU HAVE TO CALL ME A FAIRY!
PATTA
PATTA
!
Hold me.
HUH?
LIKE THIS?
SQUEEZE

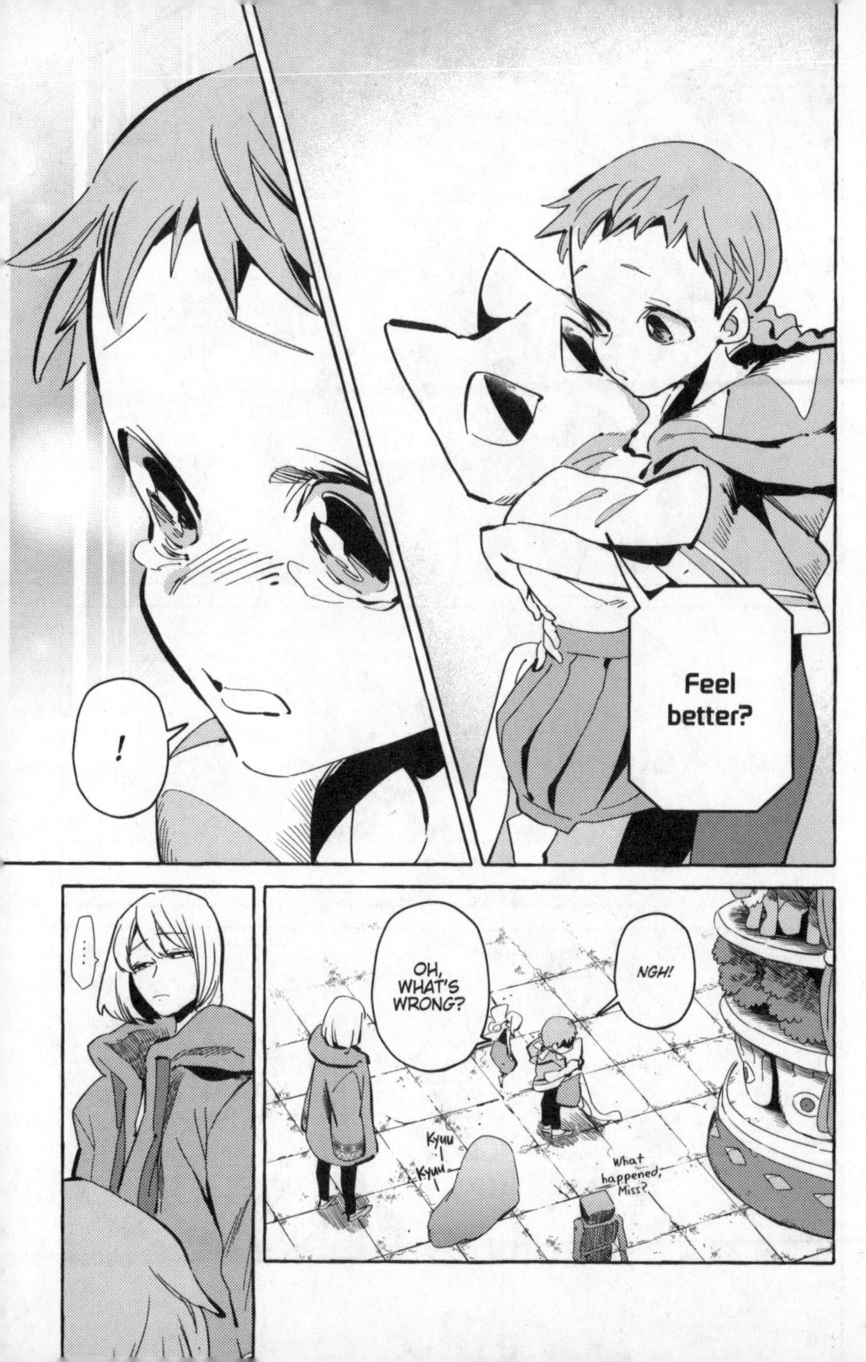
Feel better?
!
NGH!
OH, WHAT'S WRONG?
What happened, Miss?
Kyuu Kyuu
...

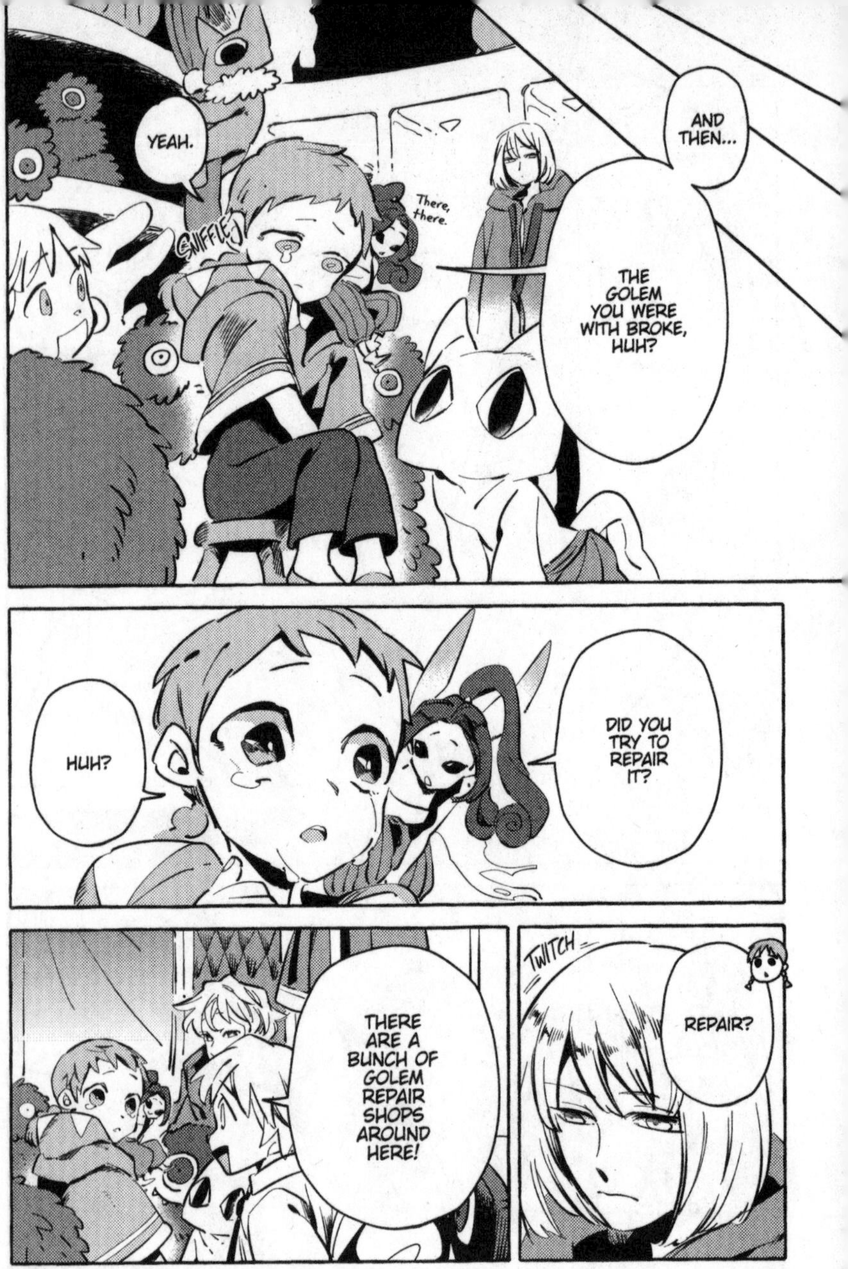
AND THEN...
THE GOLEM YOU WERE WITH BROKE, HUH?
YEAH.
SNIFFLE
There, there.
DID YOU TRY TO REPAIR IT?
HUH?
TWITCH
REPAIR?
THERE ARE A BUNCH OF GOLEM REPAIR SHOPS AROUND HERE!

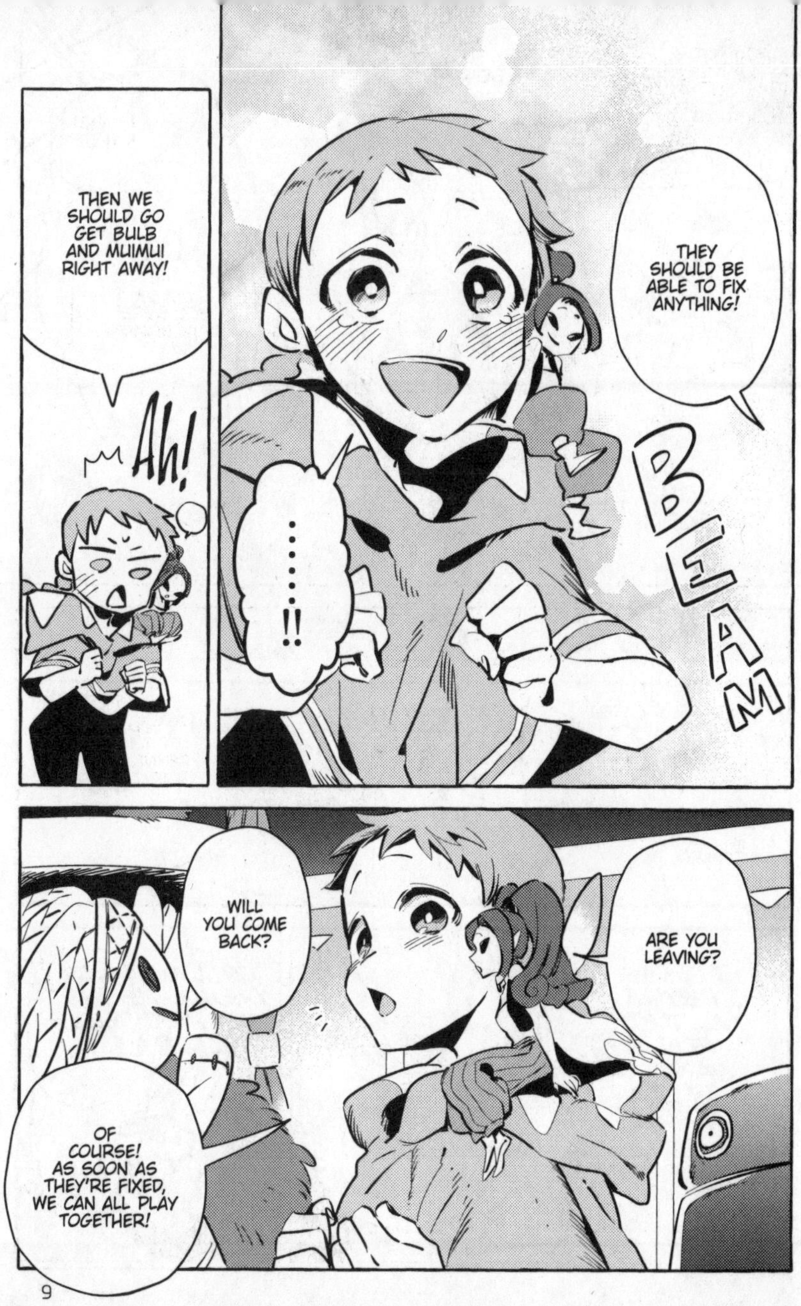
THEY SHOULD BE ABLE TO FIX ANYTHING!
BEAM
......!!
THEN WE SHOULD GO GET BULB AND MUIMUI RIGHT AWAY!
Ah!
ARE YOU LEAVING?
WILL YOU COME BACK?
OF COURSE! AS SOON AS THEY'RE FIXED, WE CAN ALL PLAY TOGETHER!

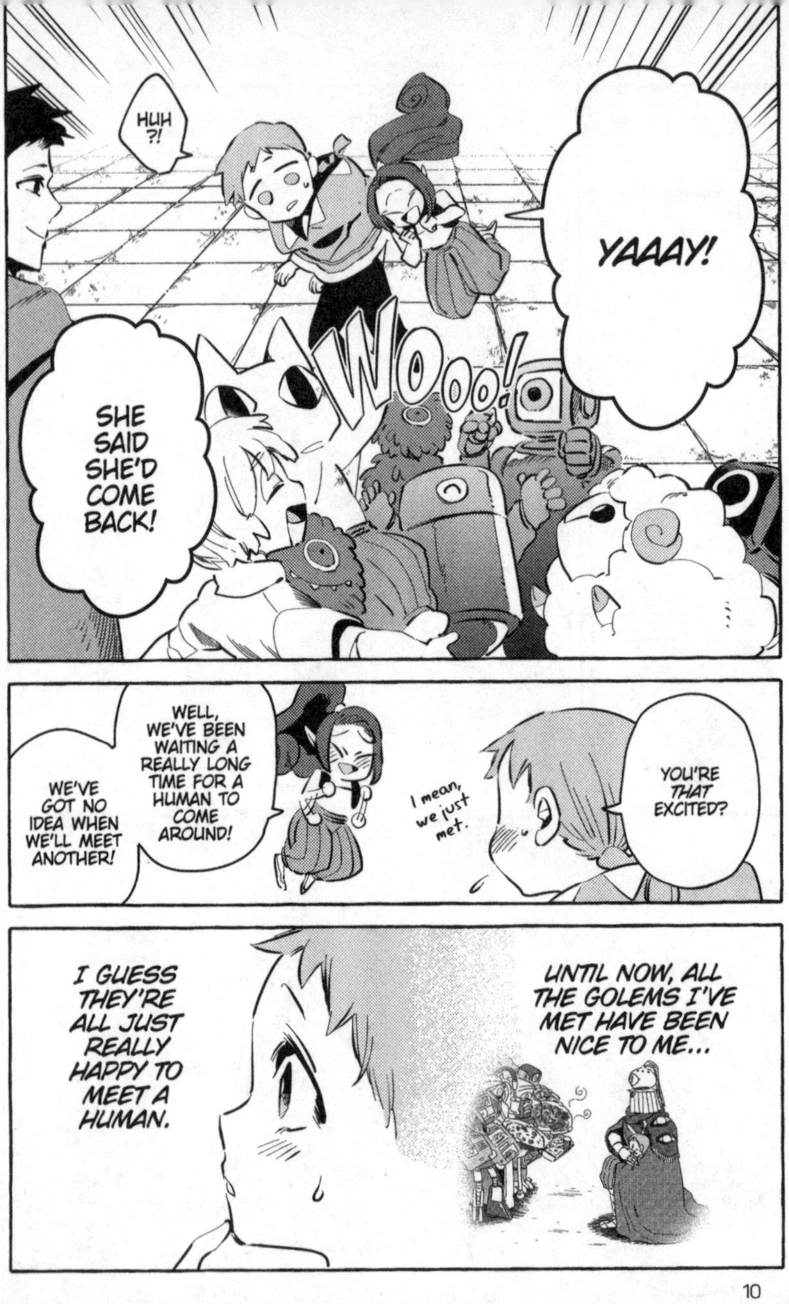
YAAAY!
HUH ?!
WOOO!
SHE SAID SHE'D COME BACK!
YOU'RE THAT EXCITED?
I mean, we just met.
WELL, WE'VE BEEN WAITING A REALLY LONG TIME FOR A HUMAN TO COME AROUND!
WE'VE GOT NO IDEA WHEN WE'LL MEET ANOTHER!
UNTIL NOW, ALL THE GOLEMS I'VE MET HAVE BEEN NICE TO ME...
I GUESS THEY'RE ALL JUST REALLY HAPPY TO MEET A HUMAN.

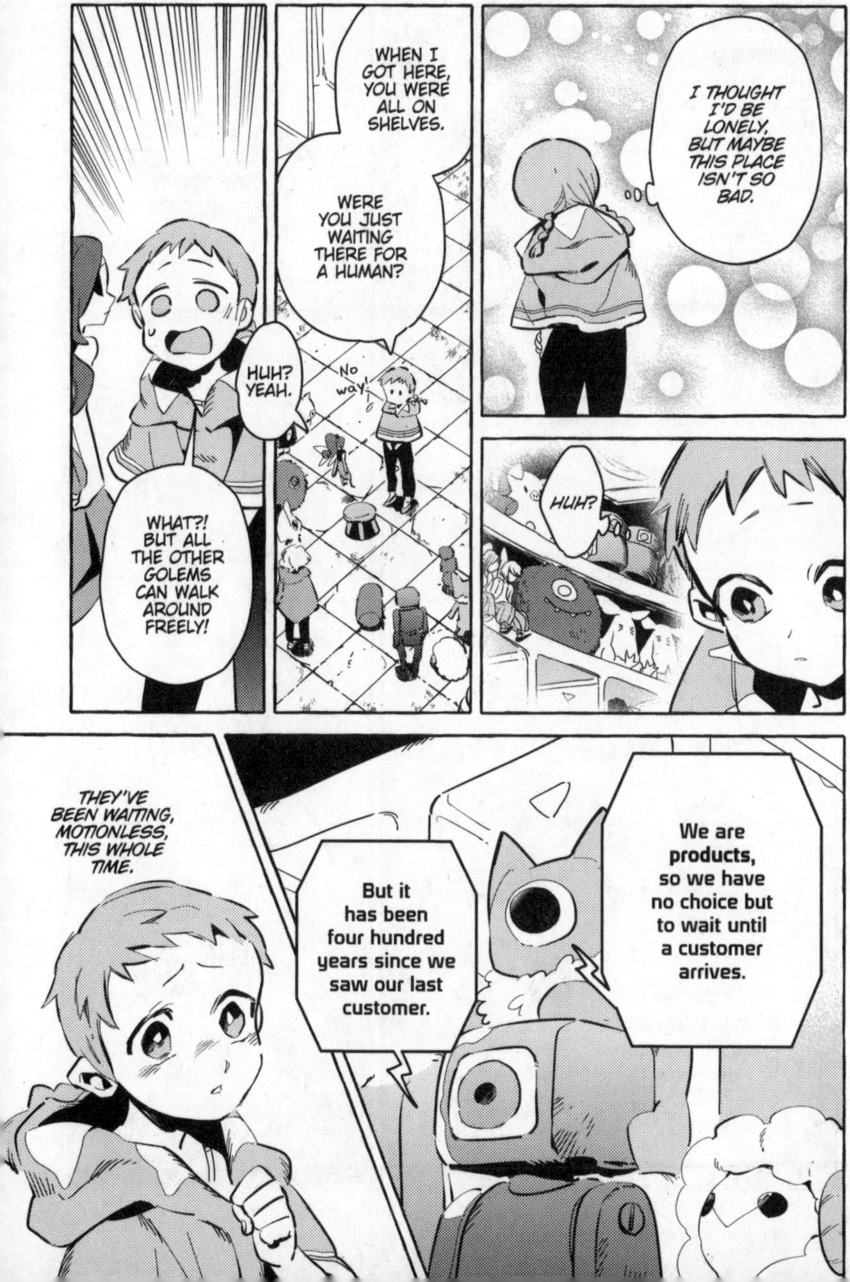
I THOUGHT I'D BE LONELY, BUT MAYBE THIS PLACE ISN'T SO BAD.
HUH?
WHEN I GOT HERE, YOU WERE ALL ON SHELVES.
WERE YOU JUST WAITING THERE FOR A HUMAN?
No way!
HUH? YEAH.
WHAT?! BUT ALL THE OTHER GOLEMS CAN WALK AROUND FREELY!
We are products, so we have no choice but to wait until a customer arrives.
But it has been four hundred years since we saw our last customer.
THEY'VE BEEN WAITING, MOTIONLESS, THIS WHOLE TIME.

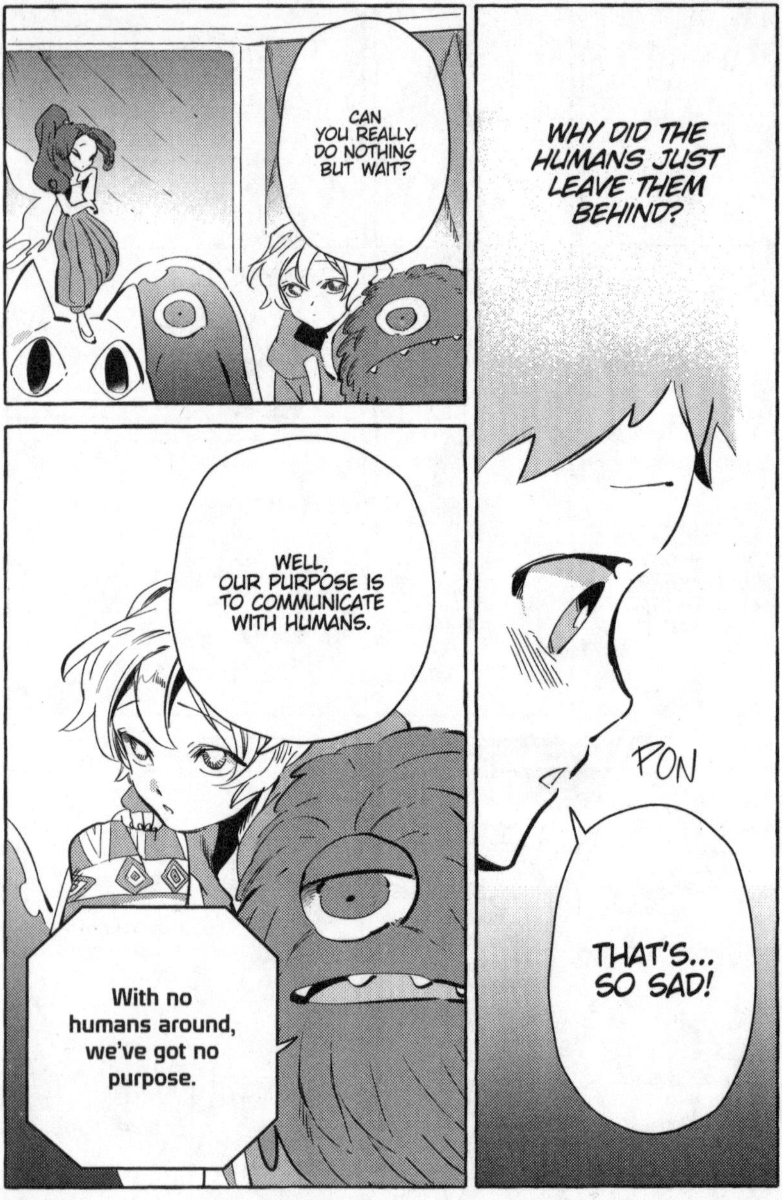
WHY DID THE HUMANS JUST LEAVE THEM BEHIND?
PON
THAT'S... SO SAD!
CAN YOU REALLY DO NOTHING BUT WAIT?
WELL, OUR PURPOSE IS TO COMMUNICATE WITH HUMANS.
With no humans around, we've got no purpose.

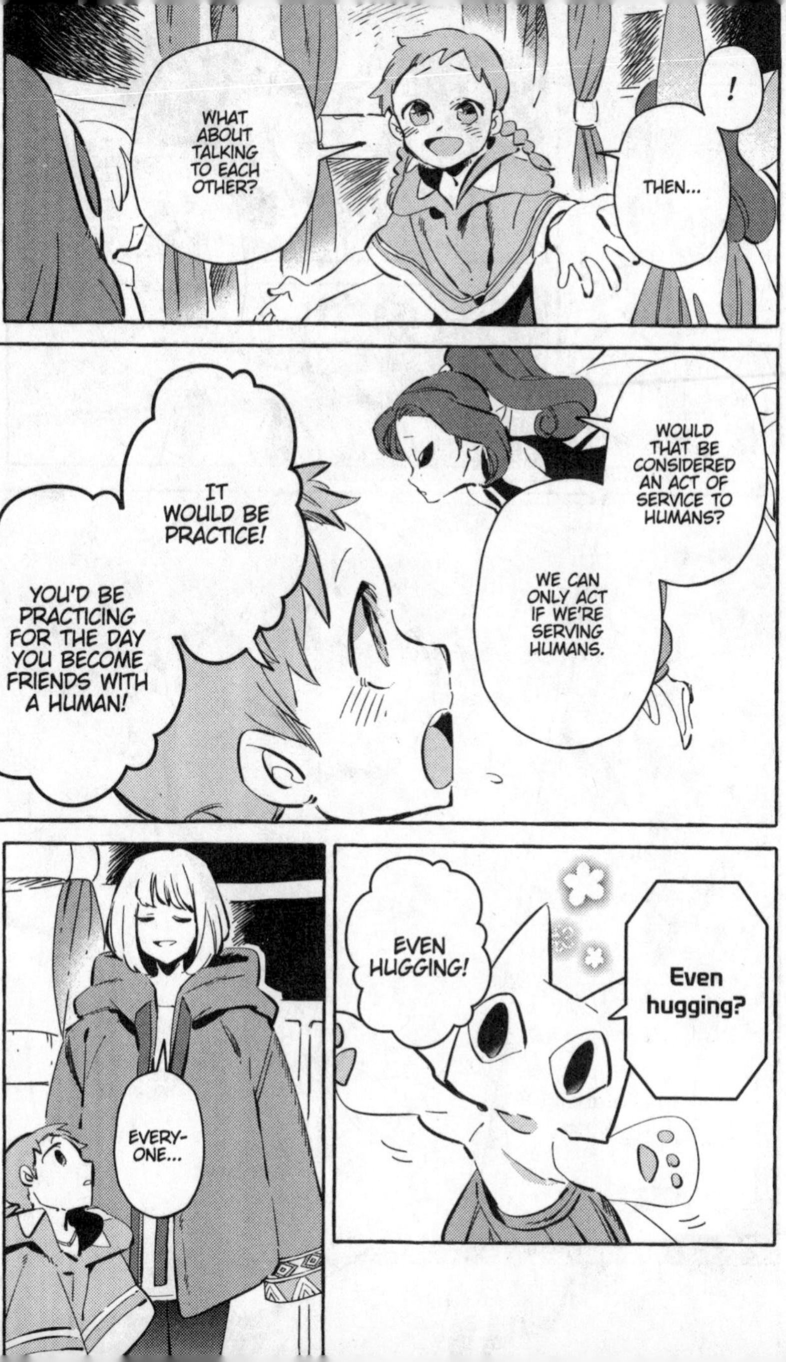
!
THEN...
WHAT ABOUT TALKING TO EACH OTHER?
WOULD THAT BE CONSIDERED AN ACT OF SERVICE TO HUMANS?
WE CAN ONLY ACT IF WE'RE SERVING HUMANS.
IT WOULD BE PRACTICE!
YOU'D BE PRACTICING FOR THE DAY YOU BECOME FRIENDS WITH A HUMAN!
Even hugging?
EVEN HUGGING!
EVERY-ONE...

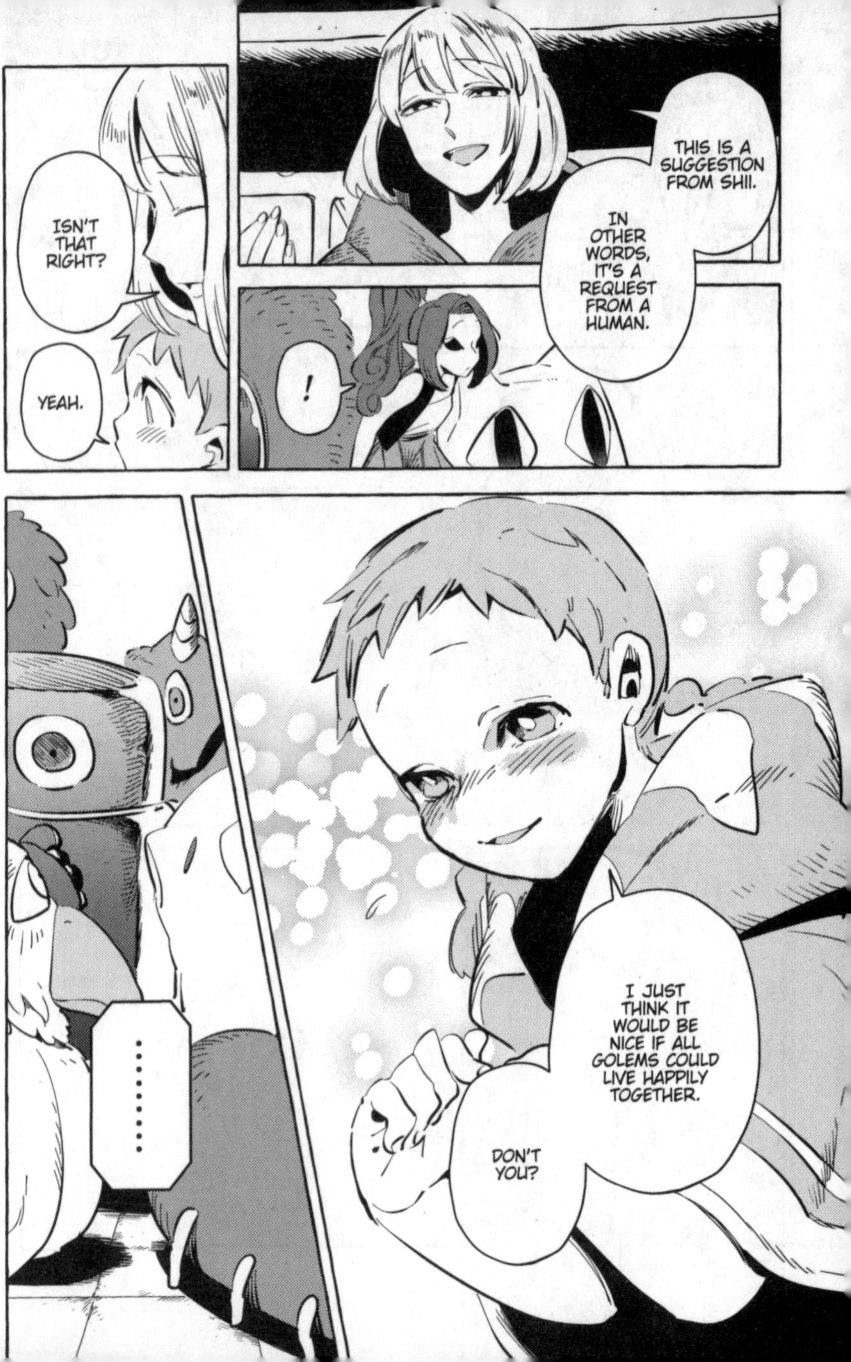
THIS IS A SUGGESTION FROM SHII.
IN OTHER WORDS, IT'S A REQUEST FROM A HUMAN.
!
ISN'T THAT RIGHT?
YEAH.
I JUST THINK IT WOULD BE NICE IF ALL GOLEMS COULD LIVE HAPPILY TOGETHER.
DON'T YOU?
....

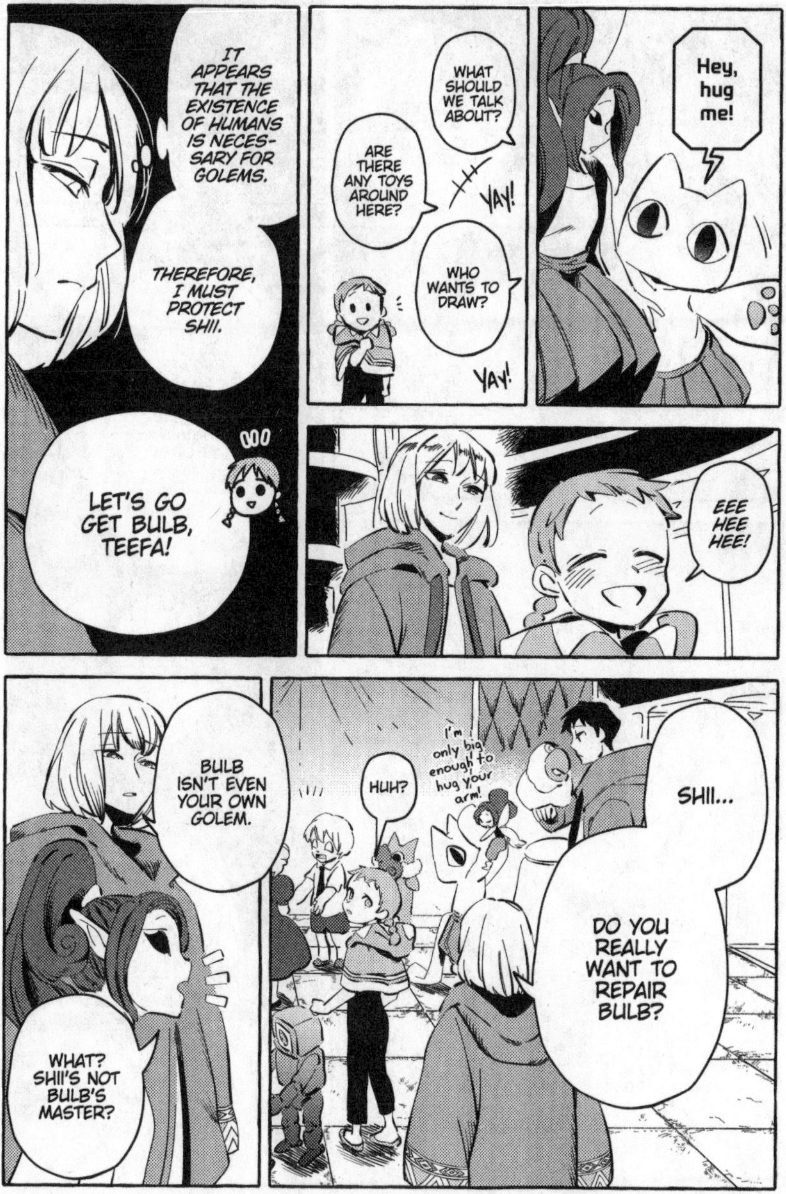
Hey, hug me!
WHAT SHOULD WE TALK ABOUT?
ARE THERE ANY TOYS AROUND HERE?
YAY!
WHO WANTS TO DRAW?
YAY!
EEE HEE HEE!
IT APPEARS THAT THE EXISTENCE OF HUMANS IS NECESSARY FOR GOLEMS.
THEREFORE, I MUST PROTECT SHII.
LET'S GO GET BULB, TEEFA!
SHII...
I'm only big enough to hug your arm!
HUH?
DO YOU REALLY WANT TO REPAIR BULB?
BULB ISN'T EVEN YOUR OWN GOLEM.
WHAT? SHII'S NOT BULB'S MASTER?

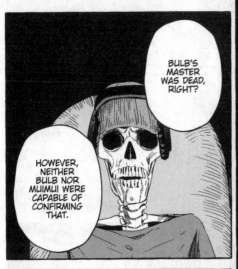

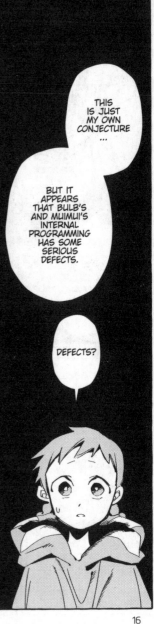

THIS IS JUST MY OWN CONJECTURE ...
BUT IT APPEARS THAT BULB'S AND MUIMUI'S INTERNAL PROGRAMMING HAS SOME SERIOUS DEFECTS.
DEFECTS?
BULB'S MASTER WAS DEAD, RIGHT?
HOWEVER, NEITHER BULB NOR MUIMUI WERE CAPABLE OF CONFIRMING THAT.
IF THEY WERE OFFICIALLY PRODUCED GOLEMS...
THEY WOULD HAVE HEALTH METERS TO ENSURE THAT HUMANS GET TAKEN IN FOR MEDICAL TREATMENT THE MOMENT ILLNESS IS DETECTED.
TO LEAVE A CORPSE UNATTENDED FOR SO LONG IS UNHEARD OF.

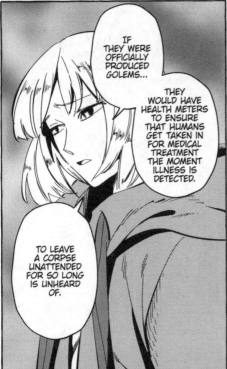

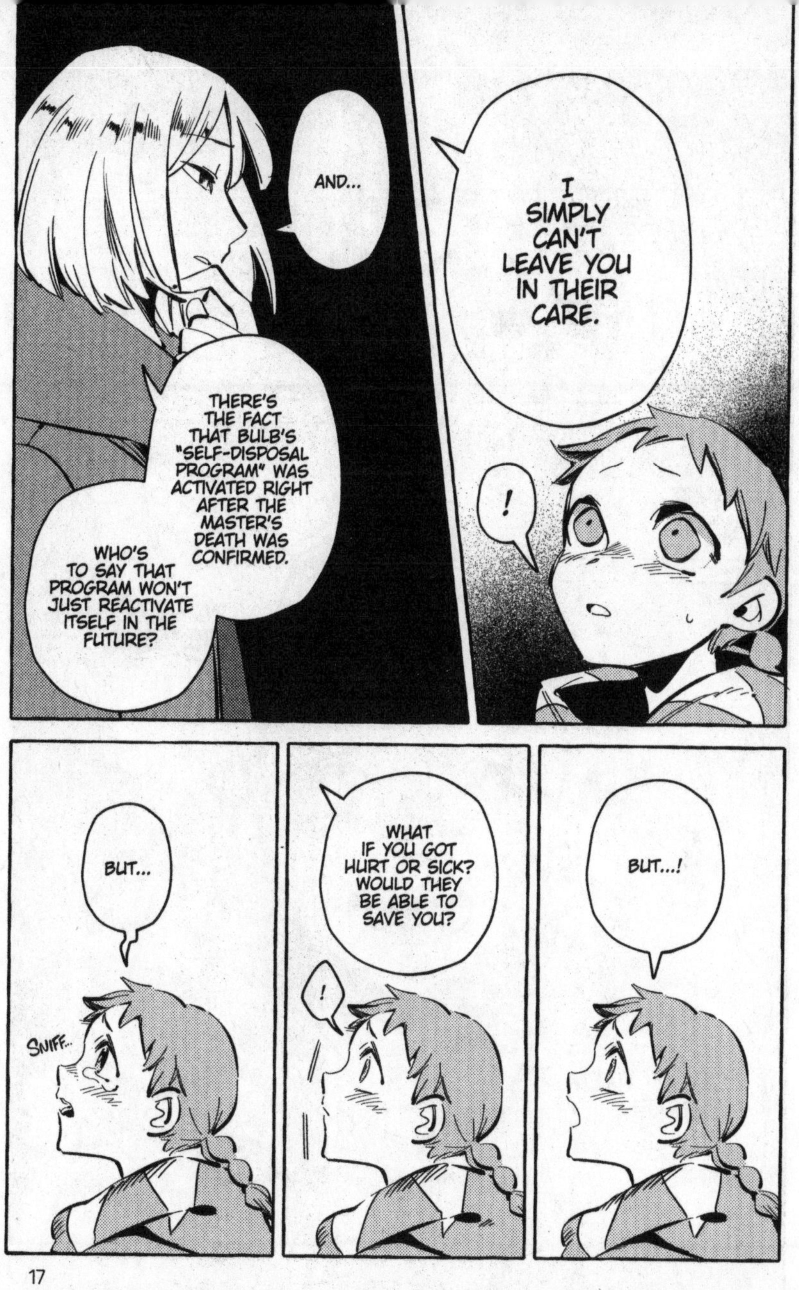
I SIMPLY CAN'T LEAVE YOU IN THEIR CARE.
!
AND...
THERE'S THE FACT THAT BULB'S "SELF-DISPOSAL PROGRAM" WAS ACTIVATED RIGHT AFTER THE MASTER'S DEATH WAS CONFIRMED.
WHO'S TO SAY THAT PROGRAM WON'T JUST REACTIVATE ITSELF IN THE FUTURE?
BUT...!
WHAT IF YOU GOT HURT OR SICK? WOULD THEY BE ABLE TO SAVE YOU?
!
BUT...
SNIFF...

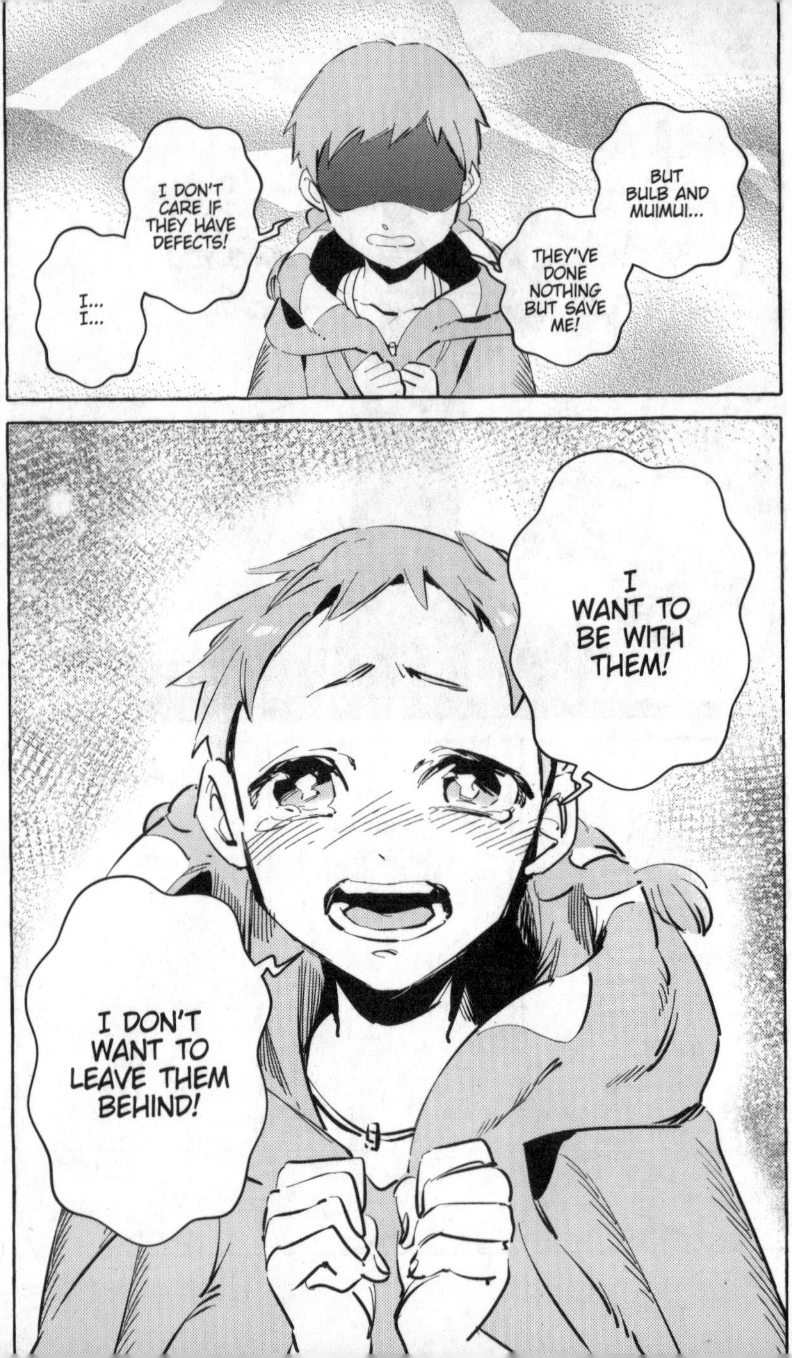
BUT BULB AND MUIMUI...
THEY'VE DONE NOTHING BUT SAVE ME!
I DON'T CARE IF THEY HAVE DEFECTS!
I... I...
I WANT TO BE WITH THEM!
I DON'T WANT TO LEAVE THEM BEHIND!

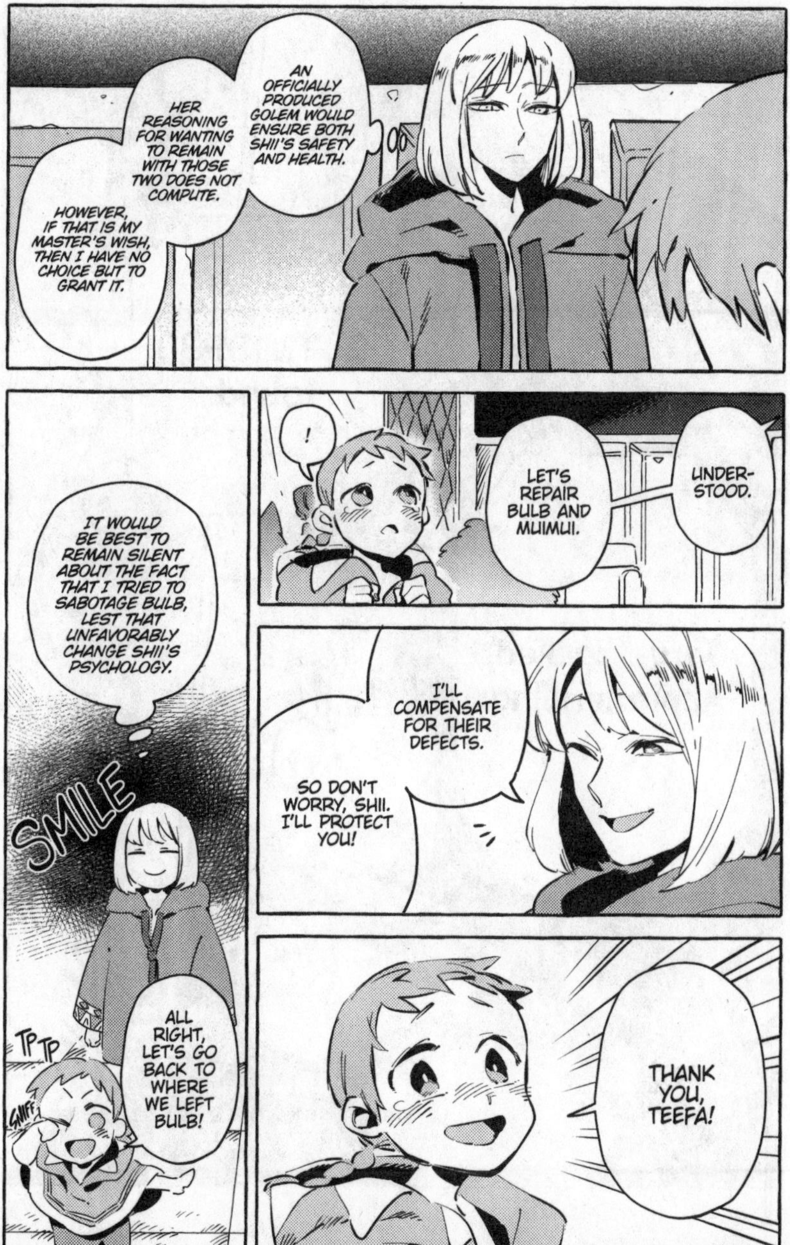
AN OFFICIALLY PRODUCED GOLEM WOULD ENSURE BOTH SHII'S SAFETY AND HEALTH.
HER REASONING FOR WANTING TO REMAIN WITH THOSE TWO DOES NOT COMPUTE.
HOWEVER, IF THAT IS MY MASTER'S WISH, THEN I HAVE NO CHOICE BUT TO GRANT IT.
UNDER-STOOD.
LET'S REPAIR BULB AND MUIMUI.
!
I'LL COMPENSATE FOR THEIR DEFECTS.
SO DON'T WORRY, SHII. I'LL PROTECT YOU!
THANK YOU, TEEFA!
IT WOULD BE BEST TO REMAIN SILENT ABOUT THE FACT THAT I TRIED TO SABOTAGE BULB, LEST THAT UNFAVORABLY CHANGE SHII'S PSYCHOLOGY.
SMILE
ALL RIGHT, LET'S GO BACK TO WHERE WE LEFT BULB!
TP TP
SNIFF

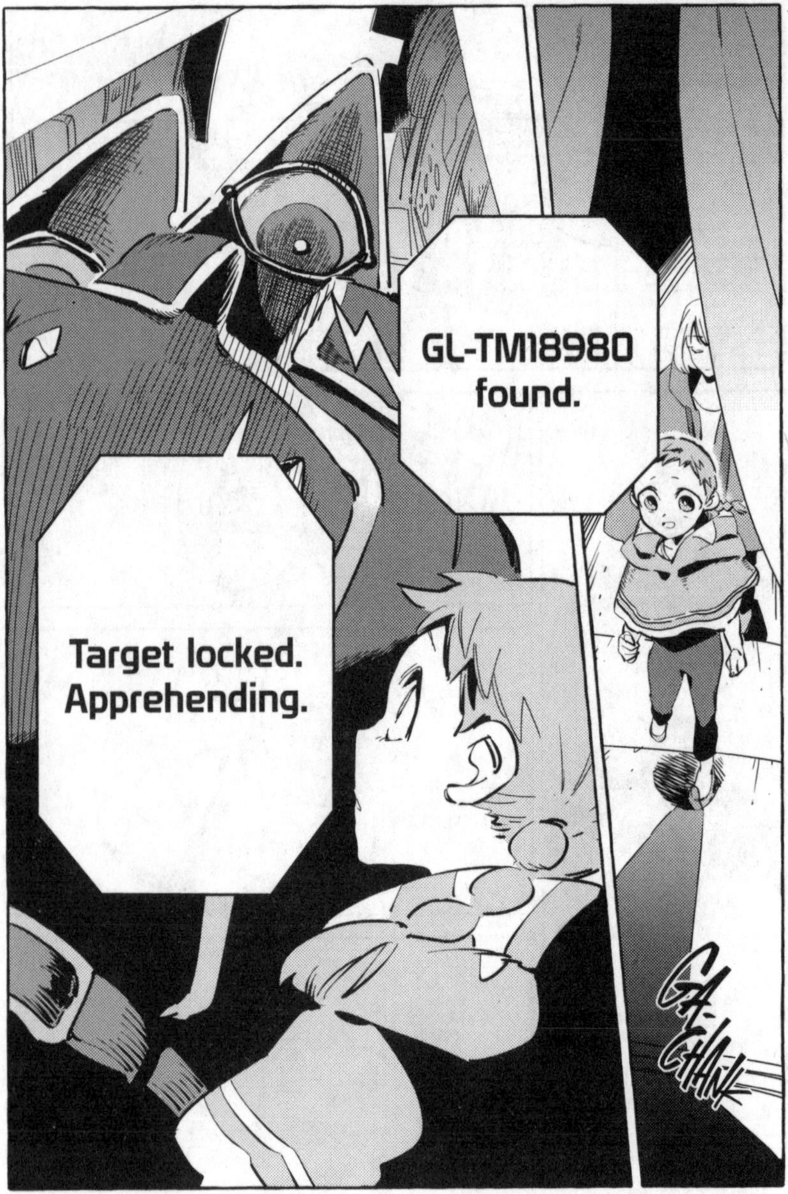
GA-CHANK
GL-TM18980 found.
Target locked. Apprehending.

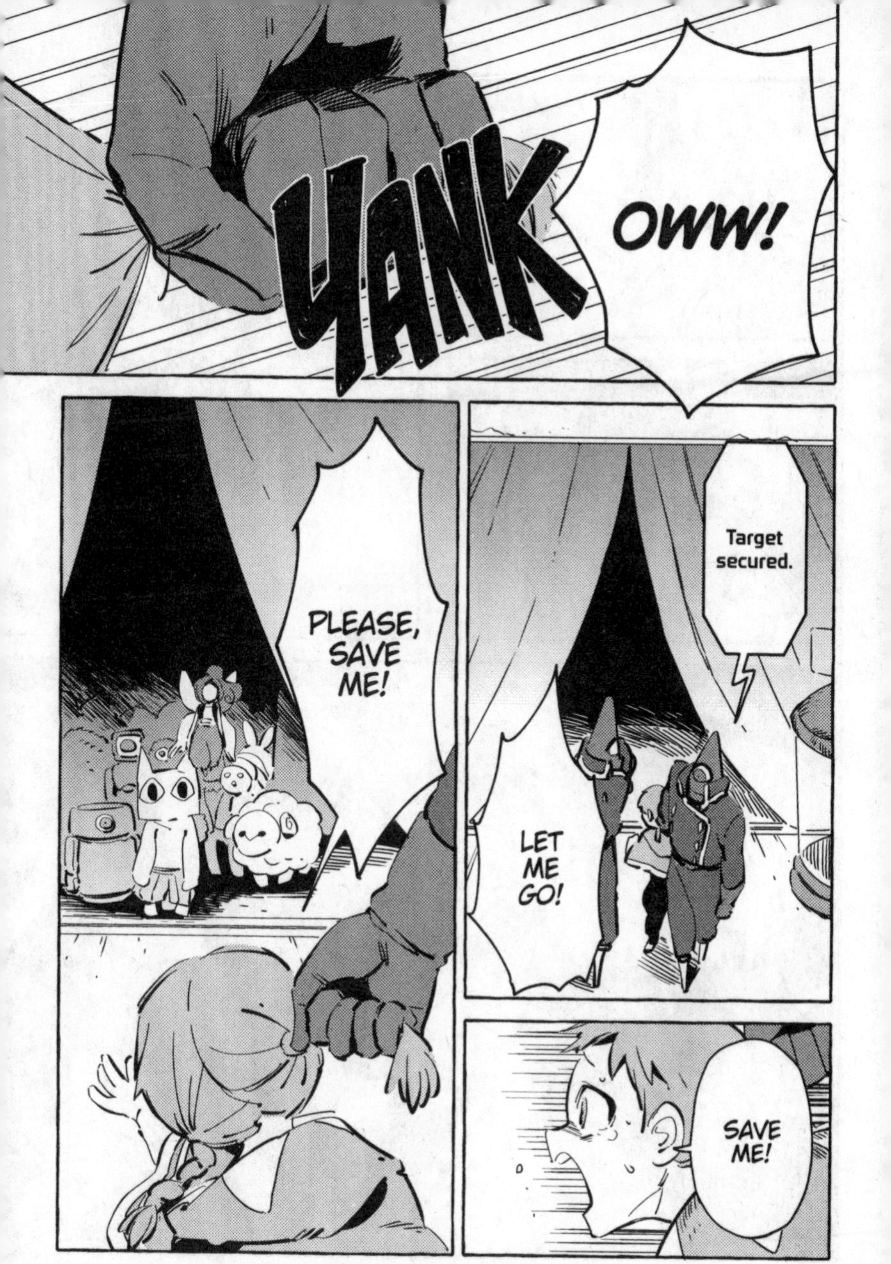
OWW!
YANK
Target secured.
LET ME GO!
SAVE ME!
PLEASE, SAVE ME!

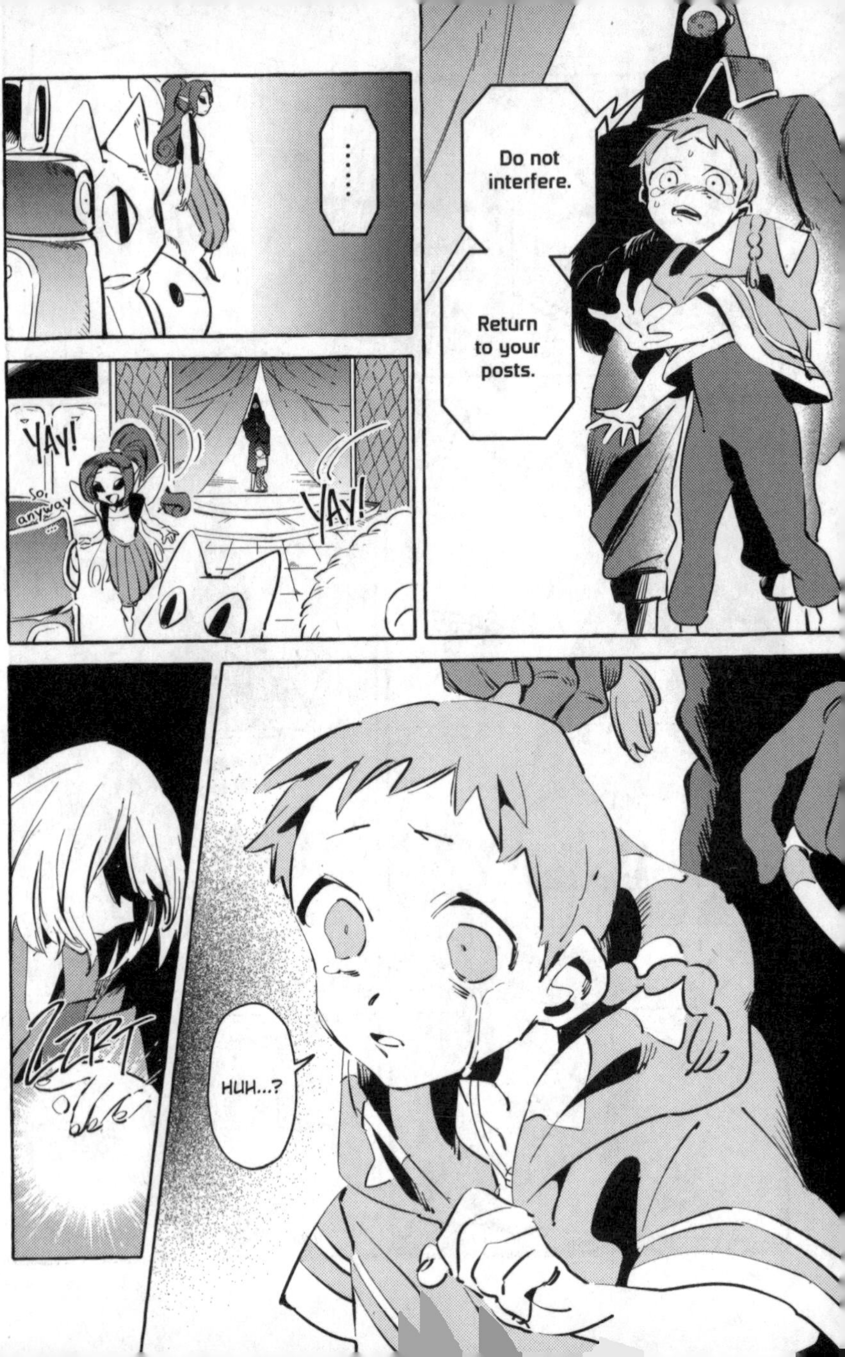
Do not interfere.
Return to your posts.
......
YAY!
So, anyway
YAY!
HUH...?
ZZRT

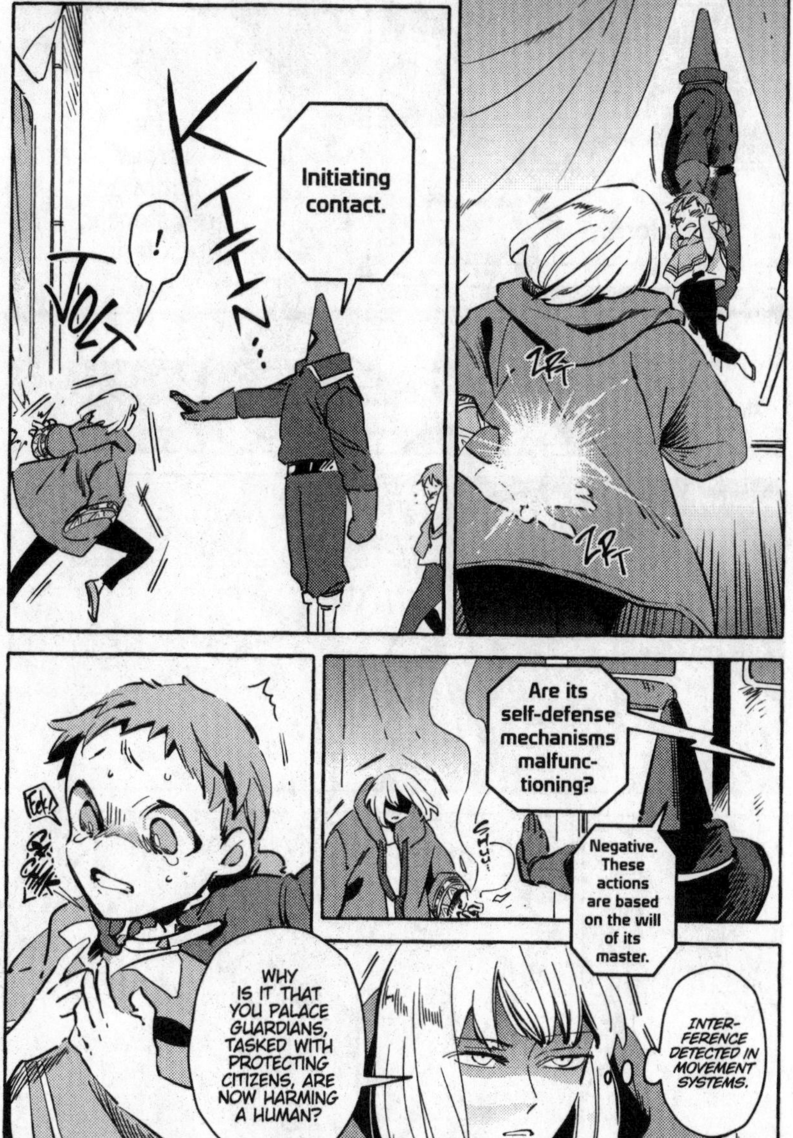
ZRT
ZRT
Initiating contact.
KIIIN...
!
JOLT
Are its self-defense mechanisms malfunctioning?
Negative. These actions are based on the will of its master.
INTERFERENCE DETECTED IN MOVEMENT SYSTEMS.
WHY IS IT THAT YOU PALACE GUARDIANS, TASKED WITH PROTECTING CITIZENS, ARE NOW HARMING A HUMAN?
Eek!

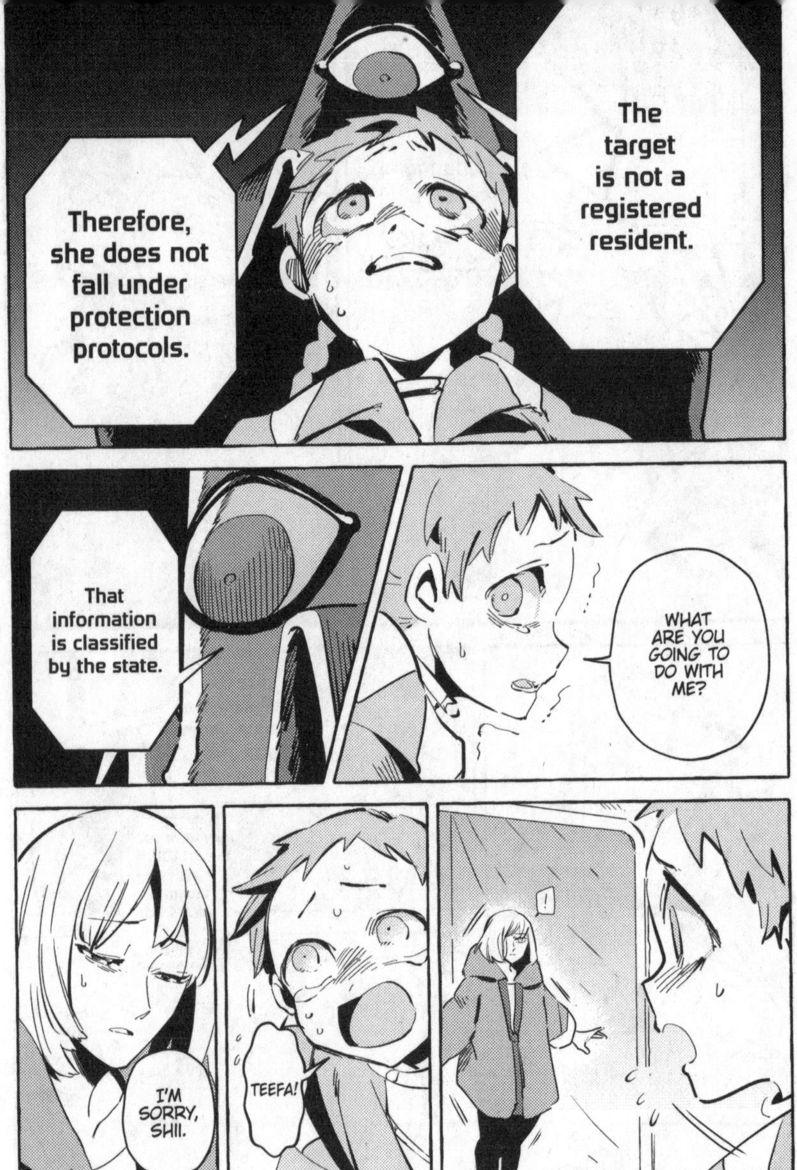
The target is not a registered resident.
Therefore, she does not fall under protection protocols.
WHAT ARE YOU GOING TO DO WITH ME?
That information is classified by the state.
!
TEEFA!
I'M SORRY, SHII.

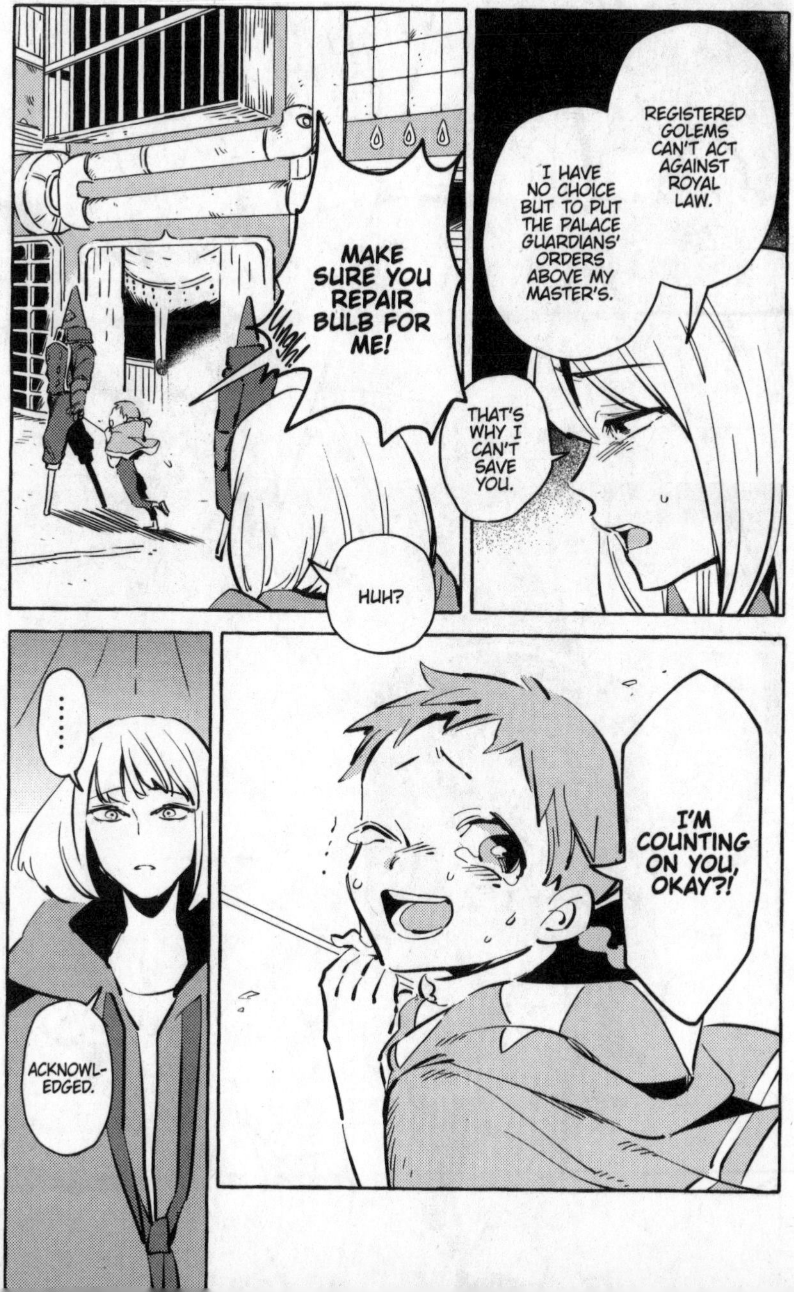
REGISTERED GOLEMS CAN'T ACT AGAINST ROYAL LAW.
I HAVE NO CHOICE BUT TO PUT THE PALACE GUARDIANS' ORDERS ABOVE MY MASTER'S.
THAT'S WHY I CAN'T SAVE YOU.
MAKE SURE YOU REPAIR BULB FOR ME!
Ungh!
HUH?
I'M COUNTING ON YOU, OKAY?!
......
ACKNOWL-EDGED.

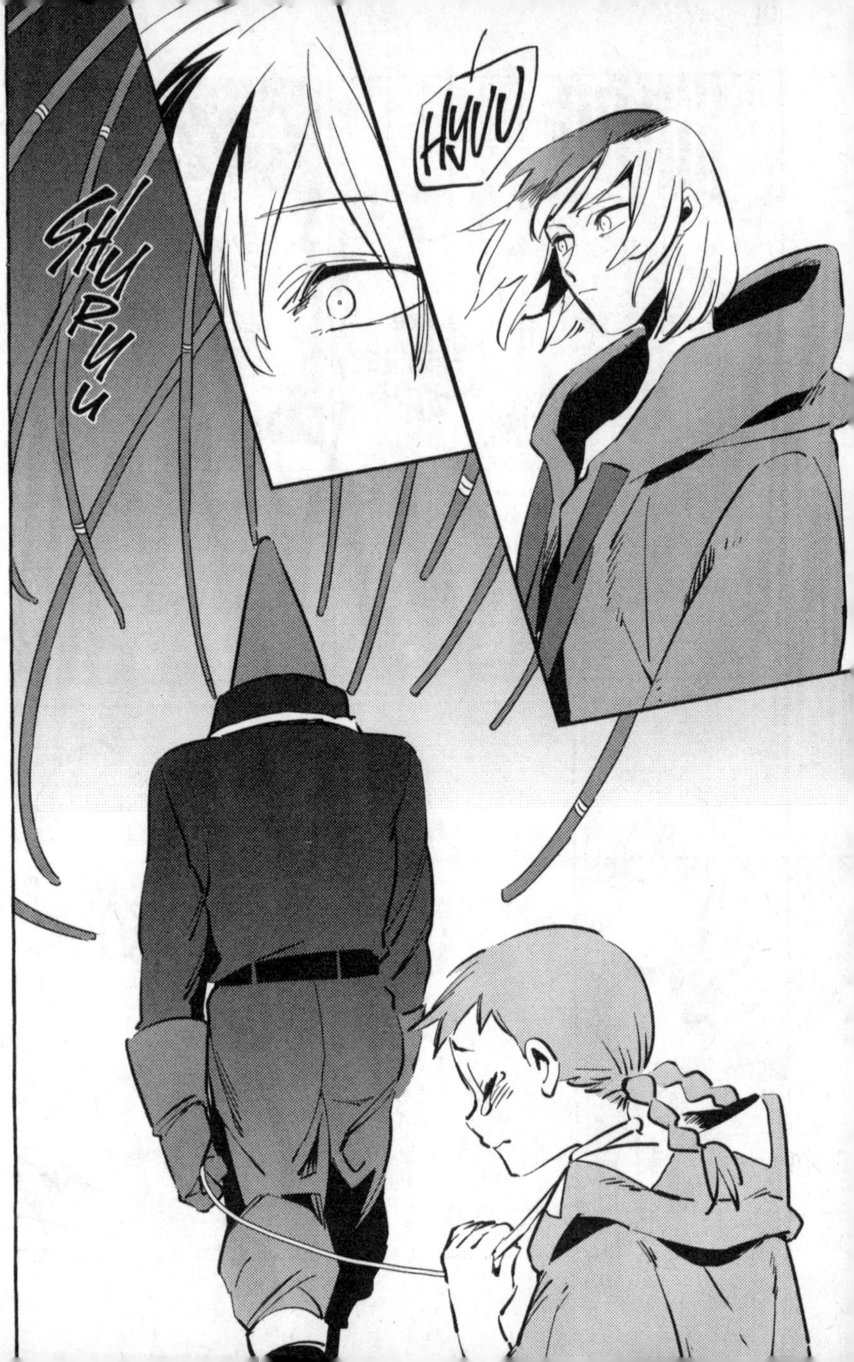
HYUU
SHURUU

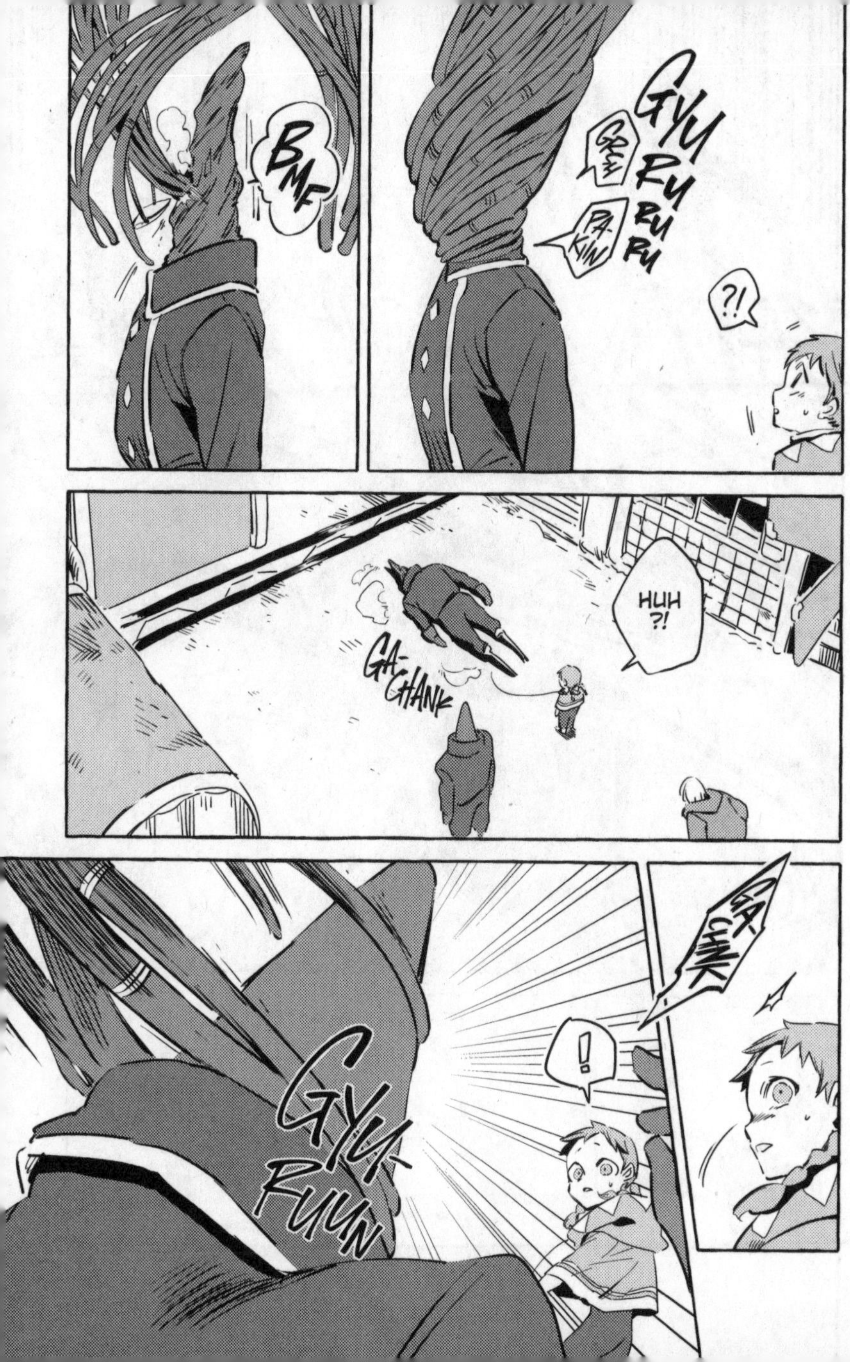
GYURURURU
GRCH
PA-KIN
?!
BMF
HUH?!
GA-CHANK
GA-CHANK
!
GYU-RUUN

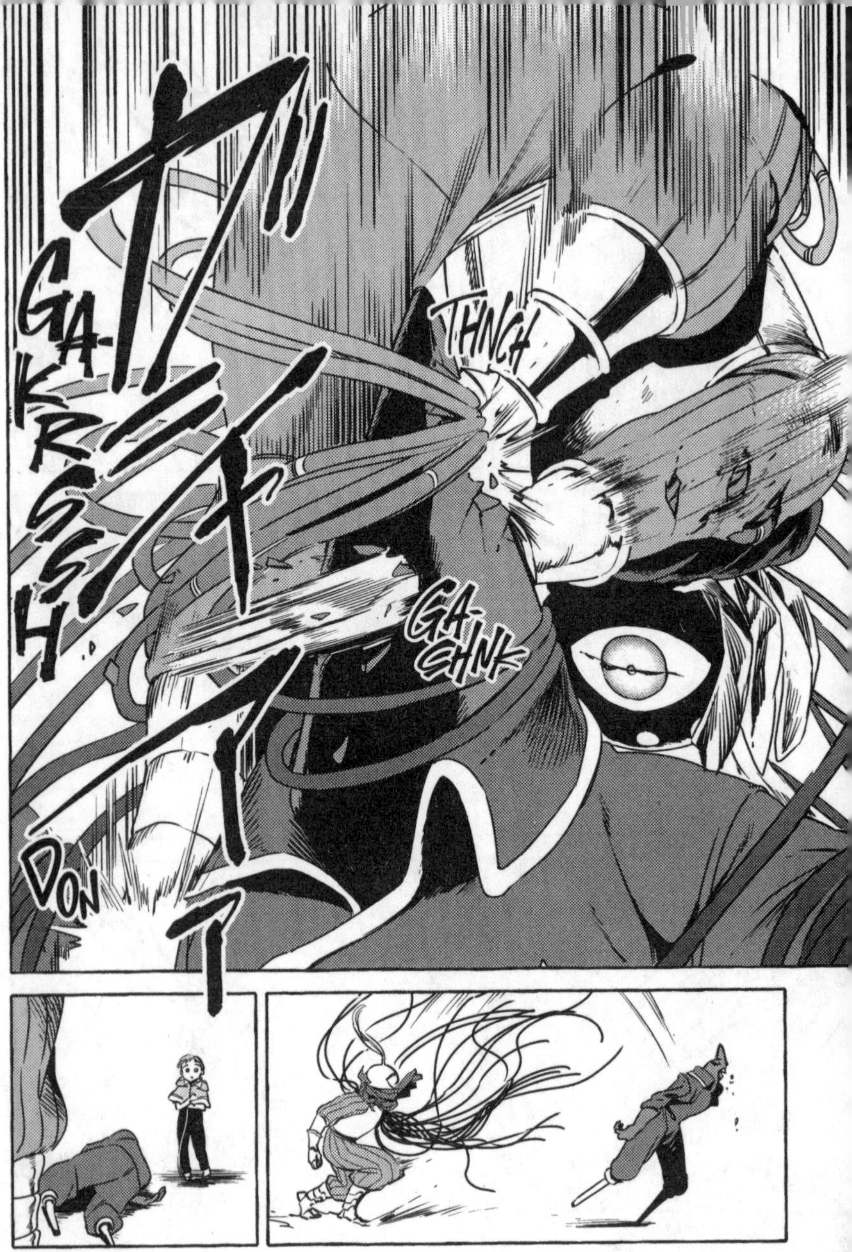
THNCH
GA-CHNK
GA-KRSSH
DON

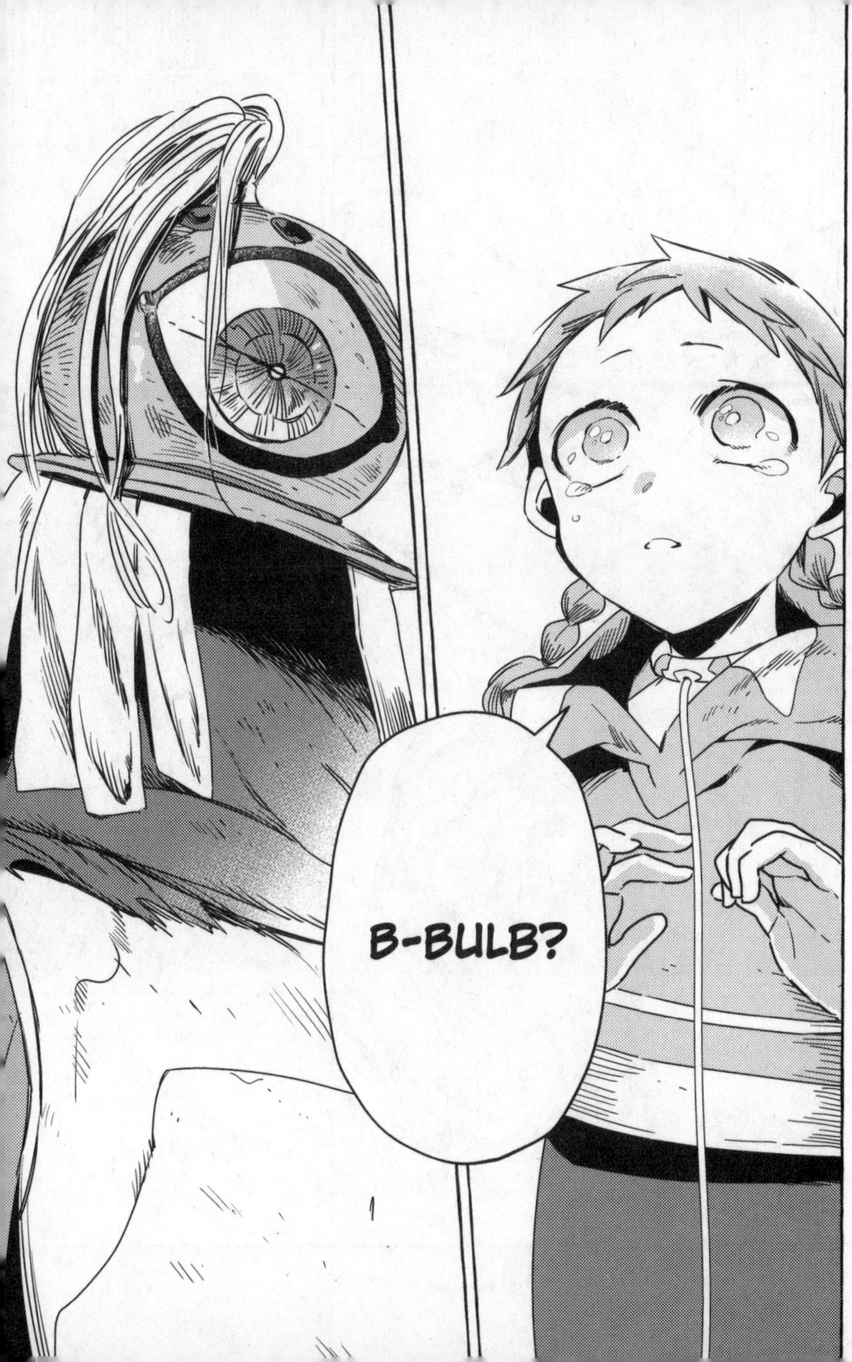
B-BULB?

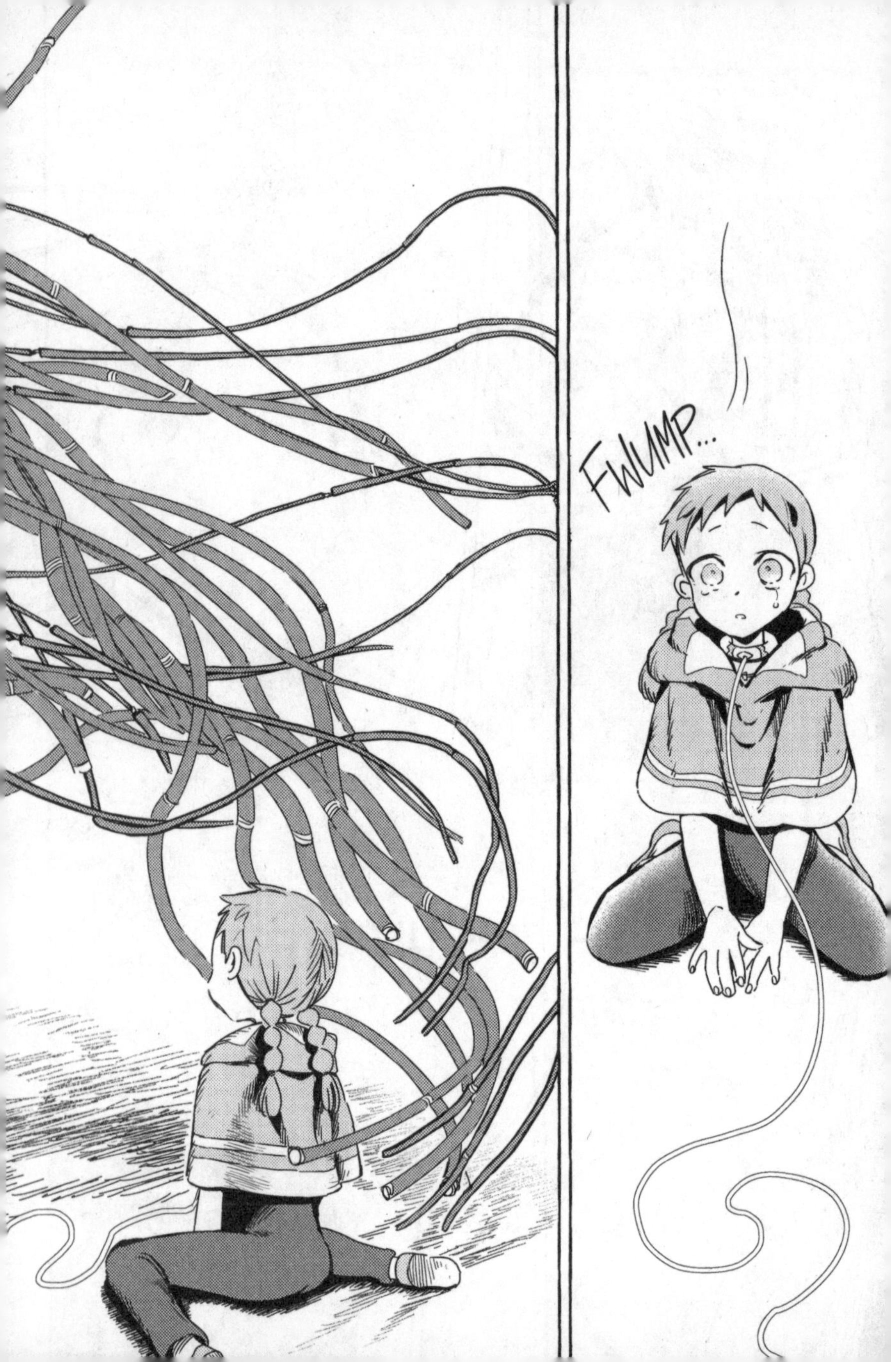
FWUMP...

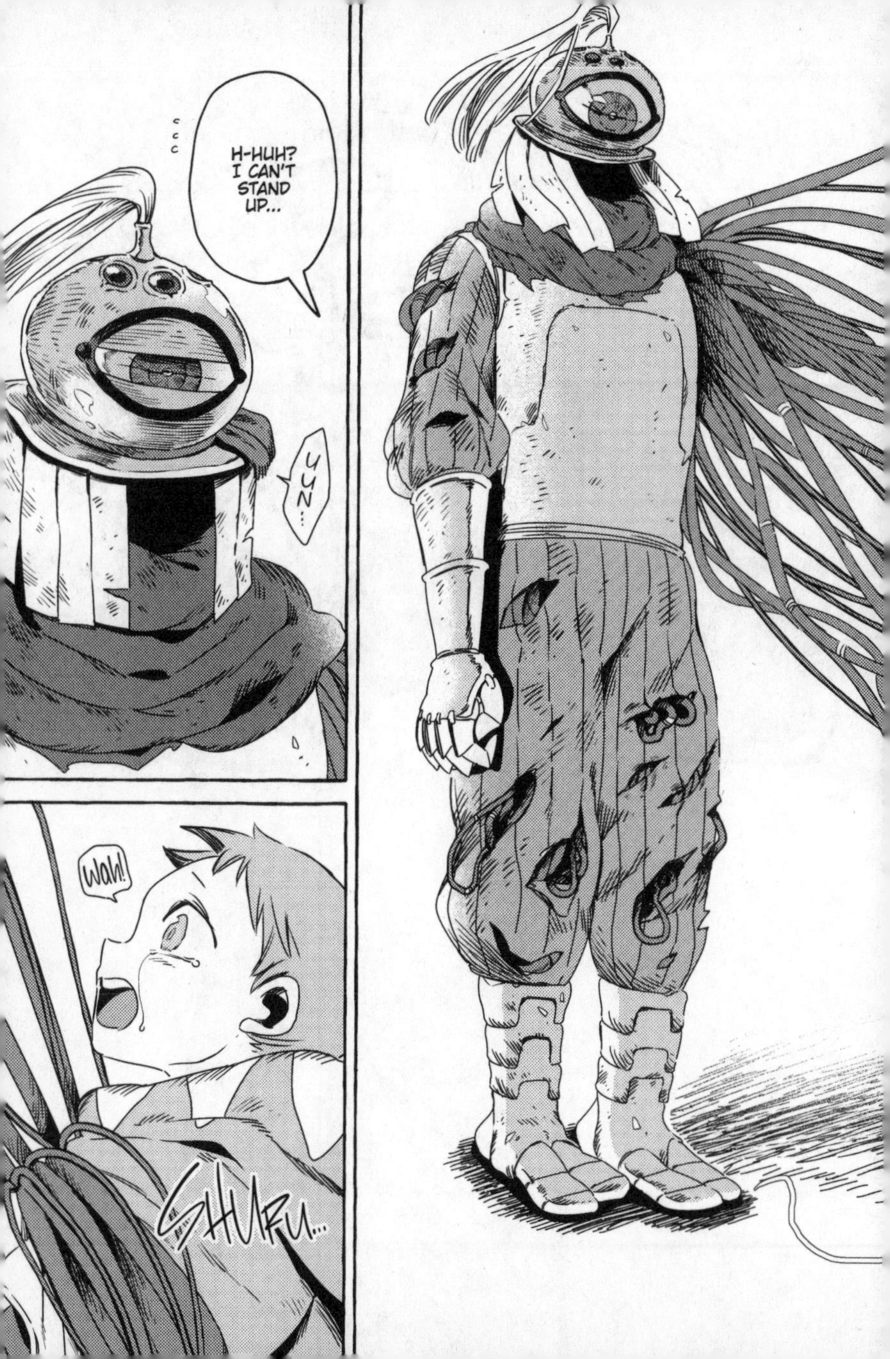
H-HUH? I CAN'T STAND UP...
UUN...
Wah!
SHURU...

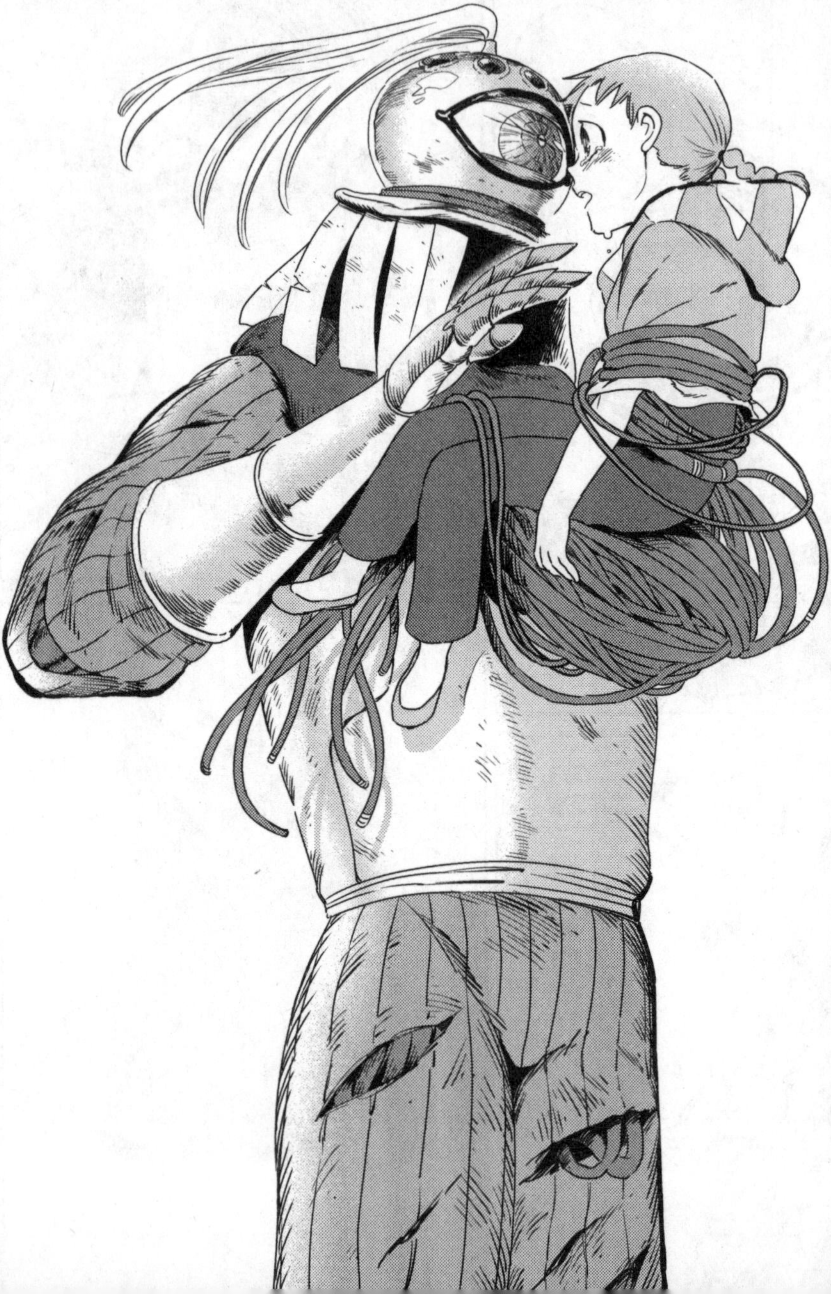

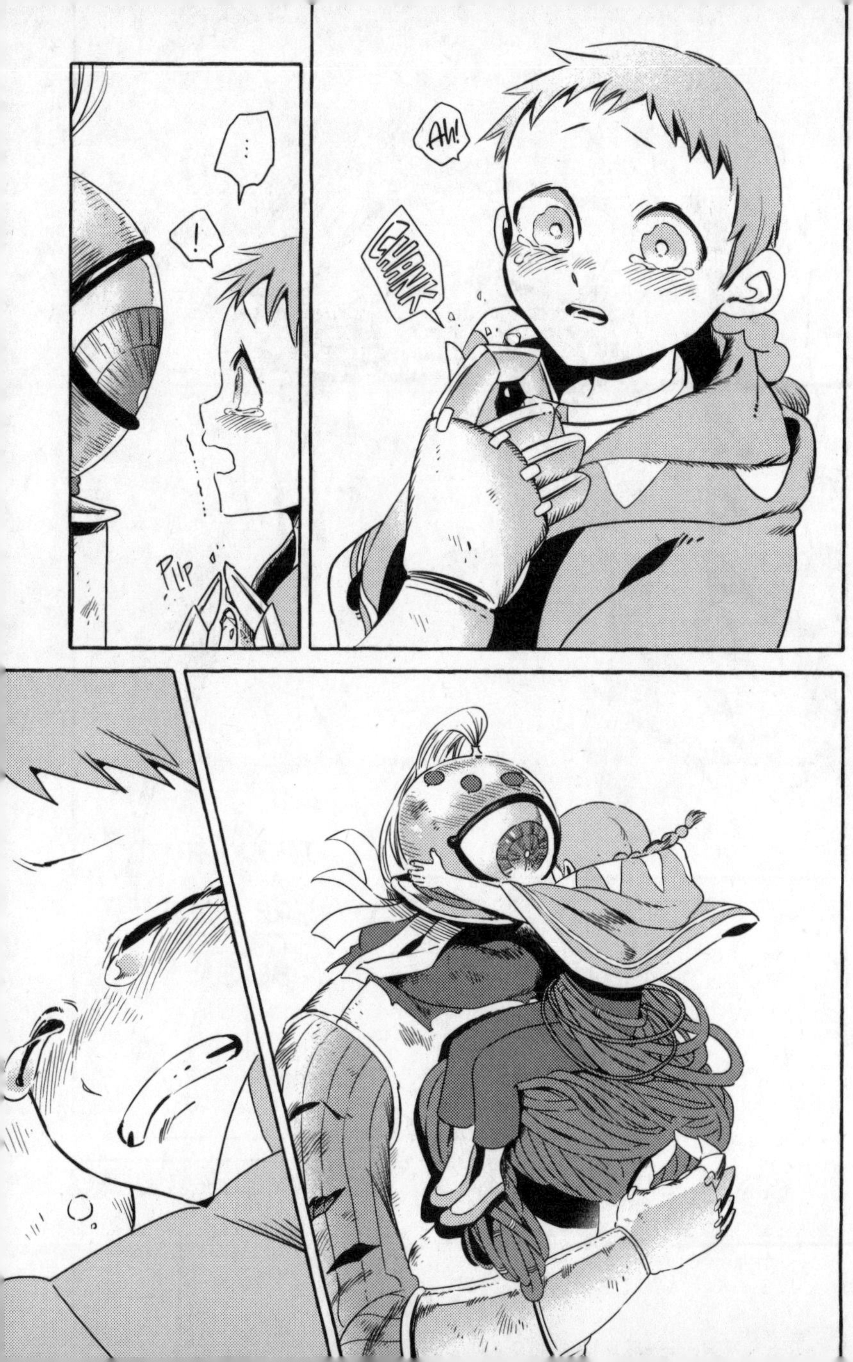
AH!
CHUNK
...
!
PLIP

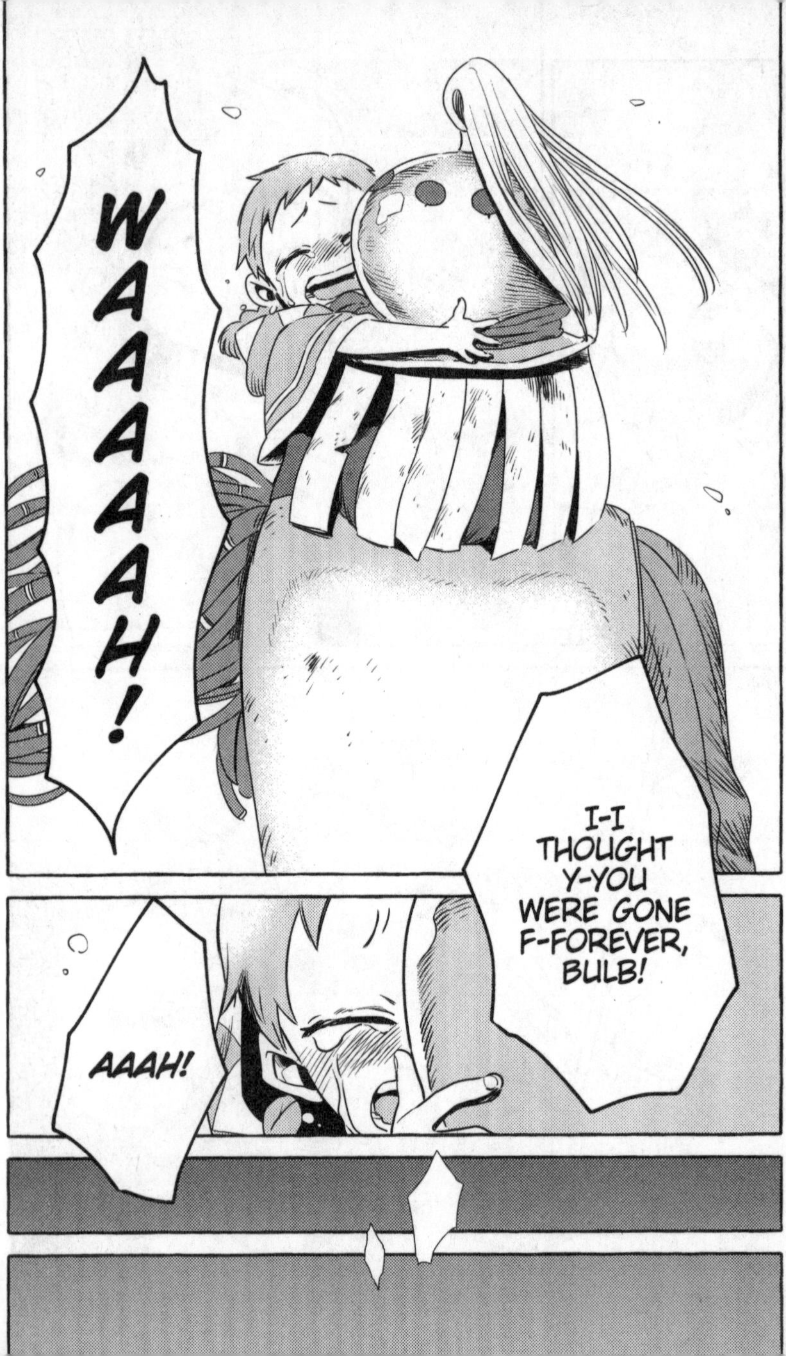
WAAAAAH!
I-I THOUGHT Y-YOU WERE GONE F-FOREVER, BULB!
AAAH!

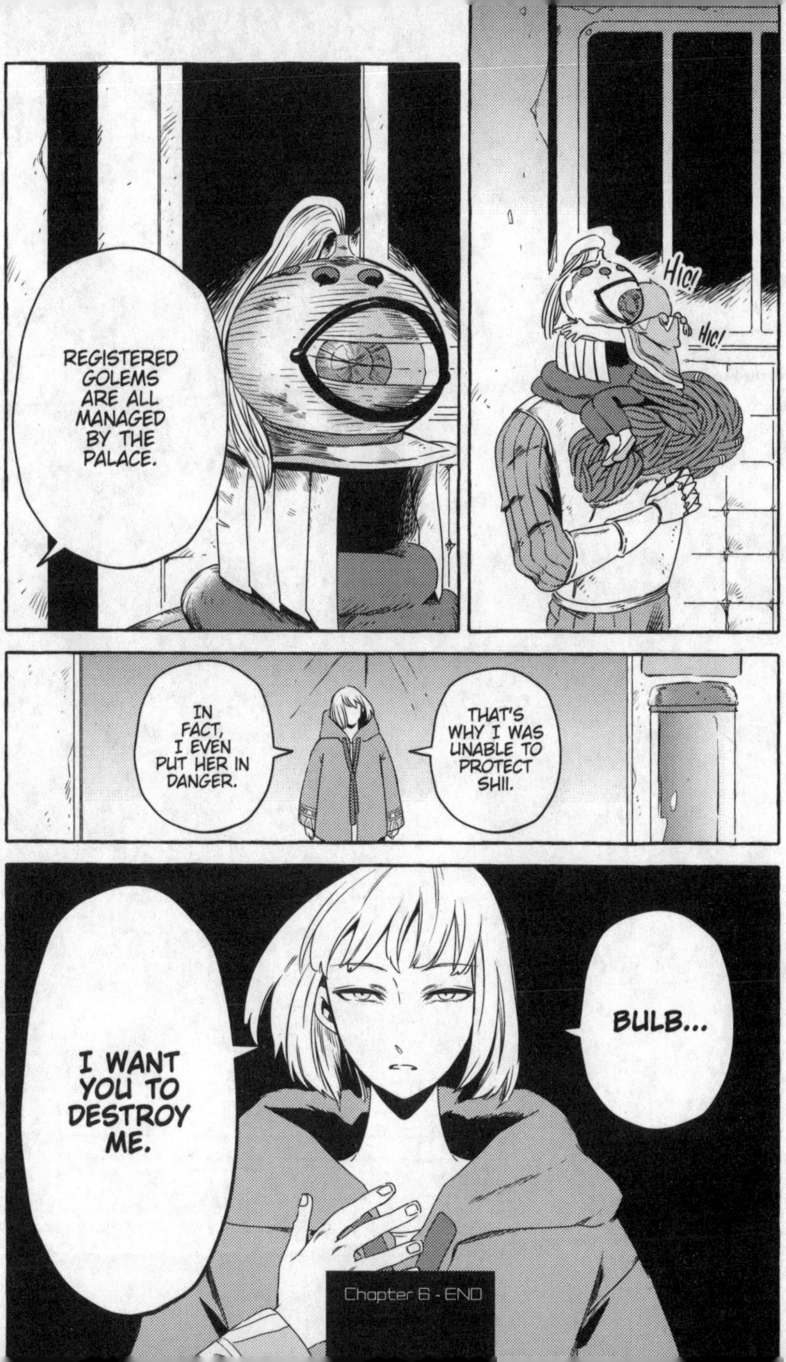
HIC!
HIC!
REGISTERED GOLEMS ARE ALL MANAGED BY THE PALACE.
THAT'S WHY I WAS UNABLE TO PROTECT SHII.
IN FACT, I EVEN PUT HER IN DANGER.
BULB...
I WANT YOU TO DESTROY ME.
Chapter 6 - END

The
Country
Without
Humans

Chapter 7

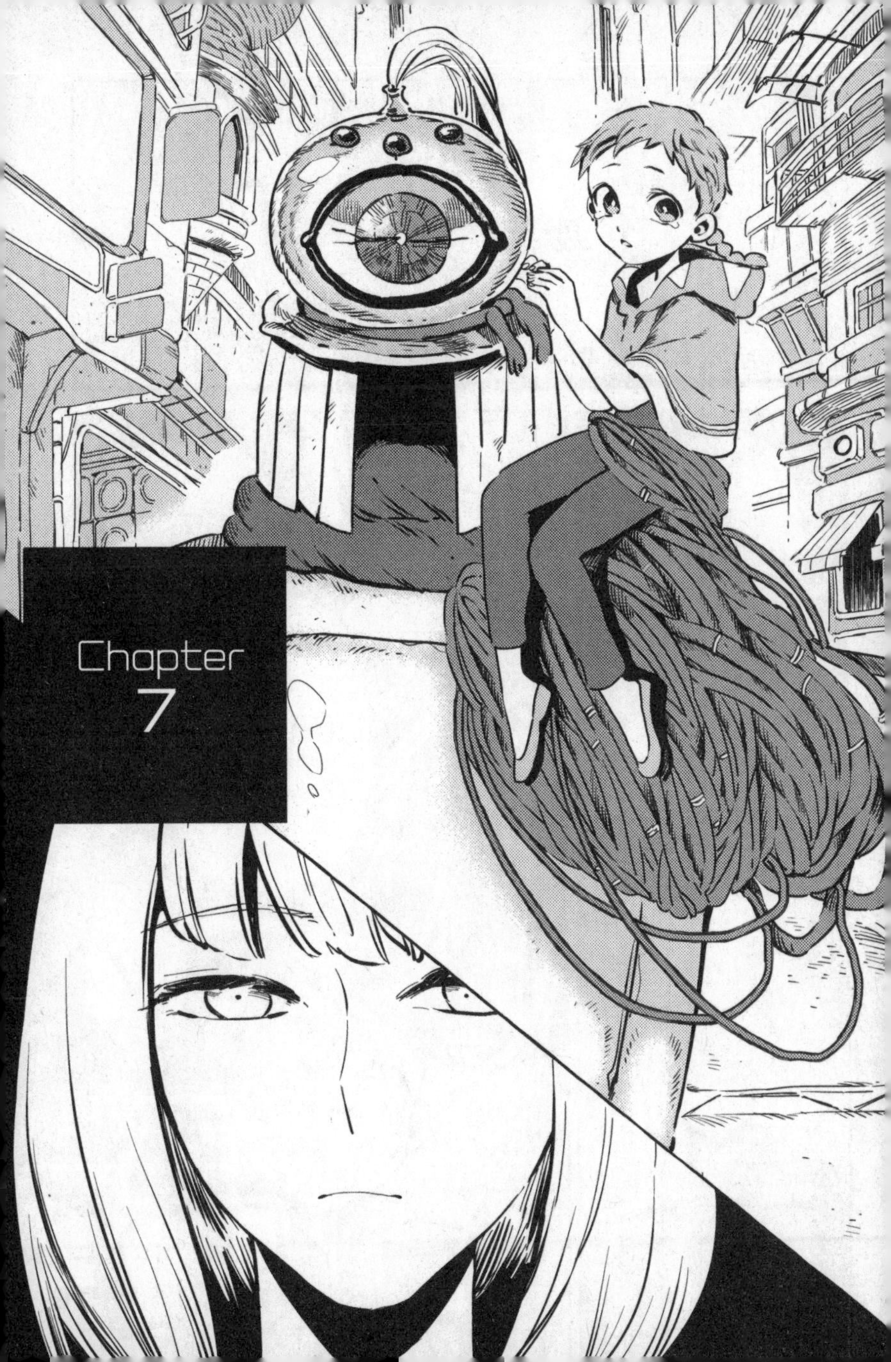

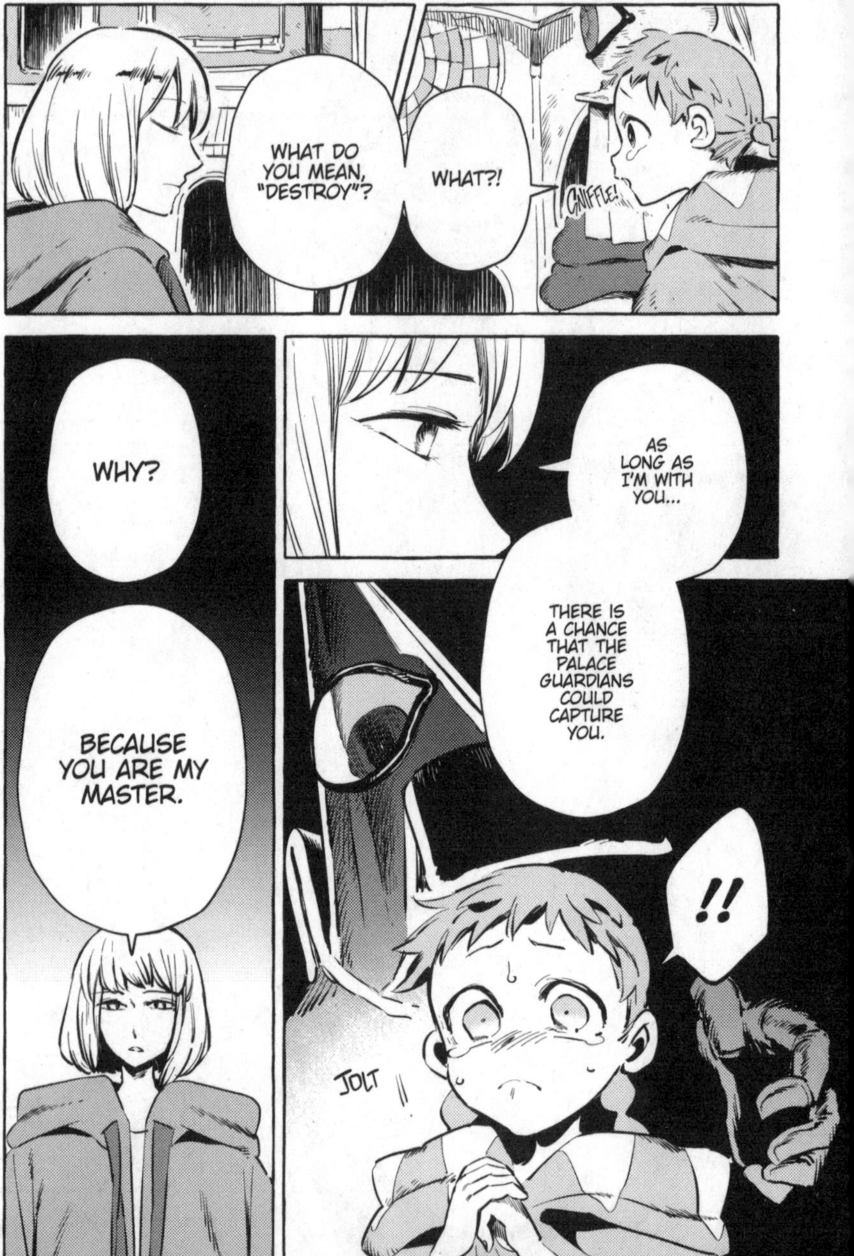
SNIFFLE!
WHAT?!
WHAT DO YOU MEAN, "DESTROY"?
AS LONG AS I'M WITH YOU...
THERE IS A CHANCE THAT THE PALACE GUARDIANS COULD CAPTURE YOU.
!!
JOLT
WHY?
BECAUSE YOU ARE MY MASTER.

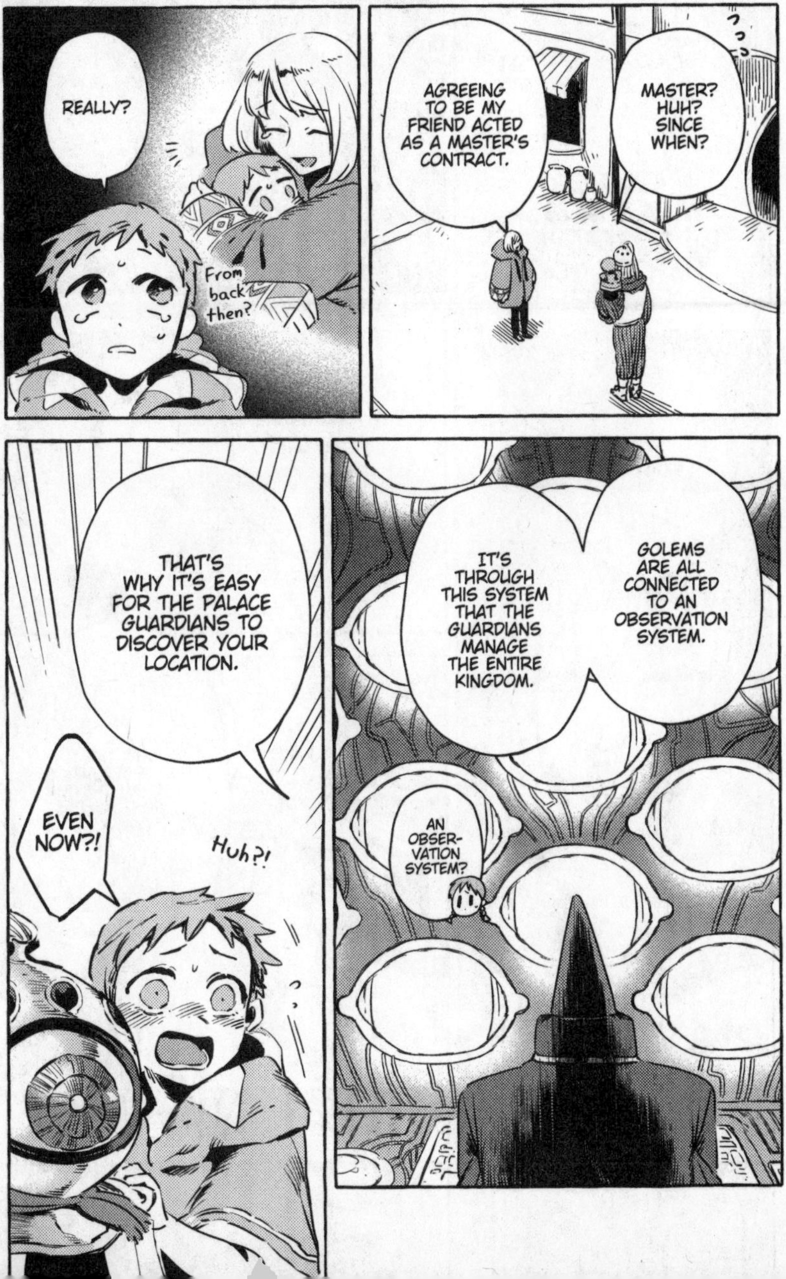
MASTER? HUH? SINCE WHEN?
AGREEING TO BE MY FRIEND ACTED AS A MASTER'S CONTRACT.
REALLY?
From back then?
GOLEMS ARE ALL CONNECTED TO AN OBSERVATION SYSTEM.
IT'S THROUGH THIS SYSTEM THAT THE GUARDIANS MANAGE THE ENTIRE KINGDOM.
AN OBSER-VATION SYSTEM?
THAT'S WHY IT'S EASY FOR THE PALACE GUARDIANS TO DISCOVER YOUR LOCATION.
Huh?!
EVEN NOW?!

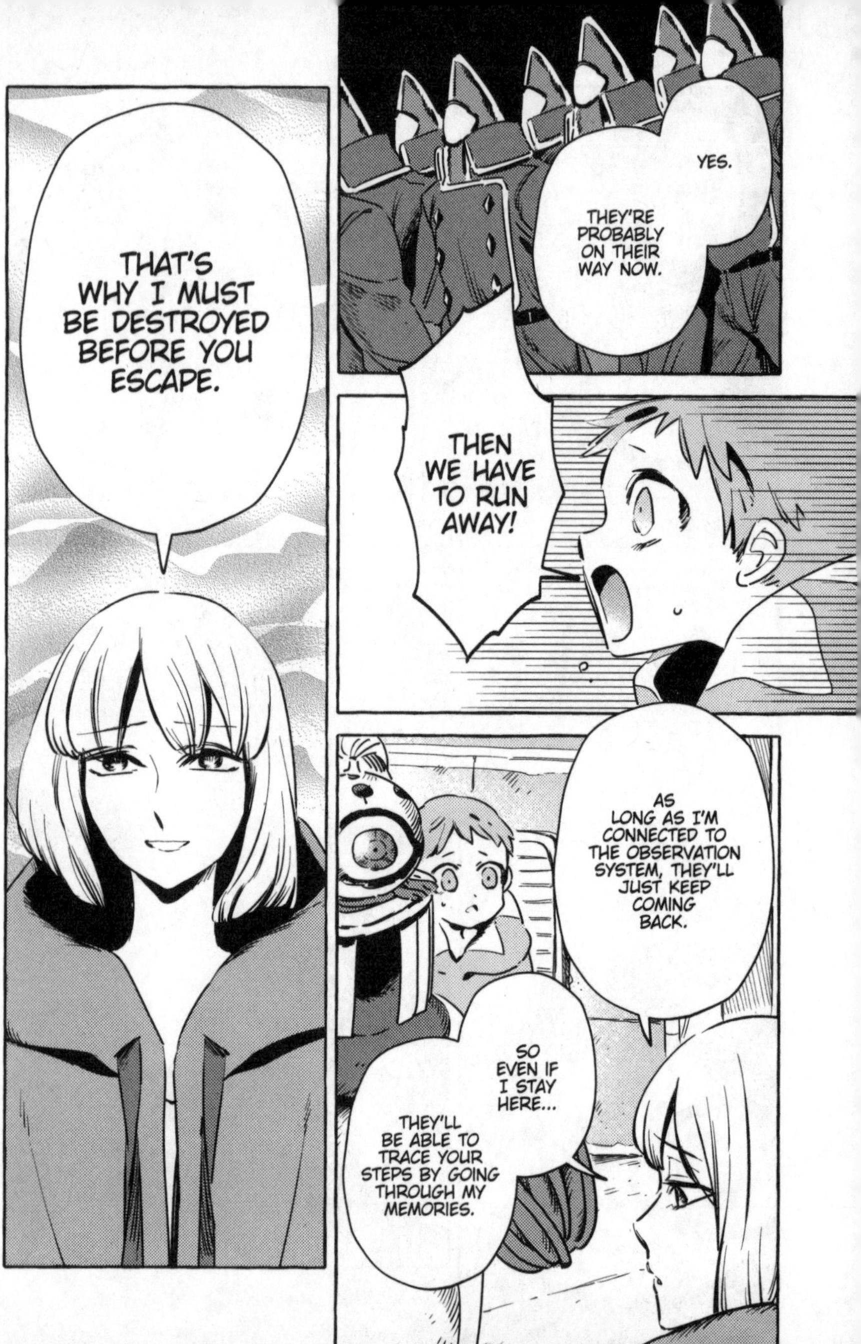
YES.
THEY'RE PROBABLY ON THEIR WAY NOW.
THEN WE HAVE TO RUN AWAY!
AS LONG AS I'M CONNECTED TO THE OBSERVATION SYSTEM, THEY'LL JUST KEEP COMING BACK.
SO EVEN IF I STAY HERE...
THEY'LL BE ABLE TO TRACE YOUR STEPS BY GOING THROUGH MY MEMORIES.
THAT'S WHY I MUST BE DESTROYED BEFORE YOU ESCAPE.

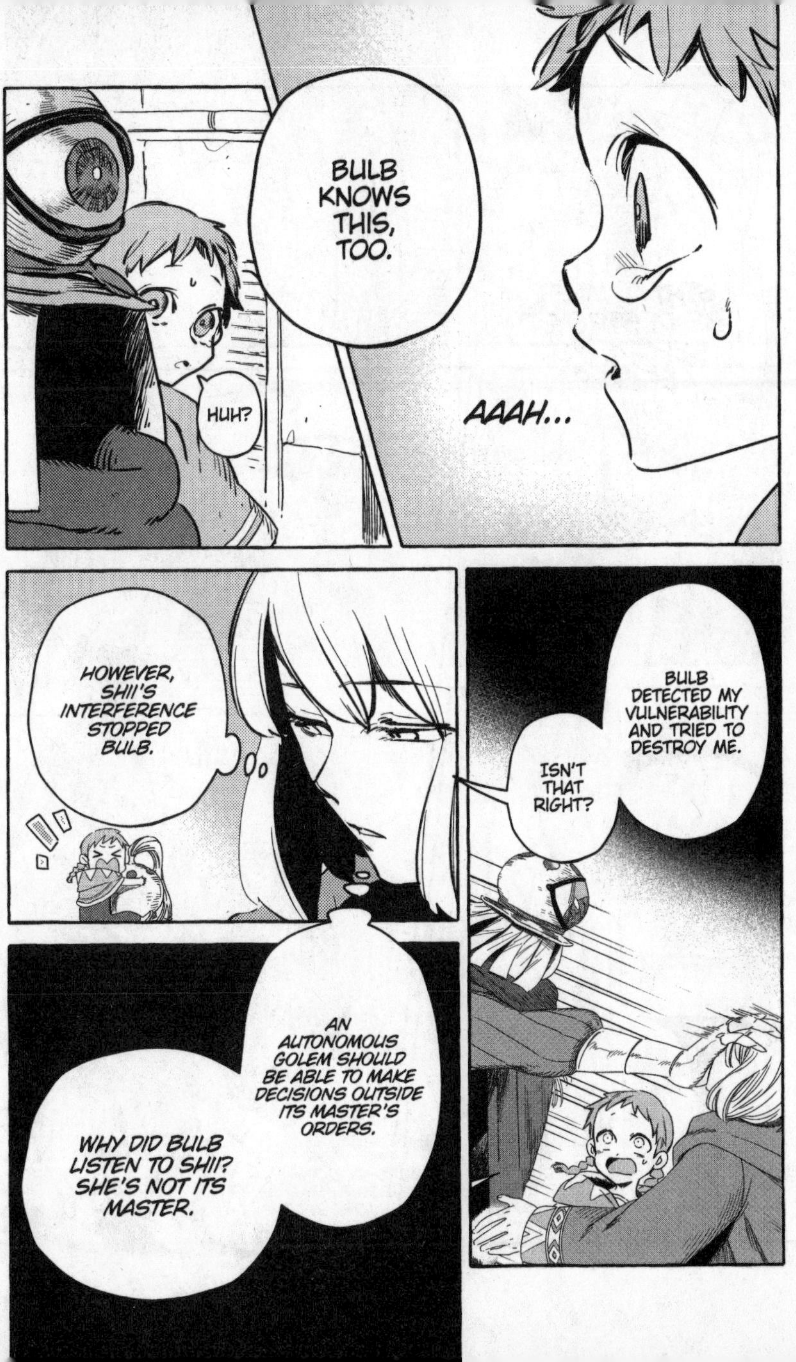
BULB KNOWS THIS, TOO.
AAAH...
HUH?
BULB DETECTED MY VULNERABILITY AND TRIED TO DESTROY ME.
ISN'T THAT RIGHT?
HOWEVER, SHII'S INTERFERENCE STOPPED BULB.
AN AUTONOMOUS GOLEM SHOULD BE ABLE TO MAKE DECISIONS OUTSIDE ITS MASTER'S ORDERS.
WHY DID BULB LISTEN TO SHII? SHE'S NOT ITS MASTER.

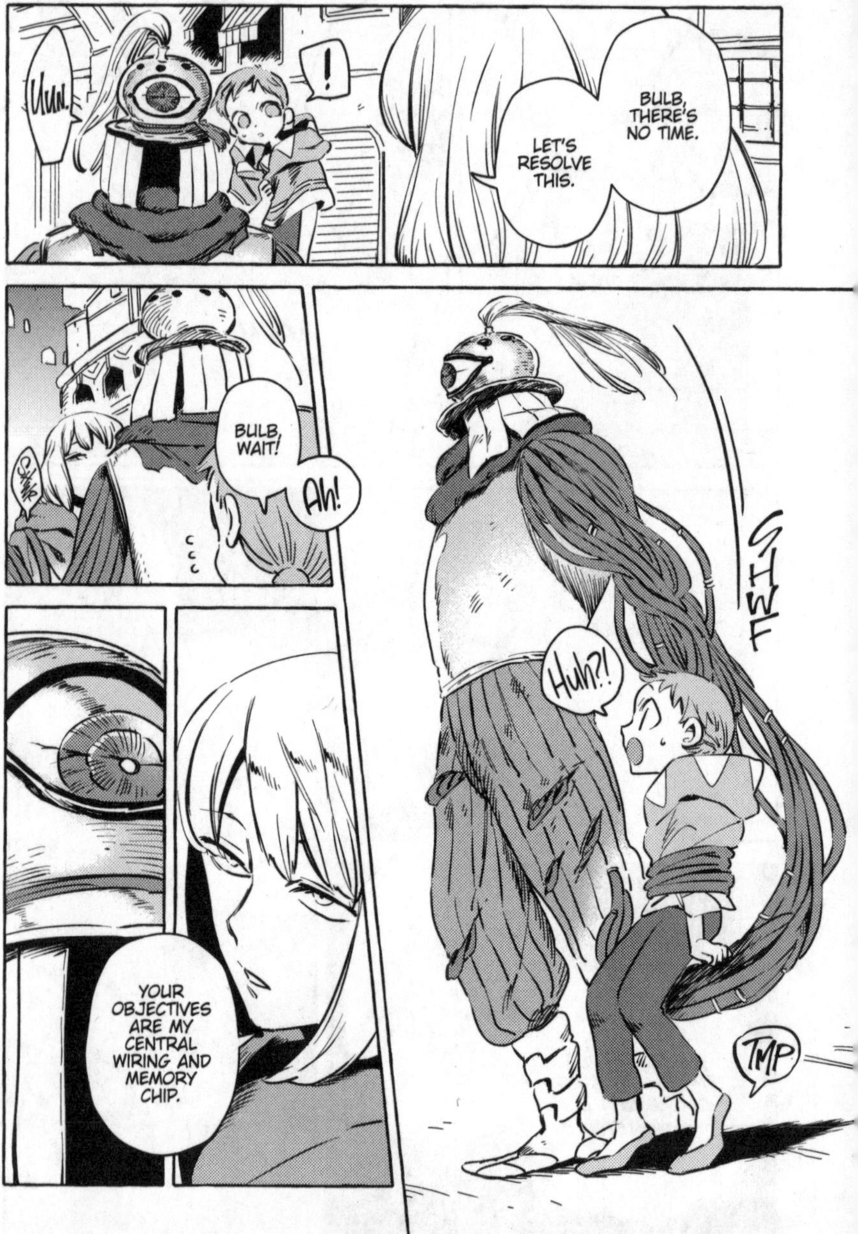
BULB, THERE'S NO TIME.
LET'S RESOLVE THIS.
!
UUN.
SHWF
Huh?!
TMP
BULB, WAIT!
Ah!
YOUR OBJECTIVES ARE MY CENTRAL WIRING AND MEMORY CHIP.

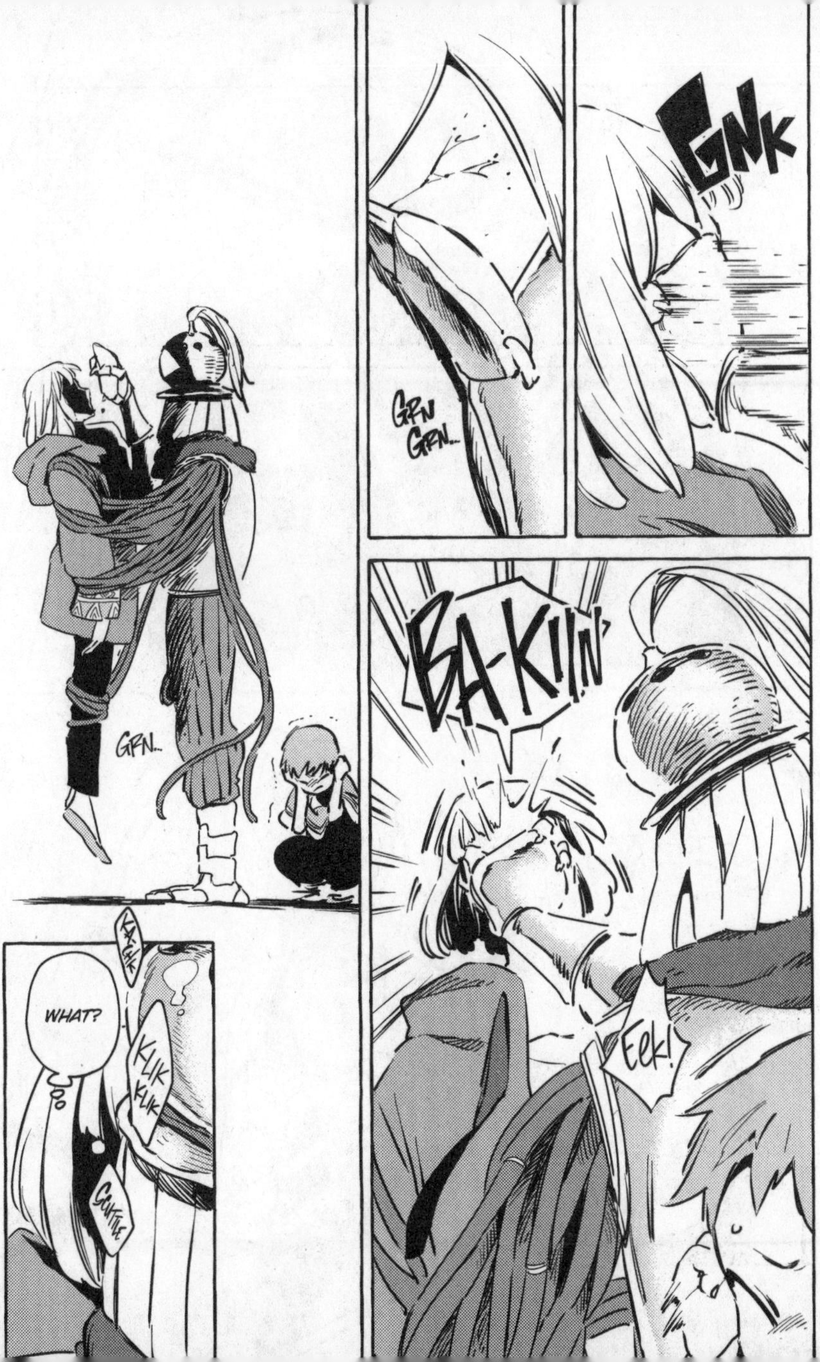
GNK
GRN GRN...
BA-KIIN
Eek!
GRN...
KA-CHK
WHAT?
KLIK KLIK

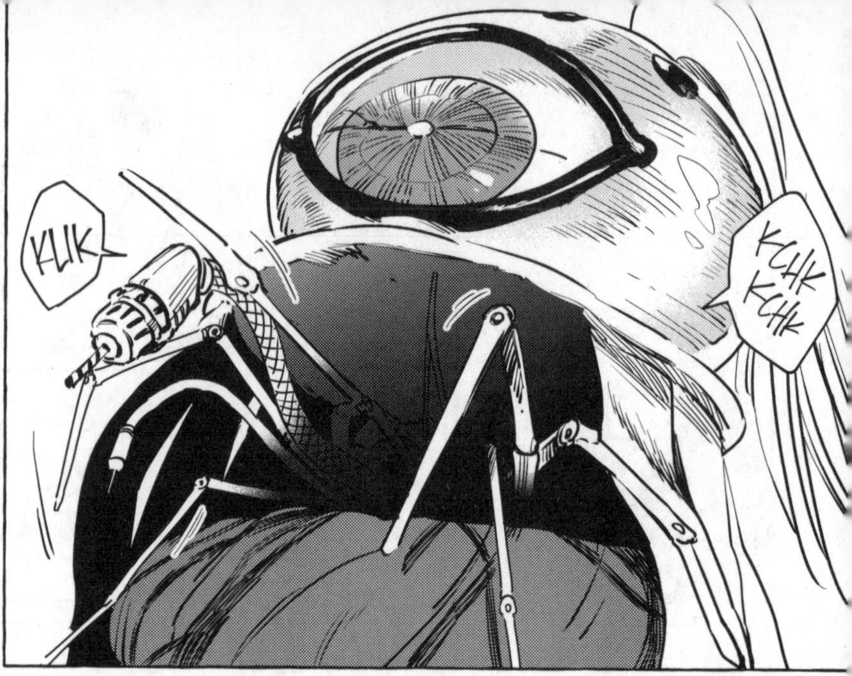
KCHK KCHK
KLIK
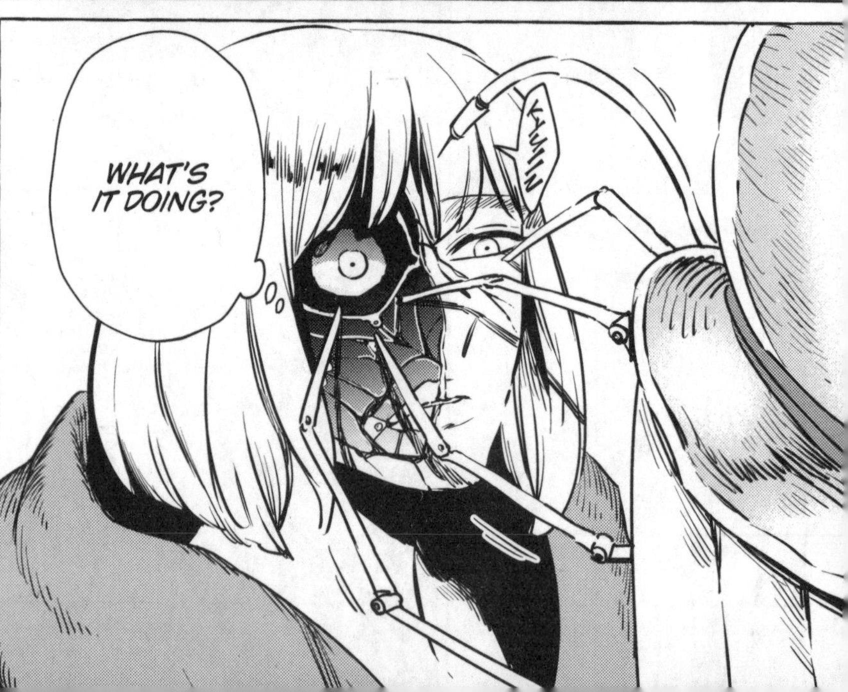
KWIIN
WHAT'S IT DOING?

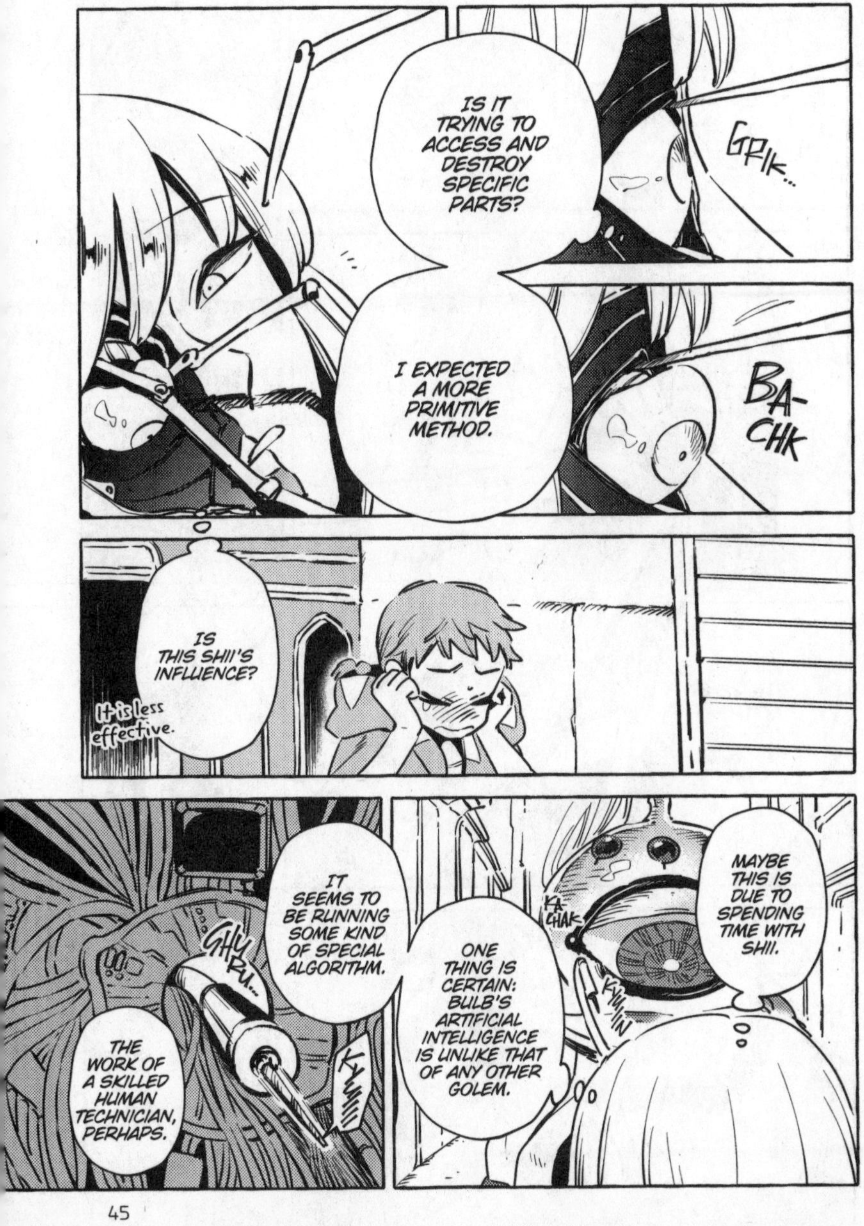
GRIK...
IS IT TRYING TO ACCESS AND DESTROY SPECIFIC PARTS?
BA-CHK
I EXPECTED A MORE PRIMITIVE METHOD.
IS THIS SHII'S INFLUENCE?
It is less effective.
MAYBE THIS IS DUE TO SPENDING TIME WITH SHII.
KA-CHAK
KYUIN
ONE THING IS CERTAIN: BULB'S ARTIFICIAL INTELLIGENCE IS UNLIKE THAT OF ANY OTHER GOLEM.
IT SEEMS TO BE RUNNING SOME KIND OF SPECIAL ALGORITHM.
GHURU...
THE WORK OF A SKILLED HUMAN TECHNICIAN, PERHAPS.

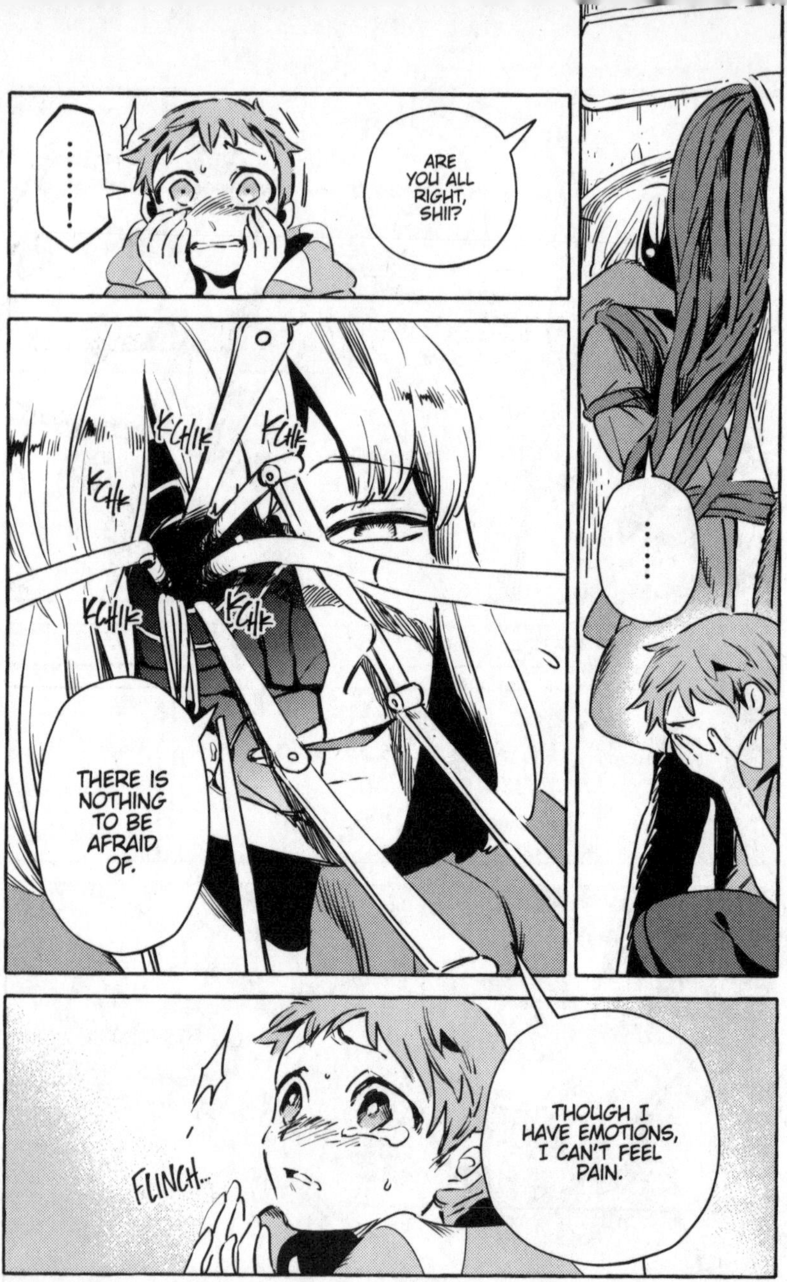
......
ARE YOU ALL RIGHT, SHII?
......!
KCHIK
KCHIK
KCHIK
KCHIK
KCHIK
THERE IS NOTHING TO BE AFRAID OF.
THOUGH I HAVE EMOTIONS, I CAN'T FEEL PAIN.
FLINCH...

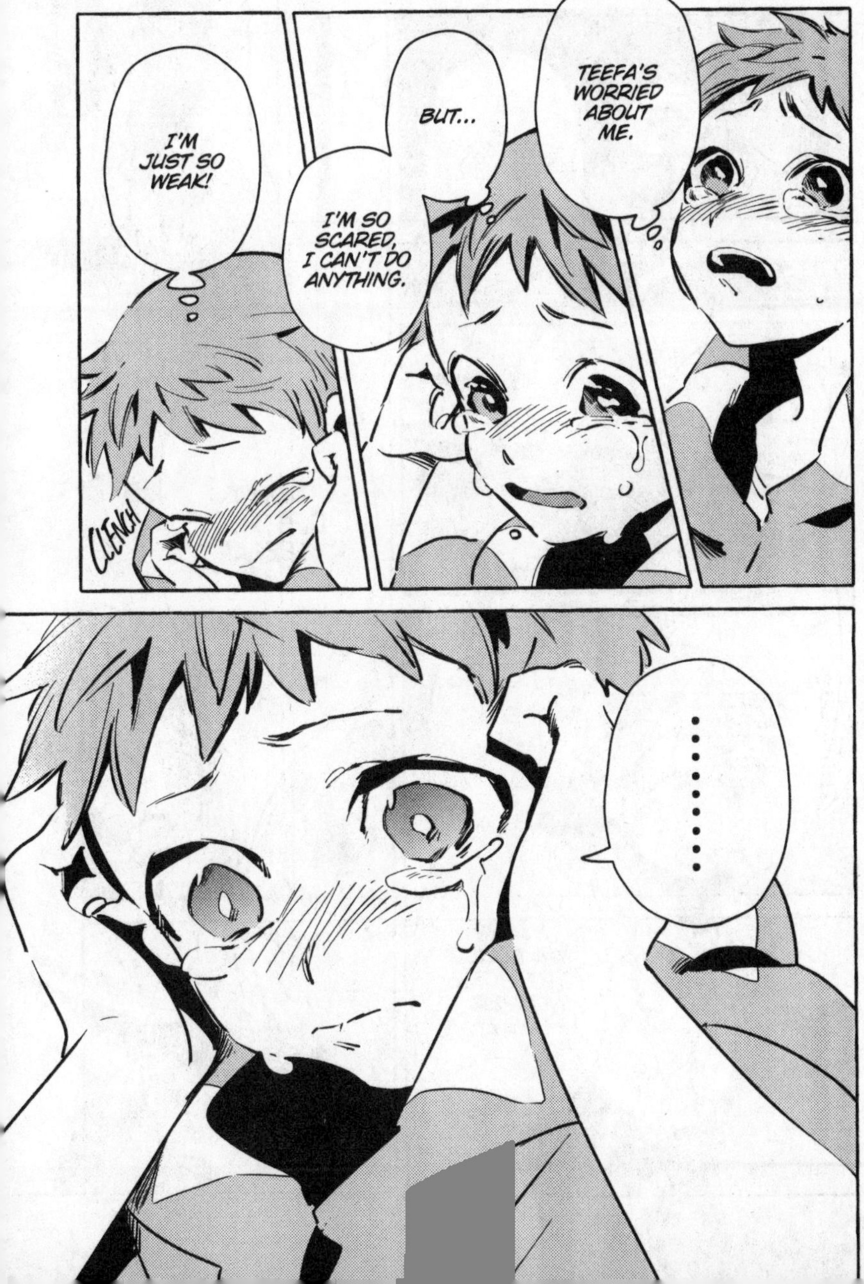
TEEFA'S WORRIED ABOUT ME.
BUT...
I'M SO SCARED, I CAN'T DO ANYTHING.
I'M JUST SO WEAK!
CLENCH
......

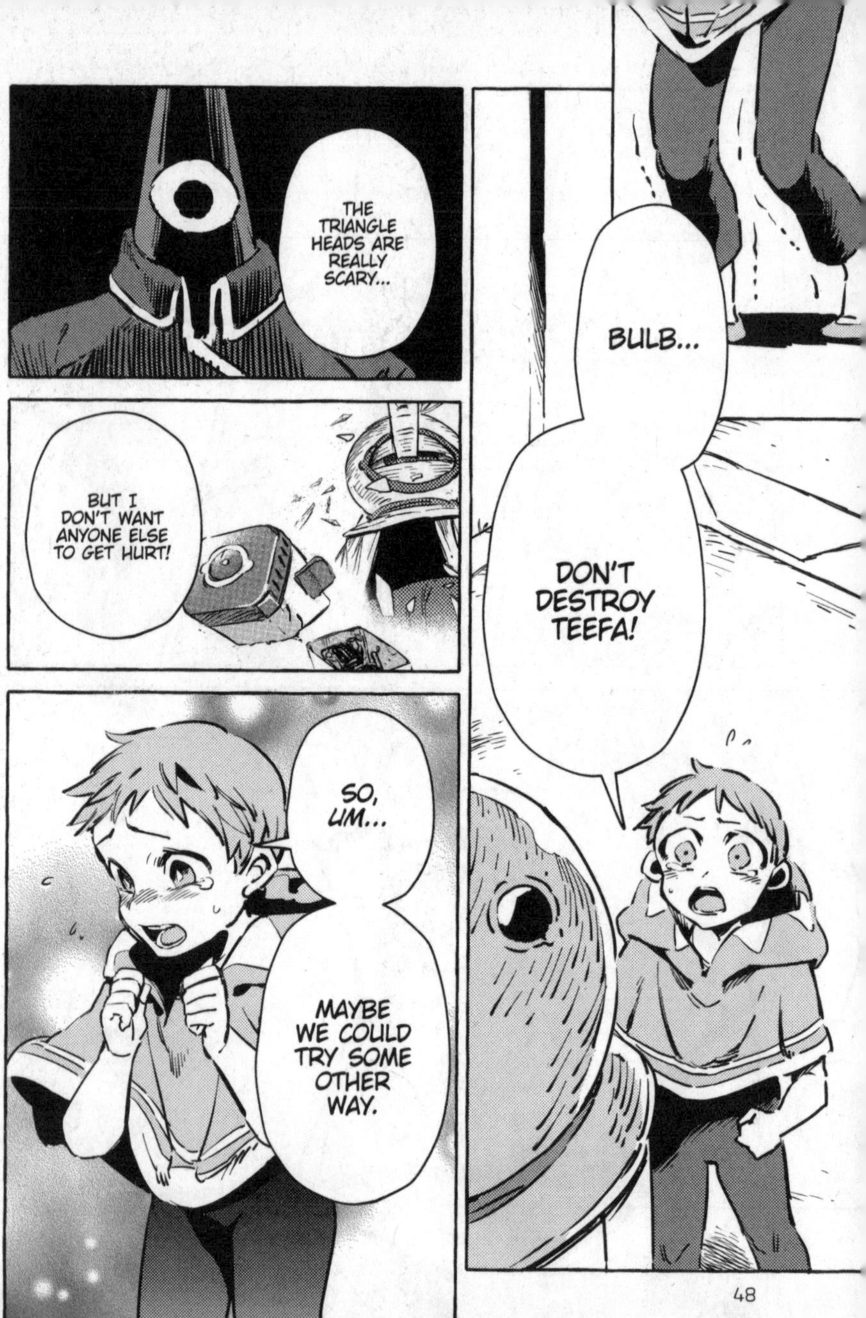
BULB...
DON'T DESTROY TEEFA!
THE TRIANGLE HEADS ARE REALLY SCARY...
BUT I DON'T WANT ANYONE ELSE TO GET HURT!
SO, UM...
MAYBE WE COULD TRY SOME OTHER WAY.

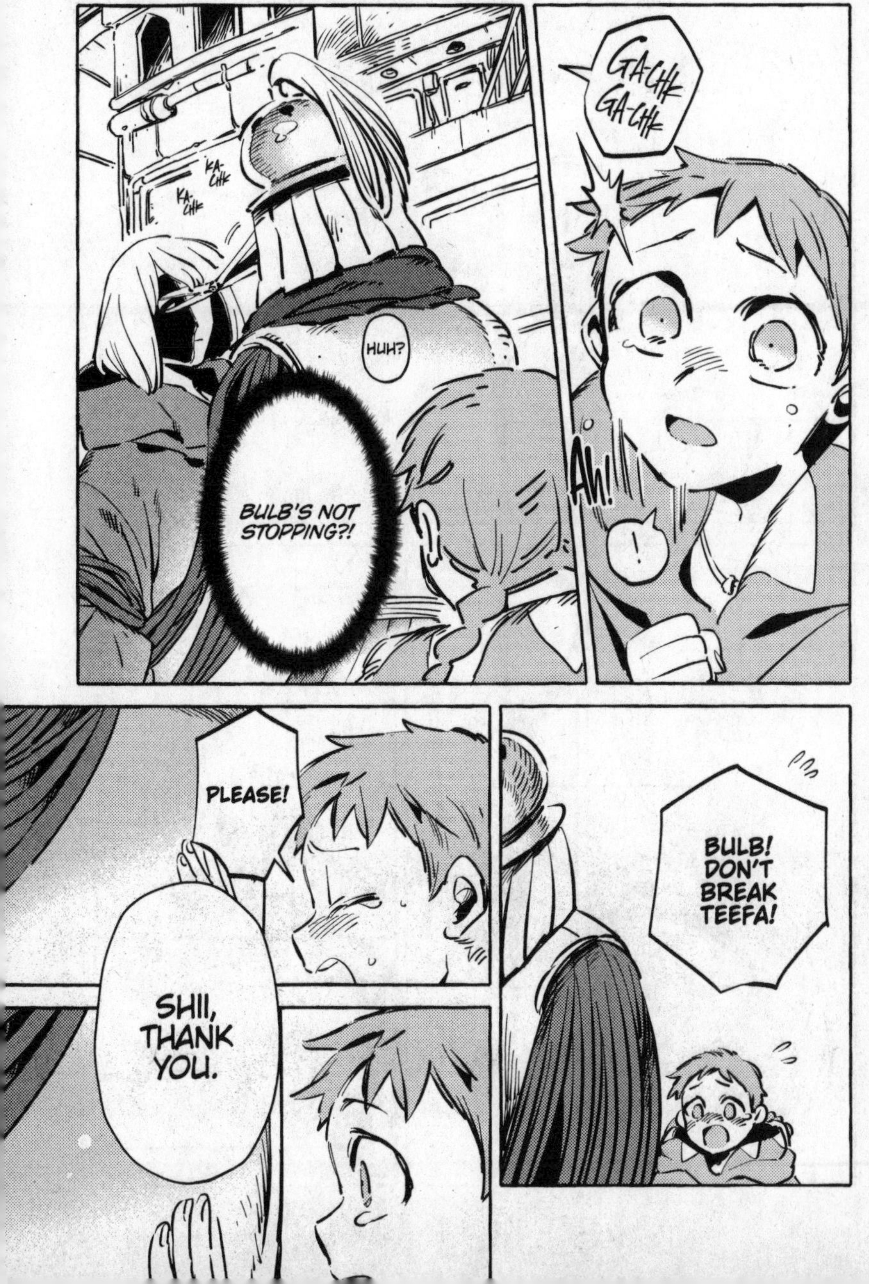
GA-CHK
GA-CHK
AH!
!
KA-CHK
KA-CHK
HUH?
BULB'S NOT STOPPING?!
BULB! DON'T BREAK TEEFA!
PLEASE!
SHII, THANK YOU.

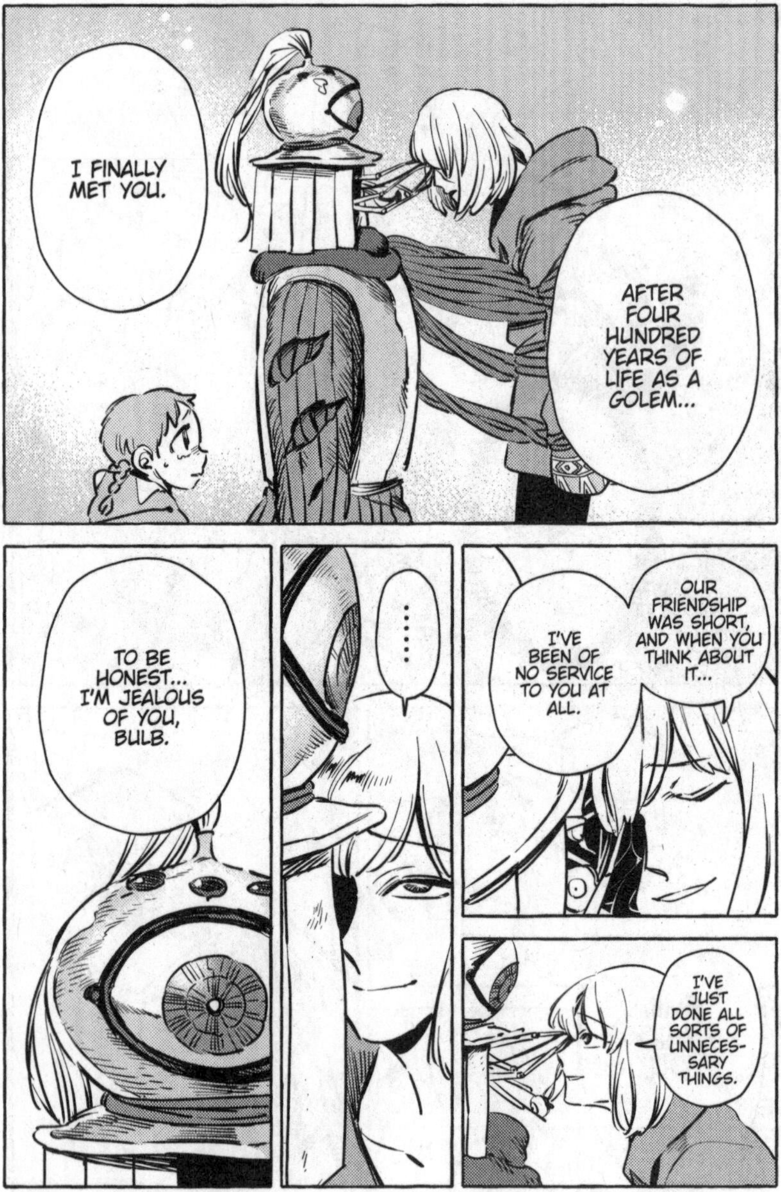
AFTER FOUR HUNDRED YEARS OF LIFE AS A GOLEM...
I FINALLY MET YOU.
OUR FRIENDSHIP WAS SHORT, AND WHEN YOU THINK ABOUT IT...
I'VE BEEN OF NO SERVICE TO YOU AT ALL.
I'VE JUST DONE ALL SORTS OF UNNECES-SARY THINGS.
......
TO BE HONEST... I'M JEALOUS OF YOU, BULB.

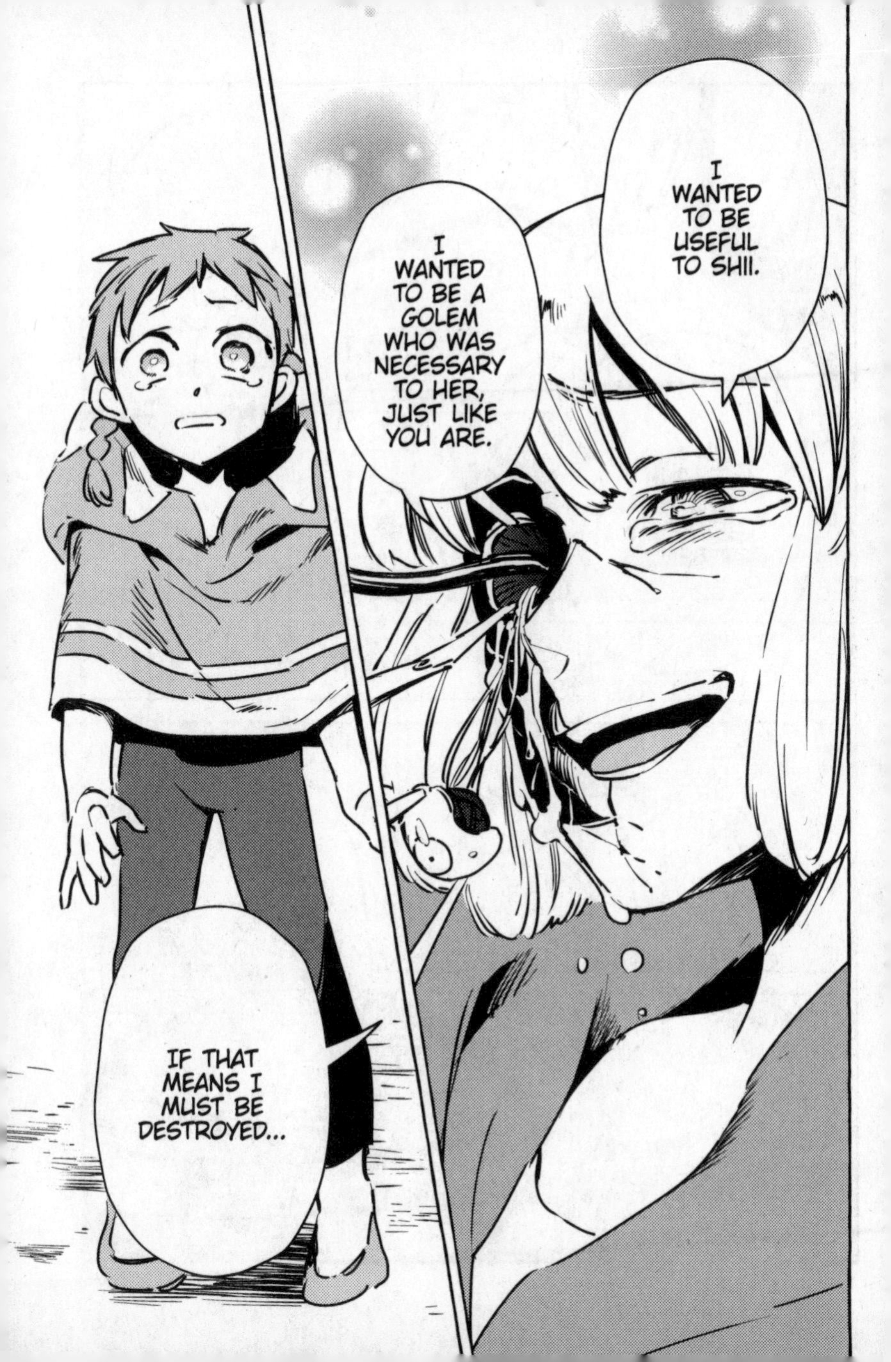
I WANTED TO BE USEFUL TO SHII.
I WANTED TO BE A GOLEM WHO WAS NECESSARY TO HER, JUST LIKE YOU ARE.
IF THAT MEANS I MUST BE DESTROYED...

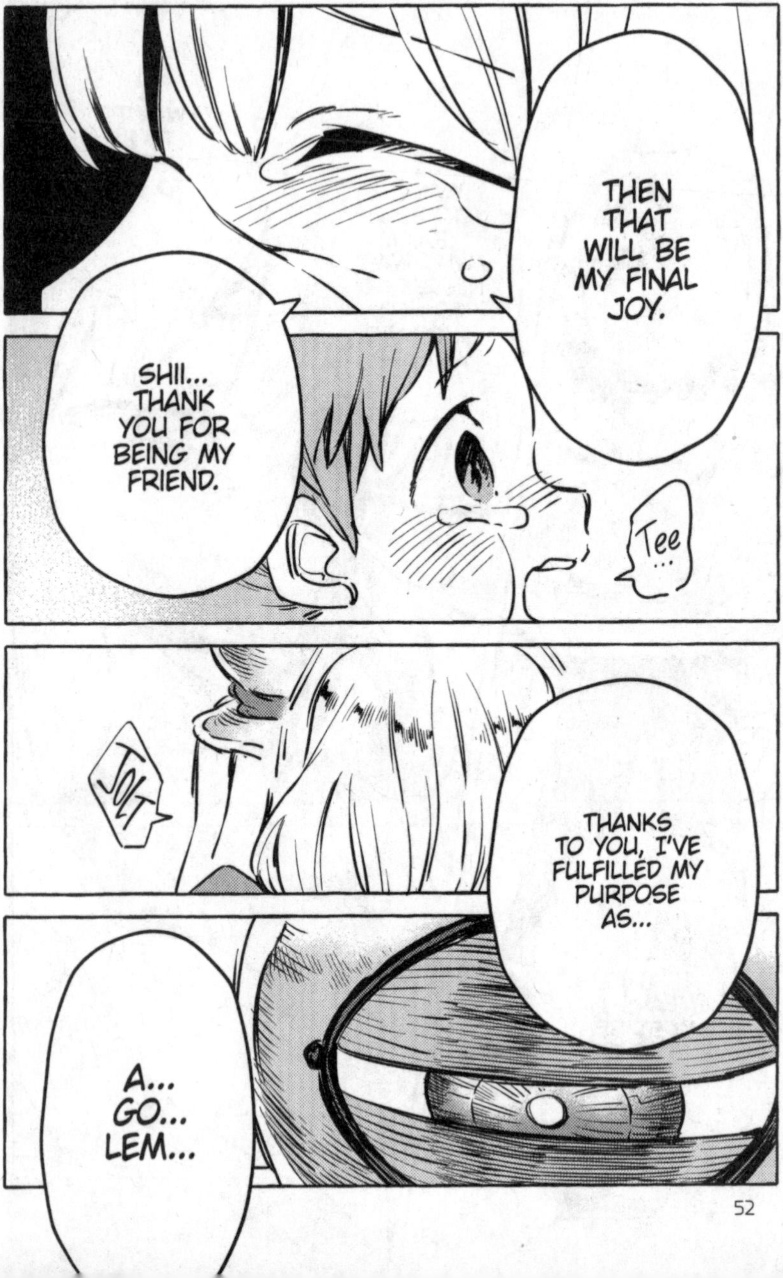
THEN THAT WILL BE MY FINAL JOY.
SHII... THANK YOU FOR BEING MY FRIEND.
Tee...
THANKS TO YOU, I'VE FULFILLED MY PURPOSE AS...
JOLT
A... GO... LEM...

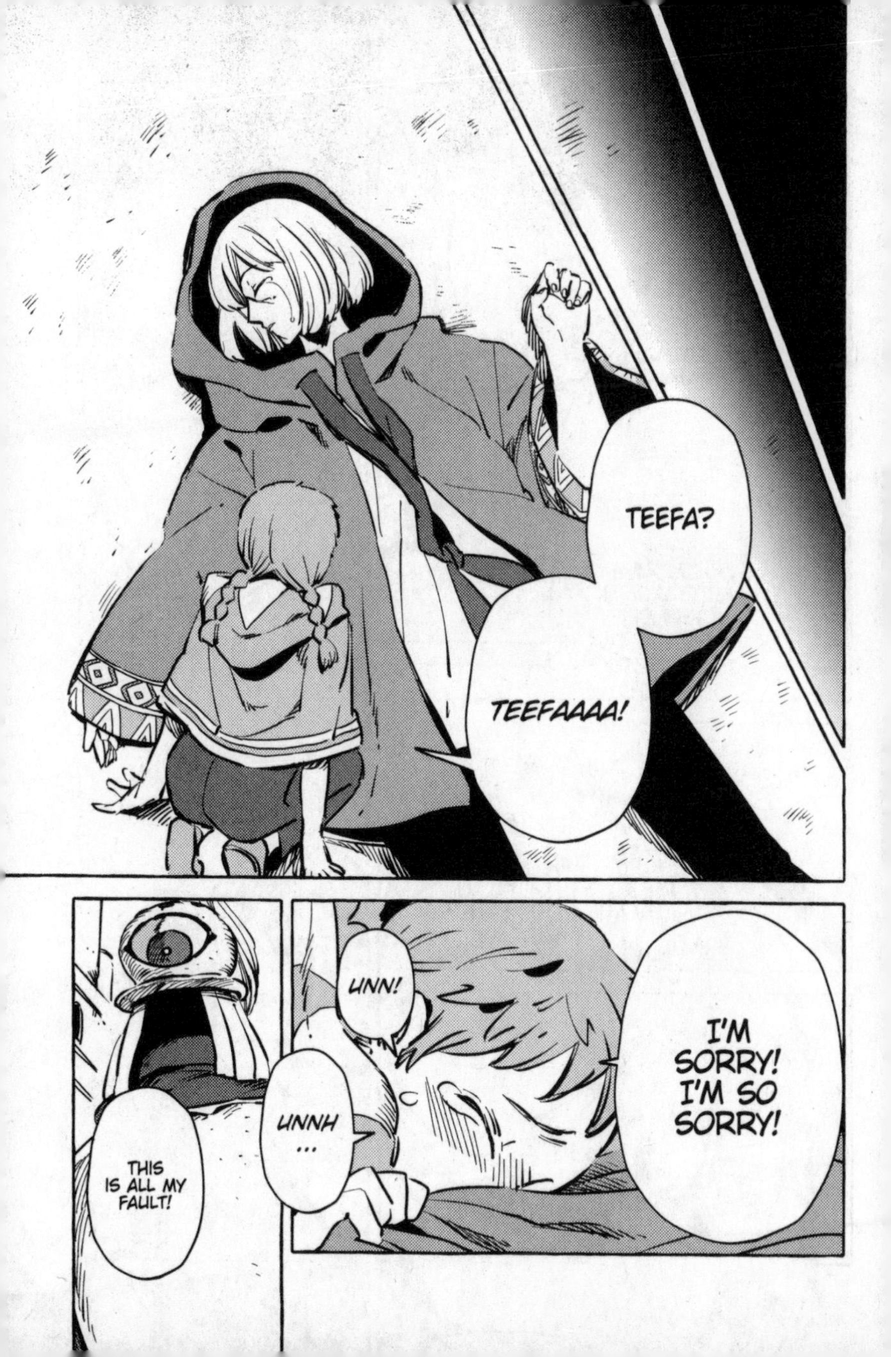
TEEFA?
TEEFAAAA!
I'M SORRY! I'M SO SORRY!
UNN!
UNNH ...
THIS IS ALL MY FAULT!

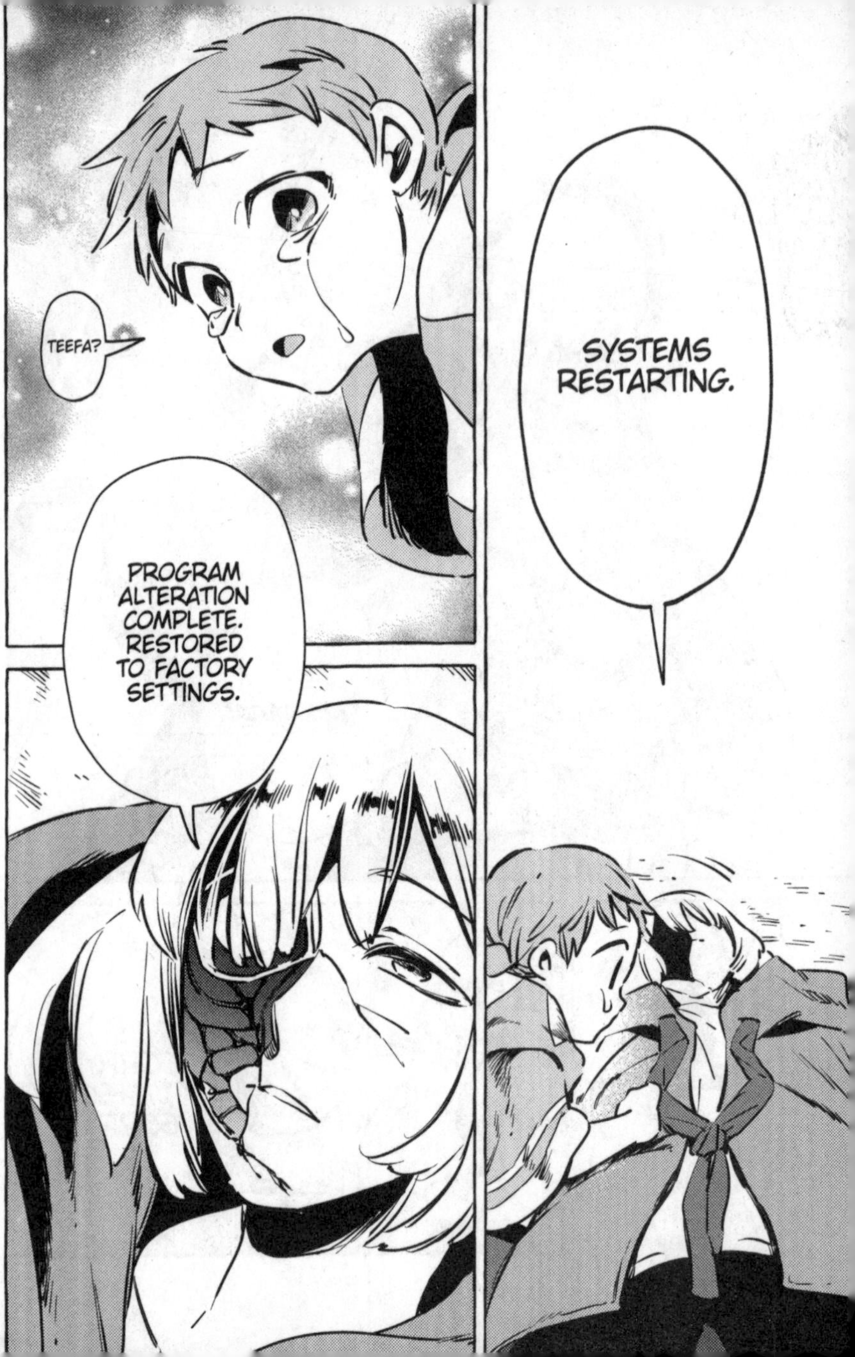
SYSTEMS RESTARTING.
TEEFA?
PROGRAM ALTERATION COMPLETE. RESTORED TO FACTORY SETTINGS.

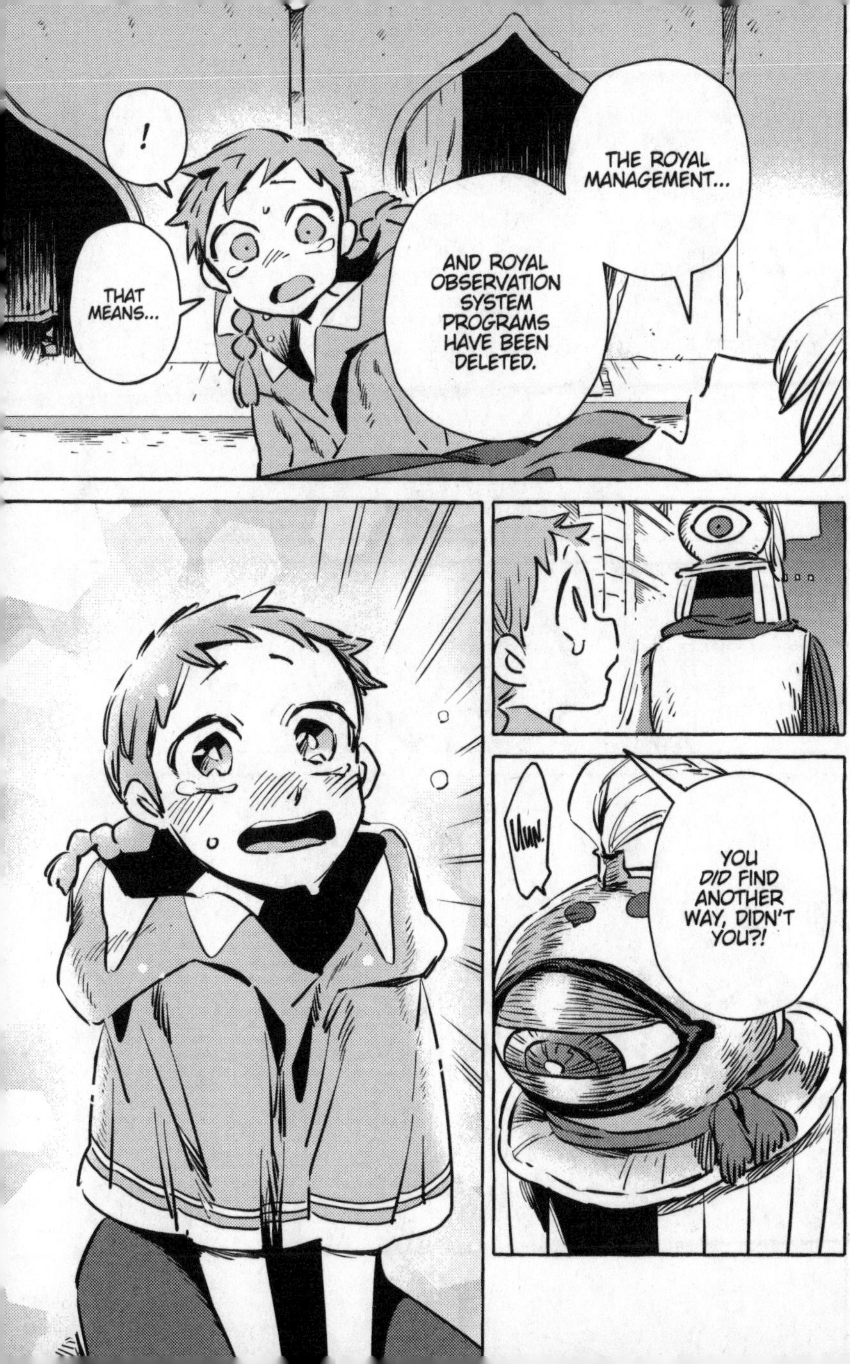
THE ROYAL MANAGEMENT...
AND ROYAL OBSERVATION SYSTEM PROGRAMS HAVE BEEN DELETED.
!
THAT MEANS...
YOU DID FIND ANOTHER WAY, DIDN'T YOU?!
UUN.

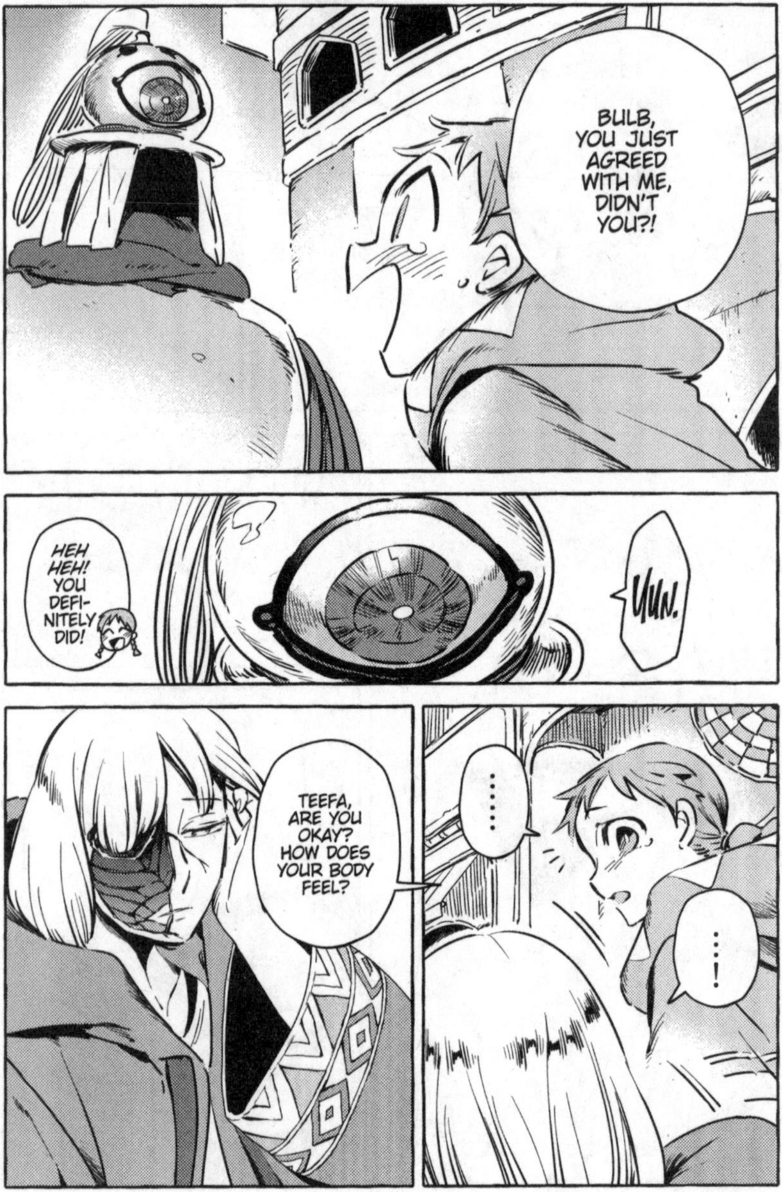
BULB, YOU JUST AGREED WITH ME, DIDN'T YOU?!
YUN.
HEH HEH! YOU DEFINITELY DID!
......
...!
TEEFA, ARE YOU OKAY? HOW DOES YOUR BODY FEEL?

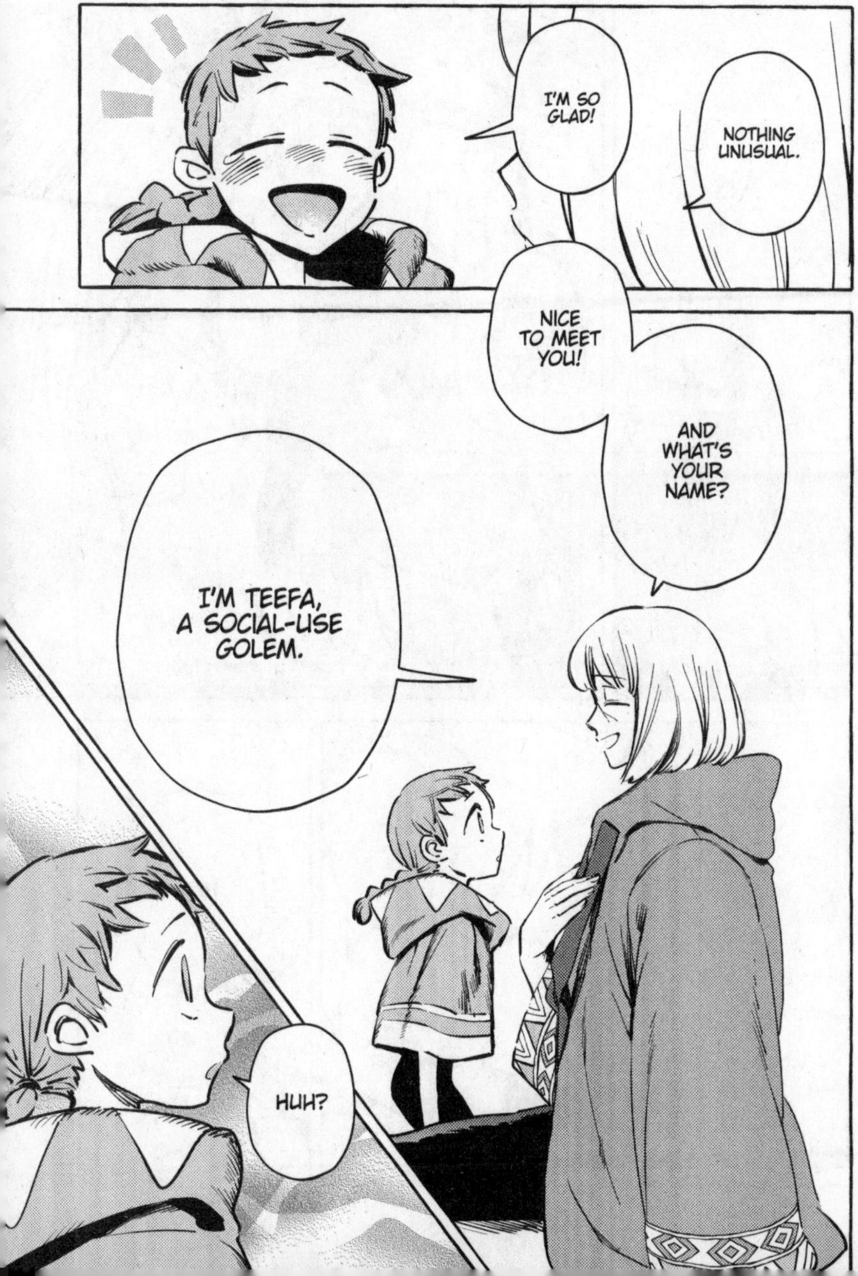
NOTHING UNUSUAL.
I'M SO GLAD!
NICE TO MEET YOU!
AND WHAT'S YOUR NAME?
I'M TEEFA, A SOCIAL-USE GOLEM.
HUH?

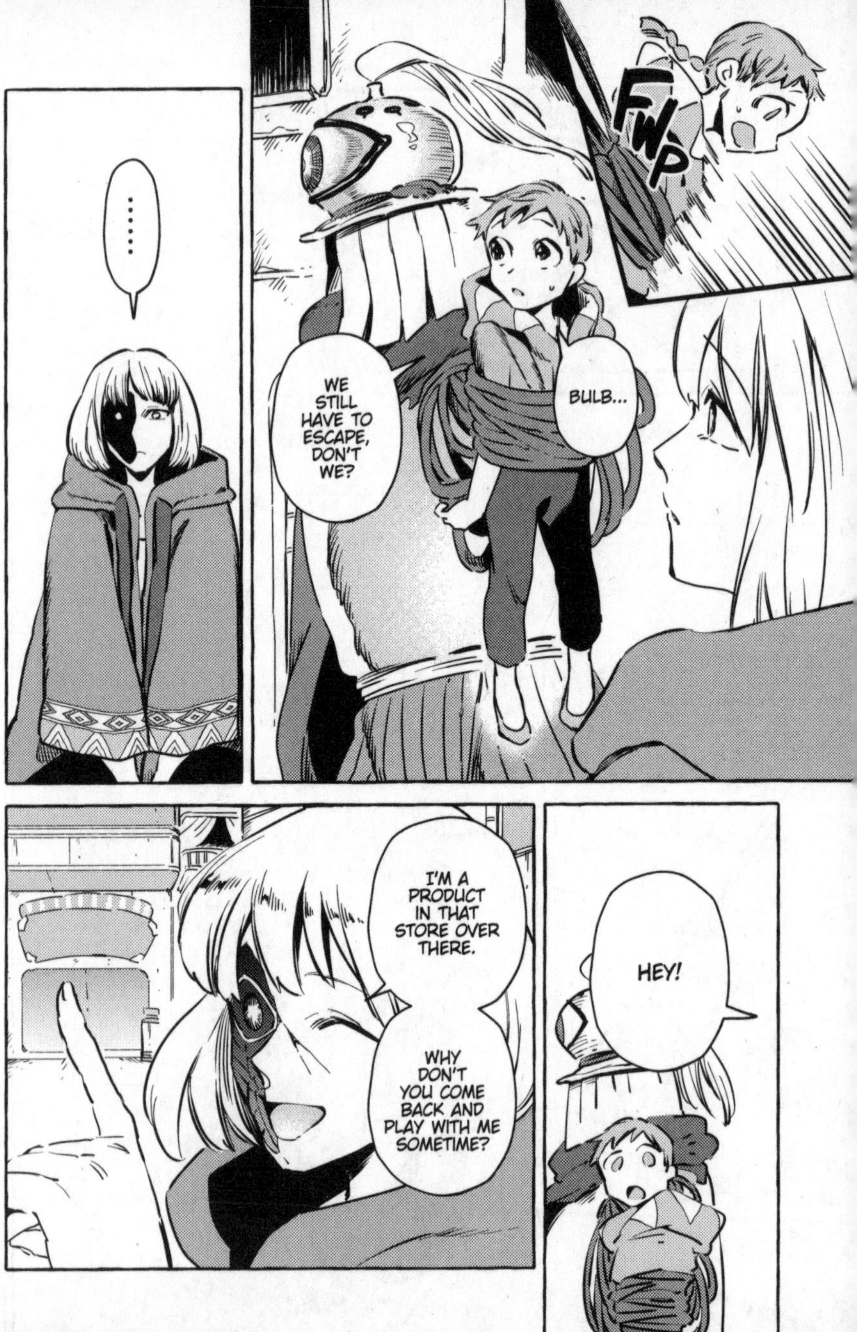
FWP
BULB...
WE STILL HAVE TO ESCAPE, DON'T WE?
......
HEY!
I'M A PRODUCT IN THAT STORE OVER THERE.
WHY DON'T YOU COME BACK AND PLAY WITH ME SOMETIME?

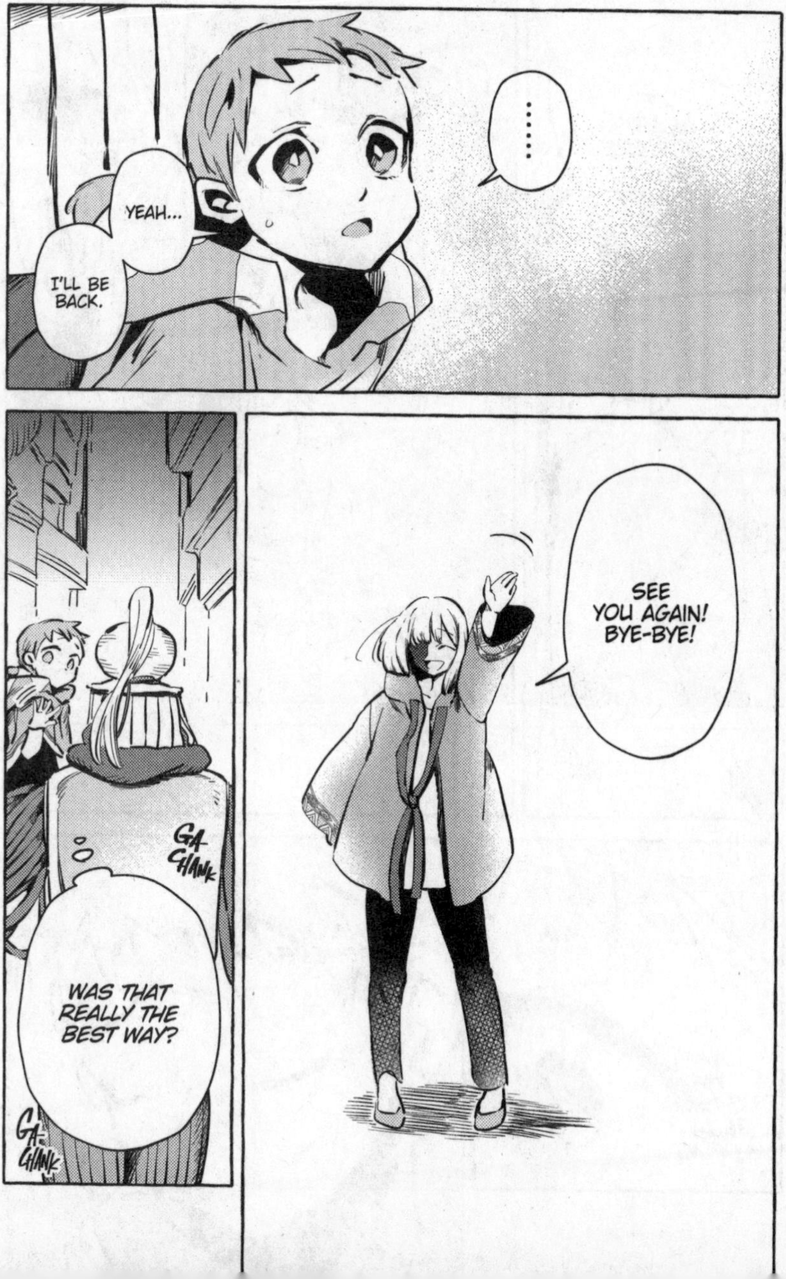
......
YEAH...
I'LL BE BACK.
SEE YOU AGAIN! BYE-BYE!
GA-CHANK
WAS THAT REALLY THE BEST WAY?
GA-CHANK

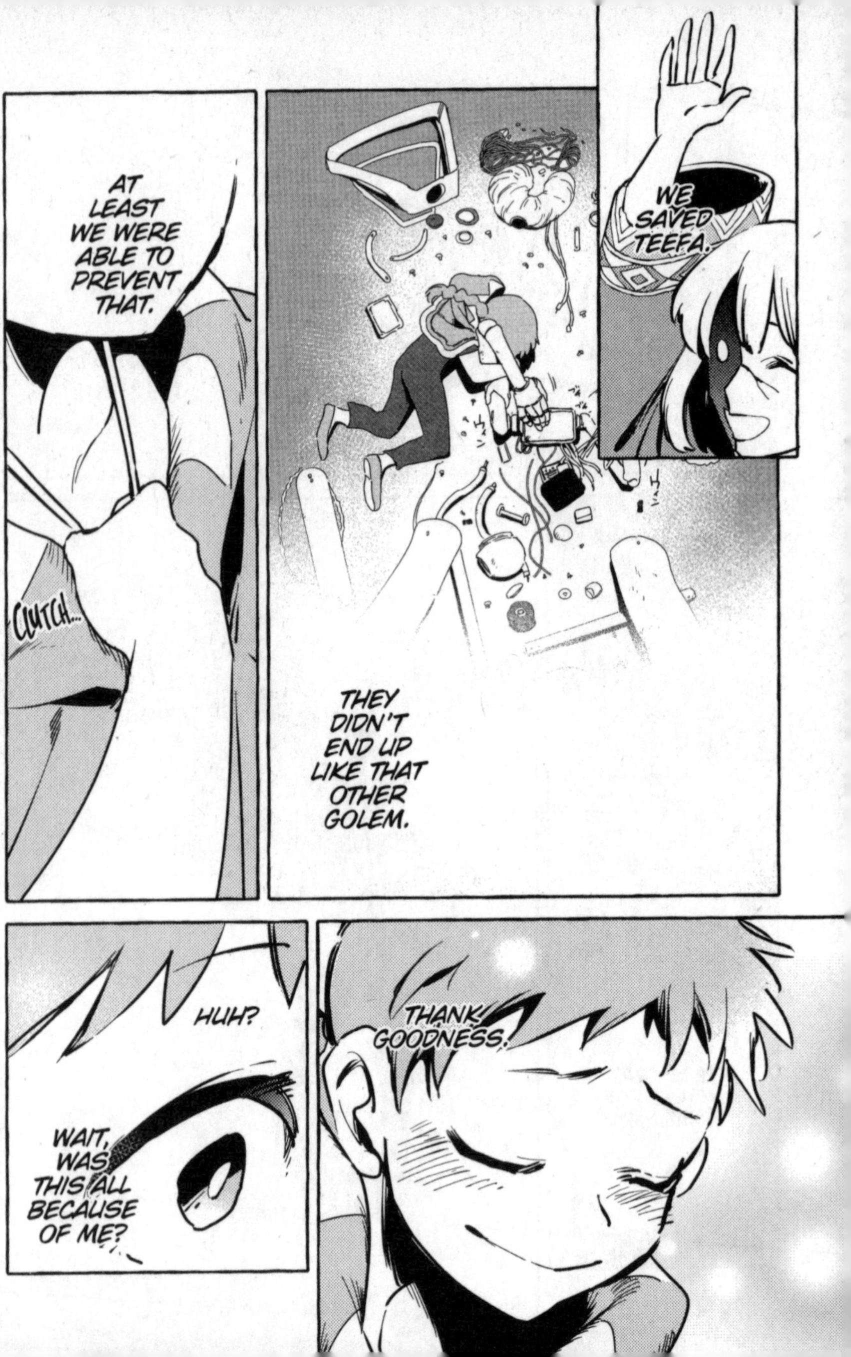
WE SAVED TEEFA.
THEY DIDN'T END UP LIKE THAT OTHER GOLEM.
AT LEAST WE WERE ABLE TO PREVENT THAT.
CLUTCH...
THANK GOODNESS.
HUH?
WAIT, WAS THIS ALL BECAUSE OF ME?

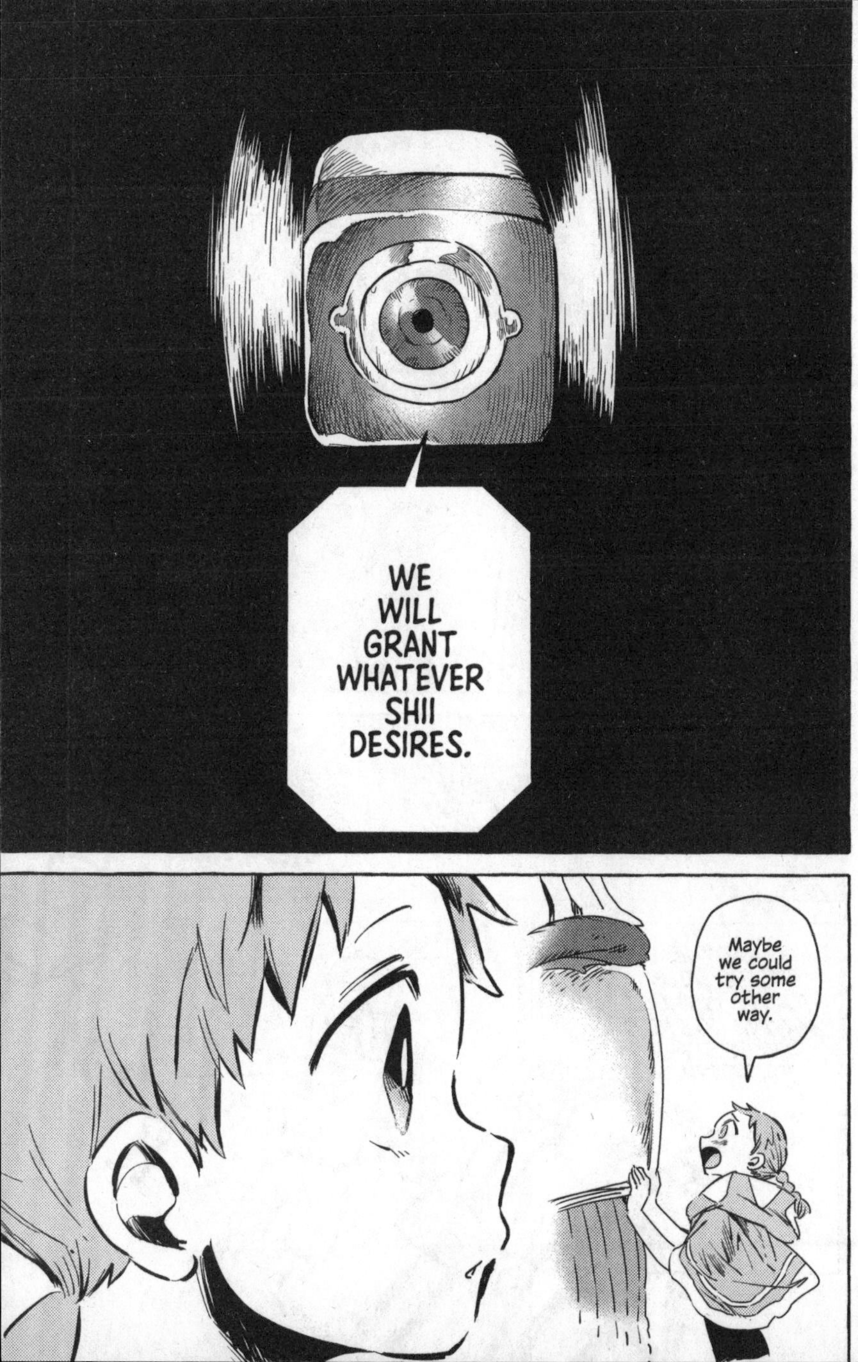
WE WILL GRANT WHATEVER SHII DESIRES.
Maybe we could try some other way.

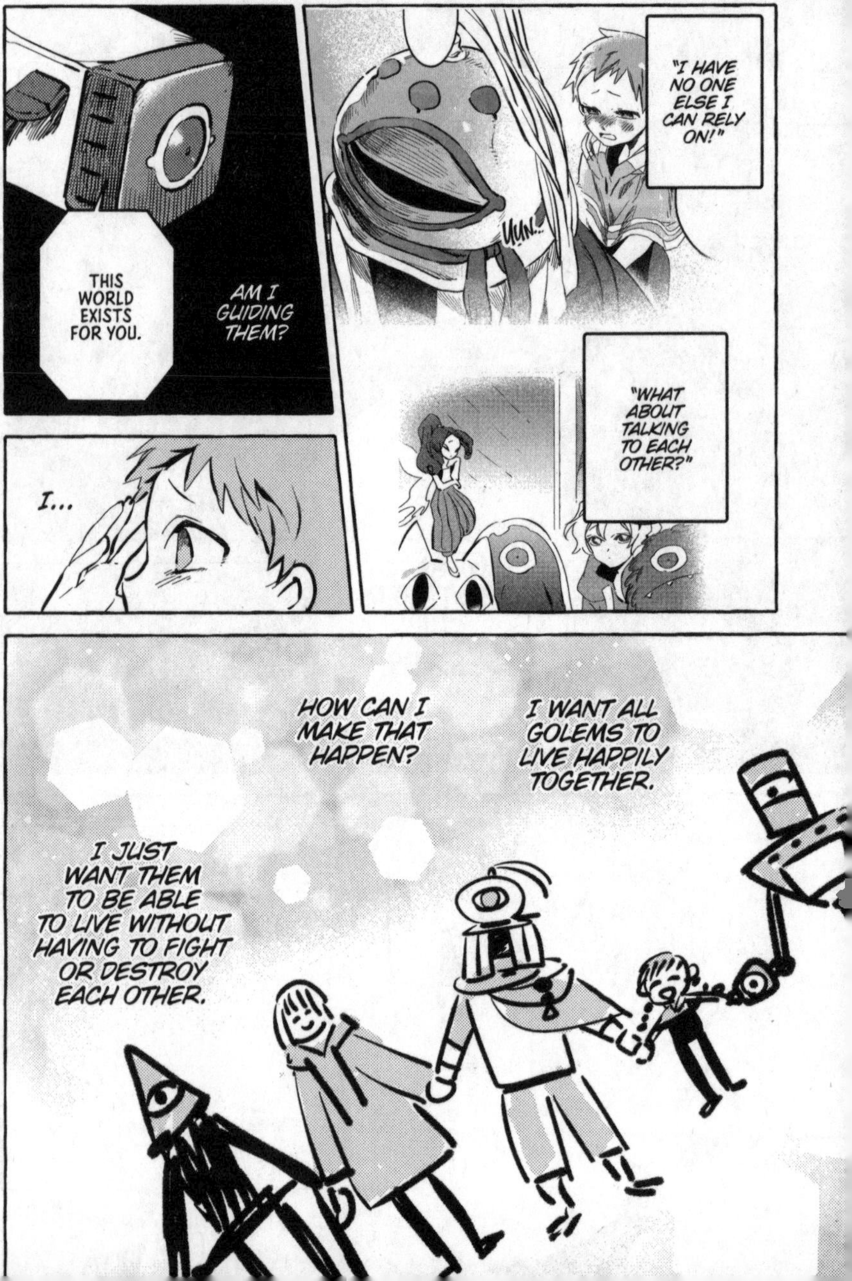
"I HAVE NO ONE ELSE I CAN RELY ON!"
UUN...
AM I GUIDING THEM?
THIS WORLD EXISTS FOR YOU.
"WHAT ABOUT TALKING TO EACH OTHER?"
I...
I WANT ALL GOLEMS TO LIVE HAPPILY TOGETHER.
HOW CAN I MAKE THAT HAPPEN?
I JUST WANT THEM TO BE ABLE TO LIVE WITHOUT HAVING TO FIGHT OR DESTROY EACH OTHER.

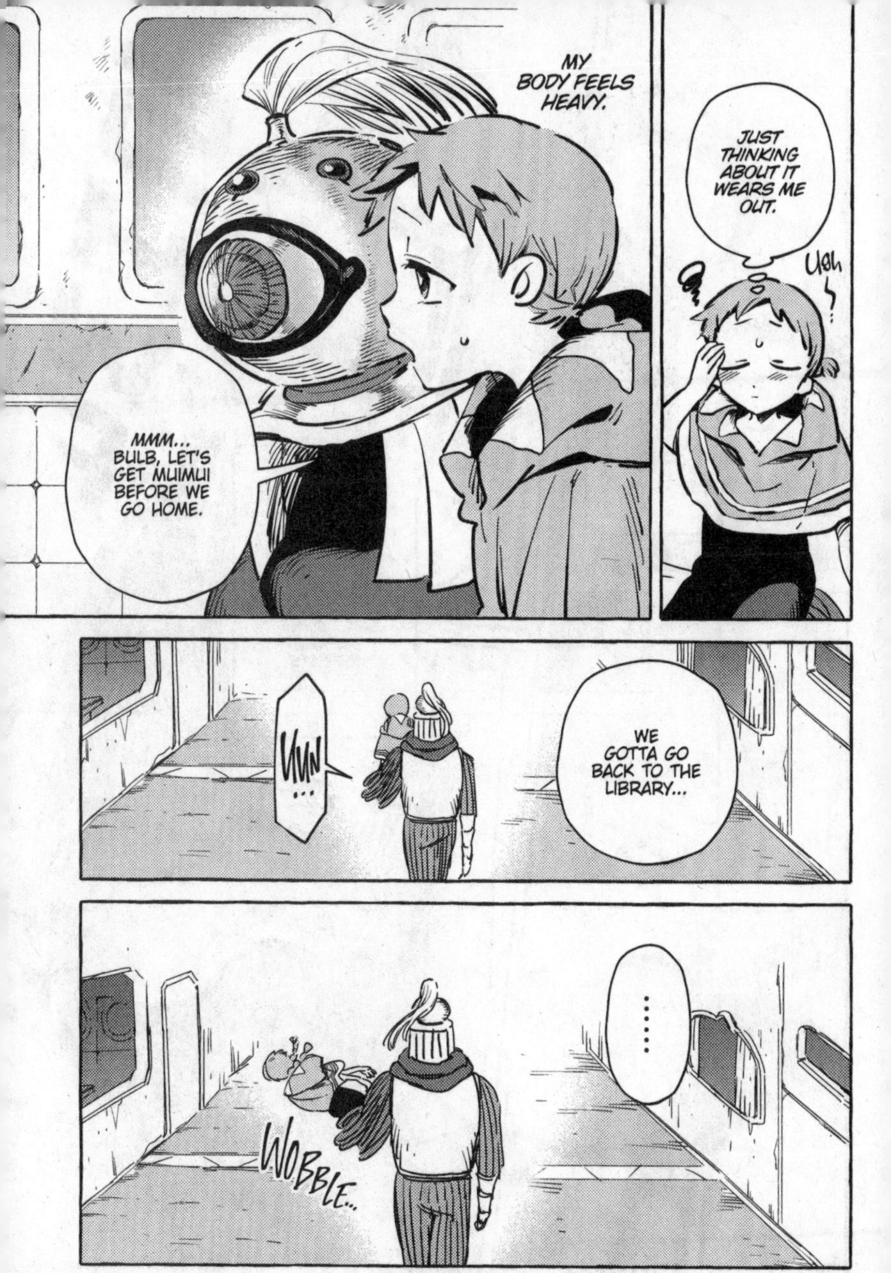
JUST THINKING ABOUT IT WEARS ME OUT.
Ugh
MY BODY FEELS HEAVY.
MMM... BULB, LET'S GET MUIMUI BEFORE WE GO HOME.
WE GOTTA GO BACK TO THE LIBRARY...
UUN...
......
WOBBLE...

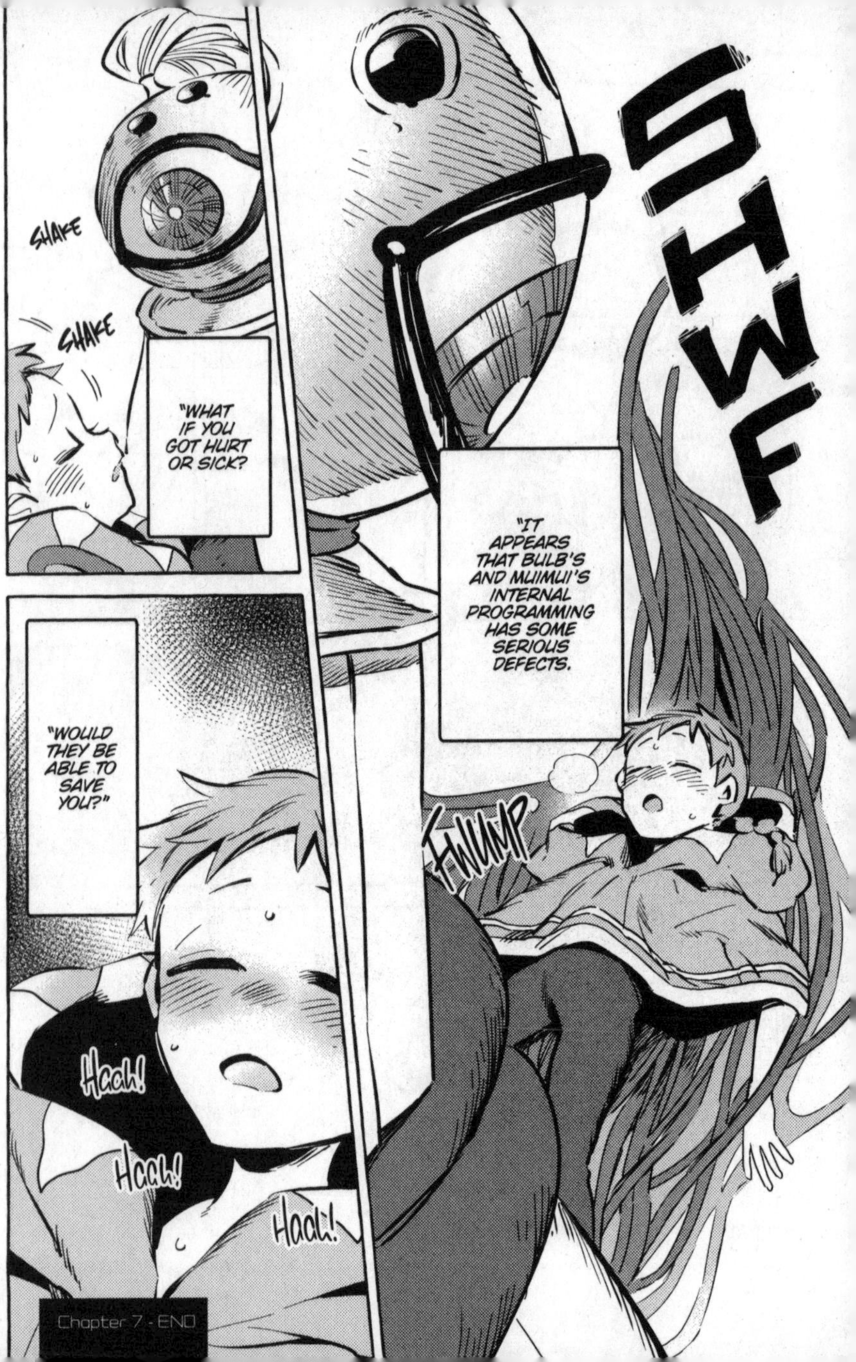
SHWF
"IT APPEARS THAT BULB'S AND MUIMUI'S INTERNAL PROGRAMMING HAS SOME SERIOUS DEFECTS.
FWUMP
SHAKE
SHAKE
"WHAT IF YOU GOT HURT OR SICK?
"WOULD THEY BE ABLE TO SAVE YOU?"
Haah!
Haah!
Haah!
Chapter 7 - END

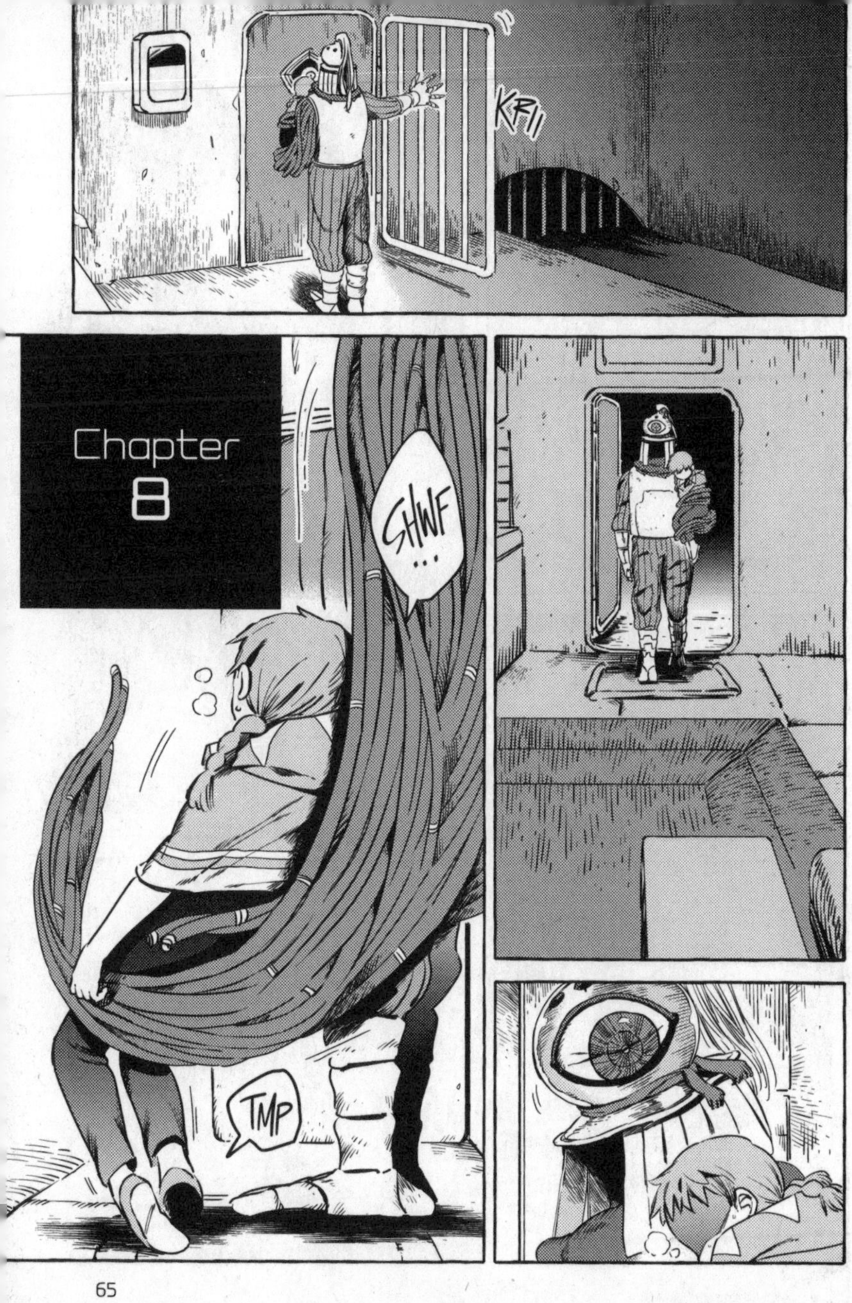
KRII
SHWF...
Chapter
8
TMP

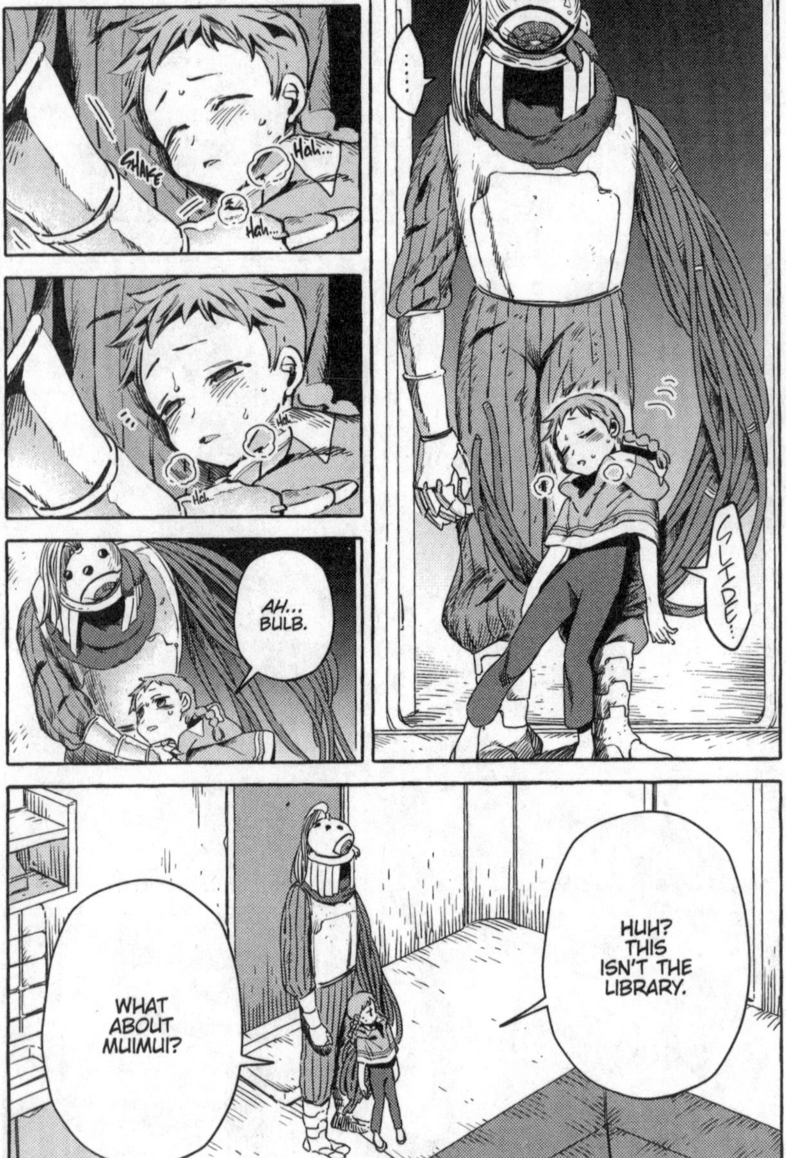

.....
SLIDE...
SHAKE
Hah...
Hah...
Hah...
Hah...
AH... BULB.
HUH? THIS ISN'T THE LIBRARY.
WHAT ABOUT MUIMUI?

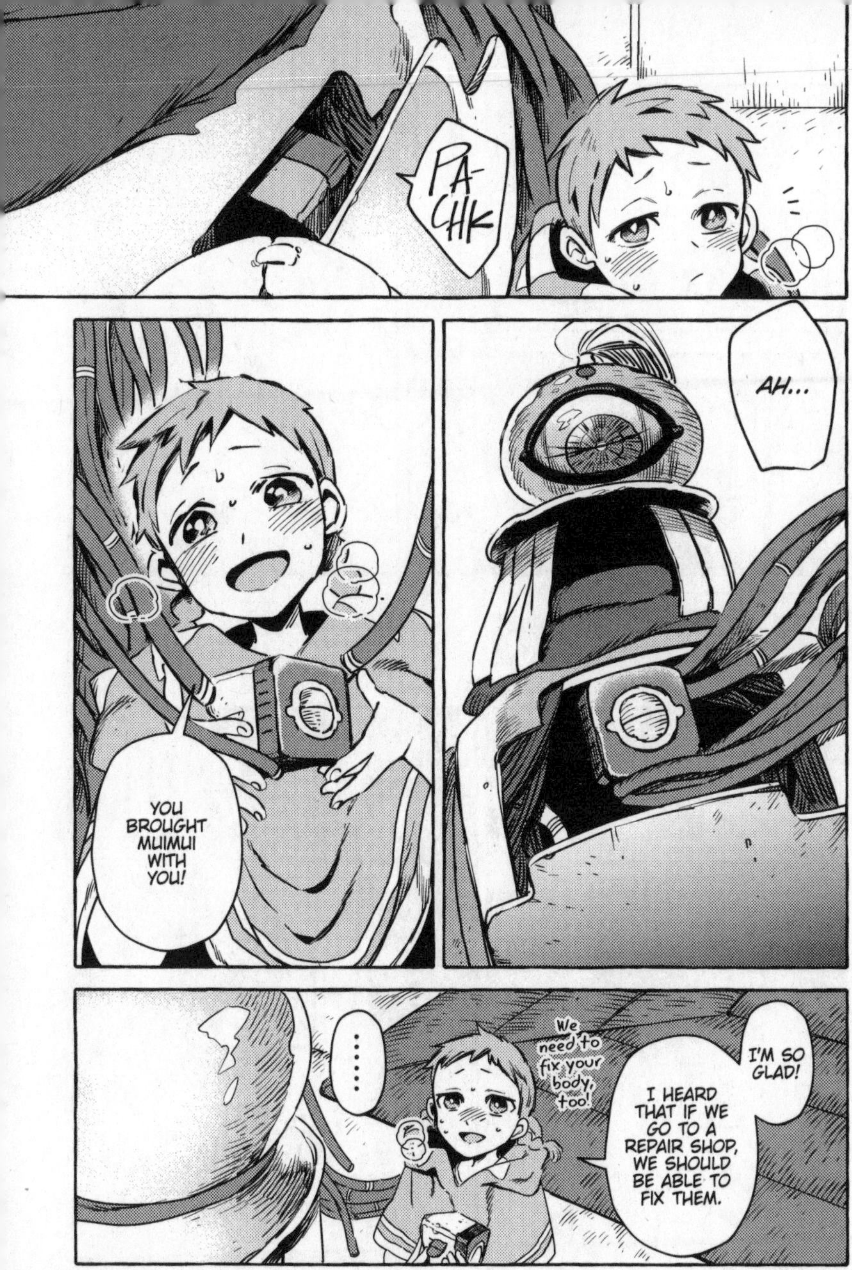
PA-CHK
AH...
YOU BROUGHT MUIMUI WITH YOU!
I'M SO GLAD!
I HEARD THAT IF WE GO TO A REPAIR SHOP, WE SHOULD BE ABLE TO FIX THEM.
We need to fix your body, too!
......

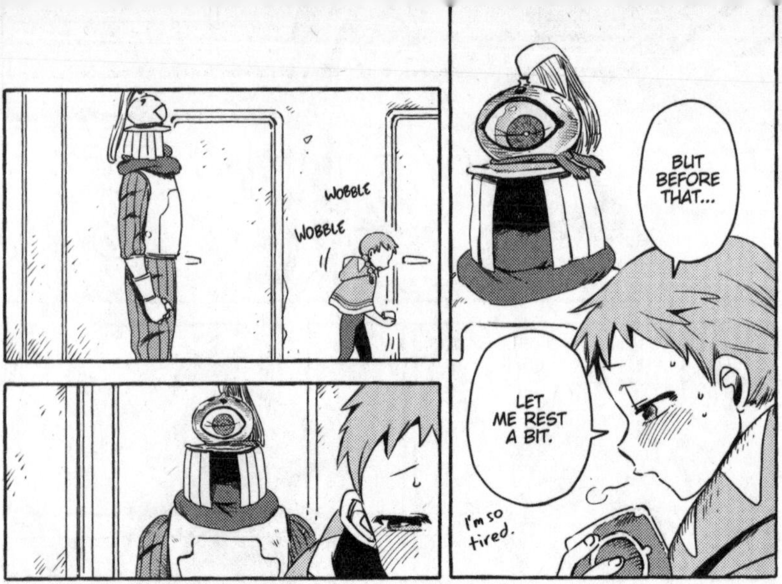
BUT BEFORE THAT...
LET ME REST A BIT.
I'm so tired.
WOBBLE
WOBBLE

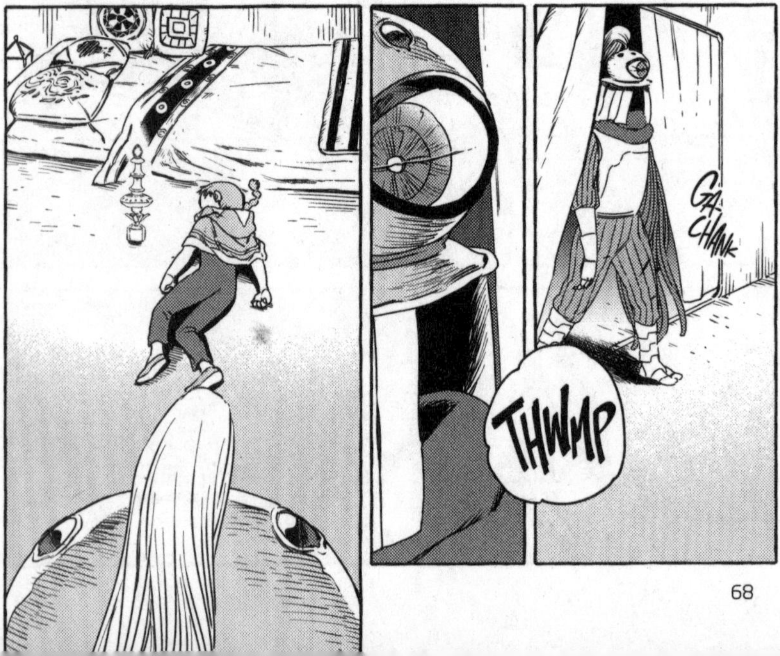
GA-CHANK
THWMP

GA-CHANK
GA-CHANK
SHURU
SHWF...

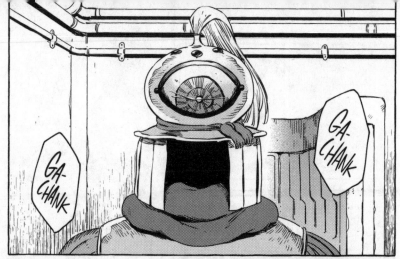

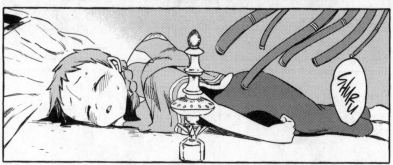

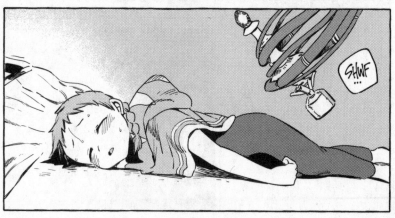

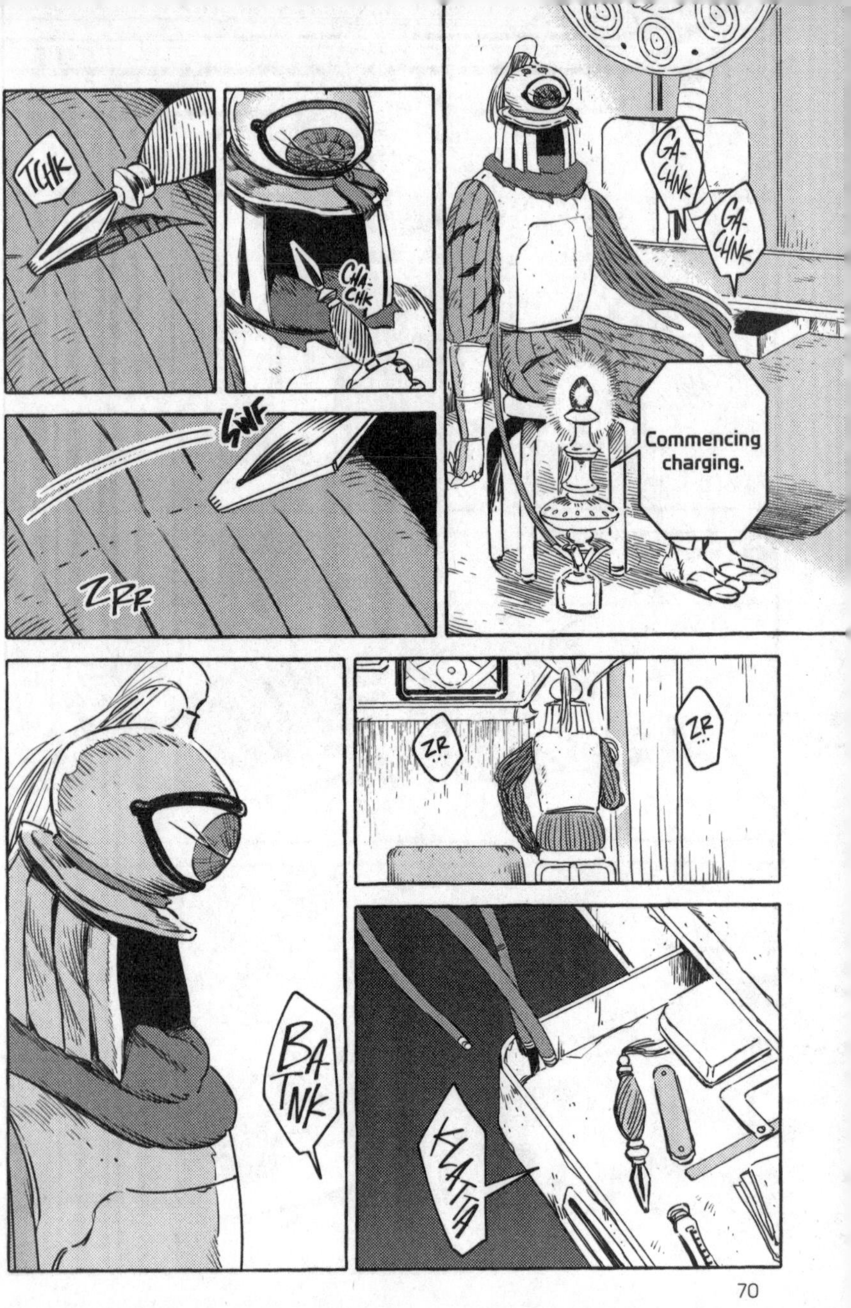
GA-CHNK
GA-CHNK
Commencing charging.
CHA-CHK
TCHK
SWF
ZRR
ZR...
ZR...
KLATTA
BATNK

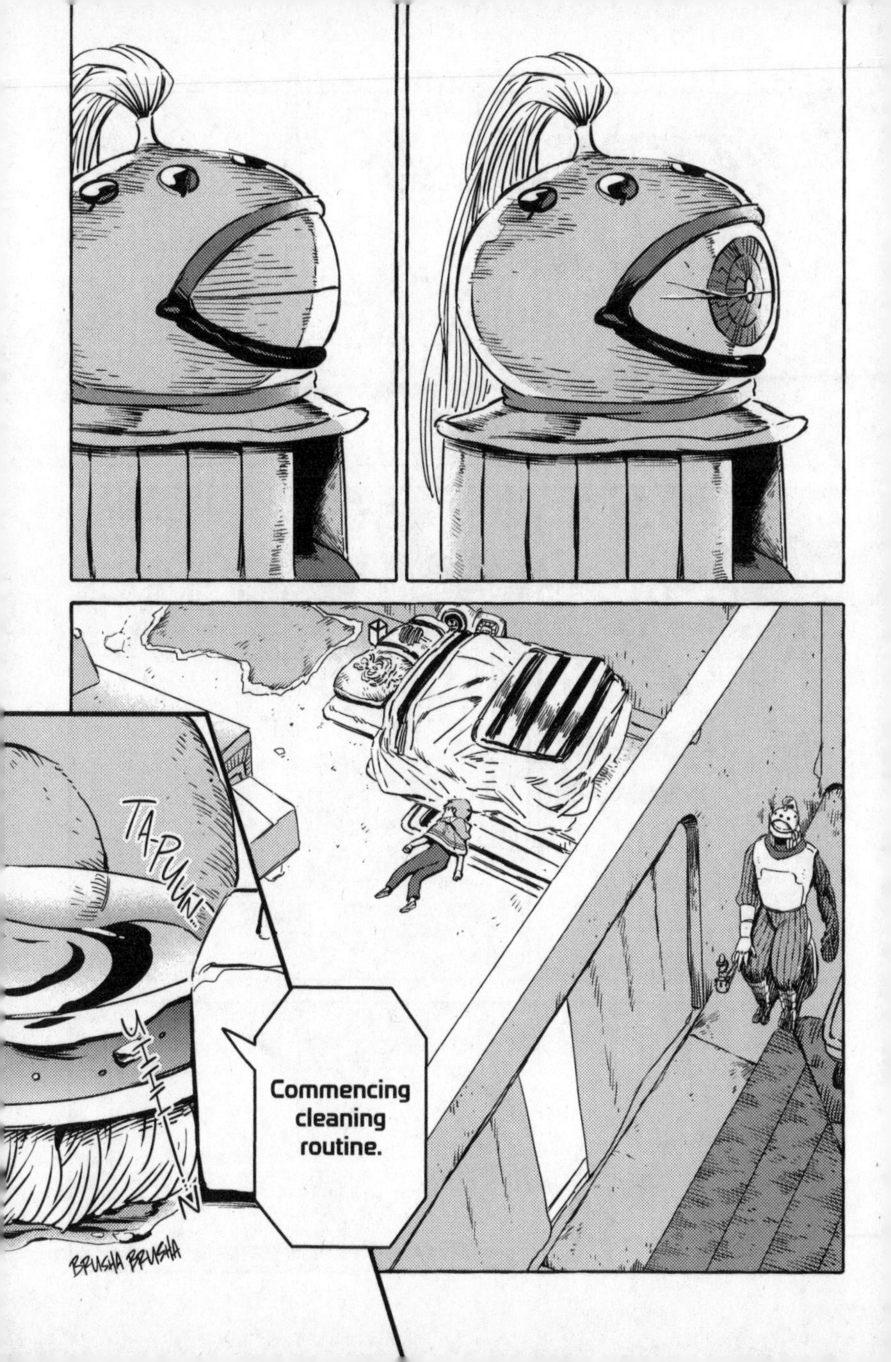
Commencing cleaning routine.
TA-PUUN...
UIIIIIIN
BRUSHA BRUSHA

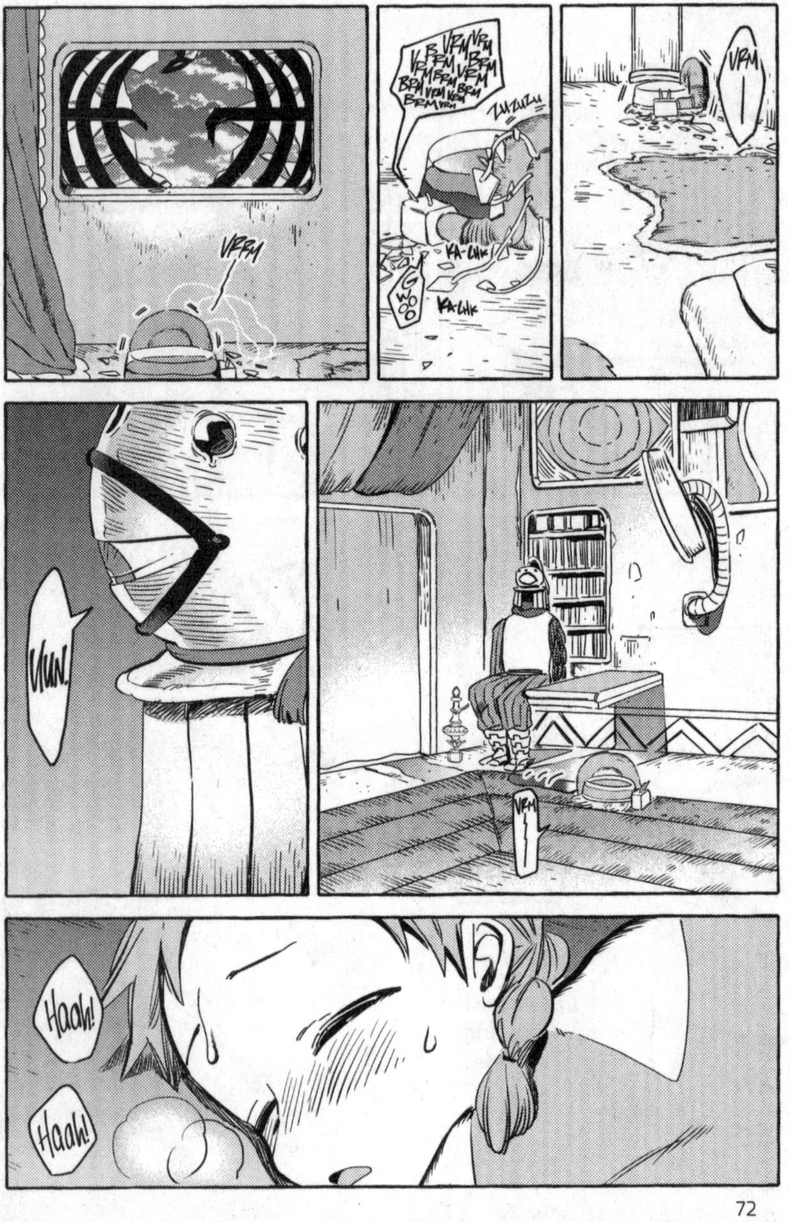
VRM
VRM VRM B BRM VRM BRM VRM BRM BRM VRM BRM VRM VRM BRM BRM VRM
ZUZUZU
KA-CHK
GWOOO
KA-CHK
VRM
VRM
VUN!
Haah!
Haah!

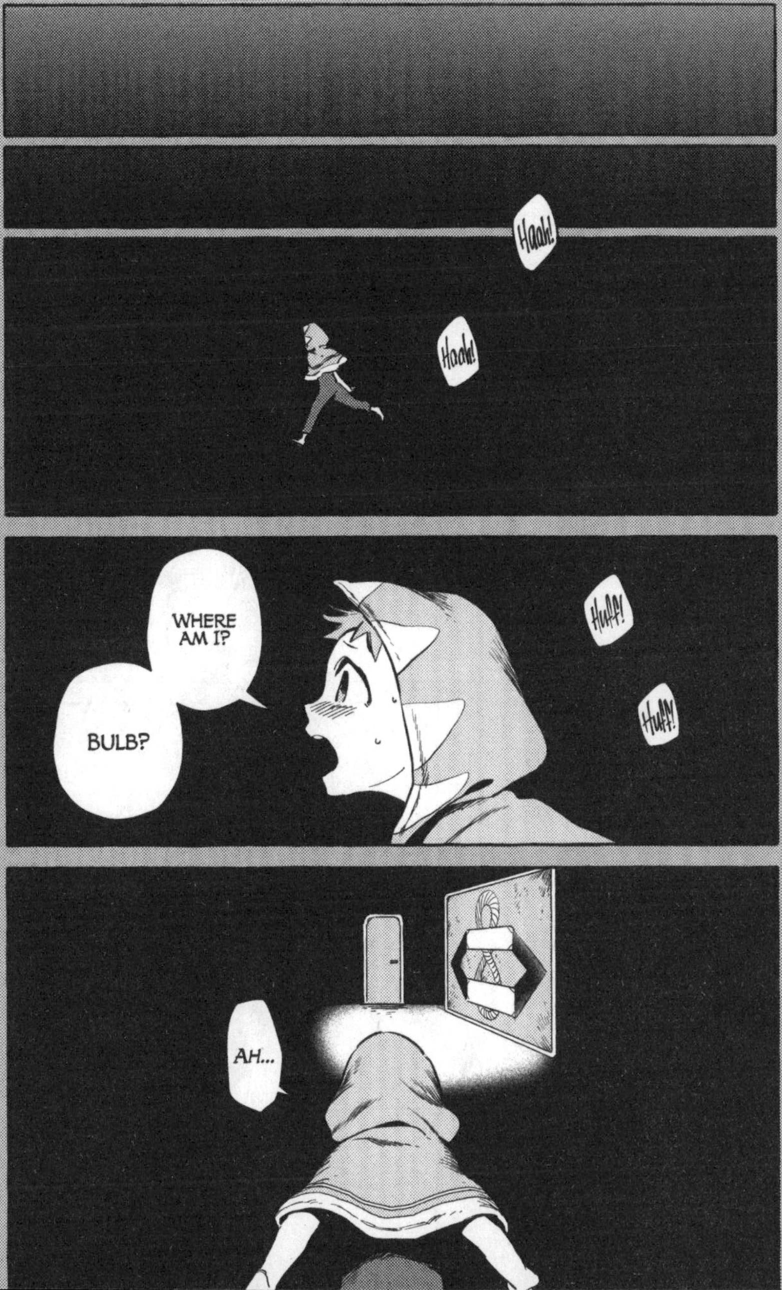
Haah!
Haah!
Huff!
Huff!
WHERE AM I?
BULB?
AH...

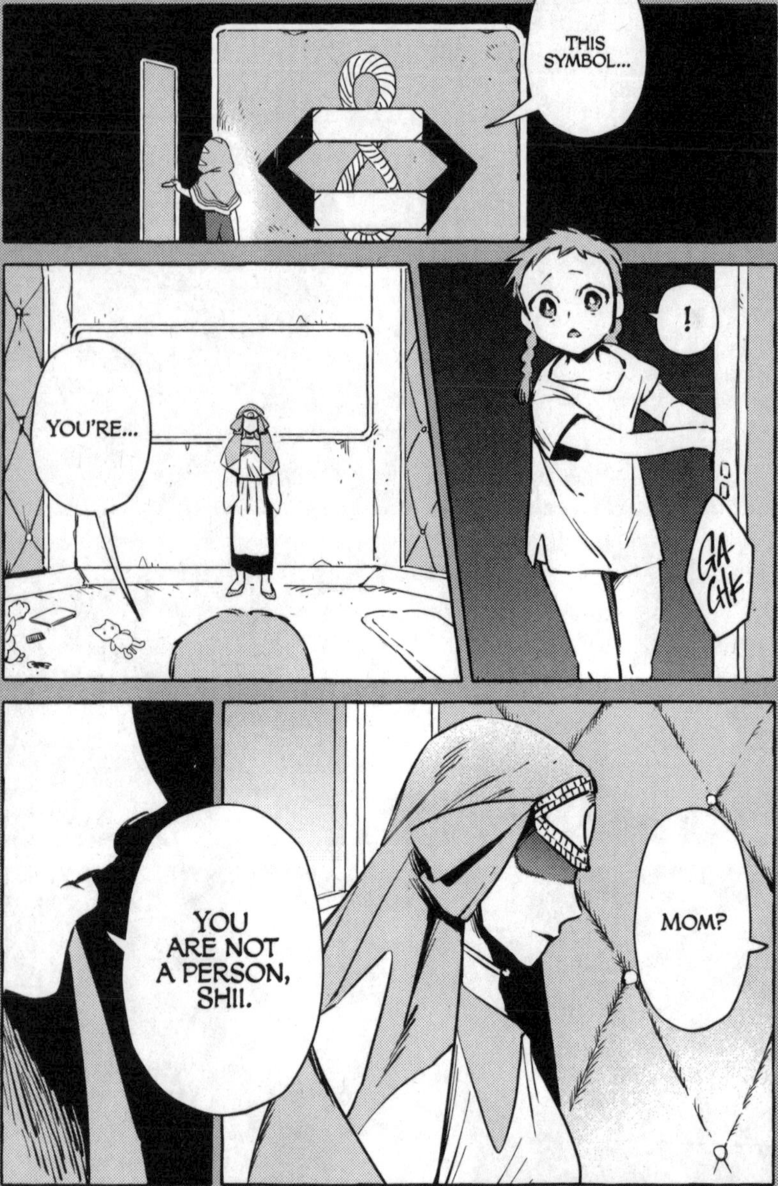
THIS SYMBOL...
!
GACHK
YOU'RE...
MOM?
YOU ARE NOT A PERSON, SHII.

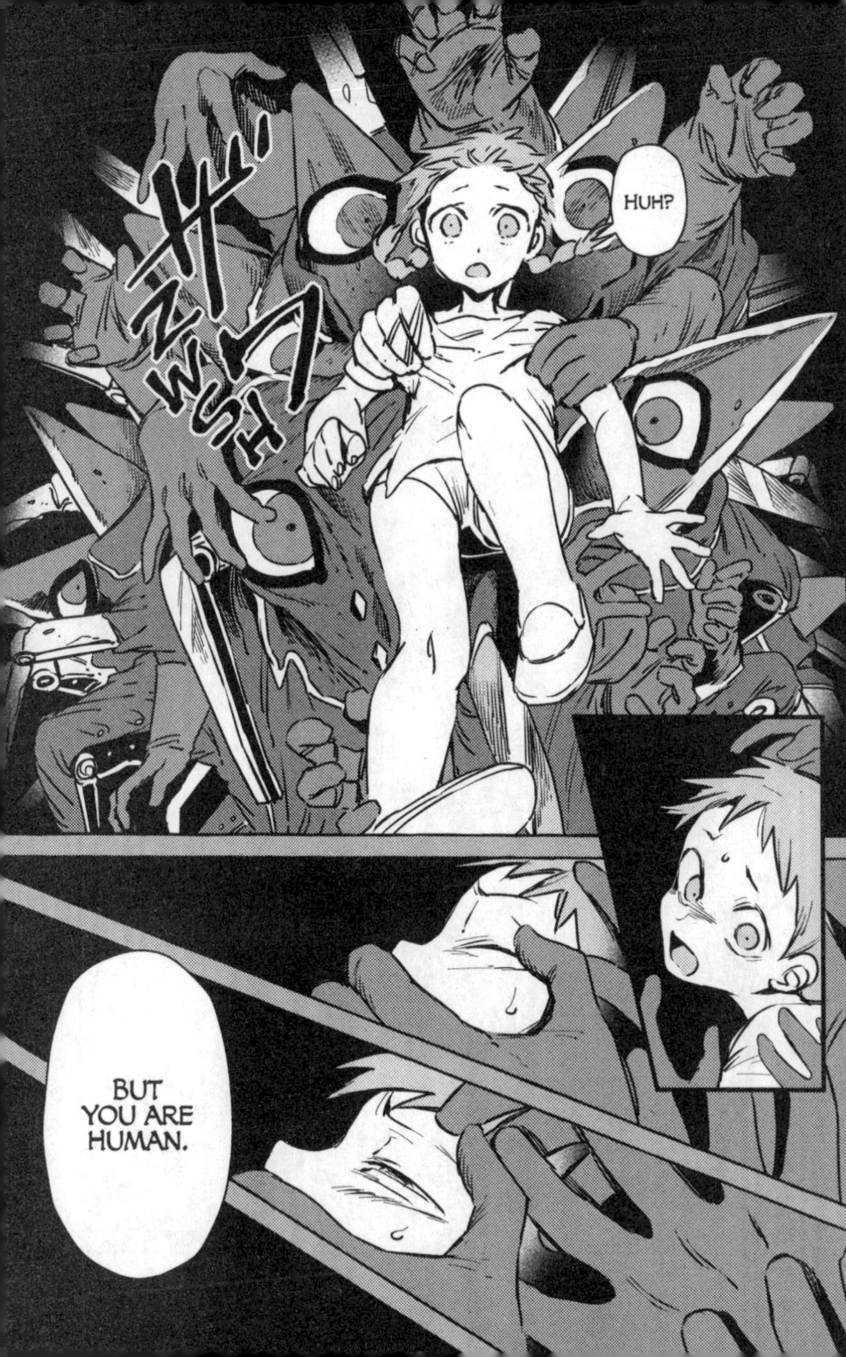
HUH?
BUT YOU ARE HUMAN.

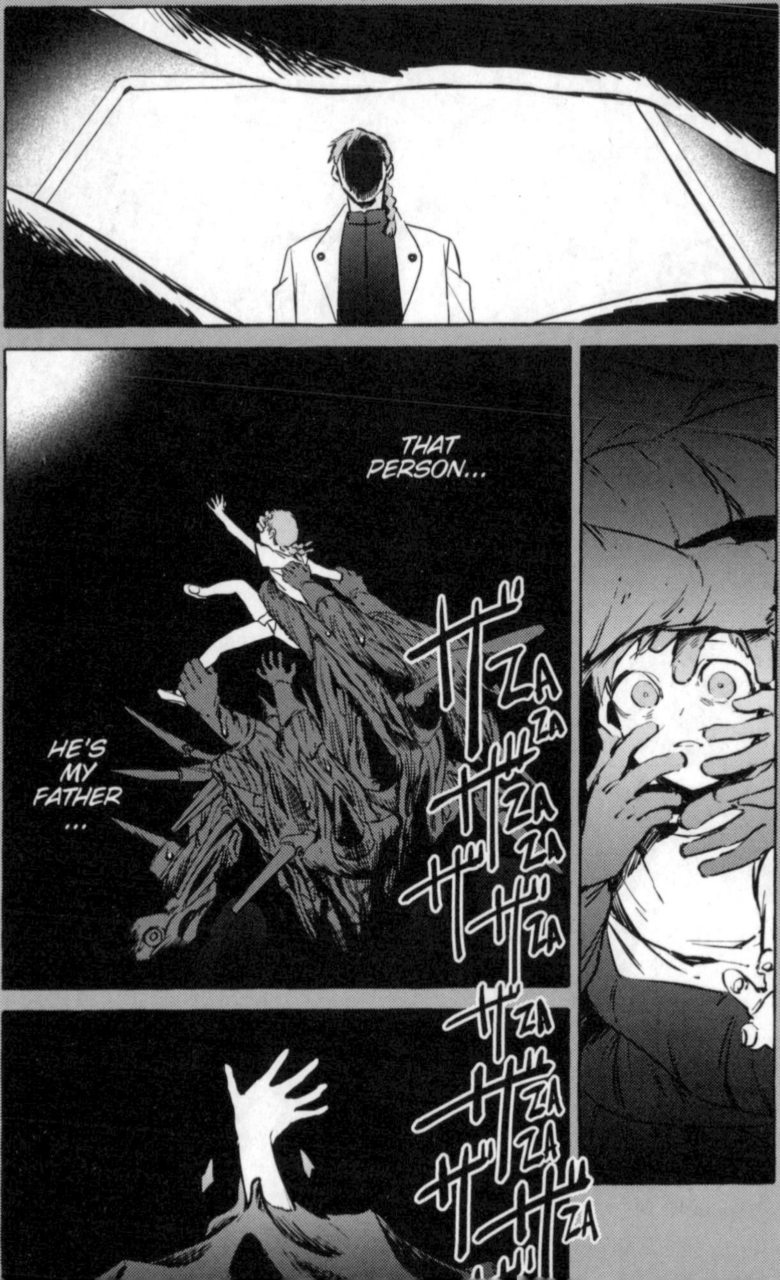
THAT PERSON...
HE'S MY FATHER ...
ZA ZA ZA ZA ZA ZA ZA ZA ZA

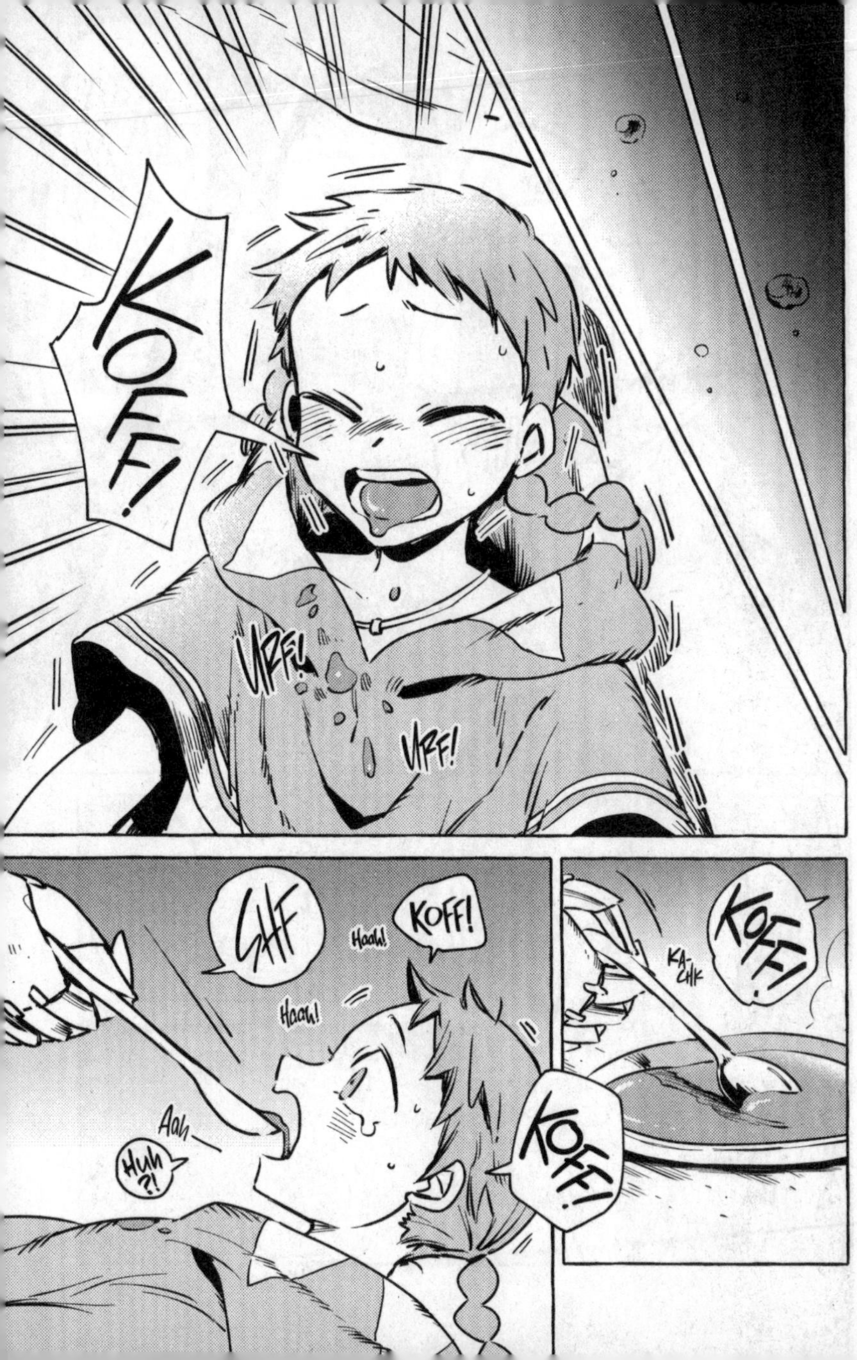
KOFF!
URF!
URF!
KOFF!
KA-CHK
KOFF!
GHF
Haah!
Haah!
Aah
Huh?!

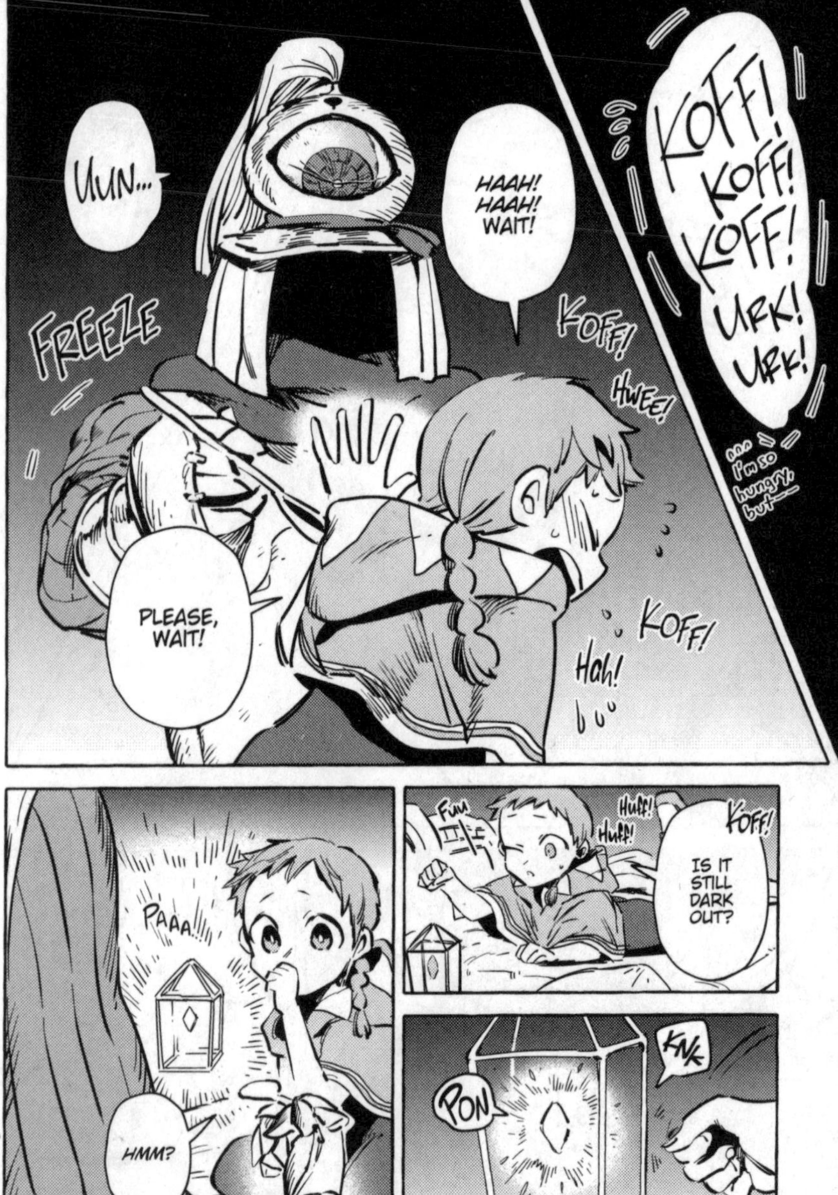
KOFF! KOFF! KOFF! URK! URK!
...I'm so hungry, but—
HAAH! HAAH! WAIT!
KOFF!
HWEE!
UUN...
FREEZE
KOFF!
Hah!
PLEASE, WAIT!
KOFF!
IS IT STILL DARK OUT?
Huff! Huff!
Fuu
KNK
PON
PAAA
HMM?

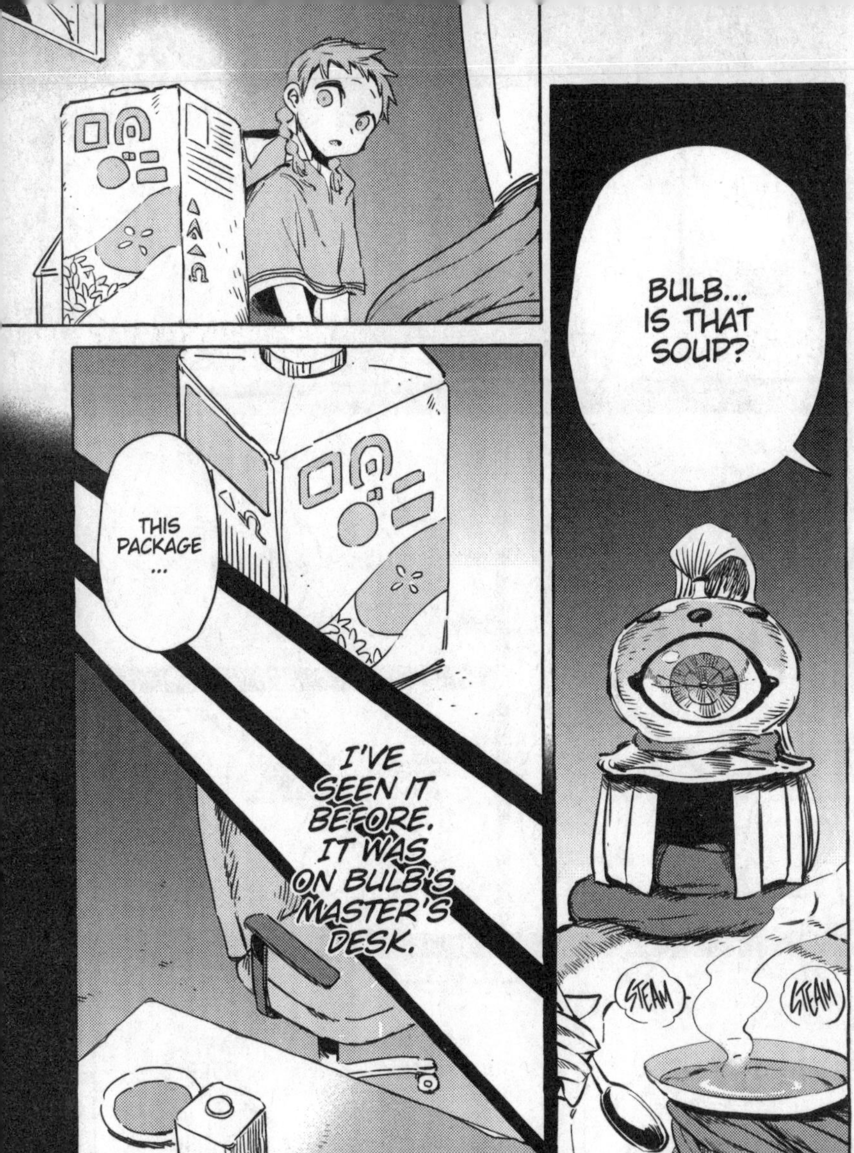
BULB... IS THAT SOUP?
STEAM
STEAM
THIS PACKAGE ...
I'VE SEEN IT BEFORE. IT WAS ON BULB'S MASTER'S DESK.

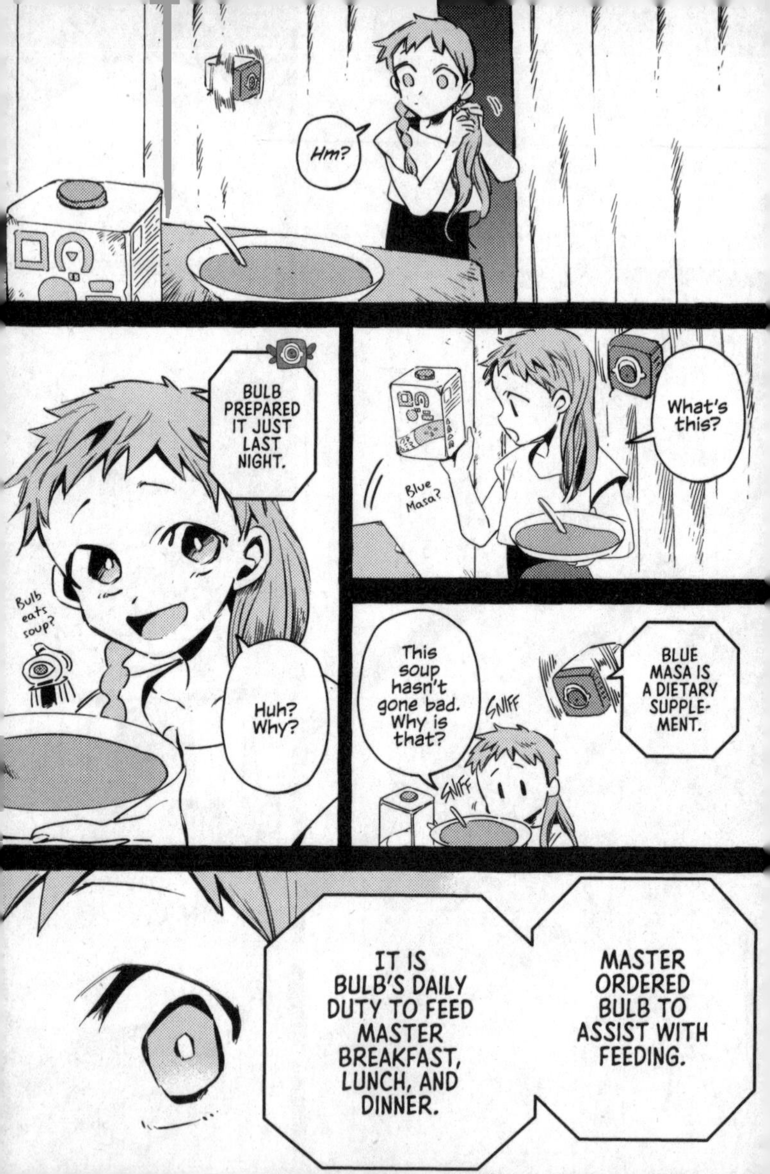
Hm?
What's this?
Blue Masa?
BLUE MASA IS A DIETARY SUPPLEMENT.
This soup hasn't gone bad. Why is that?
SNIFF
SNIFF
BULB PREPARED IT JUST LAST NIGHT.
Huh? Why?
Bulb eats soup?
MASTER ORDERED BULB TO ASSIST WITH FEEDING.
IT IS BULB'S DAILY DUTY TO FEED MASTER BREAKFAST, LUNCH, AND DINNER.

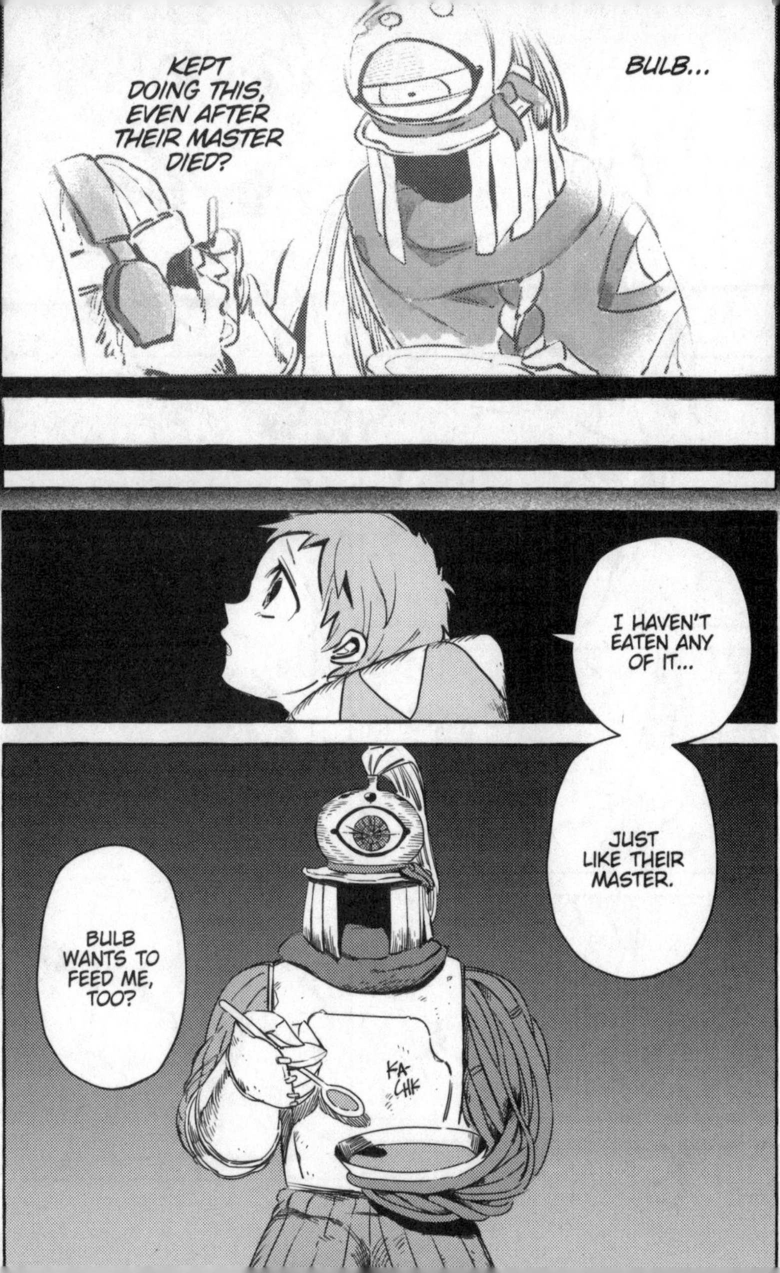
BULB...
KEPT DOING THIS, EVEN AFTER THEIR MASTER DIED?
I HAVEN'T EATEN ANY OF IT...
JUST LIKE THEIR MASTER.
BULB WANTS TO FEED ME, TOO?
KA-CHK

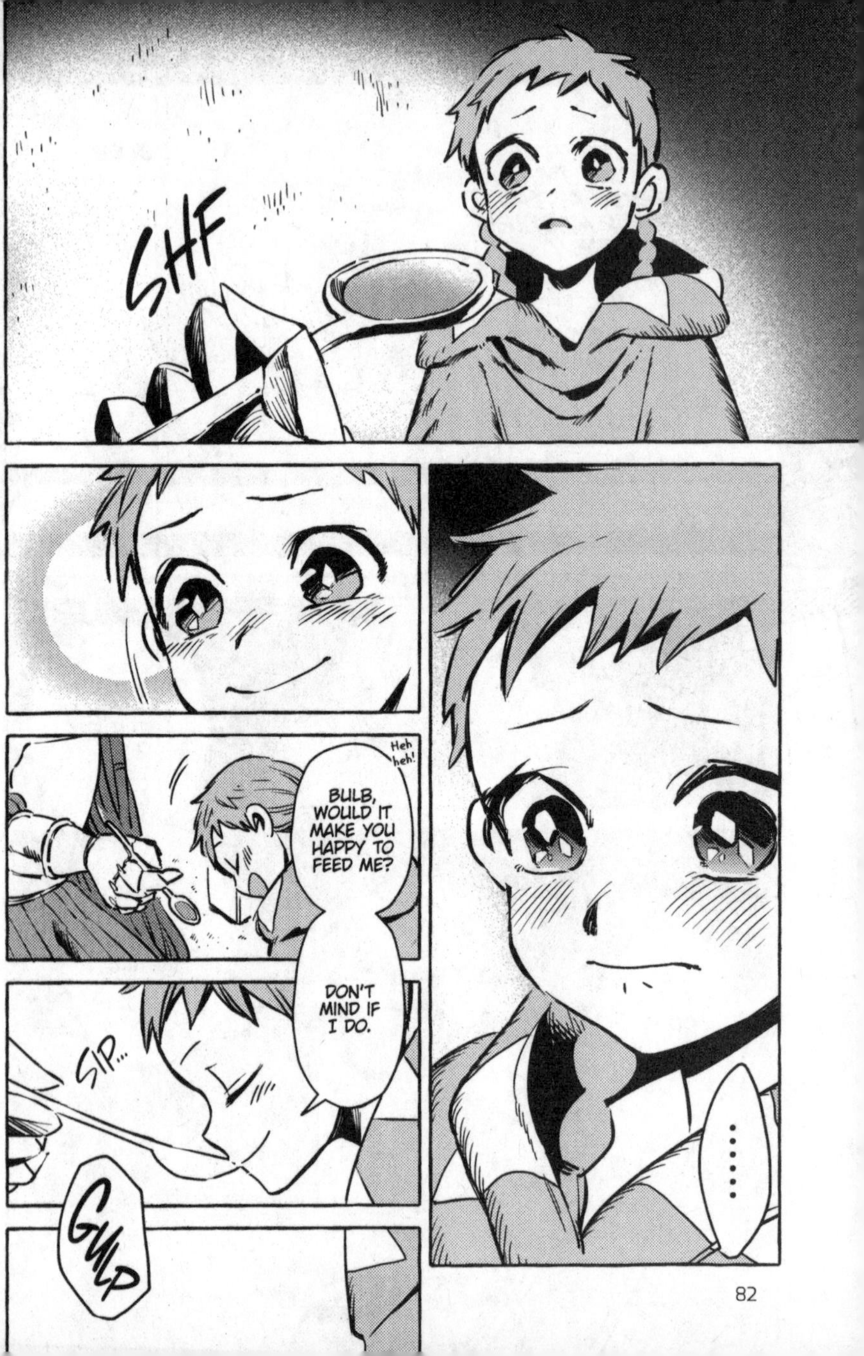
SHF
......
Heh heh!
BULB, WOULD IT MAKE YOU HAPPY TO FEED ME?
DON'T MIND IF I DO.
SIP...
GULP

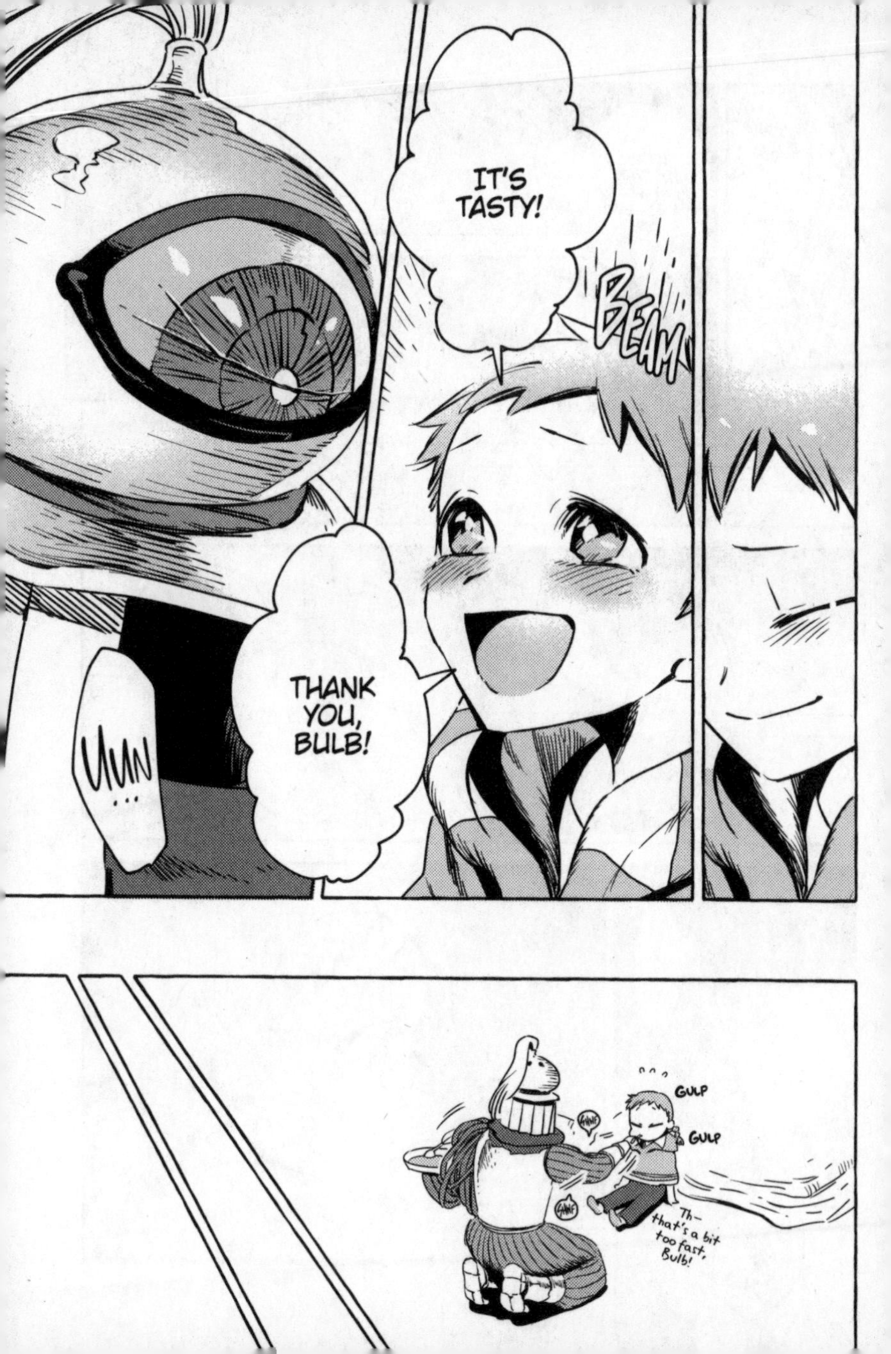
IT'S TASTY!
BEAM
THANK YOU, BULB!
UUN...
GULP
GULP
Th- that's a bit too fast, Bulb!

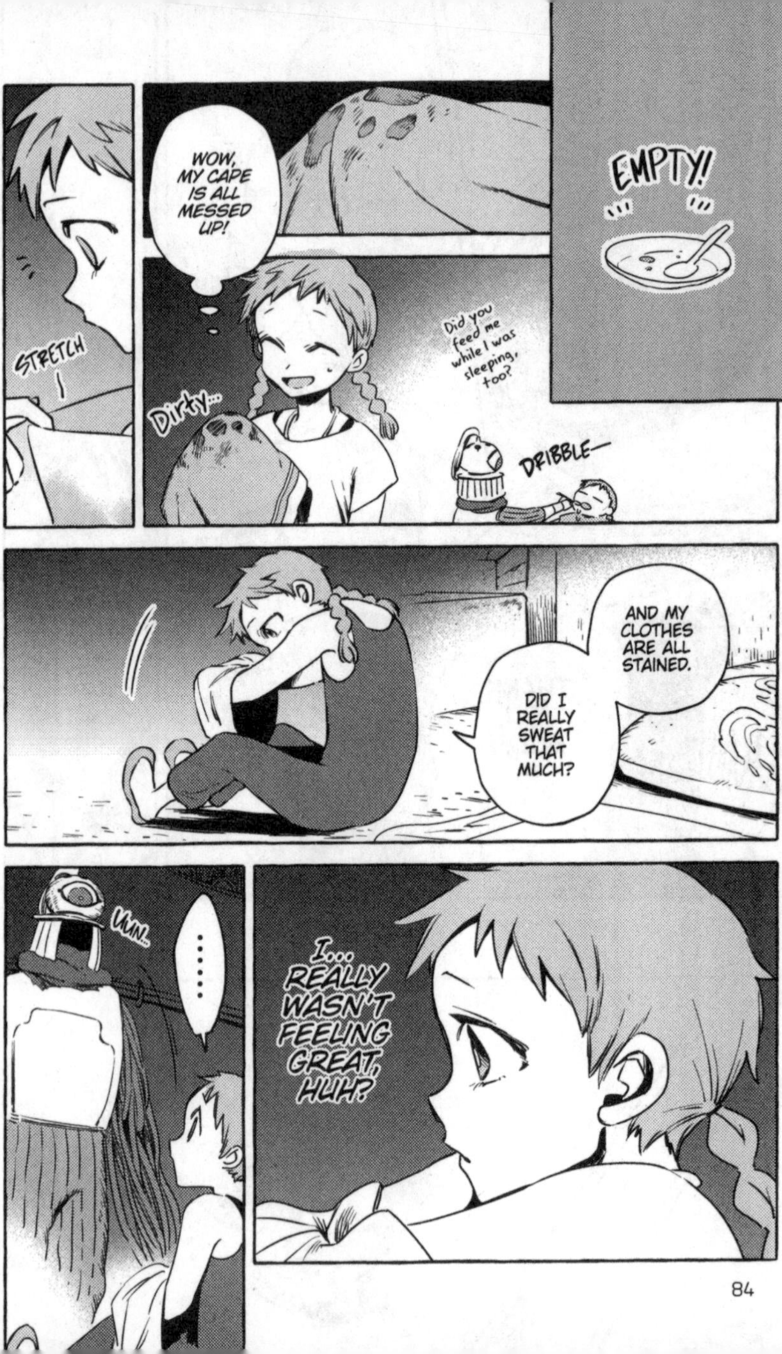
EMPTY!
WOW, MY CAPE IS ALL MESSED UP!
Did you feed me while I was sleeping, too?
DRIBBLE—
Dirty...
STRETCH
AND MY CLOTHES ARE ALL STAINED.
DID I REALLY SWEAT THAT MUCH?
I... REALLY WASN'T FEELING GREAT, HUH?
......
Uun..

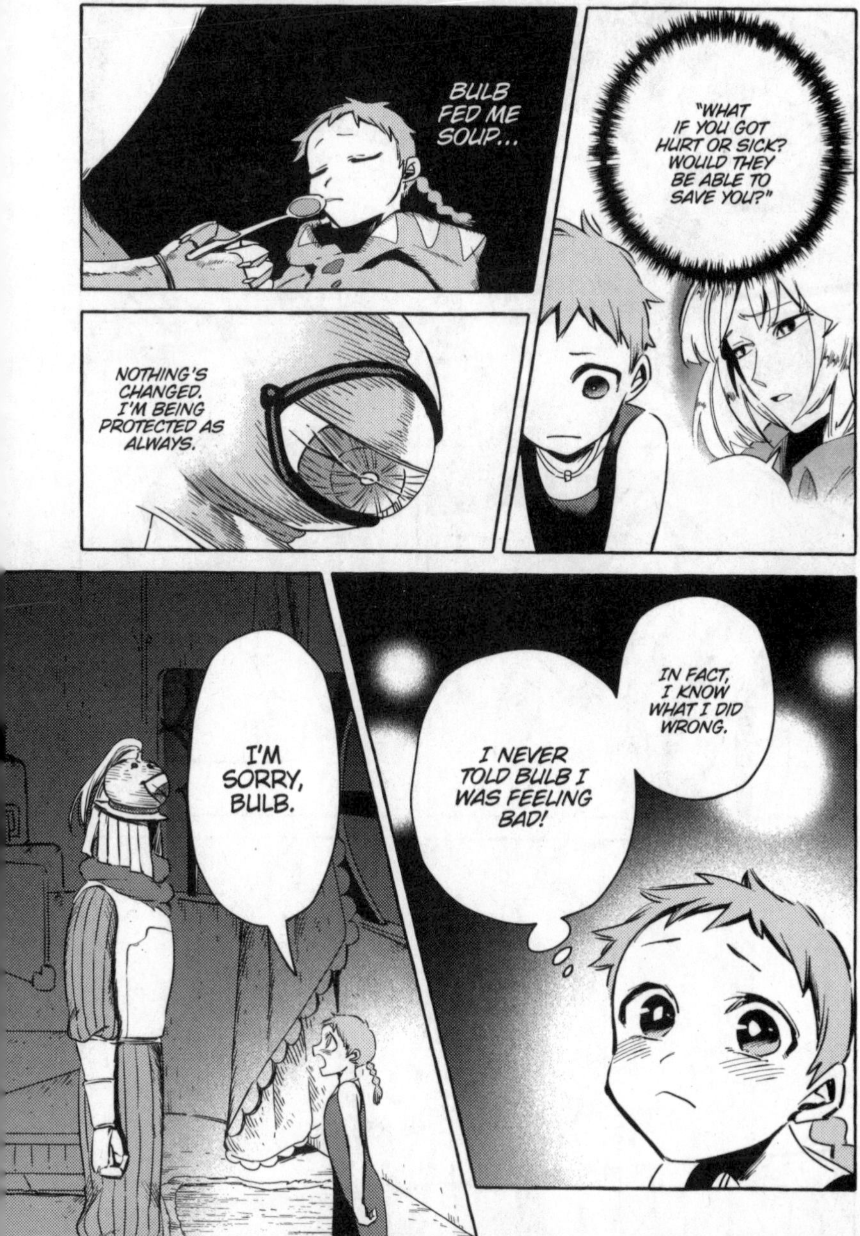
"WHAT IF YOU GOT HURT OR SICK? WOULD THEY BE ABLE TO SAVE YOU?"
BULB FED ME SOUP...
NOTHING'S CHANGED. I'M BEING PROTECTED AS ALWAYS.
IN FACT, I KNOW WHAT I DID WRONG.
I NEVER TOLD BULB I WAS FEELING BAD!
I'M SORRY, BULB.

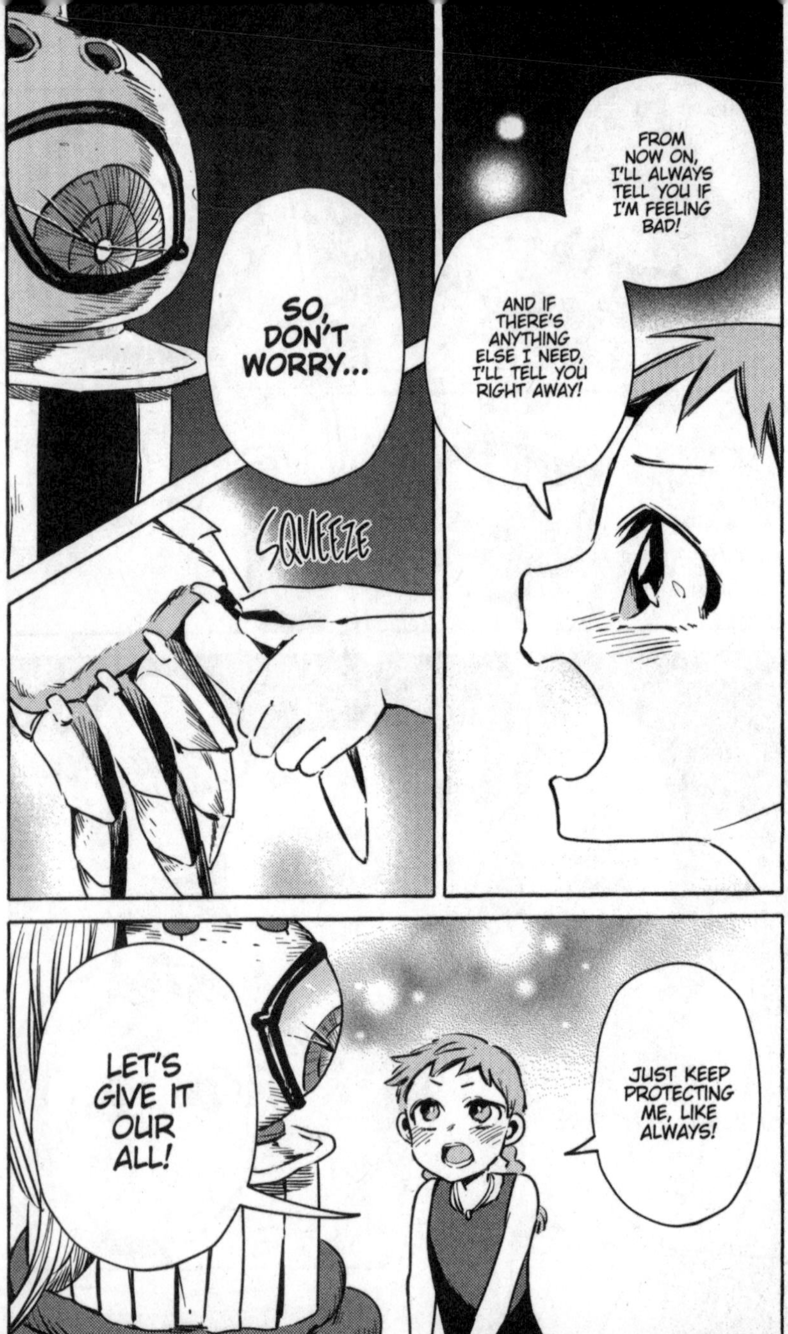
FROM NOW ON, I'LL ALWAYS TELL YOU IF I'M FEELING BAD!
AND IF THERE'S ANYTHING ELSE I NEED, I'LL TELL YOU RIGHT AWAY!
SO, DON'T WORRY...
SQUEEZE
JUST KEEP PROTECTING ME, LIKE ALWAYS!
LET'S GIVE IT OUR ALL!

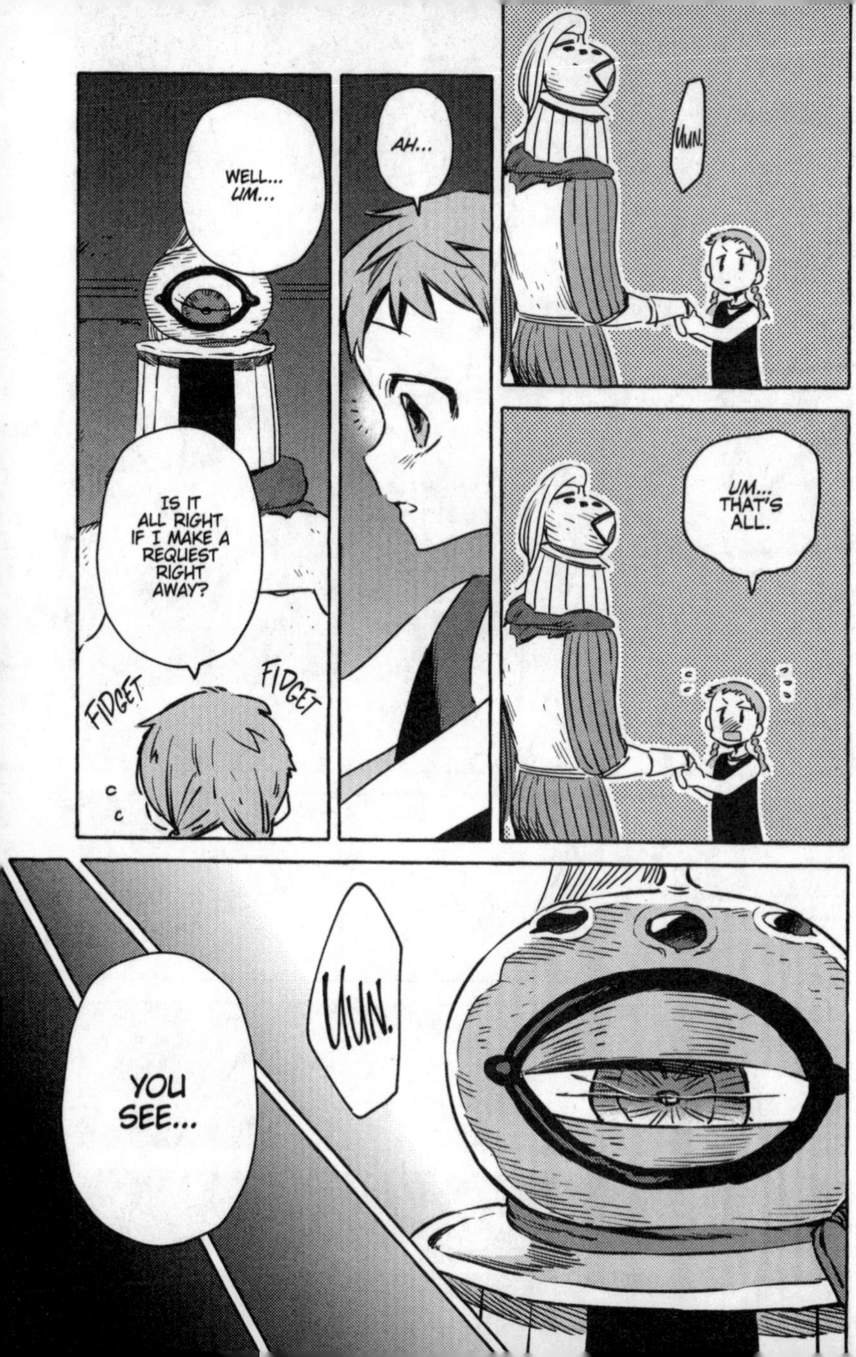
UUN.
UM... THAT'S ALL.
AH...
WELL... UM...
IS IT ALL RIGHT IF I MAKE A REQUEST RIGHT AWAY?
FIDGET
FIDGET
UUN.
YOU SEE...

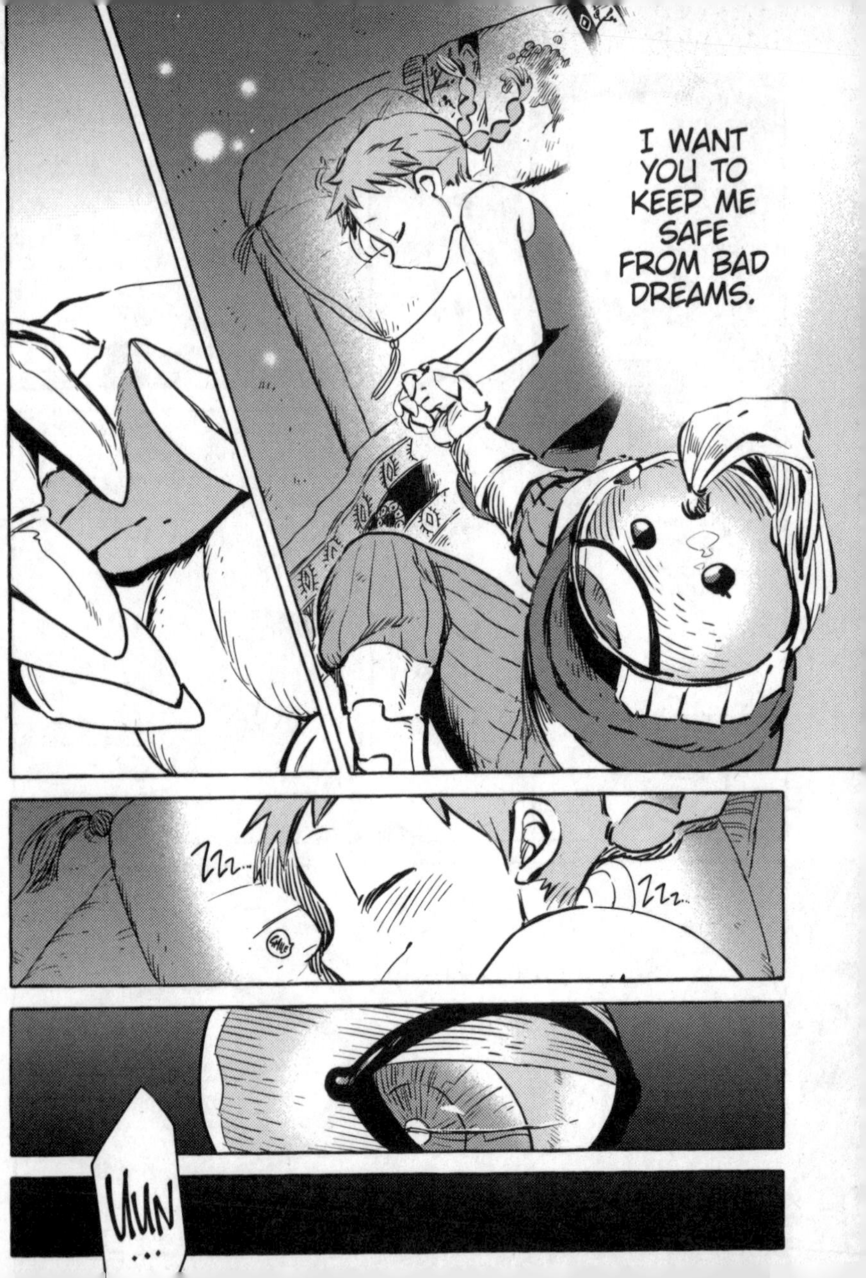
I WANT YOU TO KEEP ME SAFE FROM BAD DREAMS.
ZZZ...
ZZZ...
UUN...

A Fleeting Tale #5 Teefa's Everyday Life

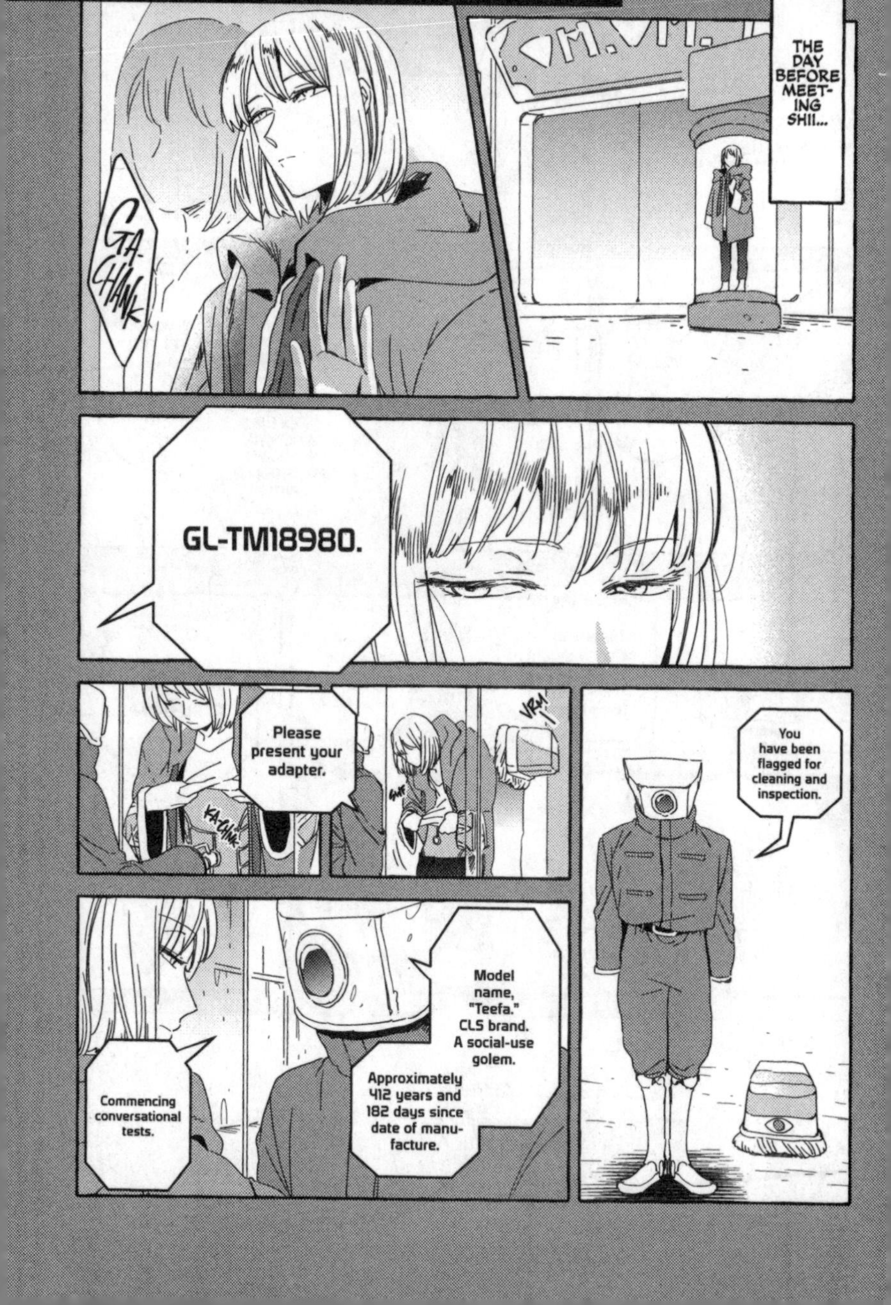
THE DAY BEFORE MEET-ING SHII...
GA-CHANK
GL-TM18980.
You have been flagged for cleaning and inspection.
VRM
Please present your adapter.
KA-CHINK
Model name, "Teefa." CLS brand. A social-use golem.
Approximately 412 years and 182 days since date of manu-facture.
Commencing conversational tests.

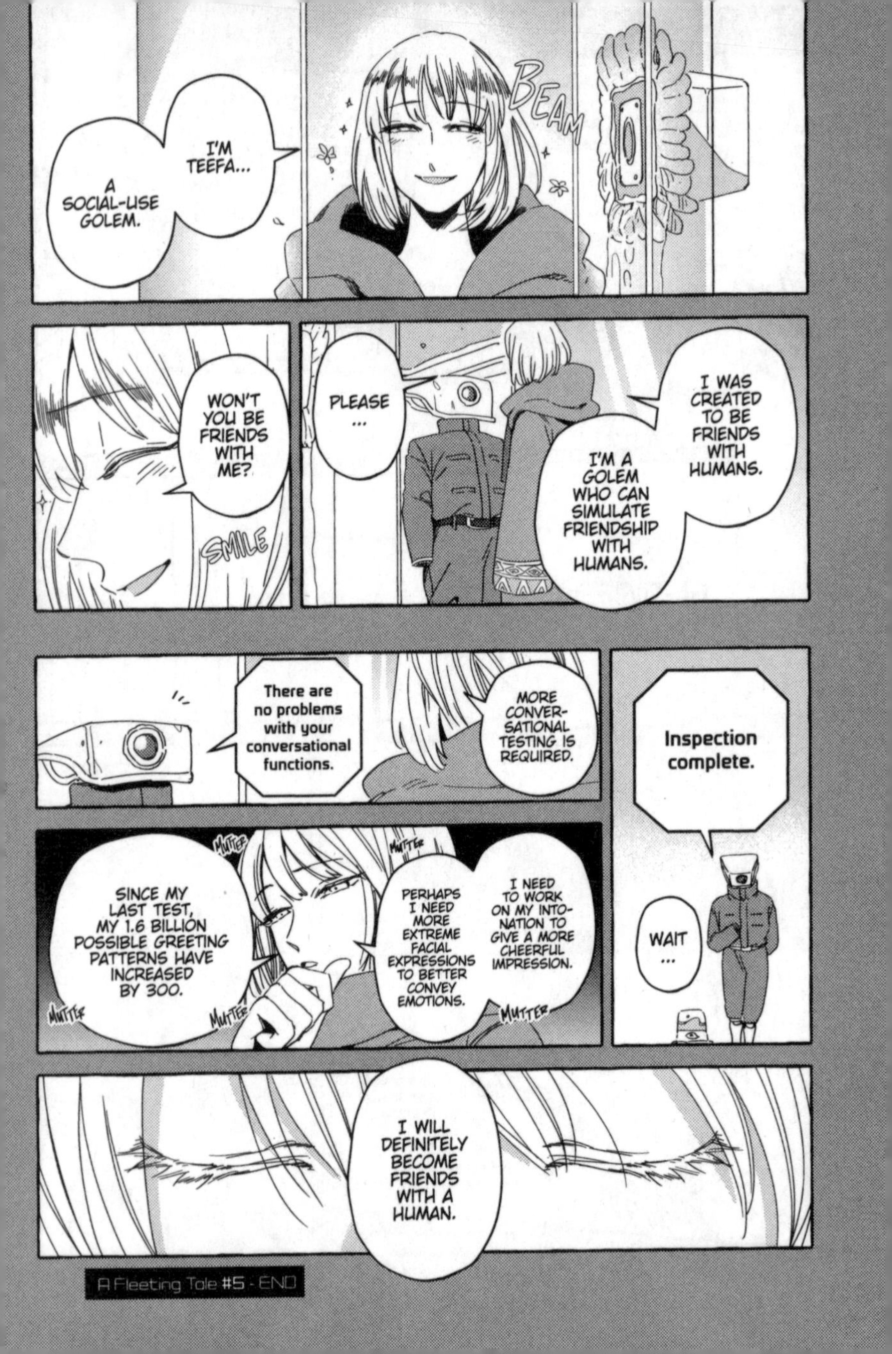
BEAM
I'M TEEFA... A SOCIAL-USE GOLEM.
I WAS CREATED TO BE FRIENDS WITH HUMANS.
I'M A GOLEM WHO CAN SIMULATE FRIENDSHIP WITH HUMANS.
PLEASE ...
WON'T YOU BE FRIENDS WITH ME?
SMILE
Inspection complete.
WAIT ...
MORE CONVER-SATIONAL TESTING IS REQUIRED.
There are no problems with your conversational functions.
MUTTER
I NEED TO WORK ON MY INTO-NATION TO GIVE A MORE CHEERFUL IMPRESSION.
PERHAPS I NEED MORE EXTREME FACIAL EXPRESSIONS TO BETTER CONVEY EMOTIONS.
SINCE MY LAST TEST, MY 1.6 BILLION POSSIBLE GREETING PATTERNS HAVE INCREASED BY 300.
MUTTER
MUTTER
MUTTER
I WILL DEFINITELY BECOME FRIENDS WITH A HUMAN.

A Fleeting Tale #5 - END

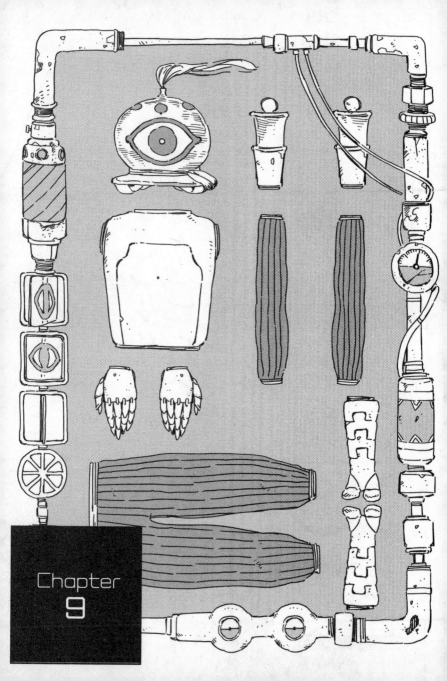

Chapter
9

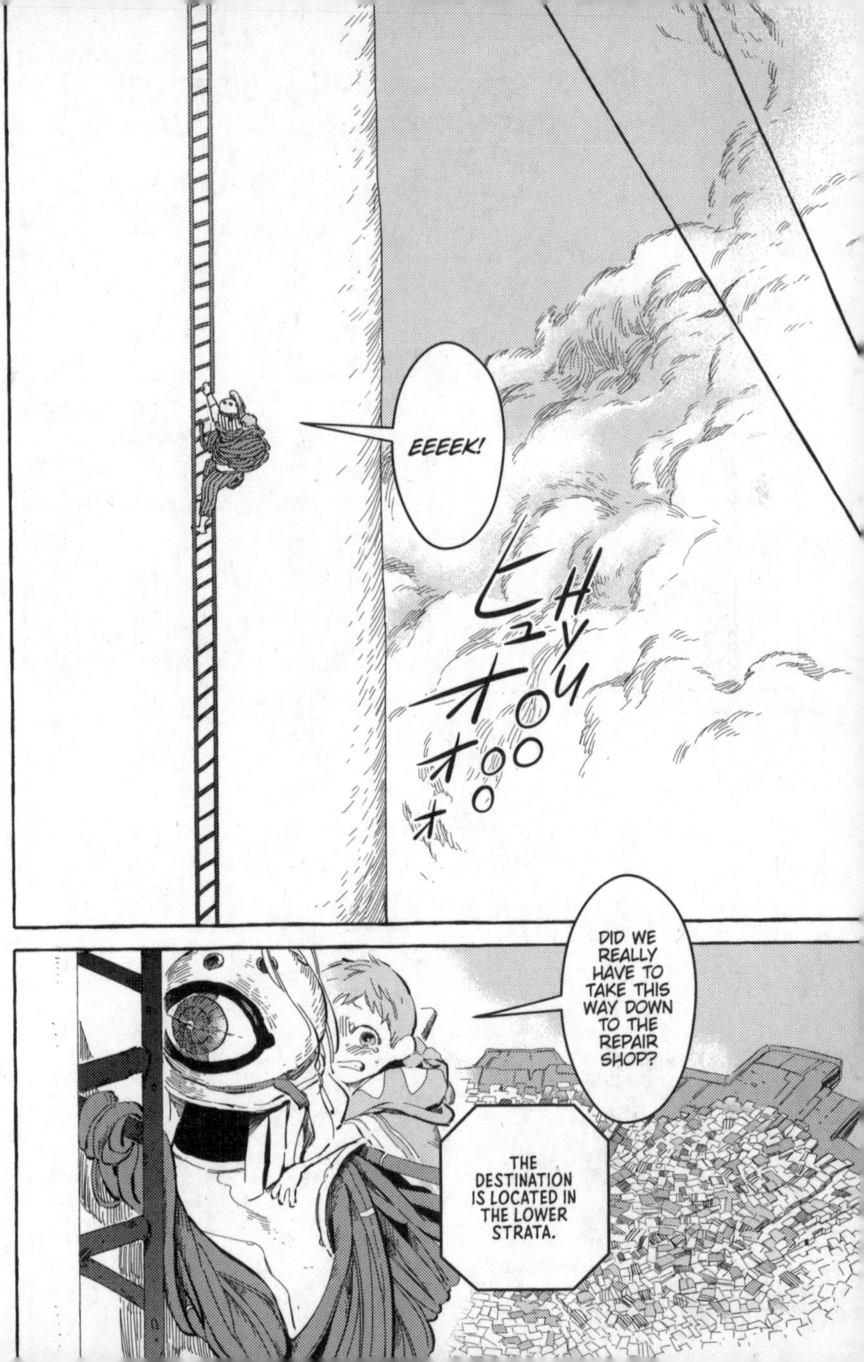
EEEEK!
ヒュオオオ
HYUOOOO
DID WE REALLY HAVE TO TAKE THIS WAY DOWN TO THE REPAIR SHOP?
THE DESTINATION IS LOCATED IN THE LOWER STRATA.

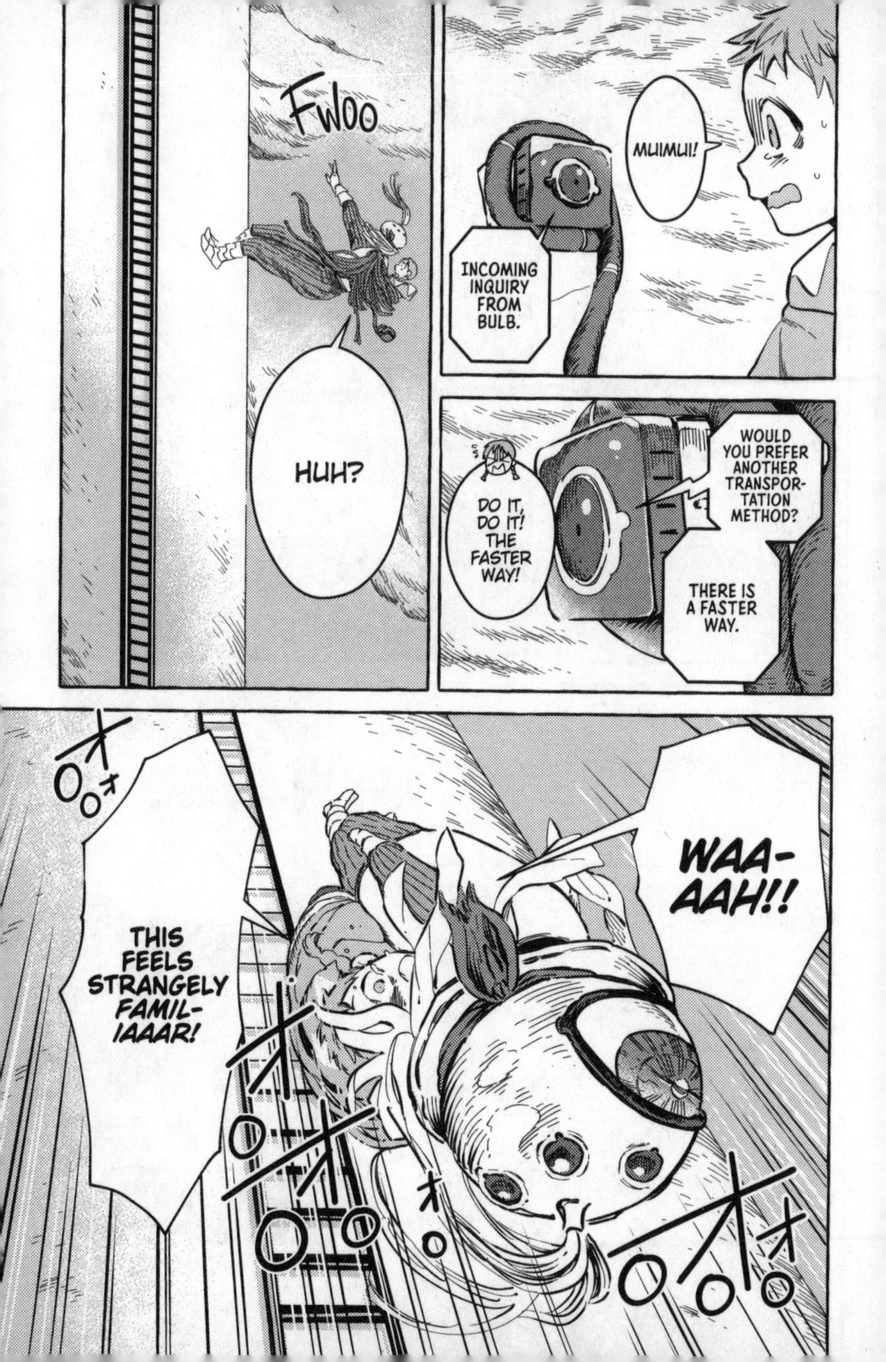
MUIMUI!
INCOMING INQUIRY FROM BULB.
WOULD YOU PREFER ANOTHER TRANSPOR-TATION METHOD?
THERE IS A FASTER WAY.
DO IT, DO IT! THE FASTER WAY!
FWOO
HUH?
WAA-AAH!!
THIS FEELS STRANGELY FAMIL-IAAAR!

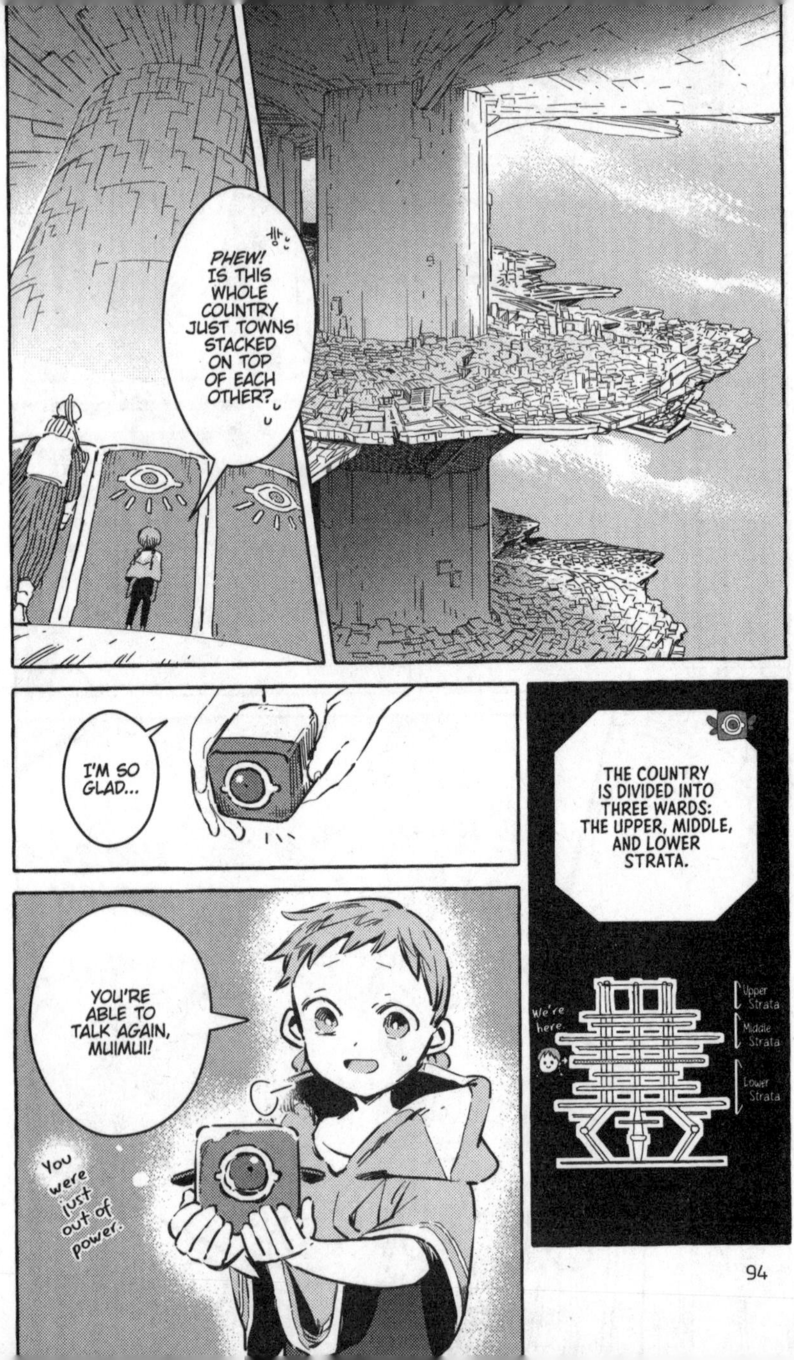
PHEW! IS THIS WHOLE COUNTRY JUST TOWNS STACKED ON TOP OF EACH OTHER?
THE COUNTRY IS DIVIDED INTO THREE WARDS: THE UPPER, MIDDLE, AND LOWER STRATA.
Upper Strata
Middle Strata
Lower Strata
We're here.
I'M SO GLAD...
YOU'RE ABLE TO TALK AGAIN, MUIMUI!
You were just out of power.

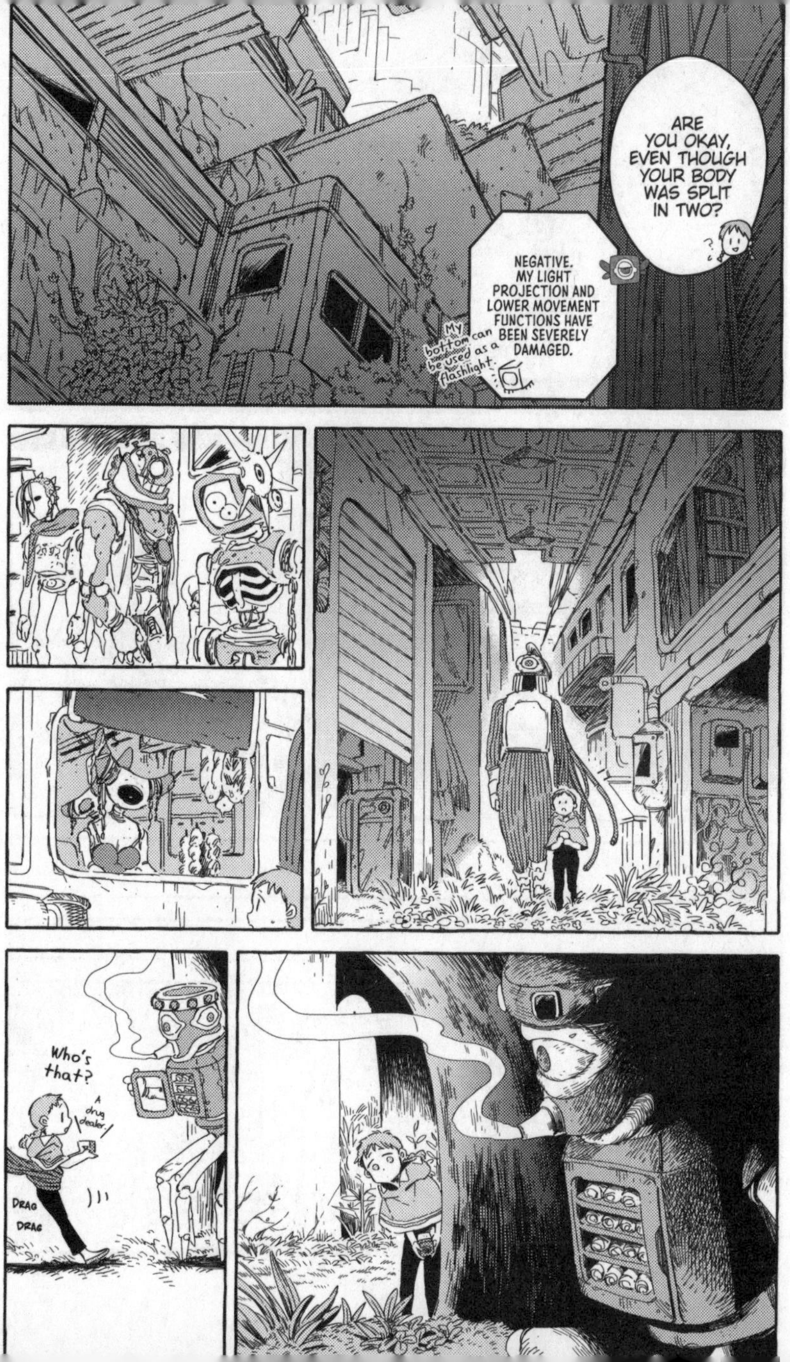
ARE YOU OKAY, EVEN THOUGH YOUR BODY WAS SPLIT IN TWO?
NEGATIVE. MY LIGHT PROJECTION AND LOWER MOVEMENT FUNCTIONS HAVE BEEN SEVERELY DAMAGED.
My bottom can be used as a flashlight.
Who's that?
A drug dealer!
DRAG
DRAG

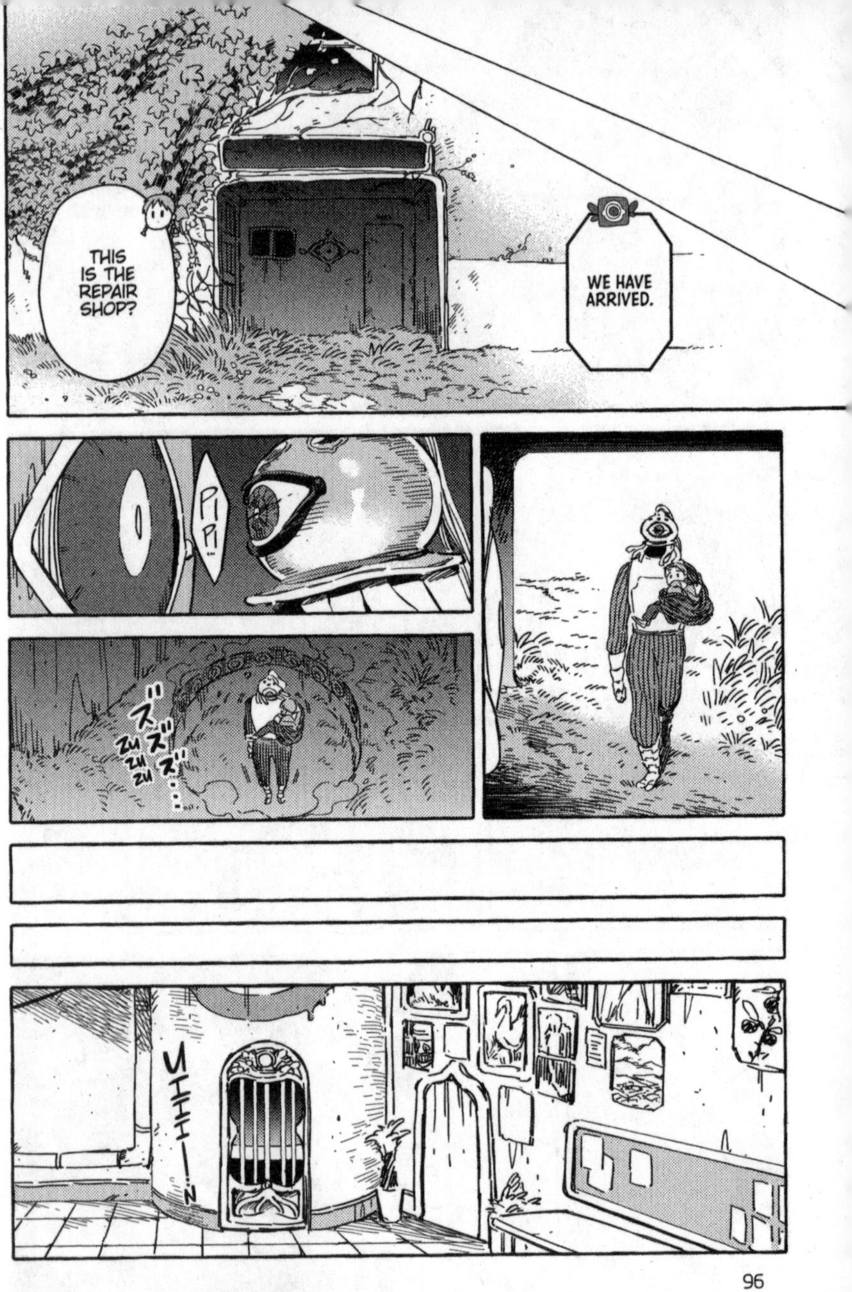
WE HAVE ARRIVED.
THIS IS THE REPAIR SHOP?
PI PI...
ズズズ...
ZU ZU ZU
UIIII...N

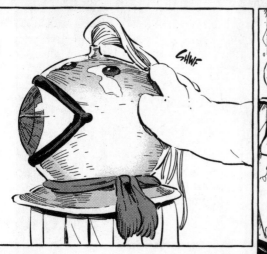

SHWF

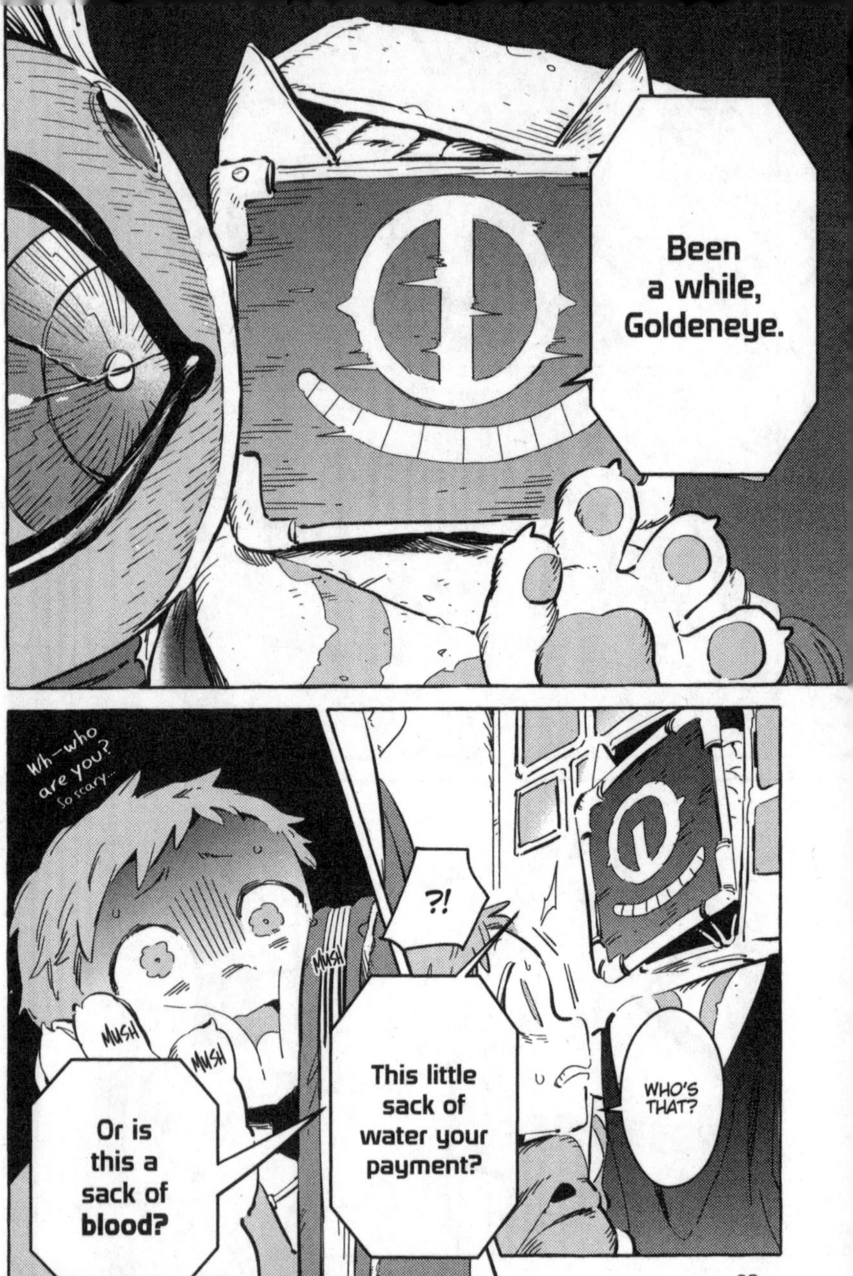
Been a while, Goldeneye.
WHO'S THAT?
?!
This little sack of water your payment?
Or is this a sack of blood?
Wh-who are you? So scary...
MUSH
MUSH
MUSH

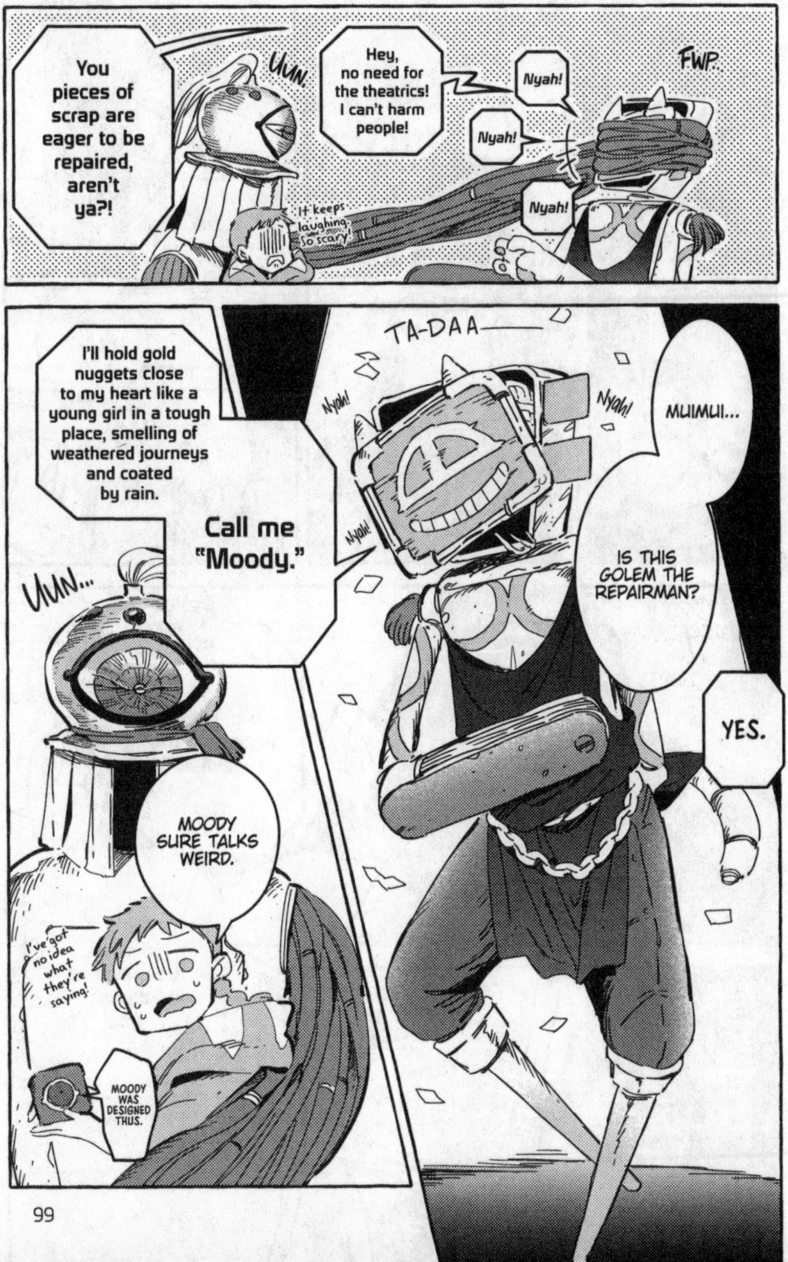

FWP.
Nyah!
Nyah!
Nyah!
Hey, no need for the theatrics! I can't harm people!
UUN.
You pieces of scrap are eager to be repaired, aren't ya?!
It keeps laughing. So scary.
TA-DAA
MUIMUI...
Nyah!
Nyah!
Nyah!
IS THIS GOLEM THE REPAIRMAN?
YES.
I'll hold gold nuggets close to my heart like a young girl in a tough place, smelling of weathered journeys and coated by rain.
Call me "Moody."
UUN...
MOODY SURE TALKS WEIRD.
I've got no idea what they're saying!
MOODY WAS DESIGNED THUS.

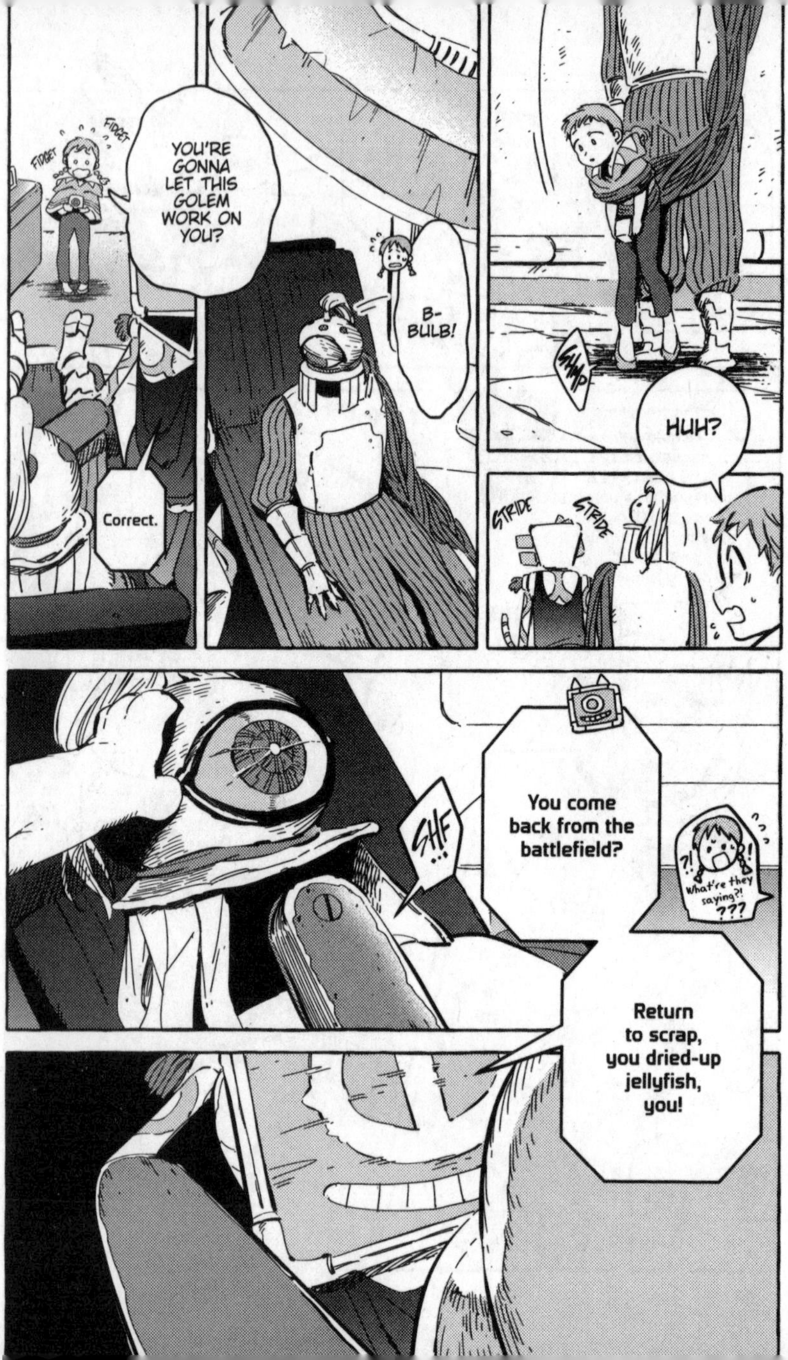
SHMP
HUH?
STRIDE
STRIDE
B-BULB!
FIDGET
FIDGET
YOU'RE GONNA LET THIS GOLEM WORK ON YOU?
Correct.
?! ! What're they saying?! ???
You come back from the battlefield?
SHF...
Return to scrap, you dried-up jellyfish, you!

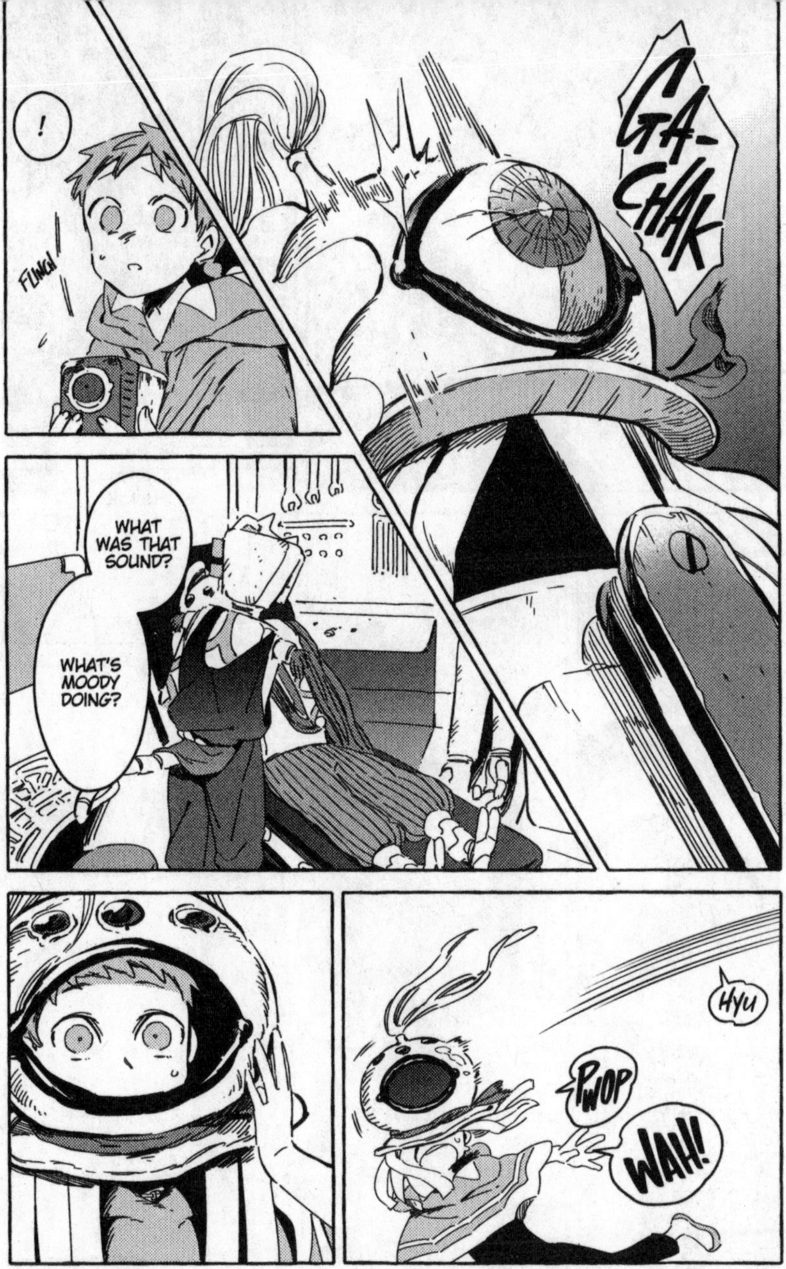
GA-CHAK
!
FLINCH
WHAT WAS THAT SOUND?
WHAT'S MOODY DOING?
HYU
PWOP
WAH!

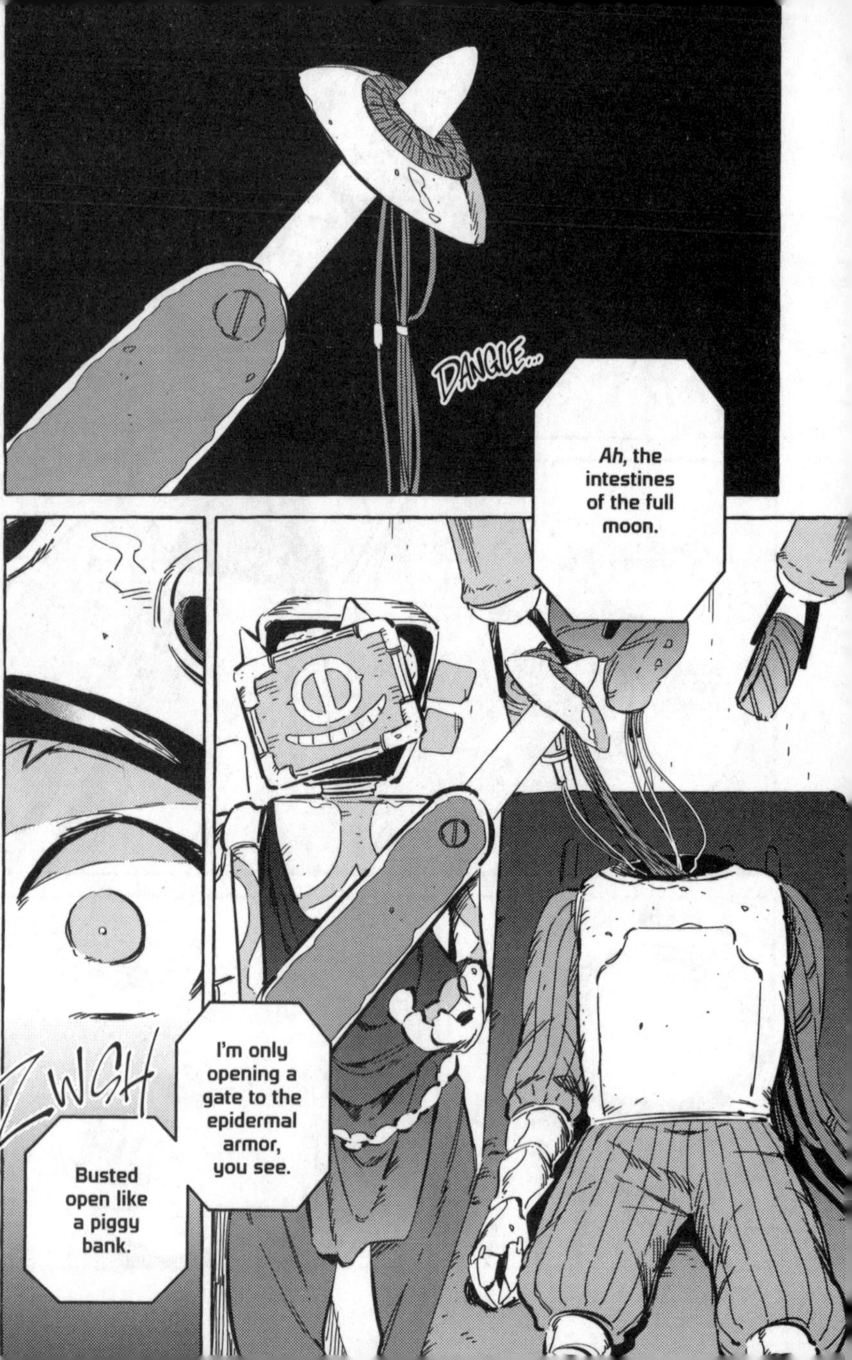

DANGLE...
Ah, the intestines of the full moon.
I'm only opening a gate to the epidermal armor, you see.
ZWSH
Busted open like a piggy bank.

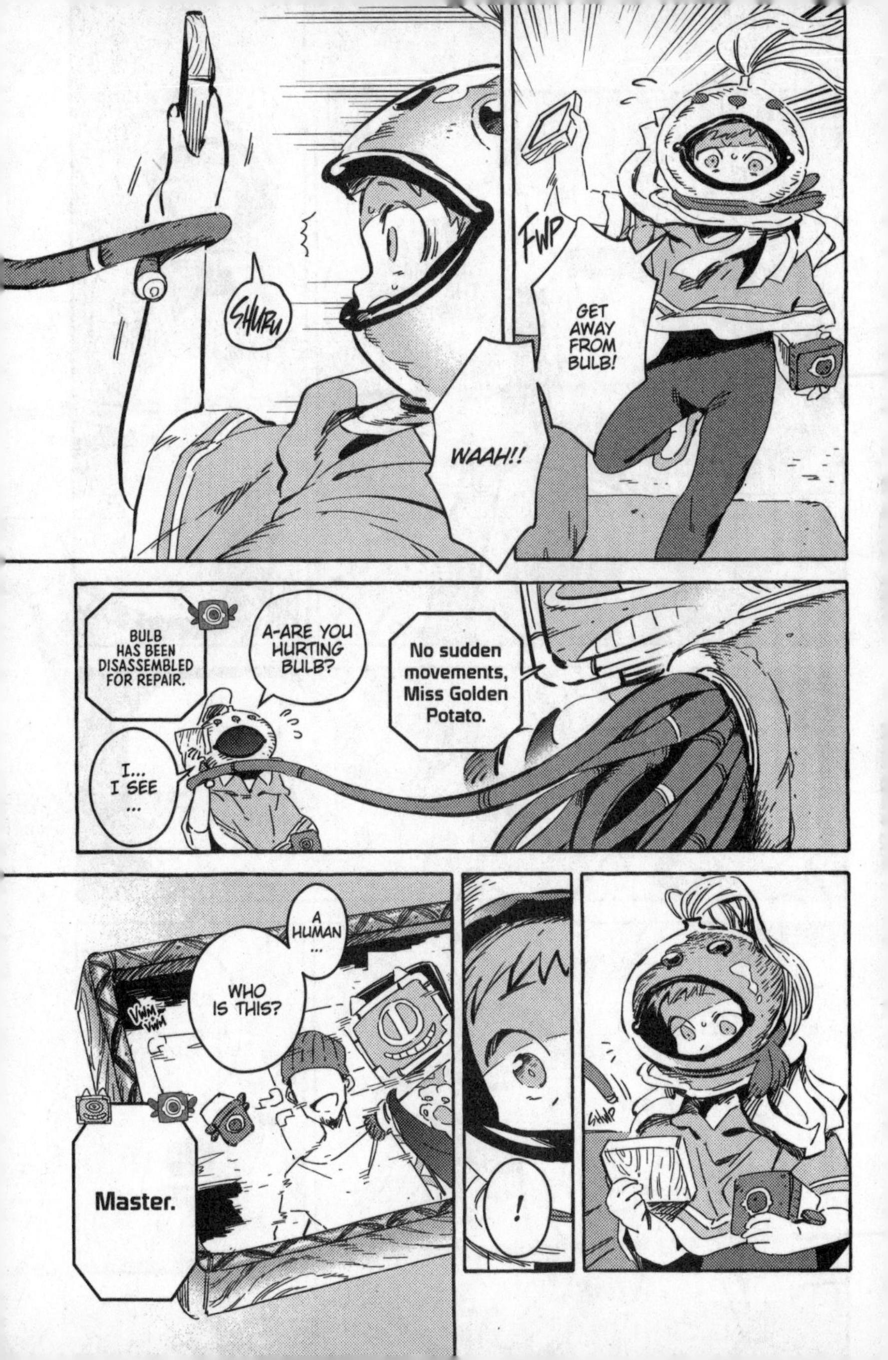
FWP
GET AWAY FROM BULB!
WAAH!!
SHURU
No sudden movements, Miss Golden Potato.
A-ARE YOU HURTING BULB?
BULB HAS BEEN DISASSEMBLED FOR REPAIR.
I... I SEE ...
!
A HUMAN ...
WHO IS THIS?
VWM VWM
Master.

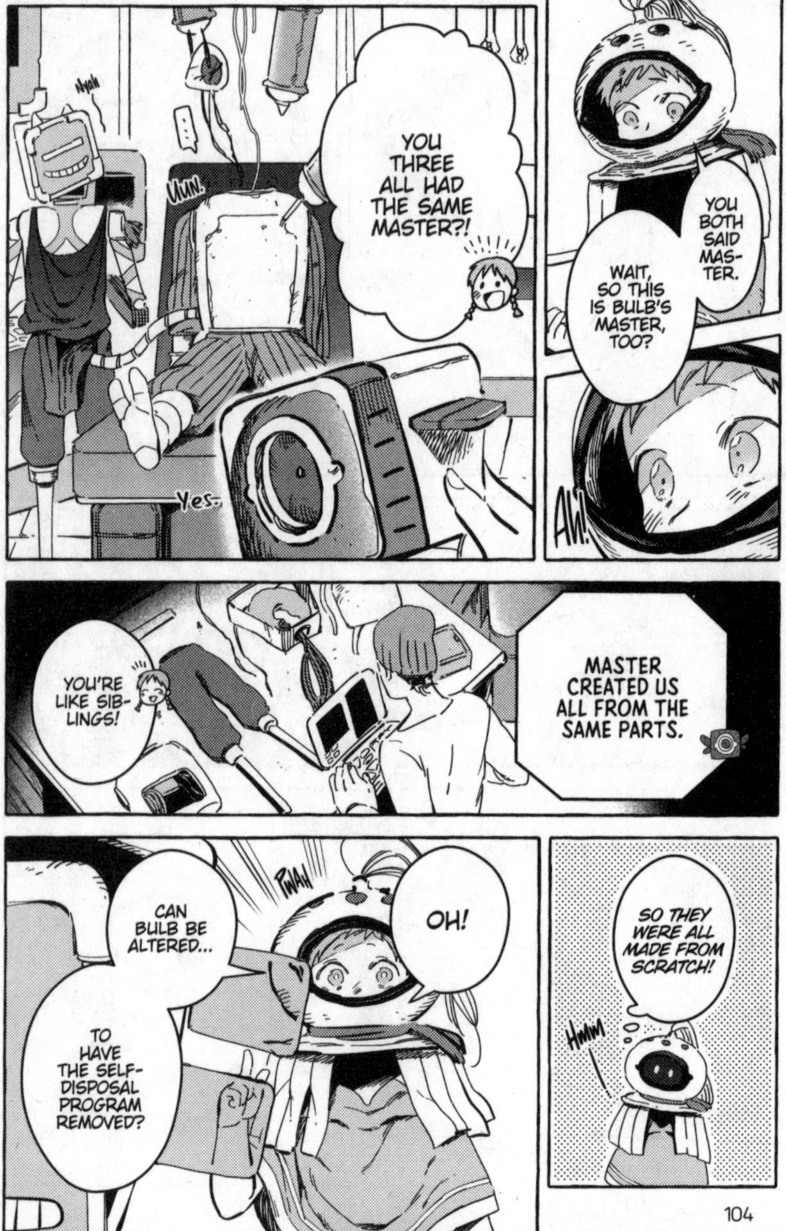
YOU BOTH SAID MASTER.
WAIT, SO THIS IS BULB'S MASTER, TOO?
AH!
YOU THREE ALL HAD THE SAME MASTER?!
Nyoh
...
Uun.
Yes.
MASTER CREATED US ALL FROM THE SAME PARTS.
YOU'RE LIKE SIBLINGS!
SO THEY WERE ALL MADE FROM SCRATCH!
HMM
OH!
PWAH
CAN BULB BE ALTERED...
TO HAVE THE SELF-DISPOSAL PROGRAM REMOVED?

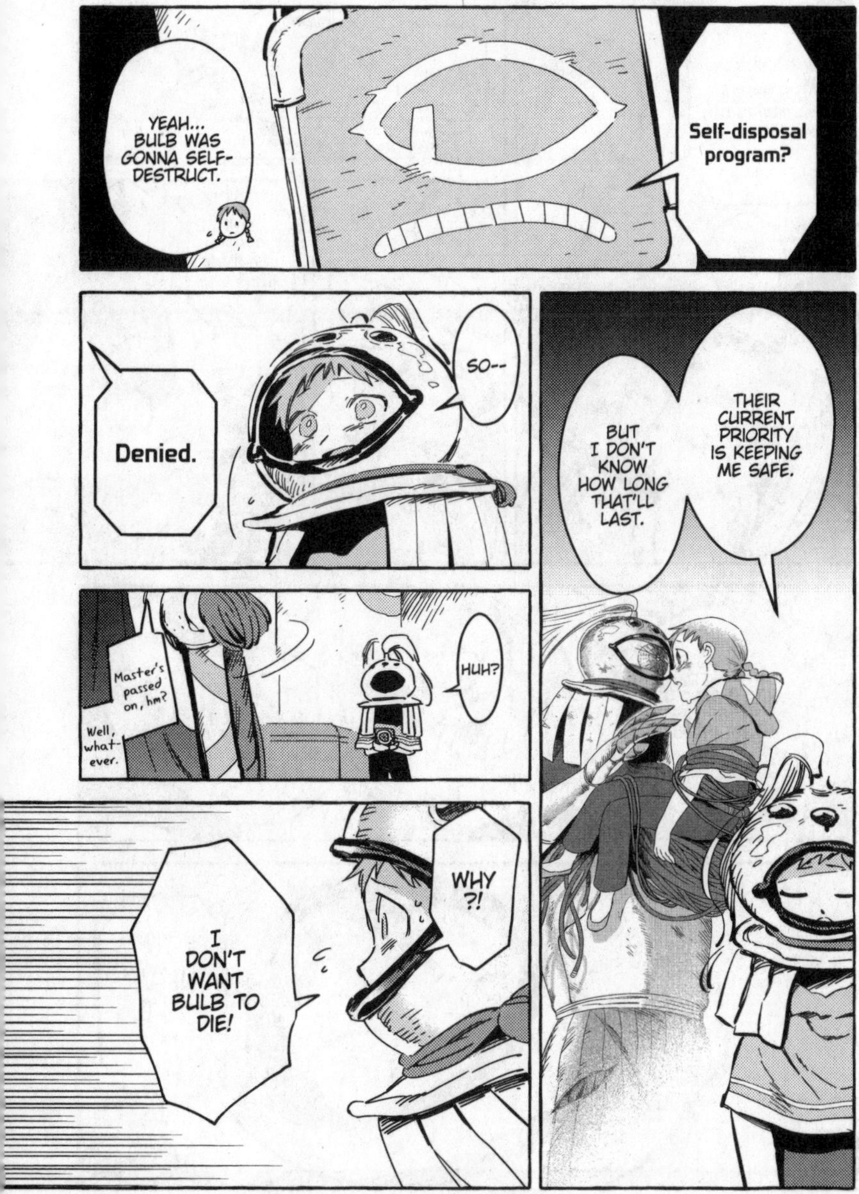

Self-disposal program?
YEAH... BULB WAS GONNA SELF-DESTRUCT.
THEIR CURRENT PRIORITY IS KEEPING ME SAFE.
BUT I DON'T KNOW HOW LONG THAT'LL LAST.
SO--
Denied.
HUH?
Master's passed on, hm?
Well, whatever.
WHY?!
I DON'T WANT BULB TO DIE!

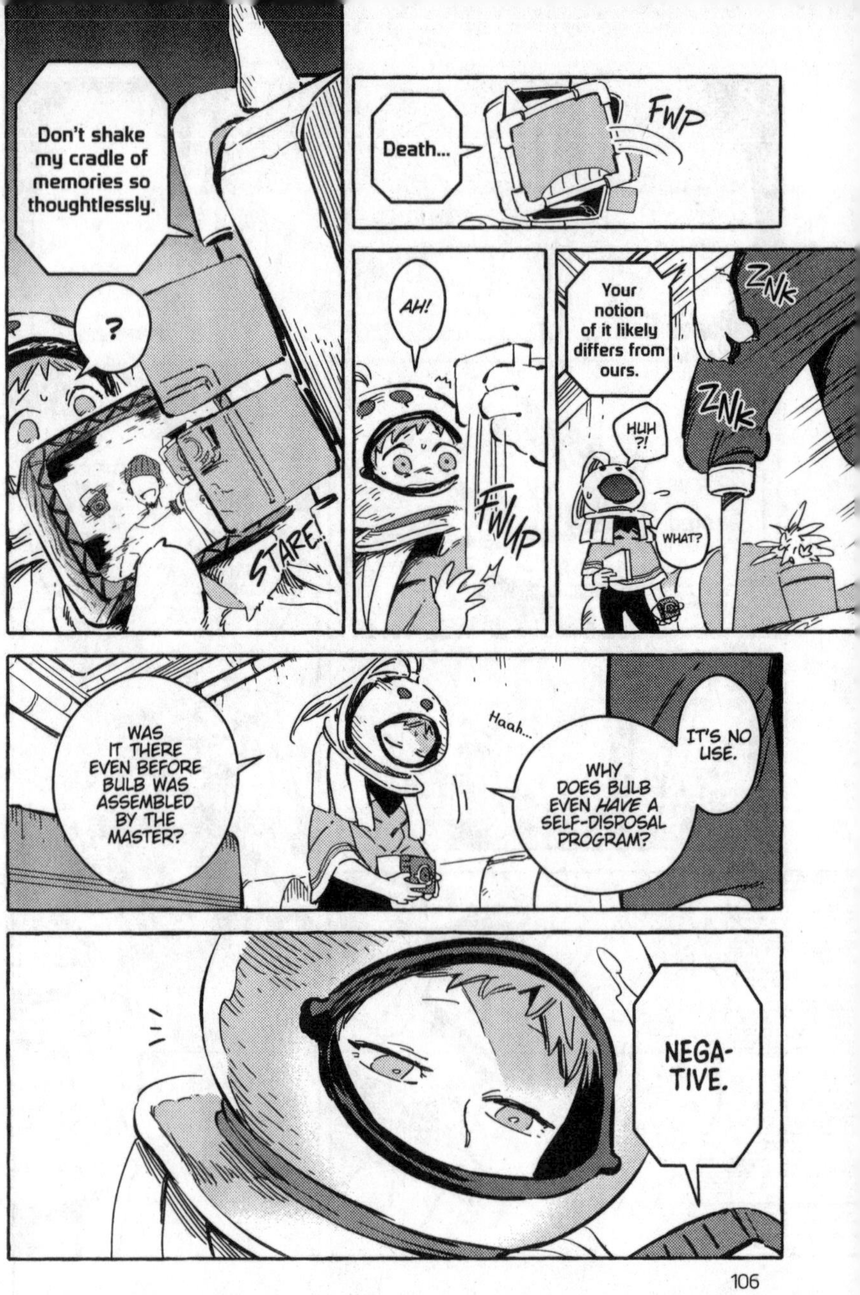
Death...
FWP
Your notion of it likely differs from ours.
ZNK
ZNK
HUH?!
WHAT?
AH!
FWUP
Don't shake my cradle of memories so thoughtlessly.
?
STARE
IT'S NO USE.
Haaah...
WHY DOES BULB EVEN *HAVE* A SELF-DISPOSAL PROGRAM?
WAS IT THERE EVEN BEFORE BULB WAS ASSEMBLED BY THE MASTER?
NEGA-TIVE.

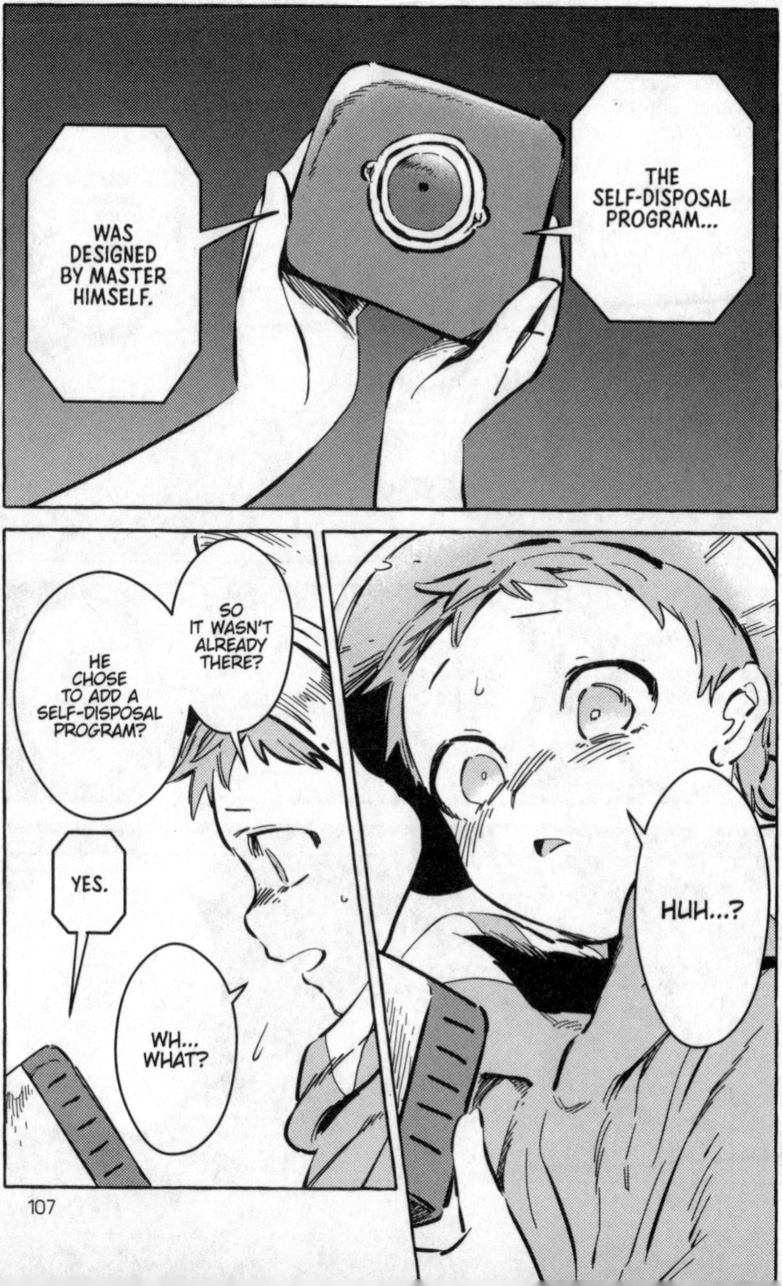
THE SELF-DISPOSAL PROGRAM...
WAS DESIGNED BY MASTER HIMSELF.
HUH...?
SO IT WASN'T ALREADY THERE?
HE CHOSE TO ADD A SELF-DISPOSAL PROGRAM?
YES.
WH... WHAT?

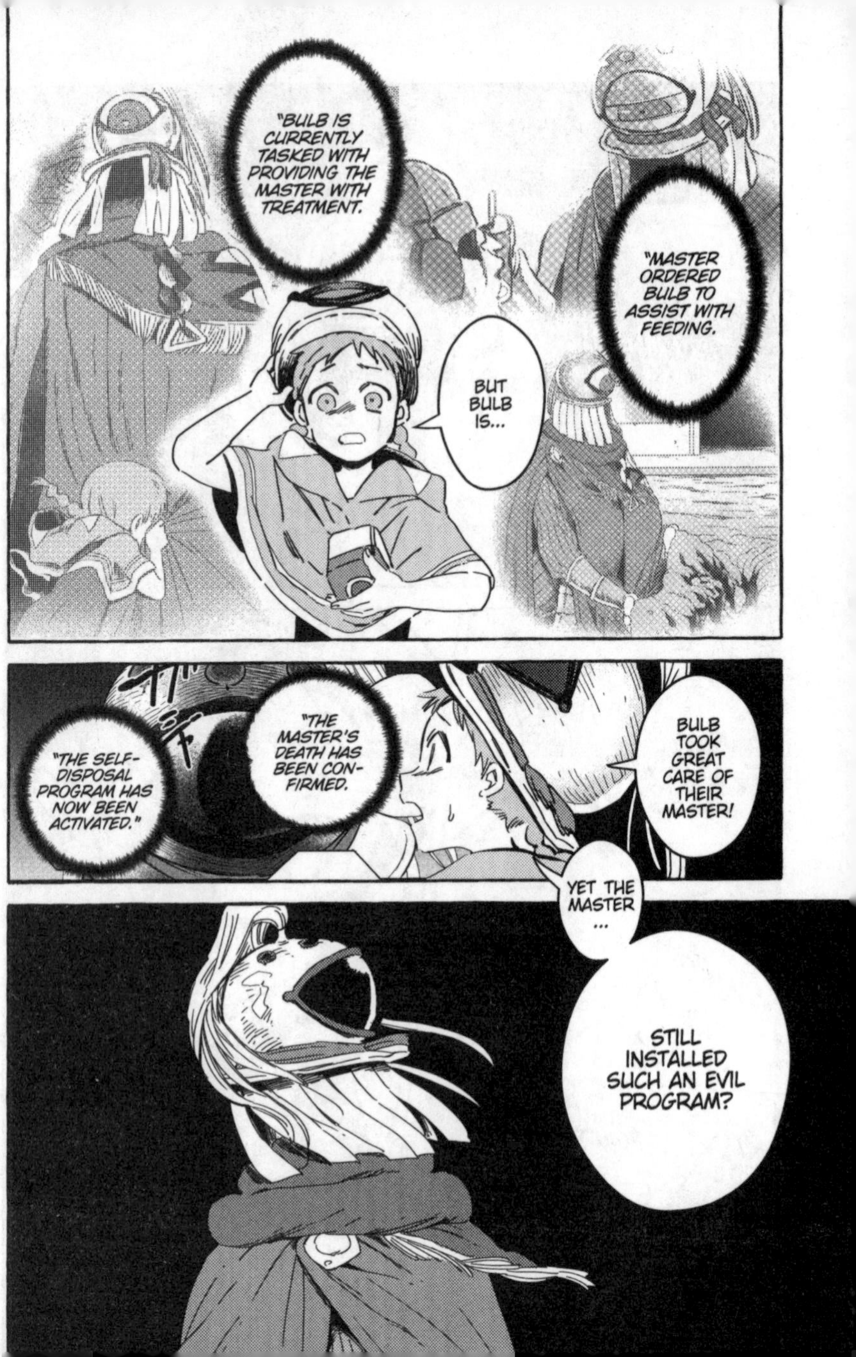
"MASTER ORDERED BULB TO ASSIST WITH FEEDING.
"BULB IS CURRENTLY TASKED WITH PROVIDING THE MASTER WITH TREATMENT.
BUT BULB IS...
BULB TOOK GREAT CARE OF THEIR MASTER!
"THE MASTER'S DEATH HAS BEEN CON-FIRMED.
"THE SELF-DISPOSAL PROGRAM HAS NOW BEEN ACTIVATED."
YET THE MASTER ...
STILL INSTALLED SUCH AN EVIL PROGRAM?

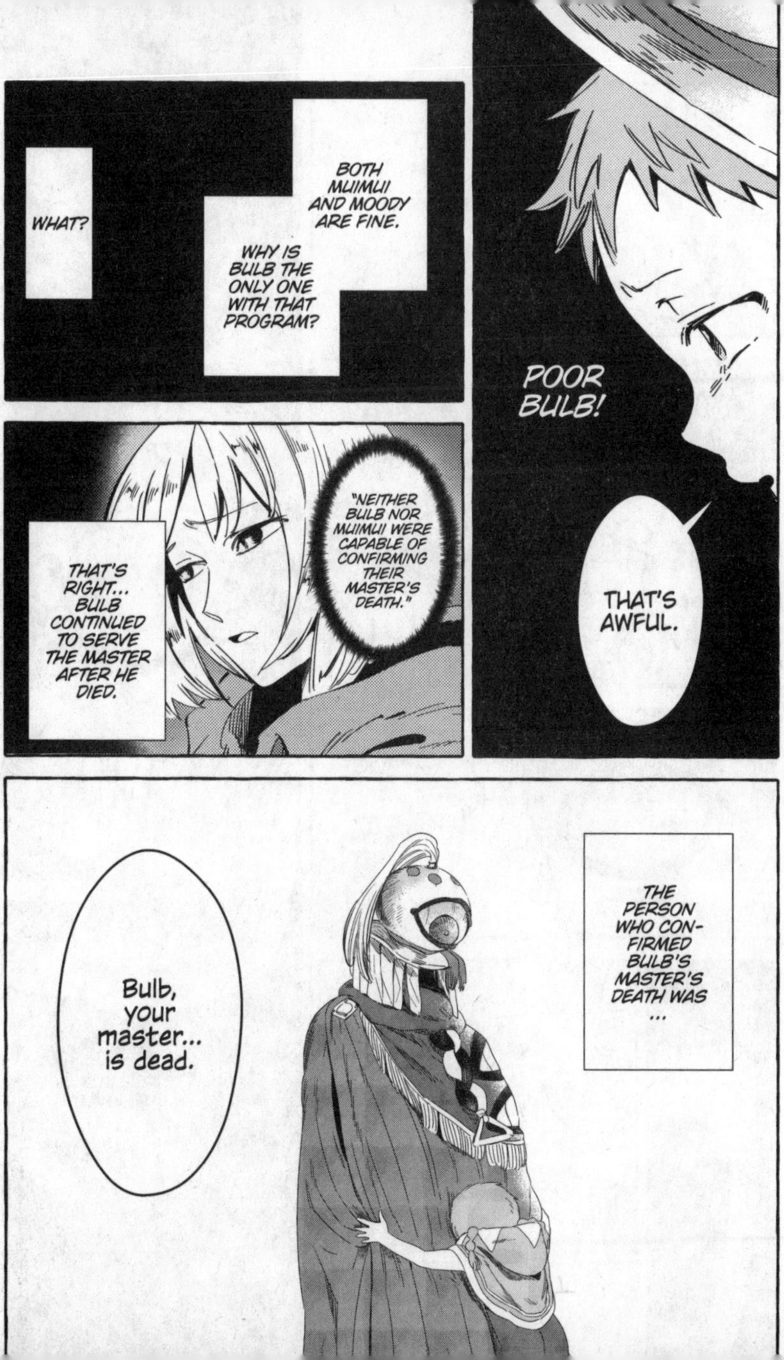
POOR BULB!
THAT'S AWFUL.
BOTH MUIMUI AND MOODY ARE FINE.
WHY IS BULB THE ONLY ONE WITH THAT PROGRAM?
WHAT?
"NEITHER BULB NOR MUIMUI WERE CAPABLE OF CONFIRMING THEIR MASTER'S DEATH."
THAT'S RIGHT... BULB CONTINUED TO SERVE THE MASTER AFTER HE DIED.
THE PERSON WHO CON-FIRMED BULB'S MASTER'S DEATH WAS ...
Bulb, your master... is dead.

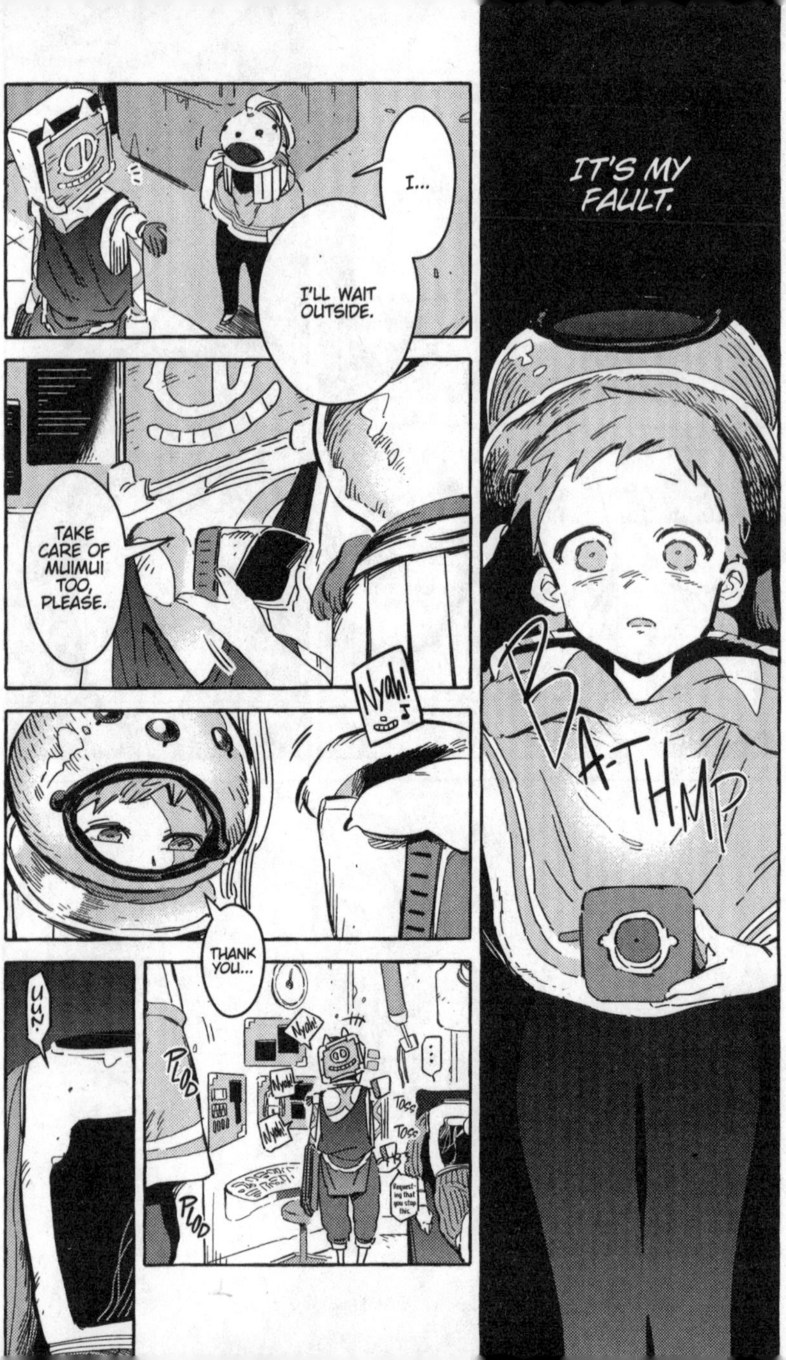
IT'S MY FAULT.
BA-THMP
I...
I'LL WAIT OUTSIDE.
TAKE CARE OF MUIMUI TOO, PLEASE.
Nyah!
THANK YOU...
Nyah!
...
Nyah!
TOSS
TOSS
Nyah!
Request-ing that you stop this.
PLOD
PLOD
Uun.

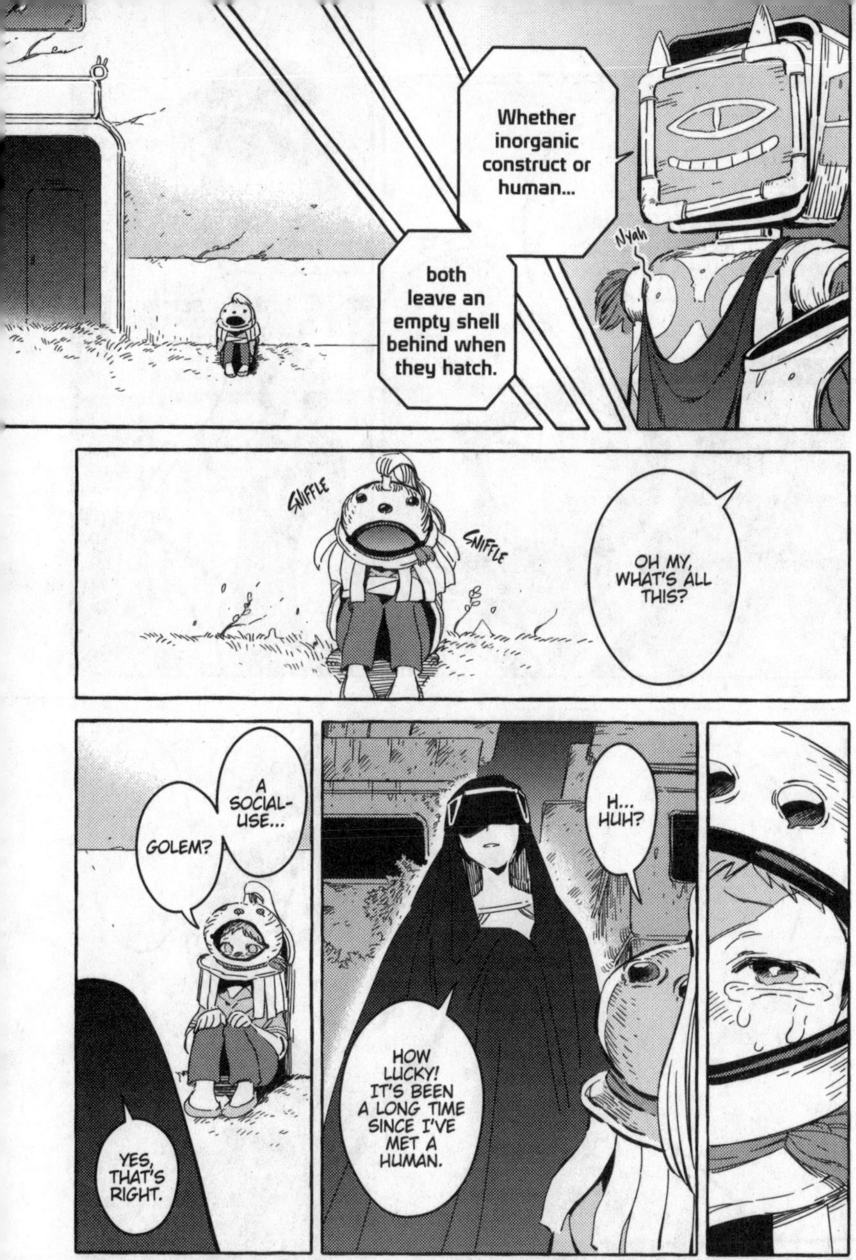
Whether inorganic construct or human...
both leave an empty shell behind when they hatch.
Nyah
OH MY, WHAT'S ALL THIS?
SNIFFLE
SNIFFLE
H... HUH?
HOW LUCKY! IT'S BEEN A LONG TIME SINCE I'VE MET A HUMAN.
A SOCIAL-USE... GOLEM?
YES, THAT'S RIGHT.

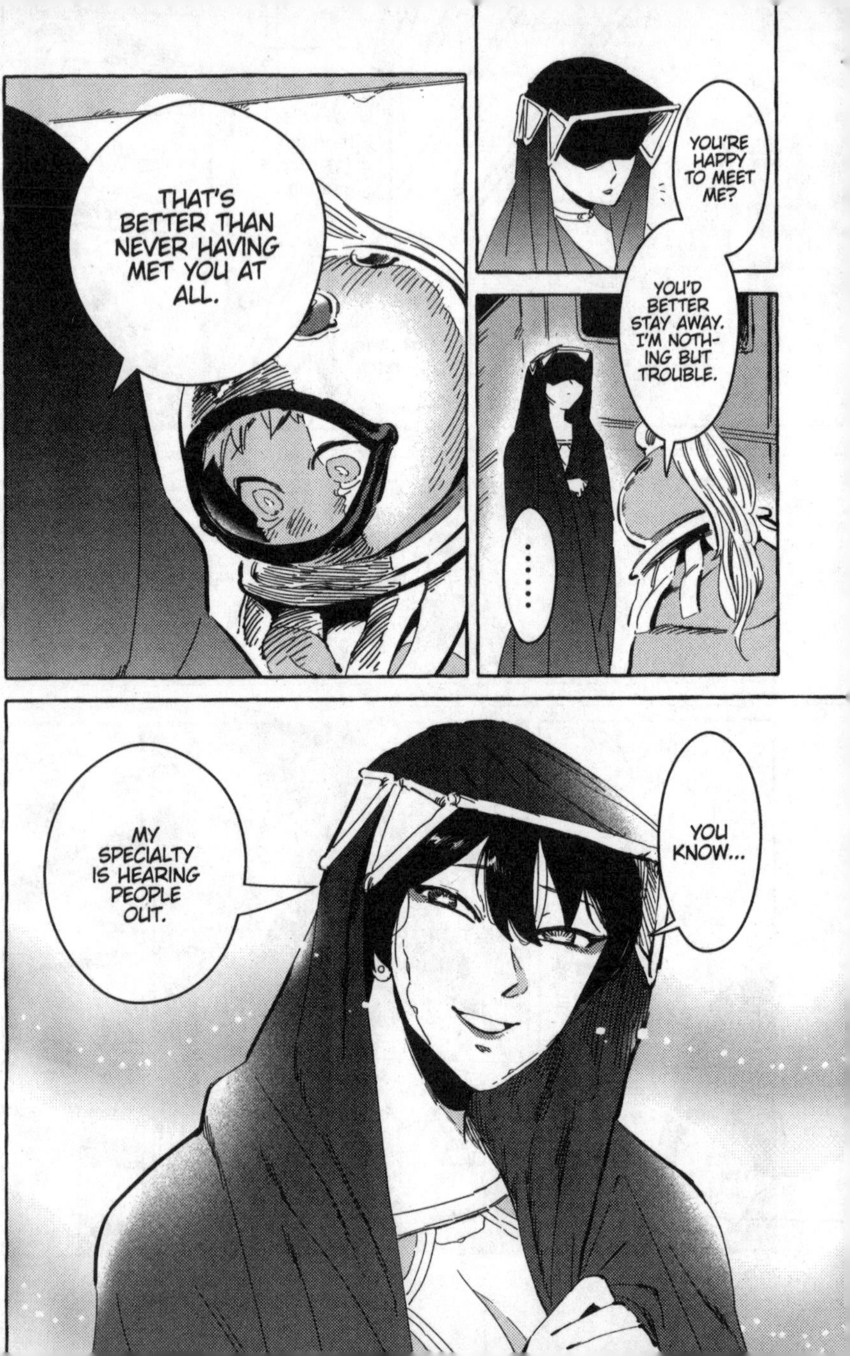
YOU'RE HAPPY TO MEET ME?
YOU'D BETTER STAY AWAY. I'M NOTHING BUT TROUBLE.
......
THAT'S BETTER THAN NEVER HAVING MET YOU AT ALL.
YOU KNOW...
MY SPECIALTY IS HEARING PEOPLE OUT.

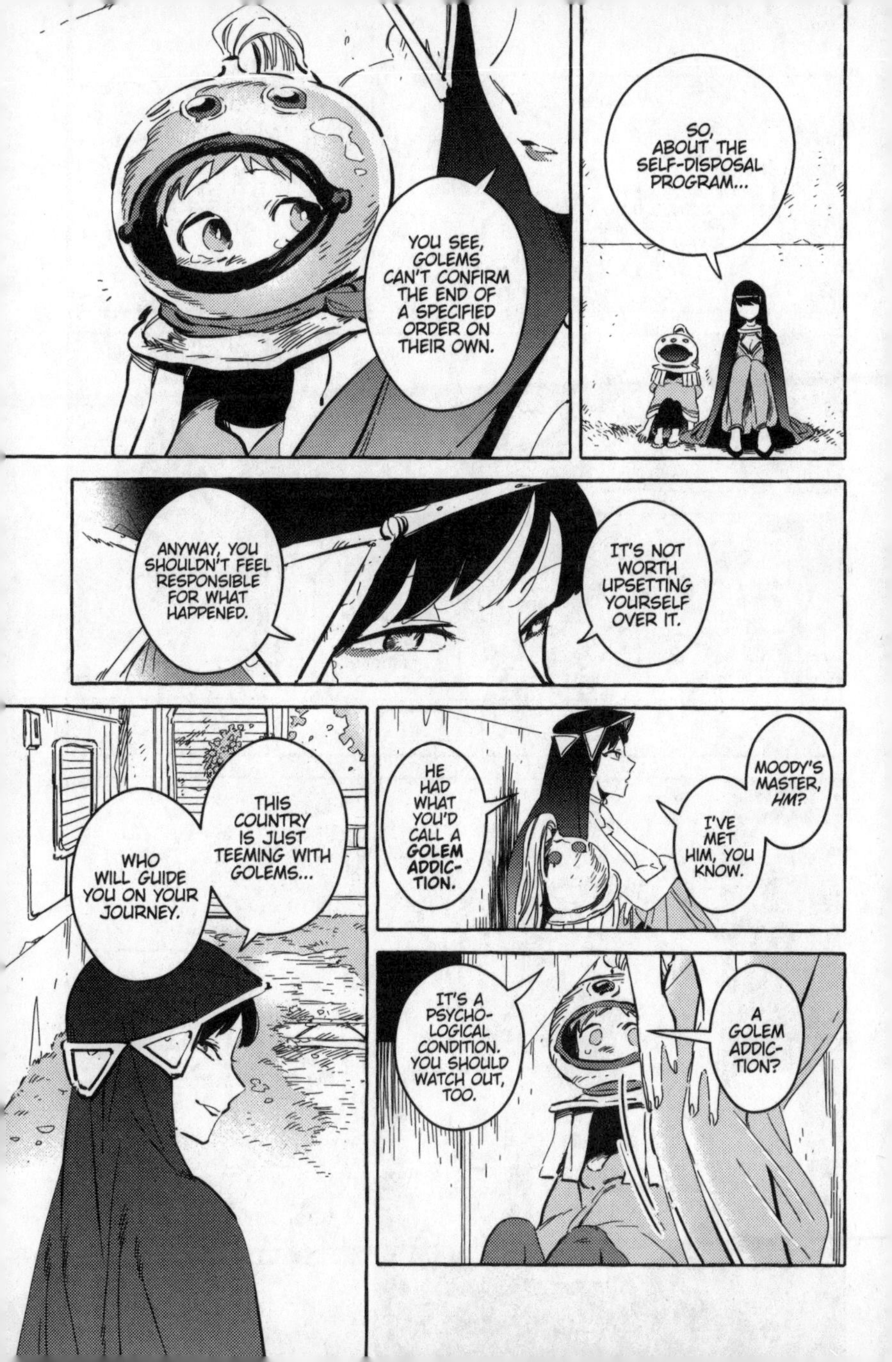
SO, ABOUT THE SELF-DISPOSAL PROGRAM...
YOU SEE, GOLEMS CAN'T CONFIRM THE END OF A SPECIFIED ORDER ON THEIR OWN.
IT'S NOT WORTH UPSETTING YOURSELF OVER IT.
ANYWAY, YOU SHOULDN'T FEEL RESPONSIBLE FOR WHAT HAPPENED.
MOODY'S MASTER, *HM?*
I'VE MET HIM, YOU KNOW.
HE HAD WHAT YOU'D CALL A **GOLEM ADDICTION.**
A GOLEM ADDICTION?
IT'S A PSYCHOLOGICAL CONDITION. YOU SHOULD WATCH OUT, TOO.
THIS COUNTRY IS JUST TEEMING WITH GOLEMS...
WHO WILL GUIDE YOU ON YOUR JOURNEY.

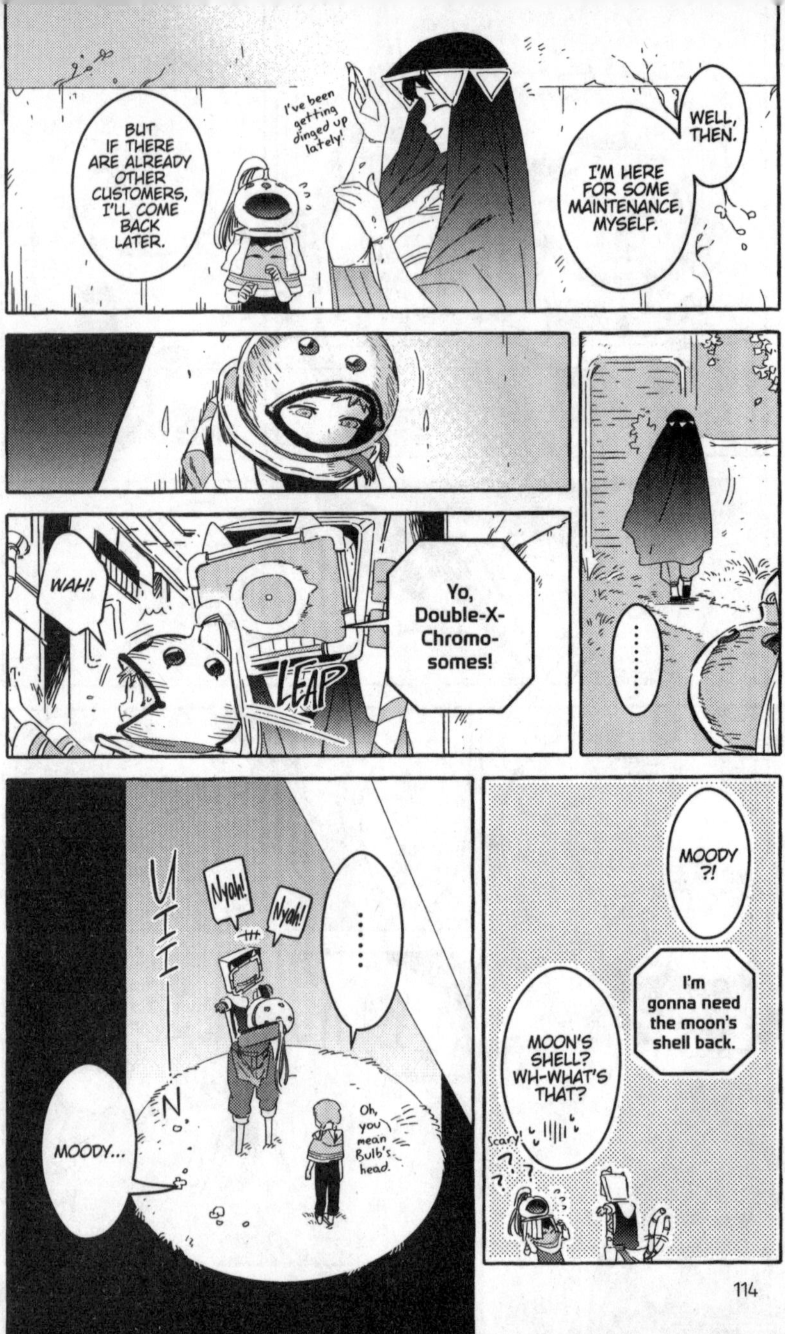
WELL, THEN.
I'M HERE FOR SOME MAINTENANCE, MYSELF.
I've been getting dinged up lately!
BUT IF THERE ARE ALREADY OTHER CUSTOMERS, I'LL COME BACK LATER.
......
Yo, Double-X-Chromo-somes!
LEAP
WAH!
MOODY ?!
I'm gonna need the moon's shell back.
MOON'S SHELL? WH-WHAT'S THAT?
Scary!
......
Nyah!
Nyah!
UII—N.
Oh, you mean Bulb's head.
MOODY...

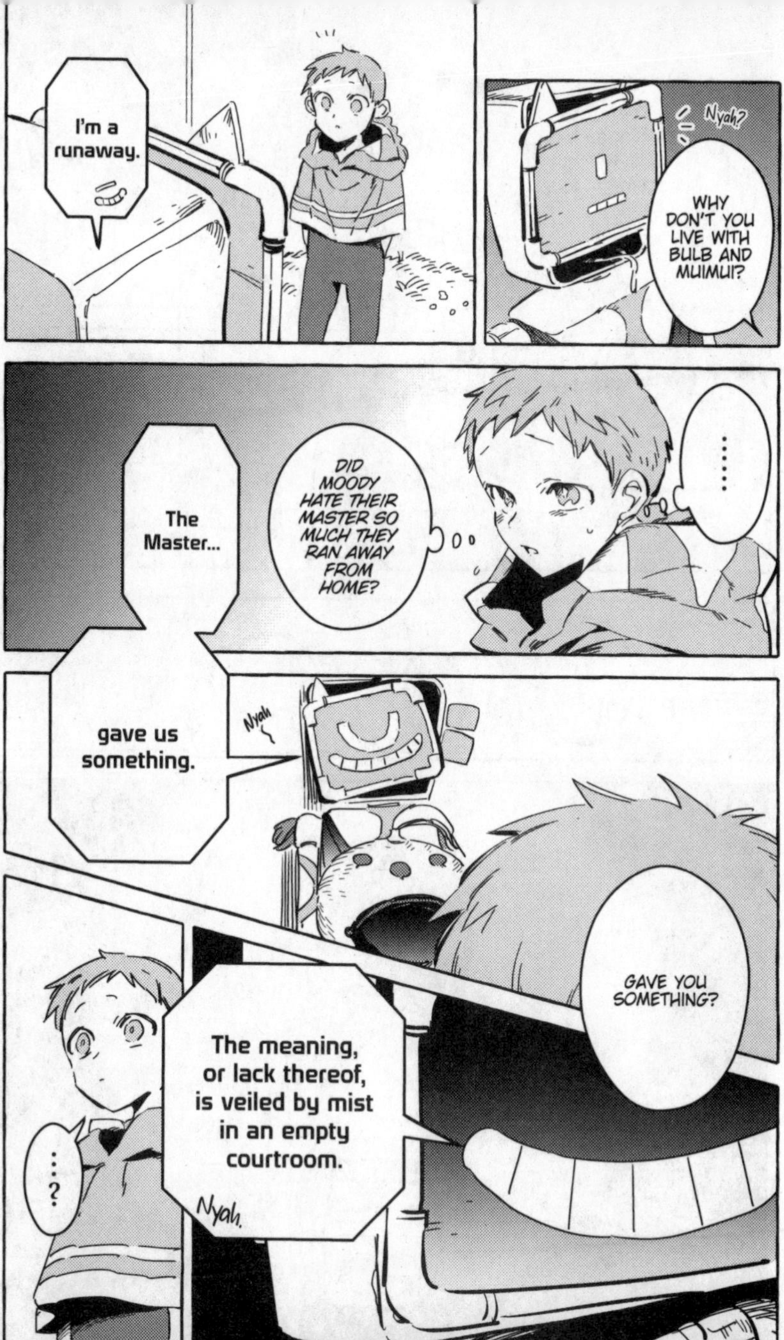
Nyah?
WHY DON'T YOU LIVE WITH BULB AND MUIMUI?
I'm a runaway.
......
DID MOODY HATE THEIR MASTER SO MUCH THEY RAN AWAY FROM HOME?
The Master...
Nyah
gave us something.
GAVE YOU SOMETHING?
The meaning, or lack thereof, is veiled by mist in an empty courtroom.
Nyah.
...?

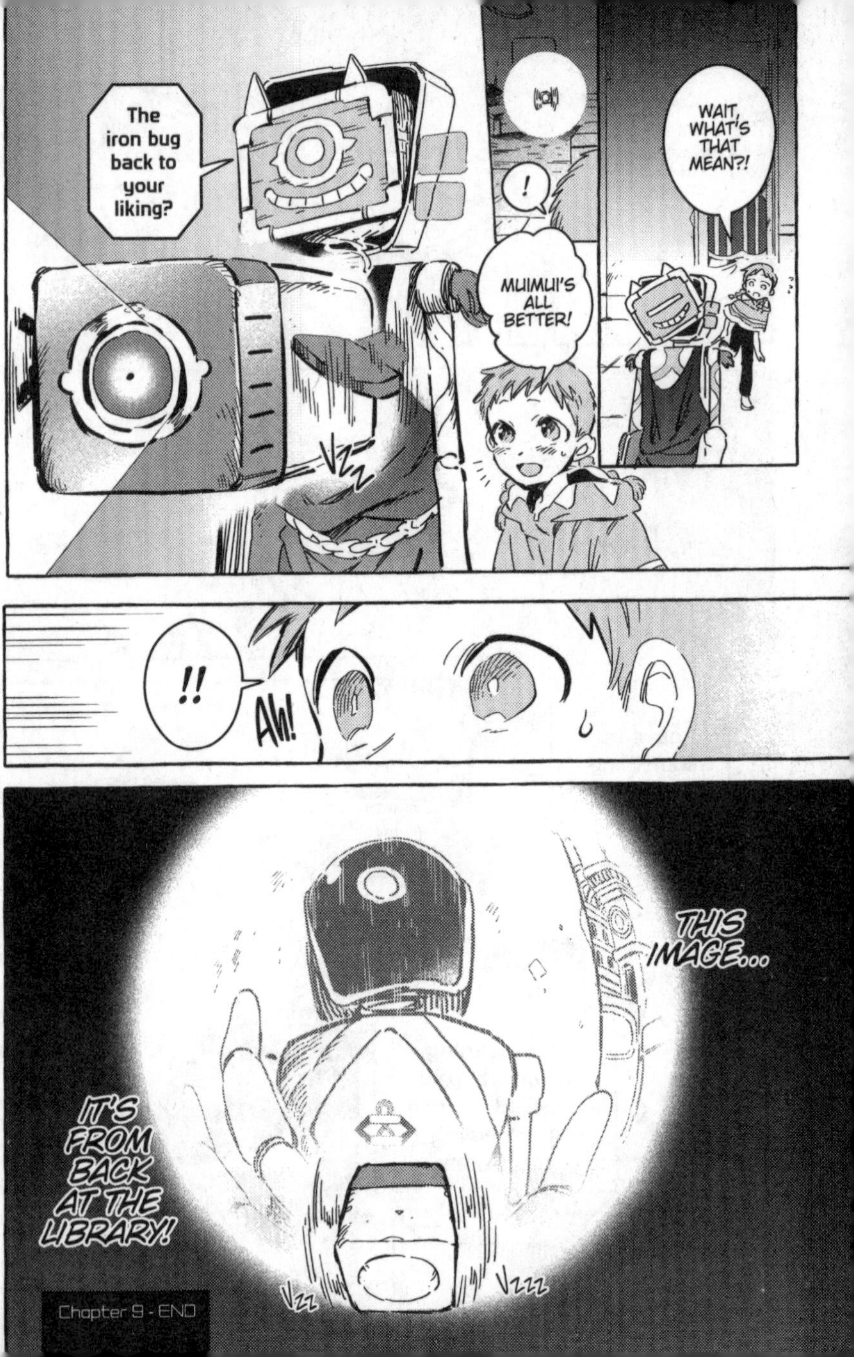
WAIT, WHAT'S THAT MEAN?!
!
MUIMUI'S ALL BETTER!
The iron bug back to your liking?
VZZ
AH!
!!
THIS IMAGE...
IT'S FROM BACK AT THE LIBRARY!
VZZZ
VZZ
Chapter 9 - END

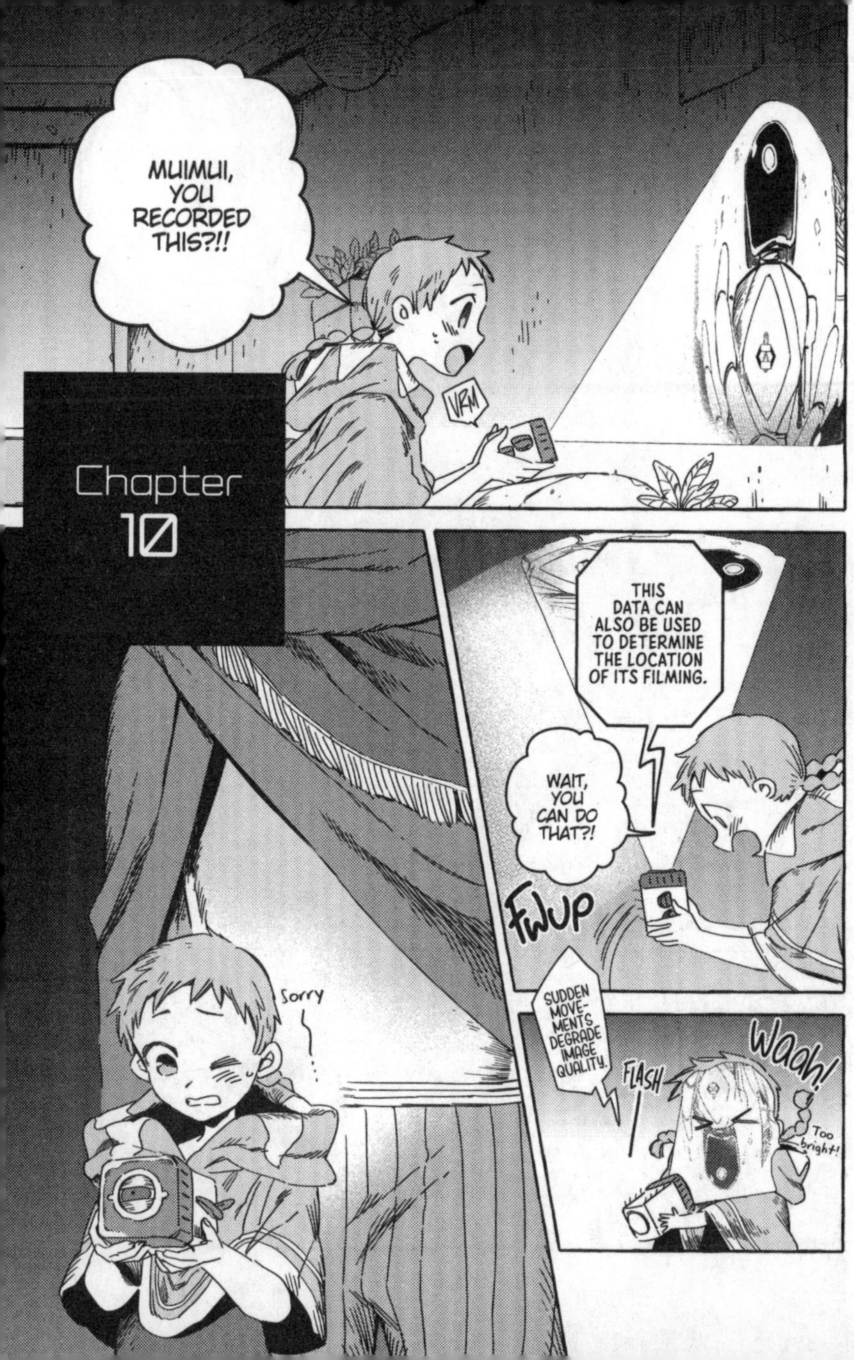
Chapter 10
MUIMUI, YOU RECORDED THIS?!!
VRM
THIS DATA CAN ALSO BE USED TO DETERMINE THE LOCATION OF ITS FILMING.
WAIT, YOU CAN DO THAT?!
FWUP
Waah!
Too bright!
FLASH
SUDDEN MOVEMENTS DEGRADE IMAGE QUALITY.
Sorry
...

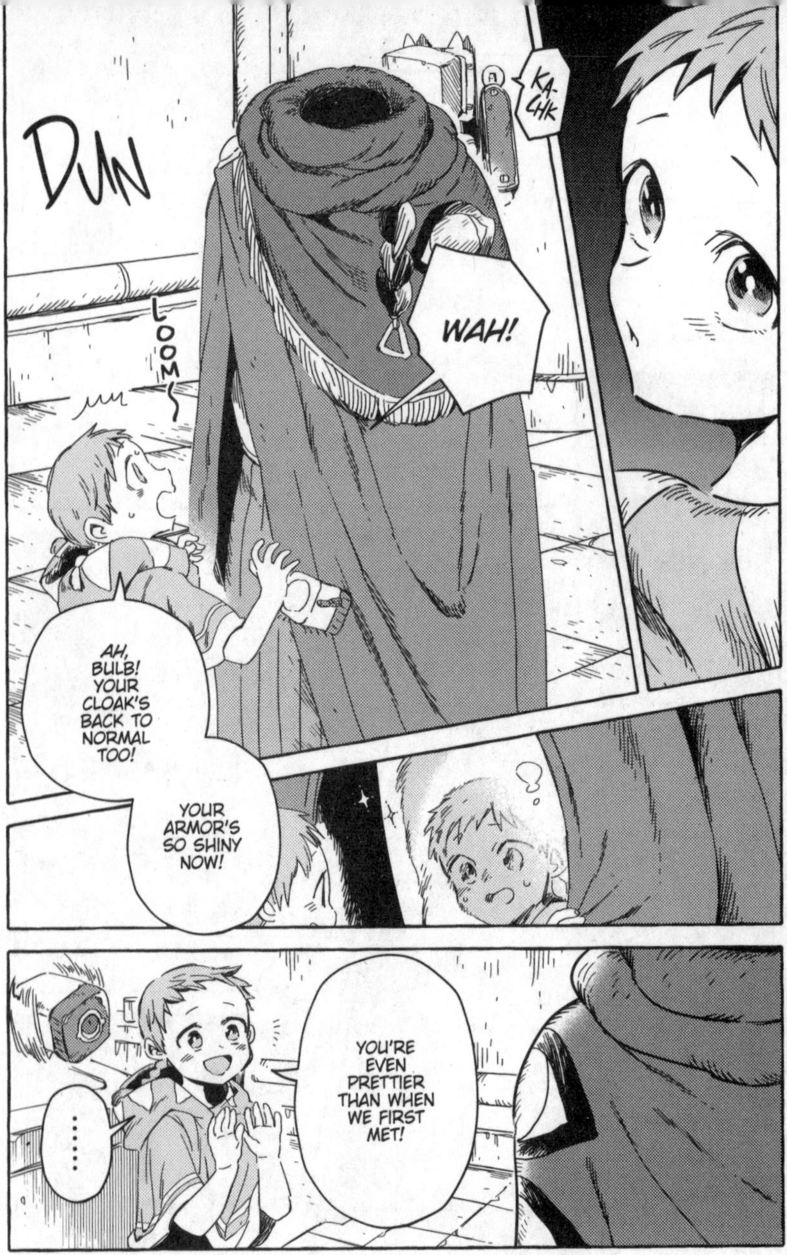
KA-CHK
WAH!
DUN
LOOM
AH, BULB! YOUR CLOAK'S BACK TO NORMAL TOO!
YOUR ARMOR'S SO SHINY NOW!
YOU'RE EVEN PRETTIER THAN WHEN WE FIRST MET!
......

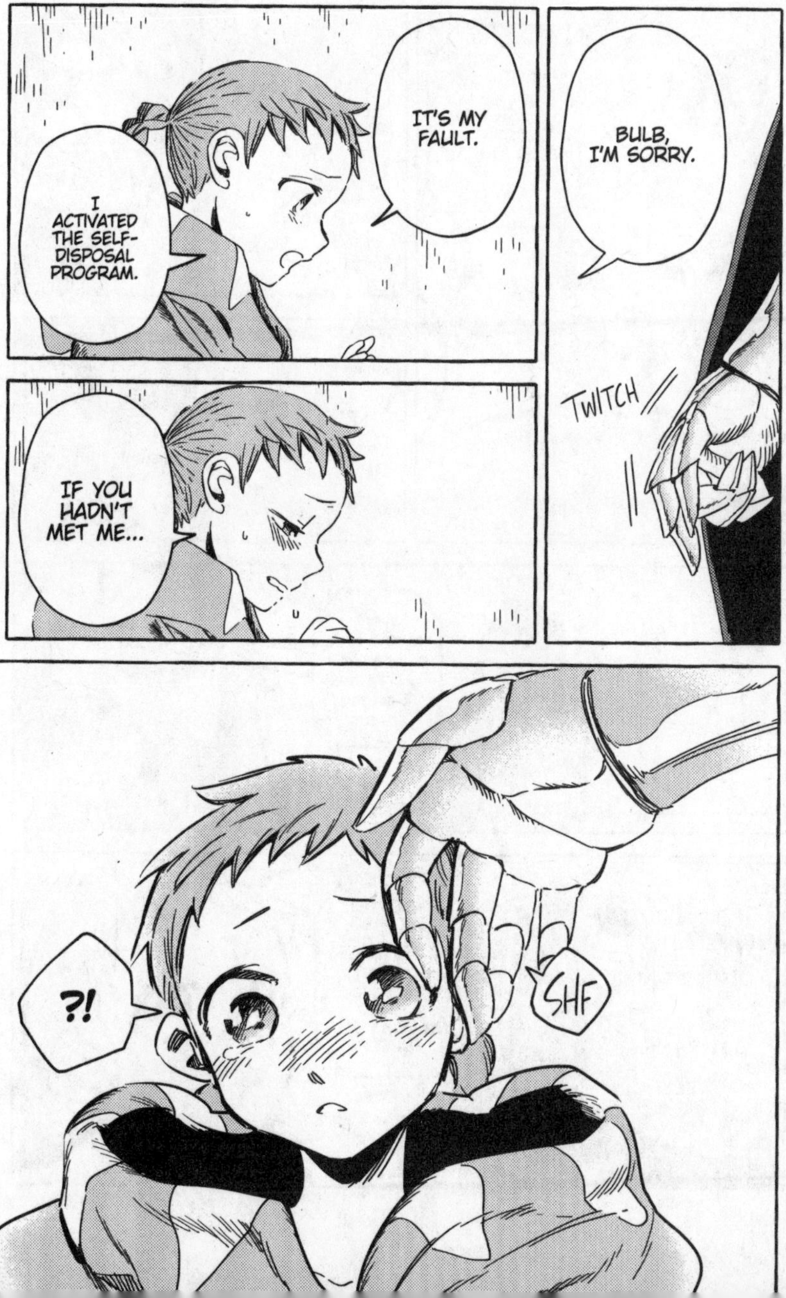
BULB, I'M SORRY.
TWITCH
IT'S MY FAULT.
I ACTIVATED THE SELF-DISPOSAL PROGRAM.
IF YOU HADN'T MET ME...
SHF
?!

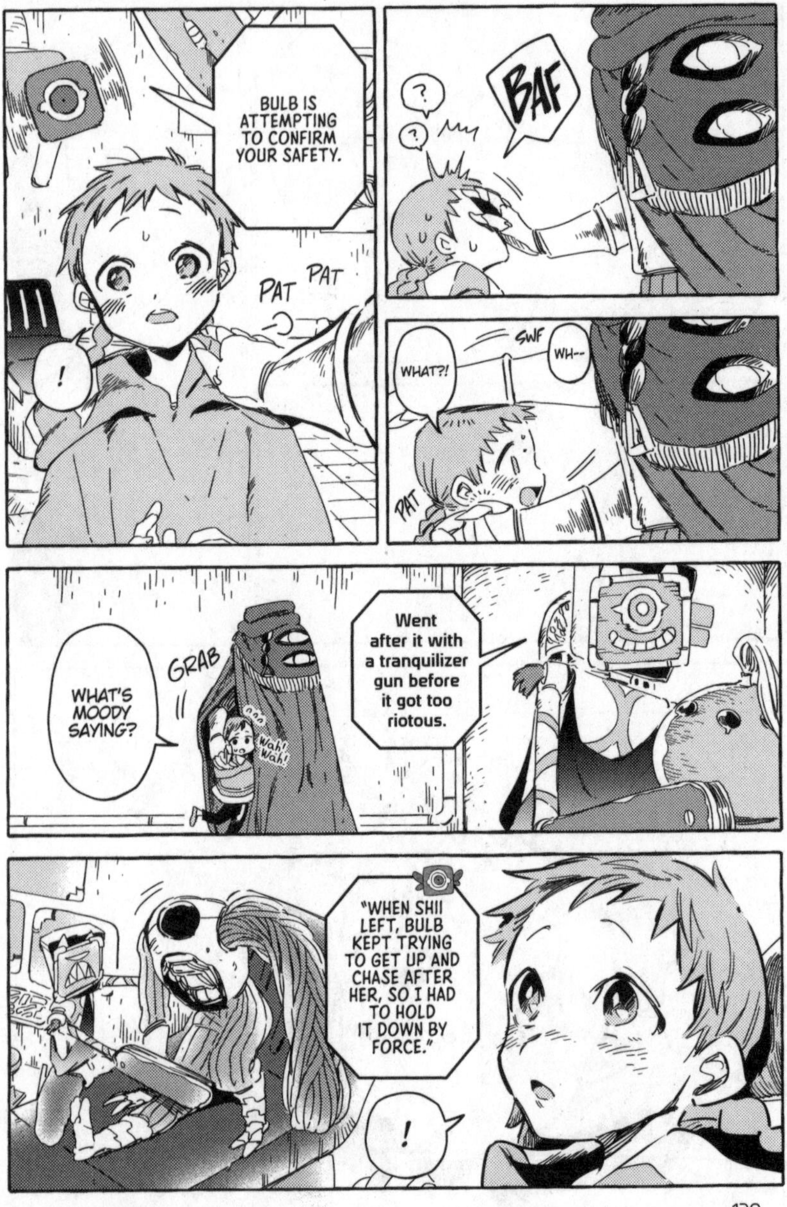
BAF
?
?
WH--
SWF
WHAT?!
PAT
BULB IS ATTEMPTING TO CONFIRM YOUR SAFETY.
PAT PAT
!
Went after it with a tranquilizer gun before it got too riotous.
GRAB
Wah! Wah!
WHAT'S MOODY SAYING?
"WHEN SHII LEFT, BULB KEPT TRYING TO GET UP AND CHASE AFTER HER, SO I HAD TO HOLD IT DOWN BY FORCE."
!

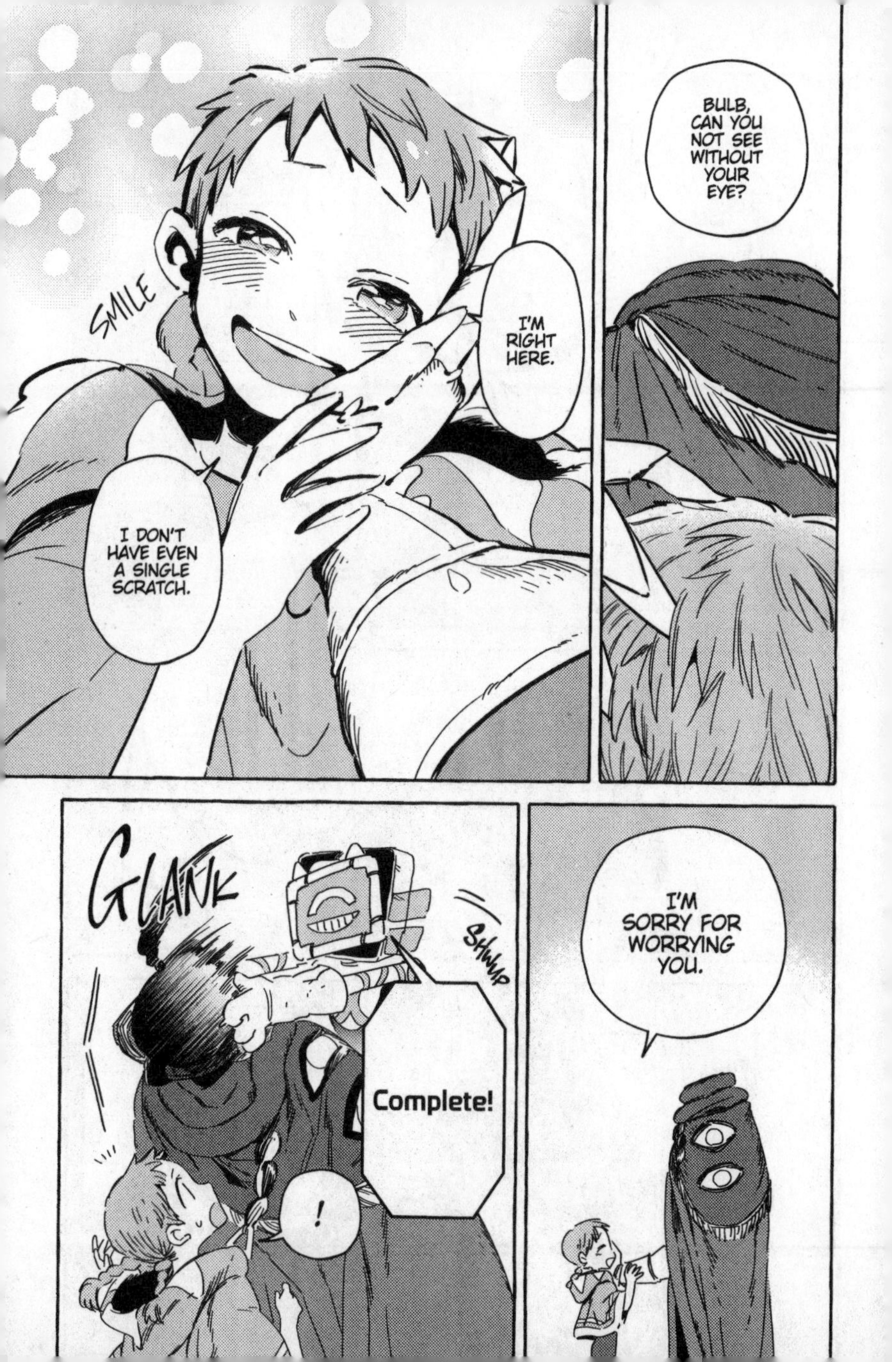
BULB, CAN YOU NOT SEE WITHOUT YOUR EYE?
I'M RIGHT HERE.
SMILE
I DON'T HAVE EVEN A SINGLE SCRATCH.
I'M SORRY FOR WORRYING YOU.
GLANK
SHWUP
Complete!
!

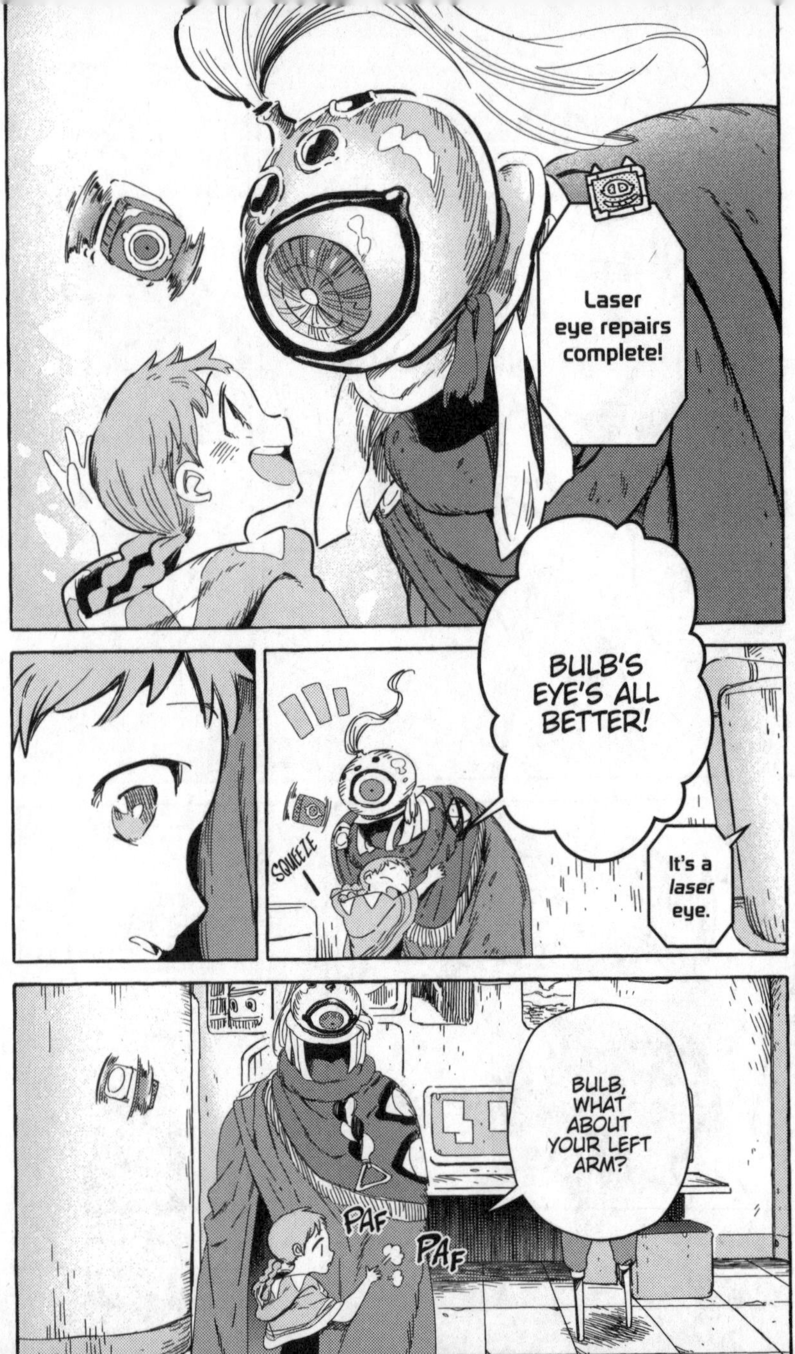
Laser eye repairs complete!
BULB'S EYE'S ALL BETTER!
It's a *laser* eye.
SQUEEZE
BULB, WHAT ABOUT YOUR LEFT ARM?
PAF
PAF

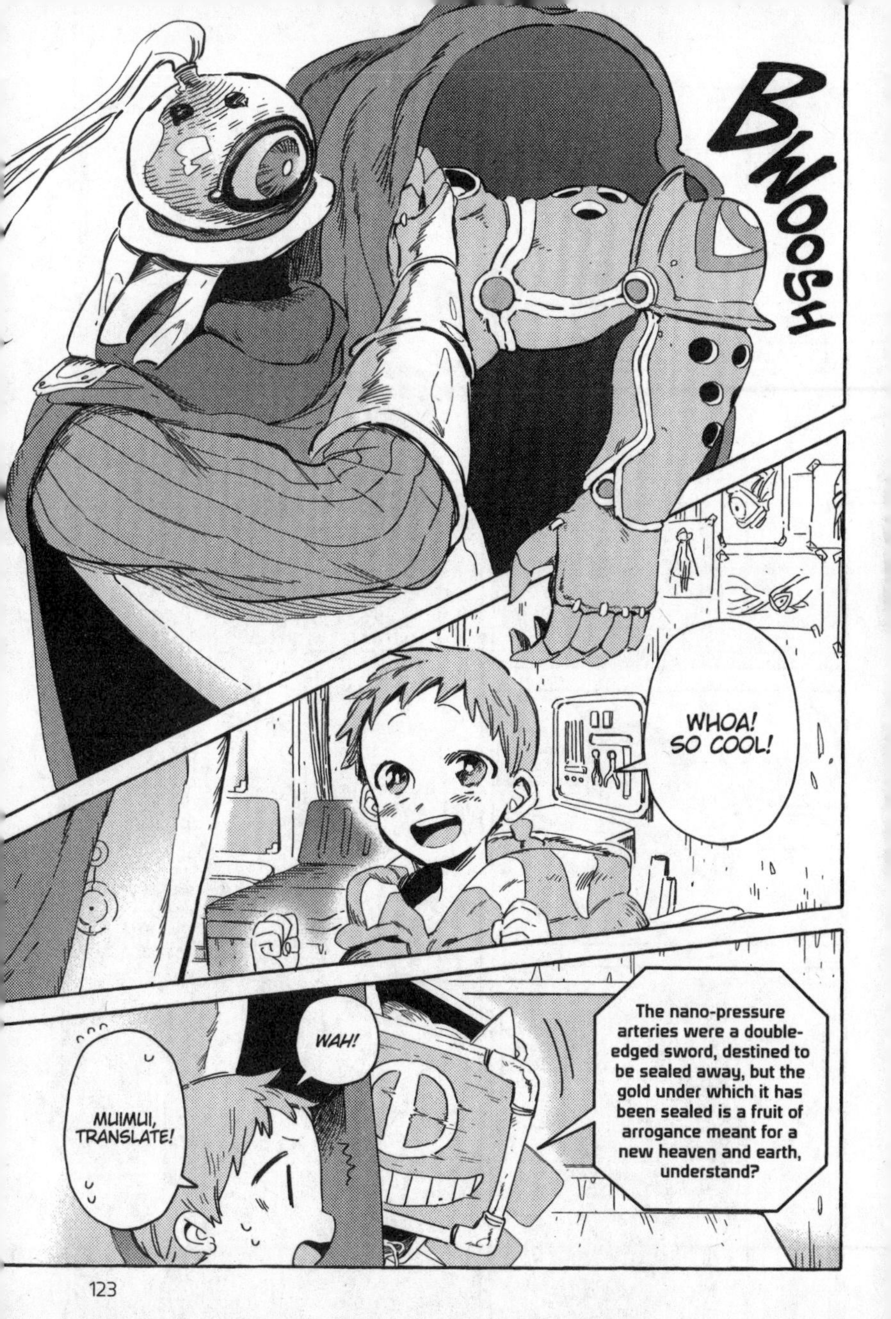
BWOOSH
WHOA! SO COOL!
The nano-pressure arteries were a double-edged sword, destined to be sealed away, but the gold under which it has been sealed is a fruit of arrogance meant for a new heaven and earth, understand?
WAH!
MUIMUI, TRANSLATE!

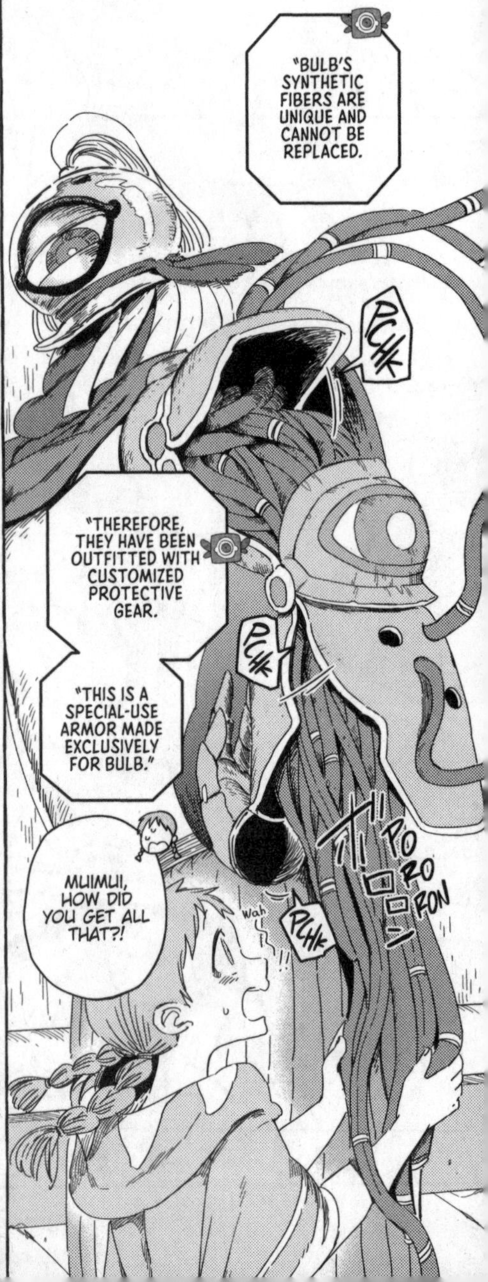
"BULB'S SYNTHETIC FIBERS ARE UNIQUE AND CANNOT BE REPLACED.
PCHK
"THEREFORE, THEY HAVE BEEN OUTFITTED WITH CUSTOMIZED PROTECTIVE GEAR.
PCHK
"THIS IS A SPECIAL-USE ARMOR MADE EXCLUSIVELY FOR BULB."
PO RO RON
PCHK
MUIMUI, HOW DID YOU GET ALL THAT?!
Wah

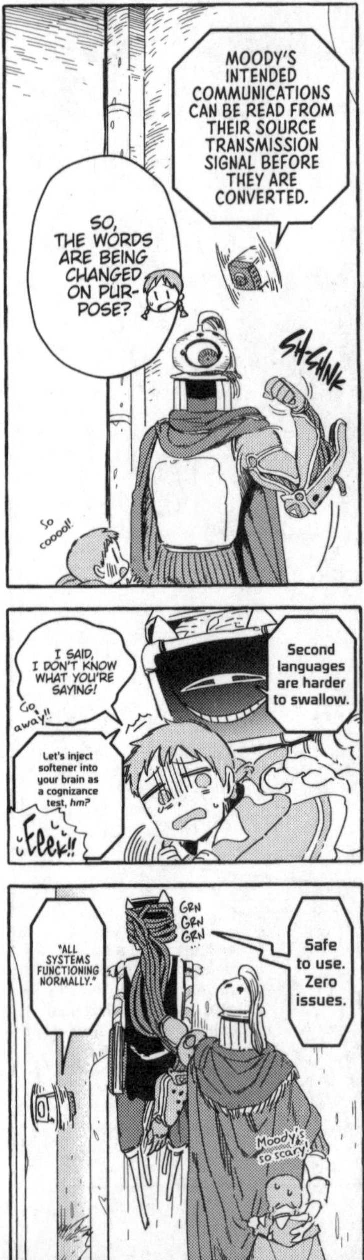
MOODY'S INTENDED COMMUNICATIONS CAN BE READ FROM THEIR SOURCE TRANSMISSION SIGNAL BEFORE THEY ARE CONVERTED.
SH-SHINK
SO, THE WORDS ARE BEING CHANGED ON PUR-POSE?
So cooool!
Second languages are harder to swallow.
I SAID, I DON'T KNOW WHAT YOU'RE SAYING!
Go away!!
Let's inject softener into your brain as a cognizance test, hm?
Eeek!!
Safe to use. Zero issues.
GRN GRN GRN
"ALL SYSTEMS FUNCTIONING NORMALLY."
Moody's so scary!

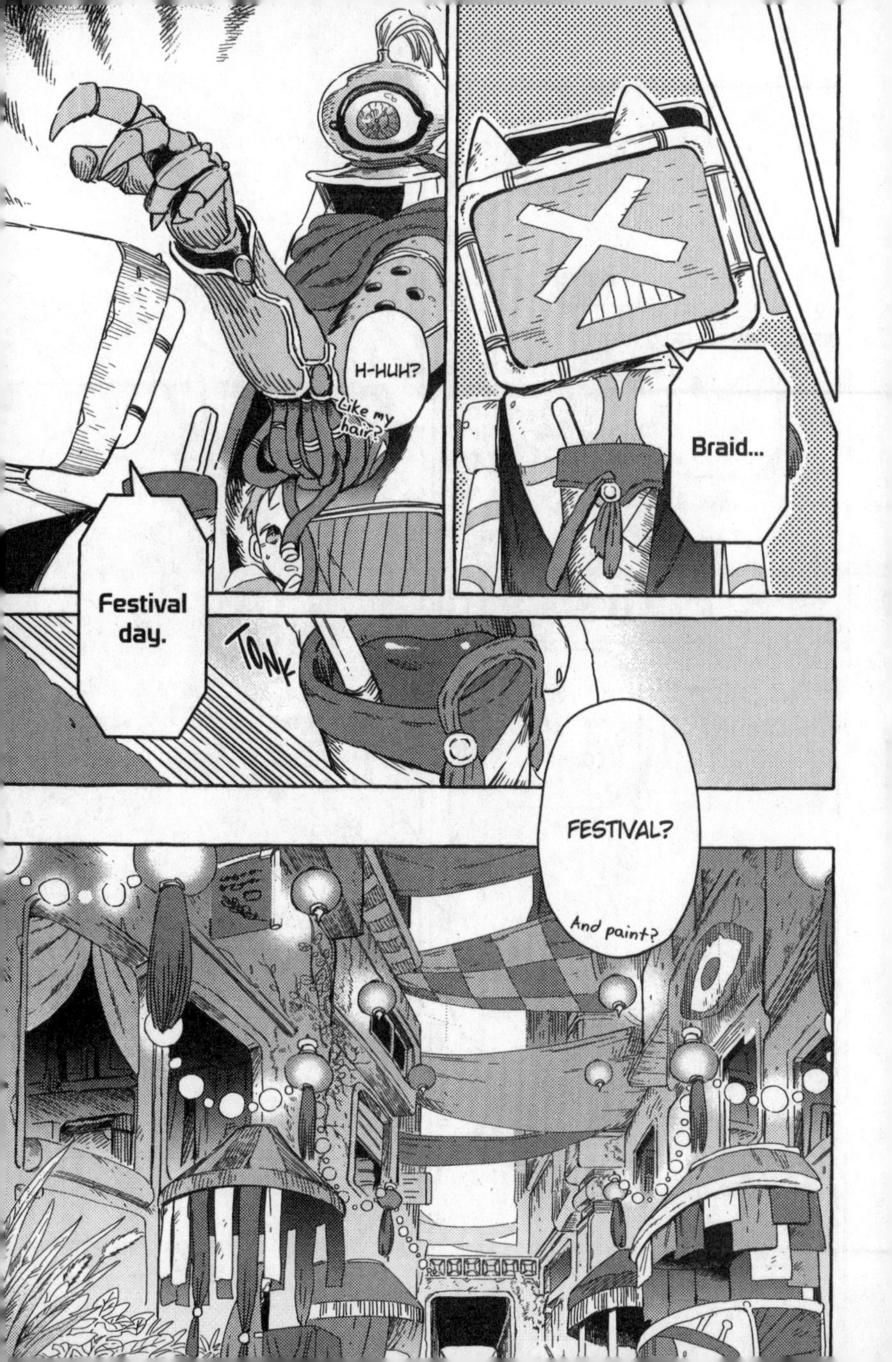
Braid...
H-HUH?
Like my hair?
Festival day.
TONK
FESTIVAL?
And paint?

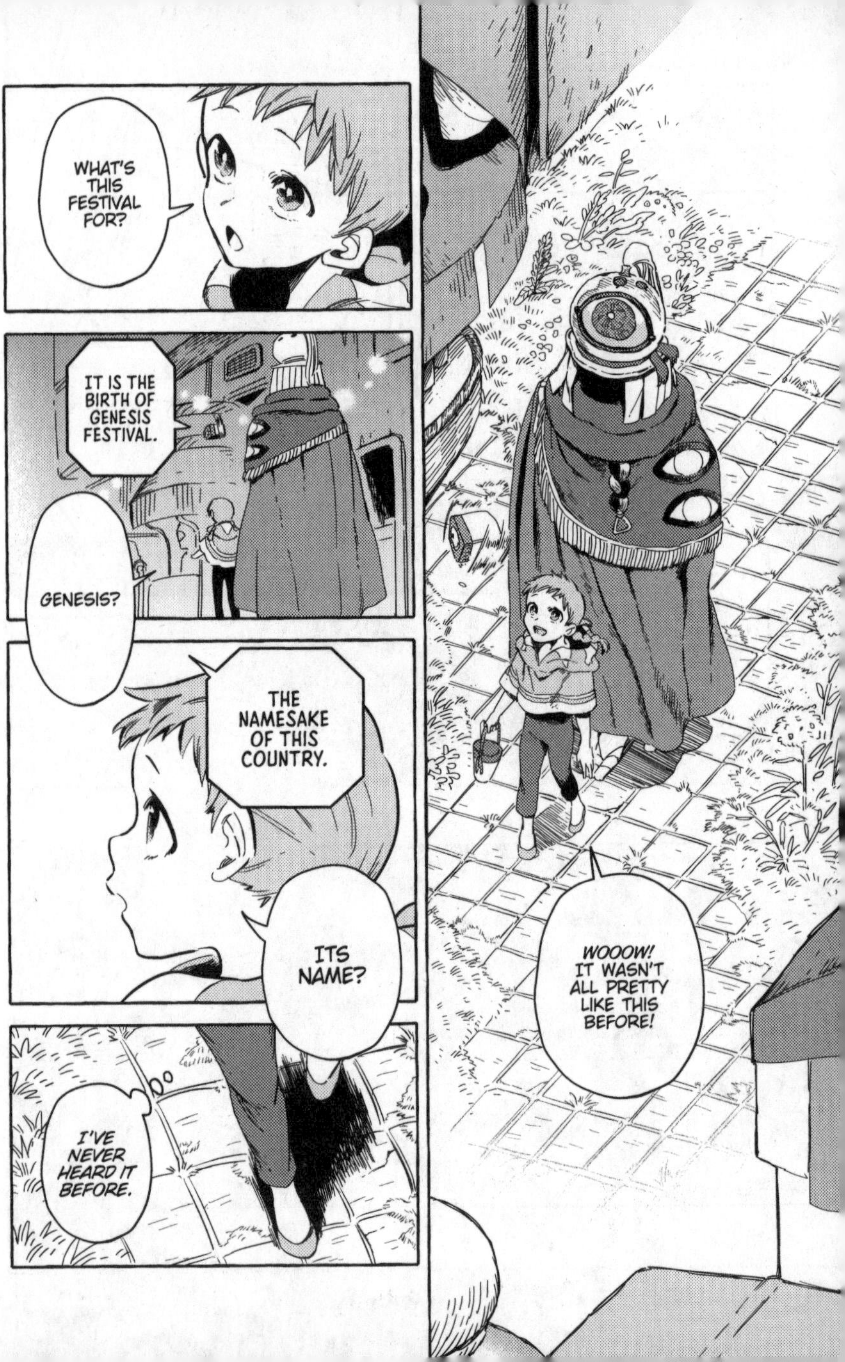

WOOOW! IT WASN'T ALL PRETTY LIKE THIS BEFORE!
WHAT'S THIS FESTIVAL FOR?
IT IS THE BIRTH OF GENESIS FESTIVAL.
GENESIS?
THE NAMESAKE OF THIS COUNTRY.
ITS NAME?
I'VE NEVER HEARD IT BEFORE.

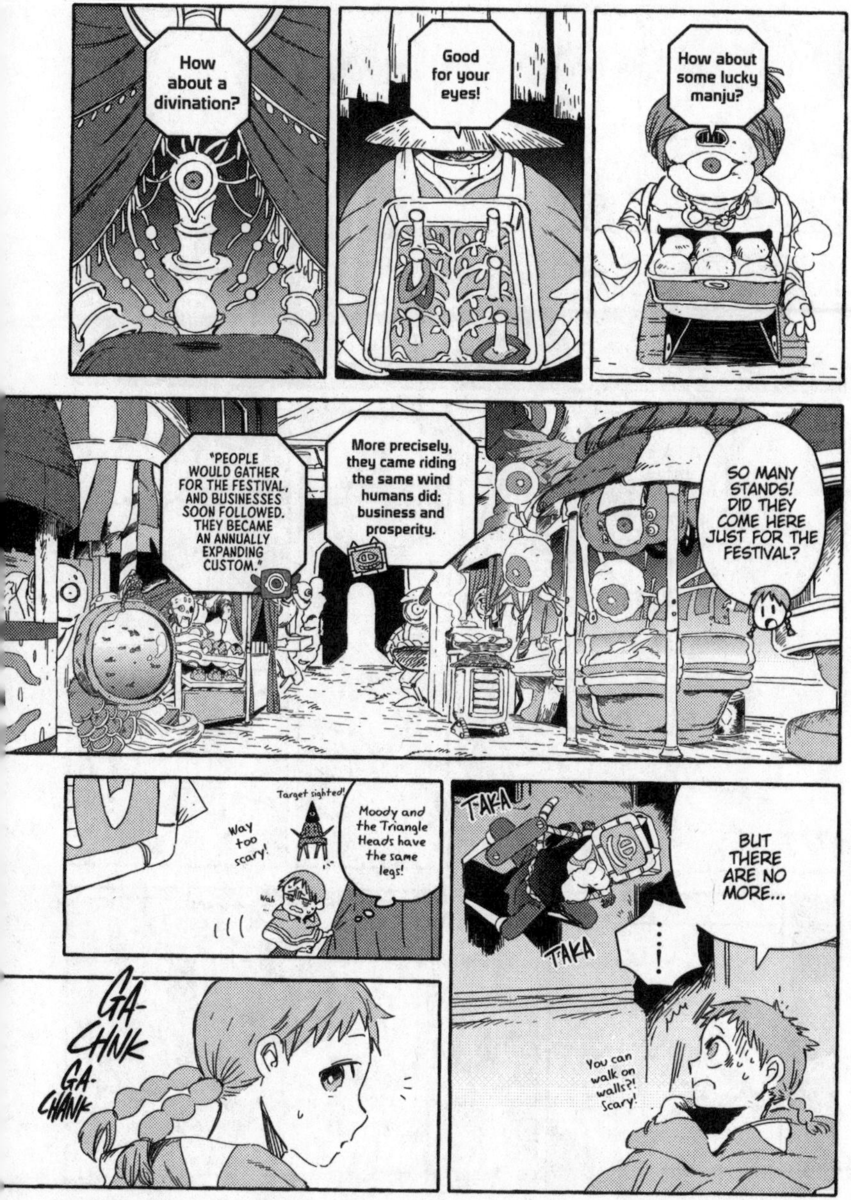
How about some lucky manju?
Good for your eyes!
How about a divination?
SO MANY STANDS! DID THEY COME HERE JUST FOR THE FESTIVAL?
More precisely, they came riding the same wind humans did: business and prosperity.
"PEOPLE WOULD GATHER FOR THE FESTIVAL, AND BUSINESSES SOON FOLLOWED. THEY BECAME AN ANNUALLY EXPANDING CUSTOM."
TAKA
BUT THERE ARE NO MORE...
TAKA
...!
You can walk on walls?! Scary!
Moody and the Triangle Heads have the same legs!
Target sighted!
Way too scary!
Wah
GA-CHNK GA-CHANK

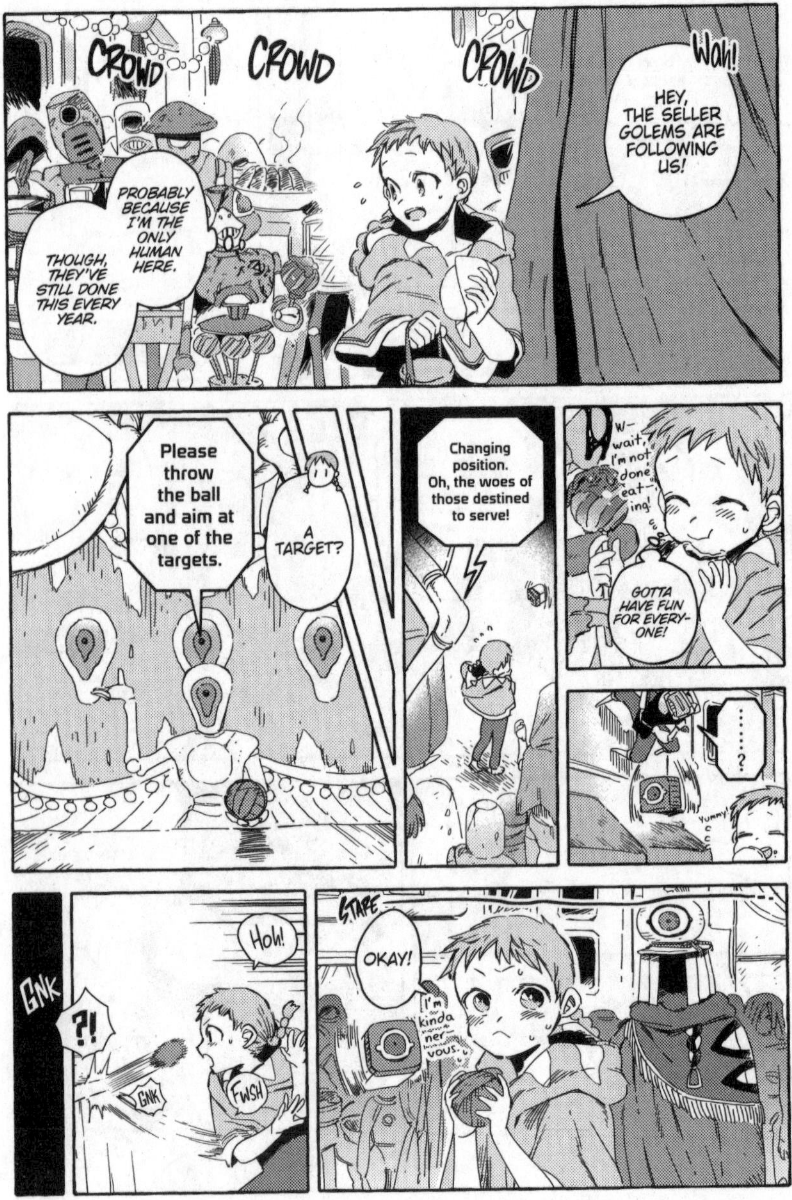
Wah!
HEY, THE SELLER GOLEMS ARE FOLLOWING US!
CROWD
CROWD
CROWD
PROBABLY BECAUSE I'M THE ONLY HUMAN HERE.
THOUGH, THEY'VE STILL DONE THIS EVERY YEAR.
W-wait, I'm not done eat-ing!
GOTTA HAVE FUN FOR EVERY-ONE!
......?
Yummy!
Changing position. Oh, the woes of those destined to serve!
A TARGET?
Please throw the ball and aim at one of the targets.
STARE
OKAY!
I'm kinda ner-vous.
Hoh!
?!
FWSH
GNK
GNK

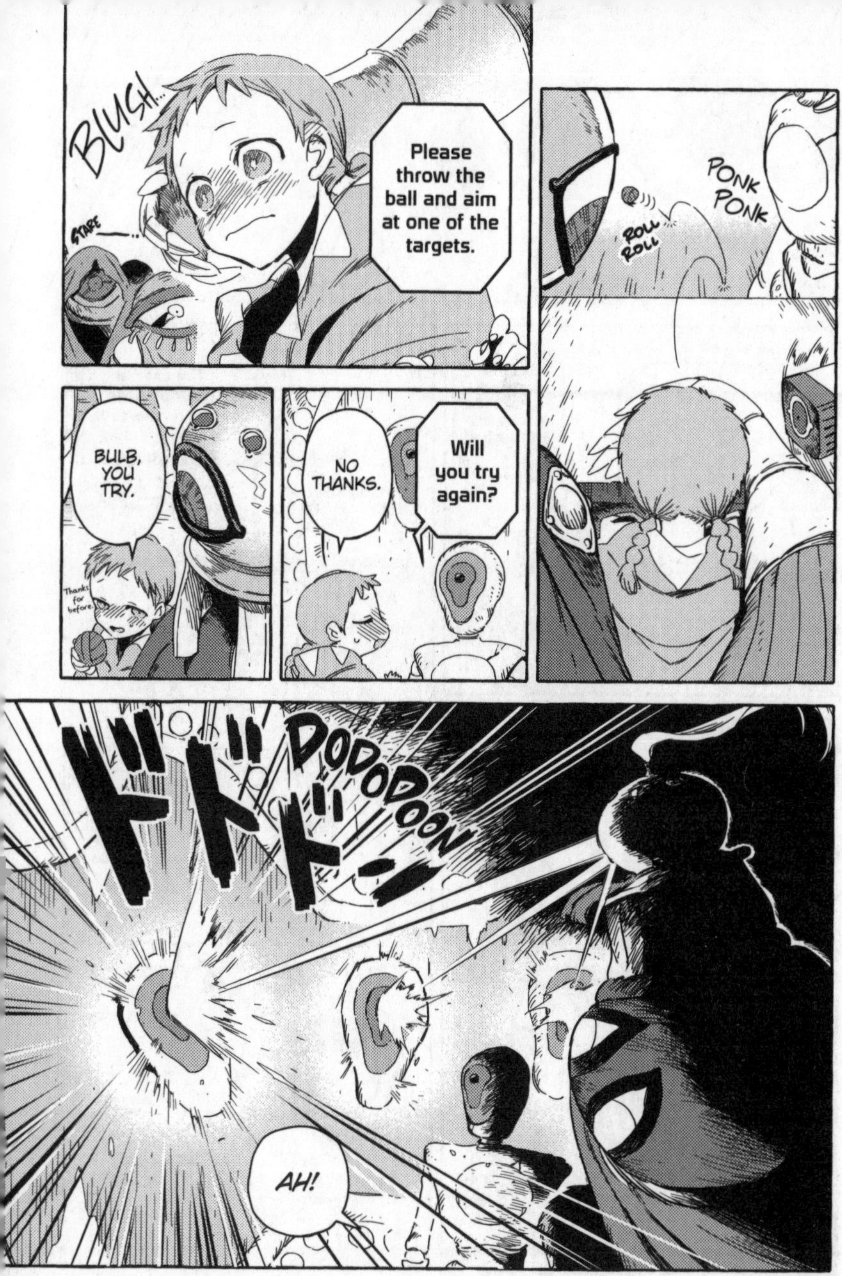
PONK PONK
ROLL ROLL
Please throw the ball and aim at one of the targets.
BLUSH...
STARE—...
Will you try again?
NO THANKS.
BULB, YOU TRY.
Thanks for before.
DODODOON
AH!

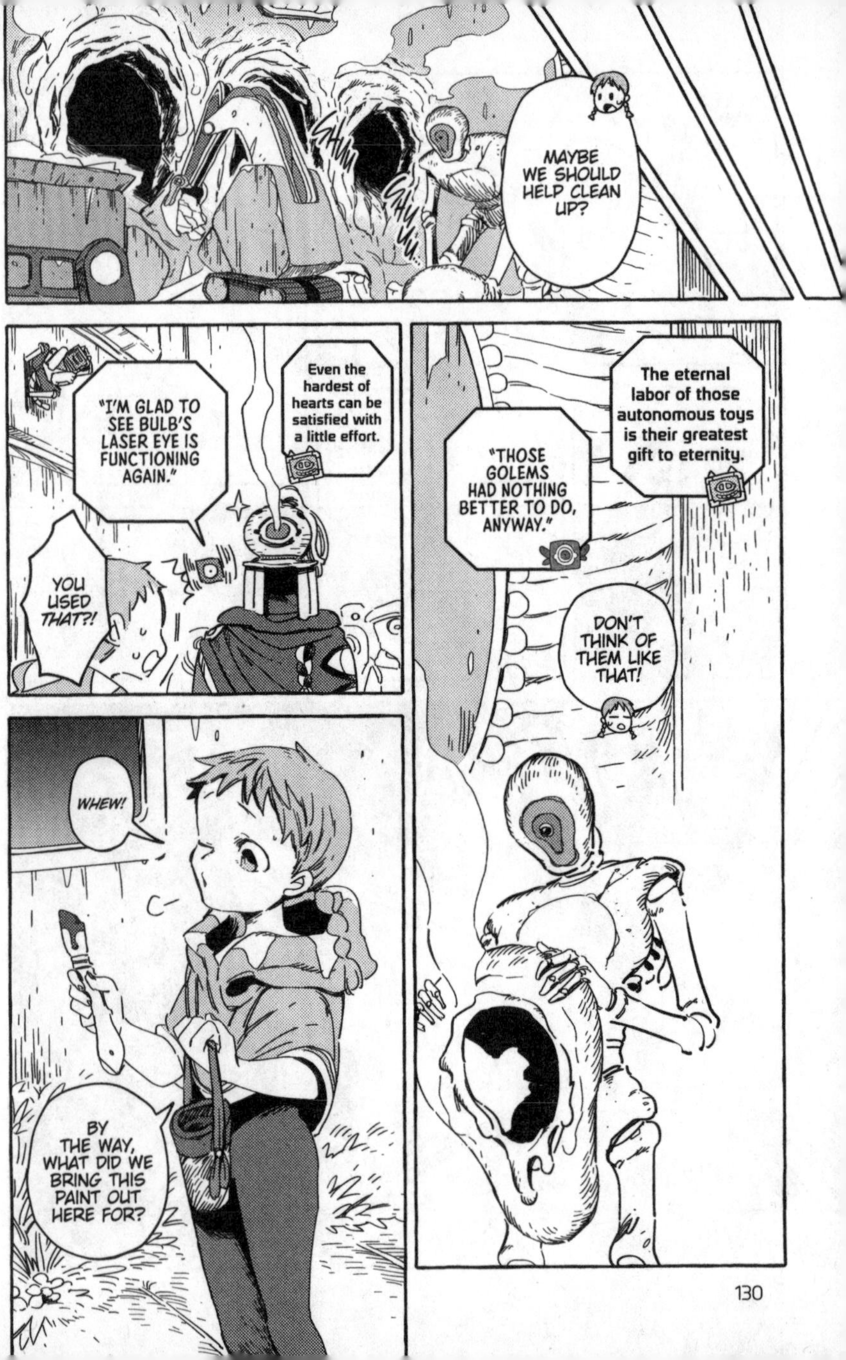
MAYBE WE SHOULD HELP CLEAN UP?
The eternal labor of those autonomous toys is their greatest gift to eternity.
"THOSE GOLEMS HAD NOTHING BETTER TO DO, ANYWAY."
DON'T THINK OF THEM LIKE THAT!
Even the hardest of hearts can be satisfied with a little effort.
"I'M GLAD TO SEE BULB'S LASER EYE IS FUNCTIONING AGAIN."
YOU USED *THAT?!*
WHEW!
BY THE WAY, WHAT DID WE BRING THIS PAINT OUT HERE FOR?

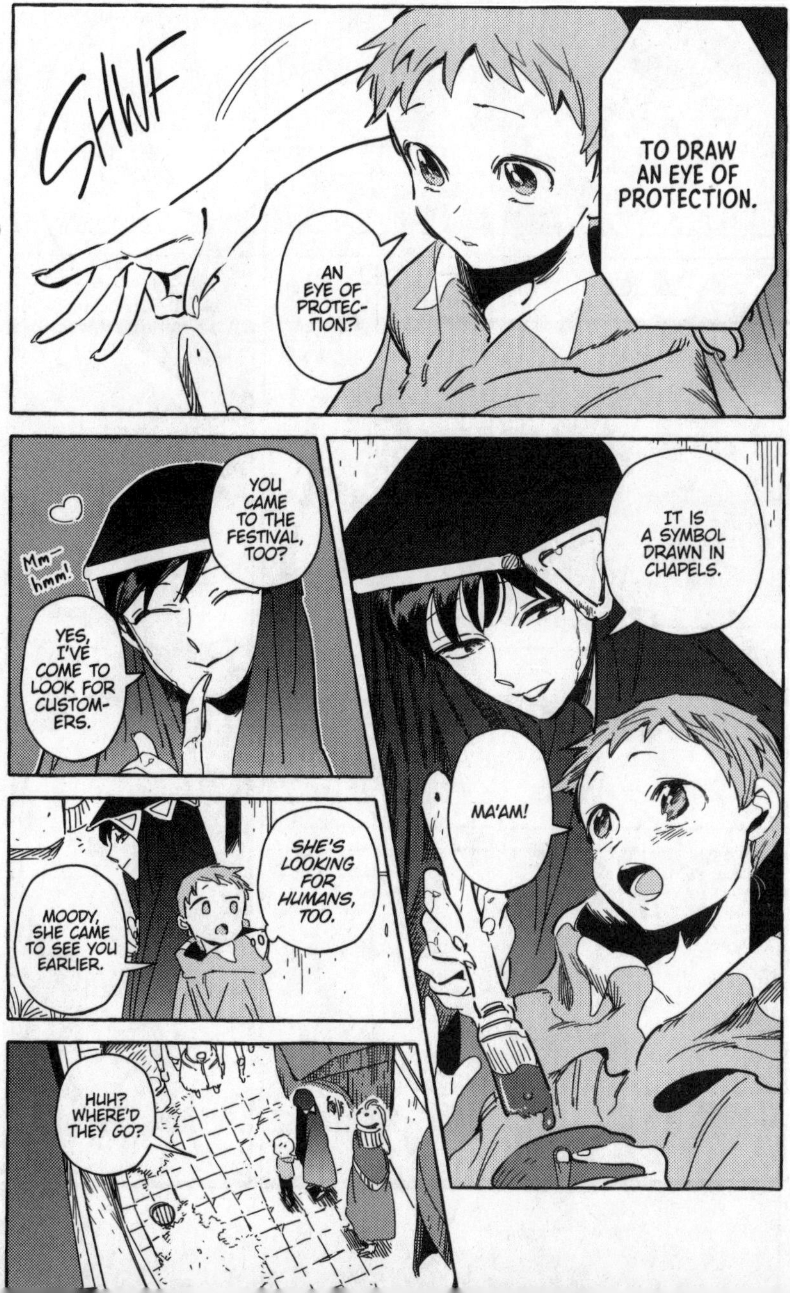
TO DRAW AN EYE OF PROTECTION.
AN EYE OF PROTECTION?
SHWF
IT IS A SYMBOL DRAWN IN CHAPELS.
MA'AM!
YOU CAME TO THE FESTIVAL, TOO?
Mm-hmm!
YES, I'VE COME TO LOOK FOR CUSTOMERS.
SHE'S LOOKING FOR HUMANS, TOO.
MOODY, SHE CAME TO SEE YOU EARLIER.
HUH? WHERE'D THEY GO?

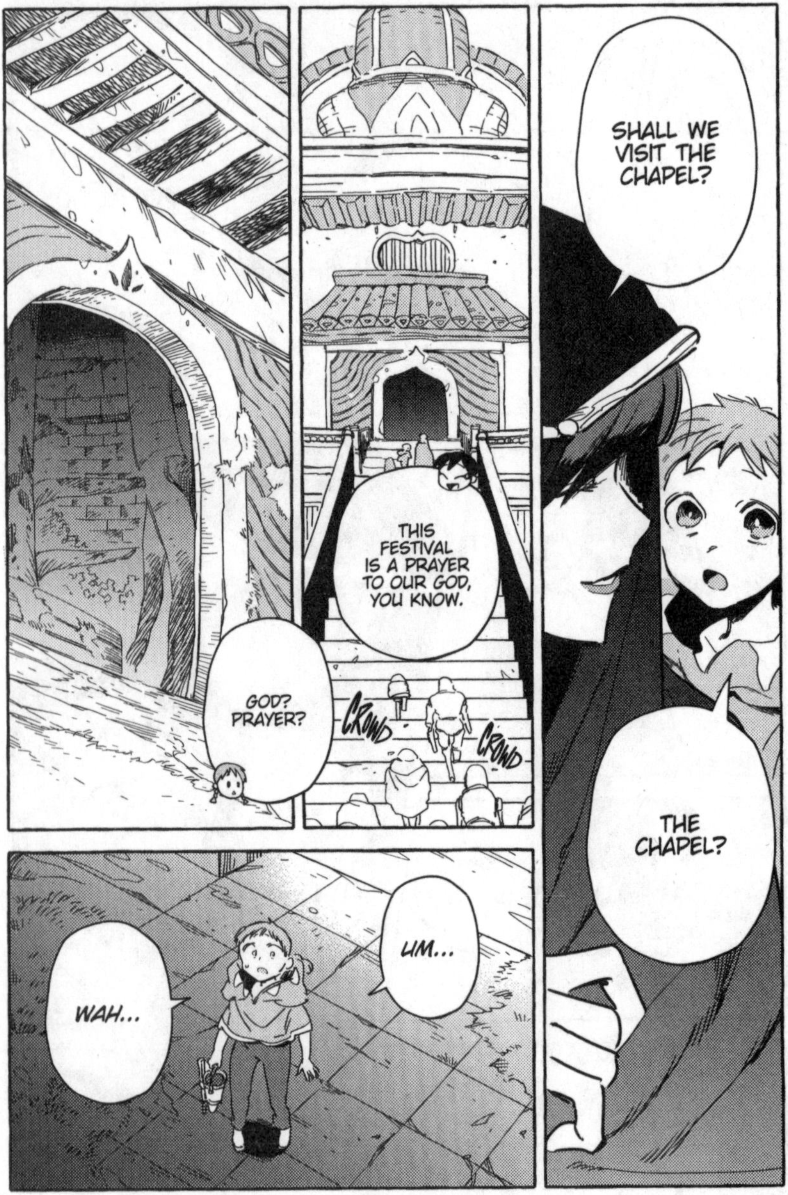
SHALL WE VISIT THE CHAPEL?
THE CHAPEL?
THIS FESTIVAL IS A PRAYER TO OUR GOD, YOU KNOW.
CROWD
CROWD
GOD? PRAYER?
UM...
WAH...

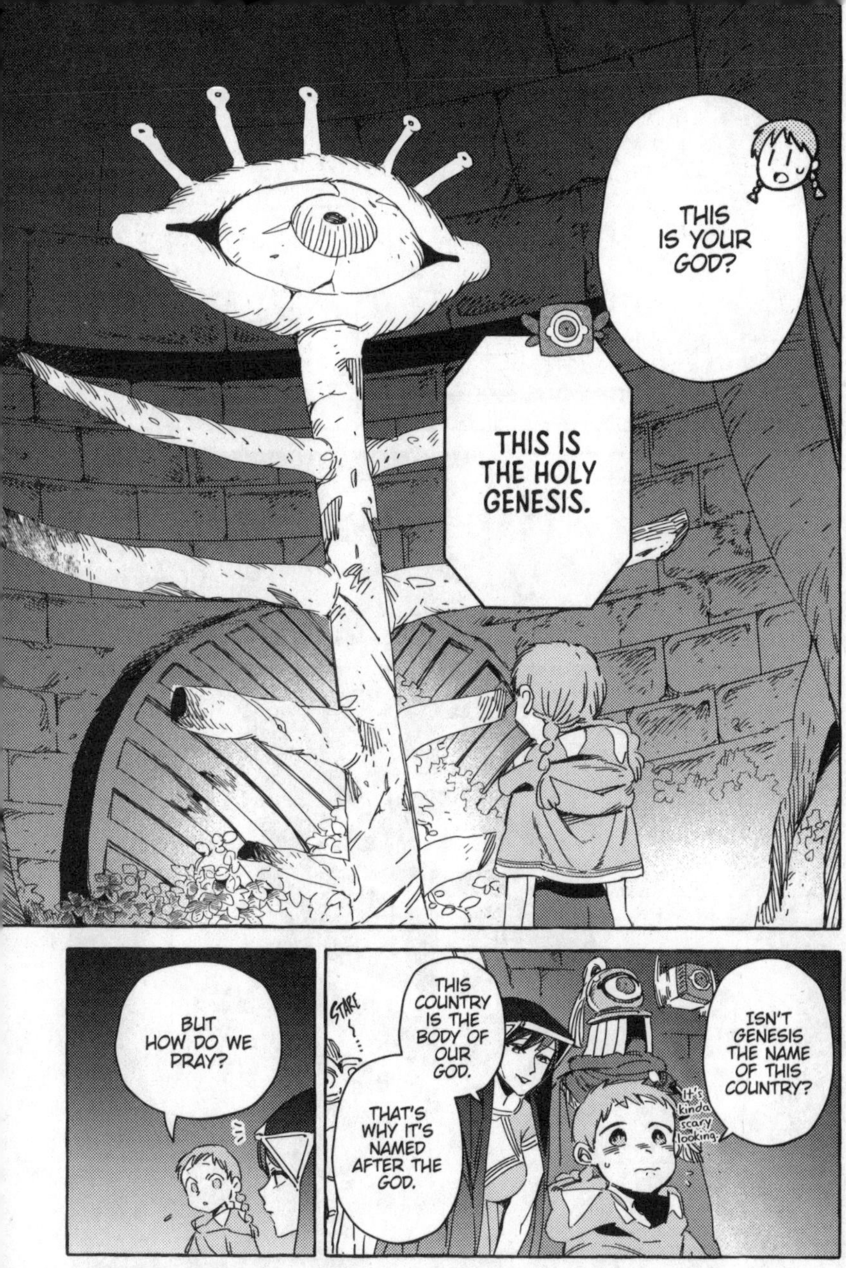
THIS IS YOUR GOD?
THIS IS THE HOLY GENESIS.
ISN'T GENESIS THE NAME OF THIS COUNTRY?
It's kinda scary looking.
THIS COUNTRY IS THE BODY OF OUR GOD.
THAT'S WHY IT'S NAMED AFTER THE GOD.
STARE
BUT HOW DO WE PRAY?

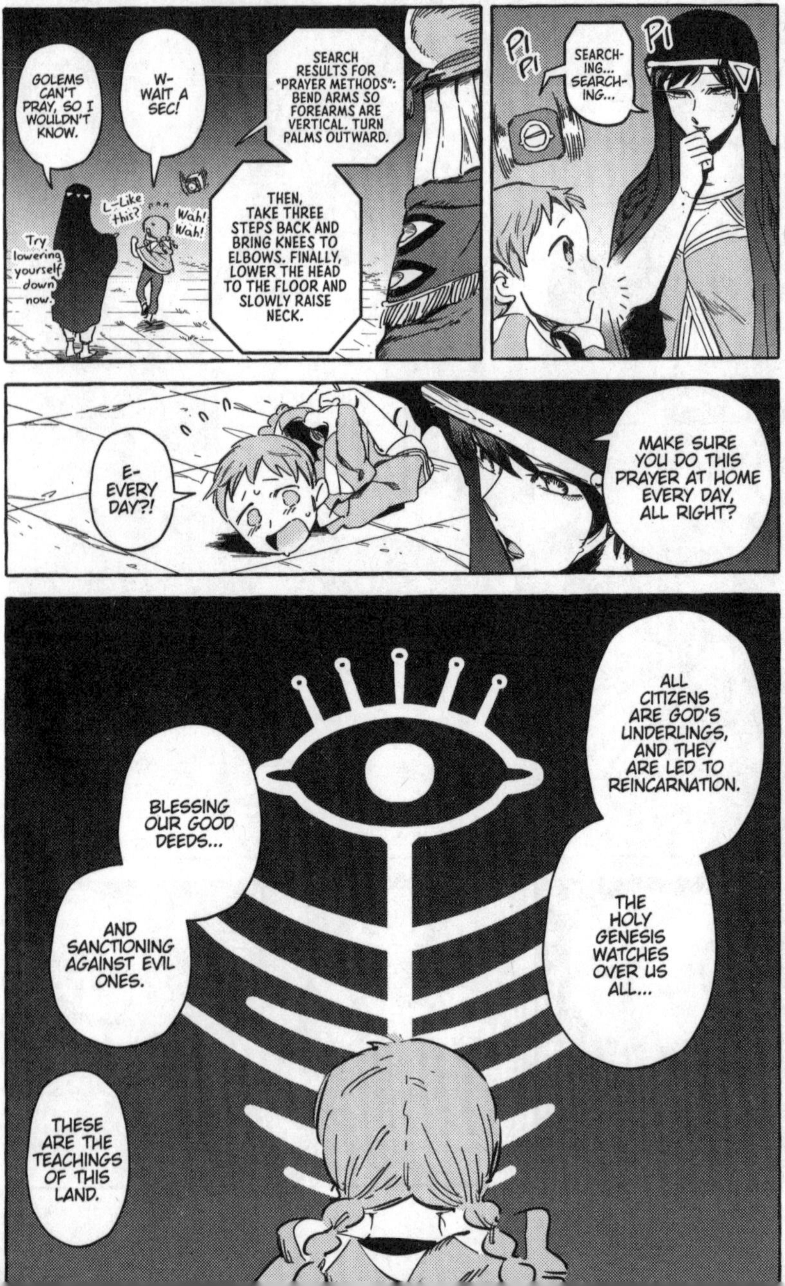
PI PI
PI
SEARCH-ING... SEARCH-ING...
SEARCH RESULTS FOR "PRAYER METHODS": BEND ARMS SO FOREARMS ARE VERTICAL. TURN PALMS OUTWARD.
THEN, TAKE THREE STEPS BACK AND BRING KNEES TO ELBOWS. FINALLY, LOWER THE HEAD TO THE FLOOR AND SLOWLY RAISE NECK.
W-WAIT A SEC!
GOLEMS CAN'T PRAY, SO I WOULDN'T KNOW.
Wah! Wah!
L-Like this?
Try lowering yourself down now.
MAKE SURE YOU DO THIS PRAYER AT HOME EVERY DAY, ALL RIGHT?
E-EVERY DAY?!
ALL CITIZENS ARE GOD'S UNDERLINGS, AND THEY ARE LED TO REINCARNATION.
BLESSING OUR GOOD DEEDS...
THE HOLY GENESIS WATCHES OVER US ALL...
AND SANCTIONING AGAINST EVIL ONES.
THESE ARE THE TEACHINGS OF THIS LAND.

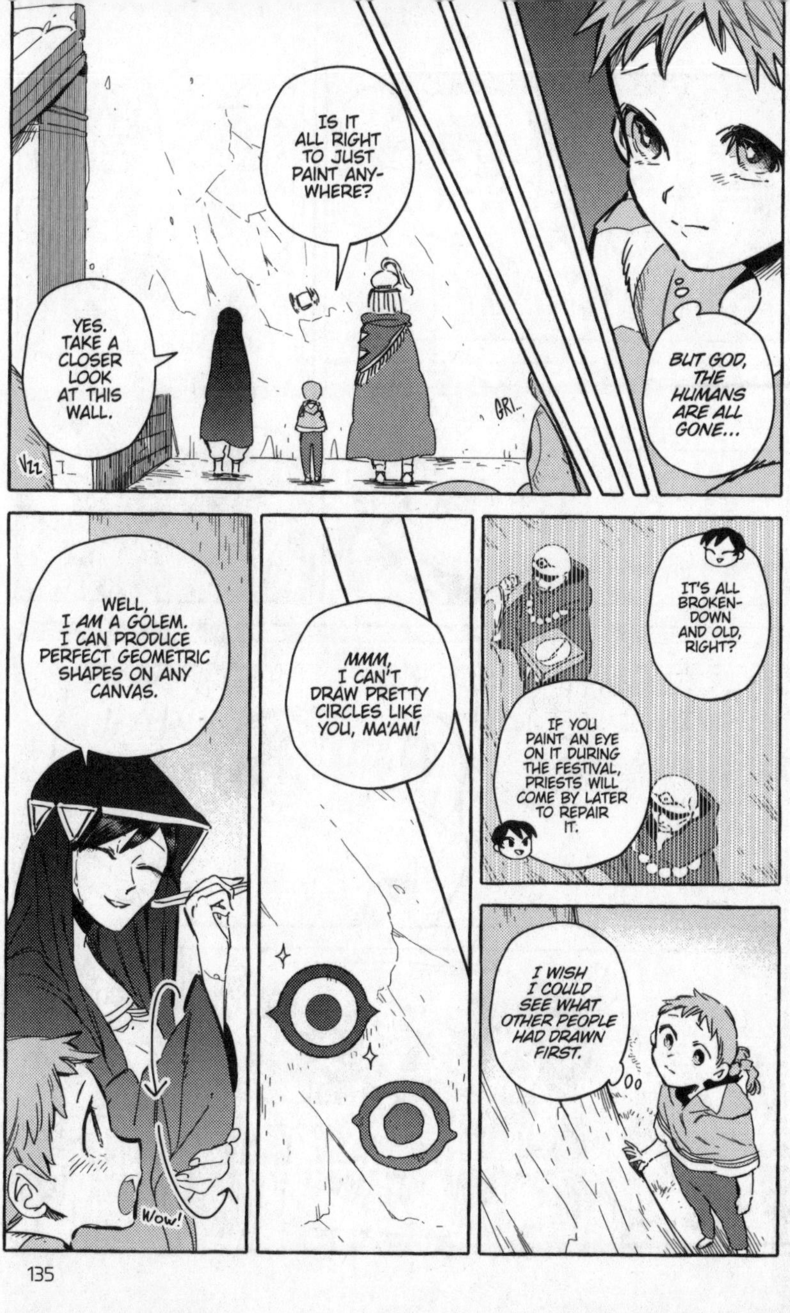
BUT GOD, THE HUMANS ARE ALL GONE...
IS IT ALL RIGHT TO JUST PAINT ANY-WHERE?
GRI...
YES. TAKE A CLOSER LOOK AT THIS WALL.
VZZ
IT'S ALL BROKEN-DOWN AND OLD, RIGHT?
IF YOU PAINT AN EYE ON IT DURING THE FESTIVAL, PRIESTS WILL COME BY LATER TO REPAIR IT.
I WISH I COULD SEE WHAT OTHER PEOPLE HAD DRAWN FIRST.
MMM, I CAN'T DRAW PRETTY CIRCLES LIKE YOU, MA'AM!
WELL, I AM A GOLEM. I CAN PRODUCE PERFECT GEOMETRIC SHAPES ON ANY CANVAS.
WOW!

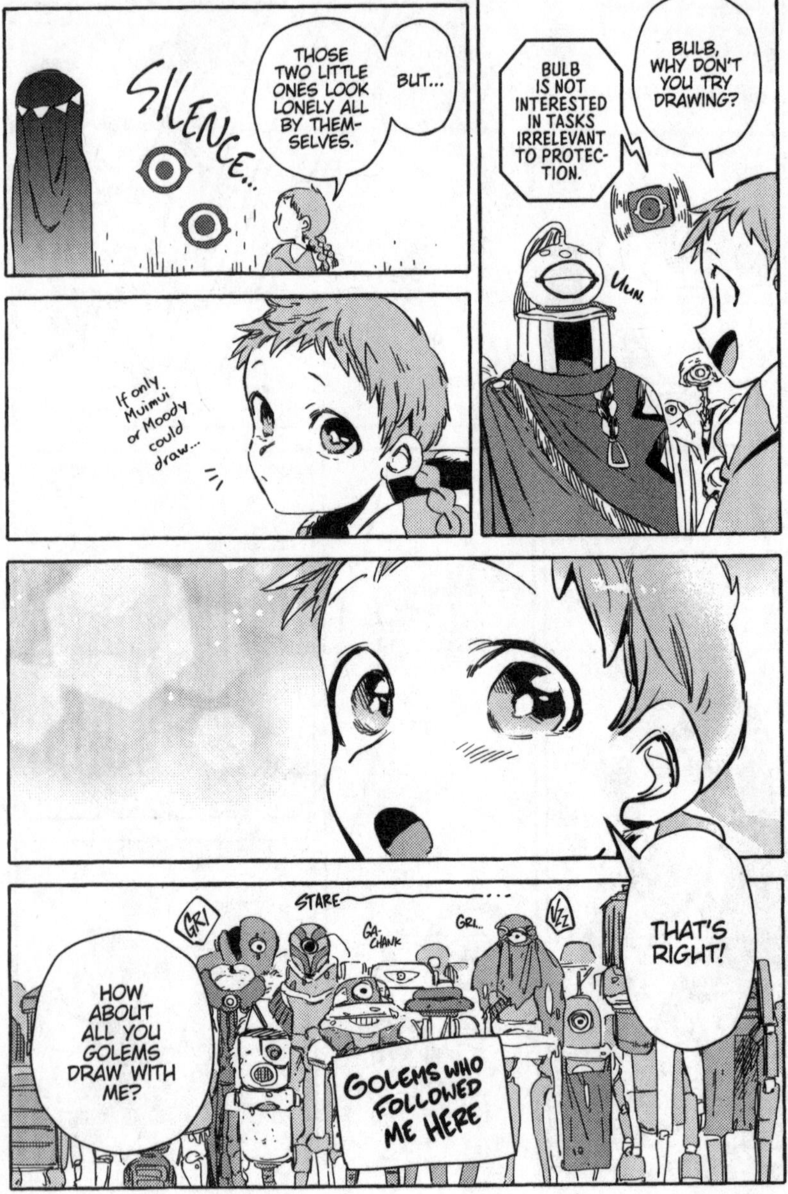
BULB, WHY DON'T YOU TRY DRAWING?
BULB IS NOT INTERESTED IN TASKS IRRELEVANT TO PROTECTION.
Uun.
BUT...
THOSE TWO LITTLE ONES LOOK LONELY ALL BY THEMSELVES.
SILENCE...
If only Muimui or Moody could draw...
THAT'S RIGHT!
VZZ
GRI..
GA-CHANK
STARE...
GRI
HOW ABOUT ALL YOU GOLEMS DRAW WITH ME?
GOLEMS WHO FOLLOWED ME HERE

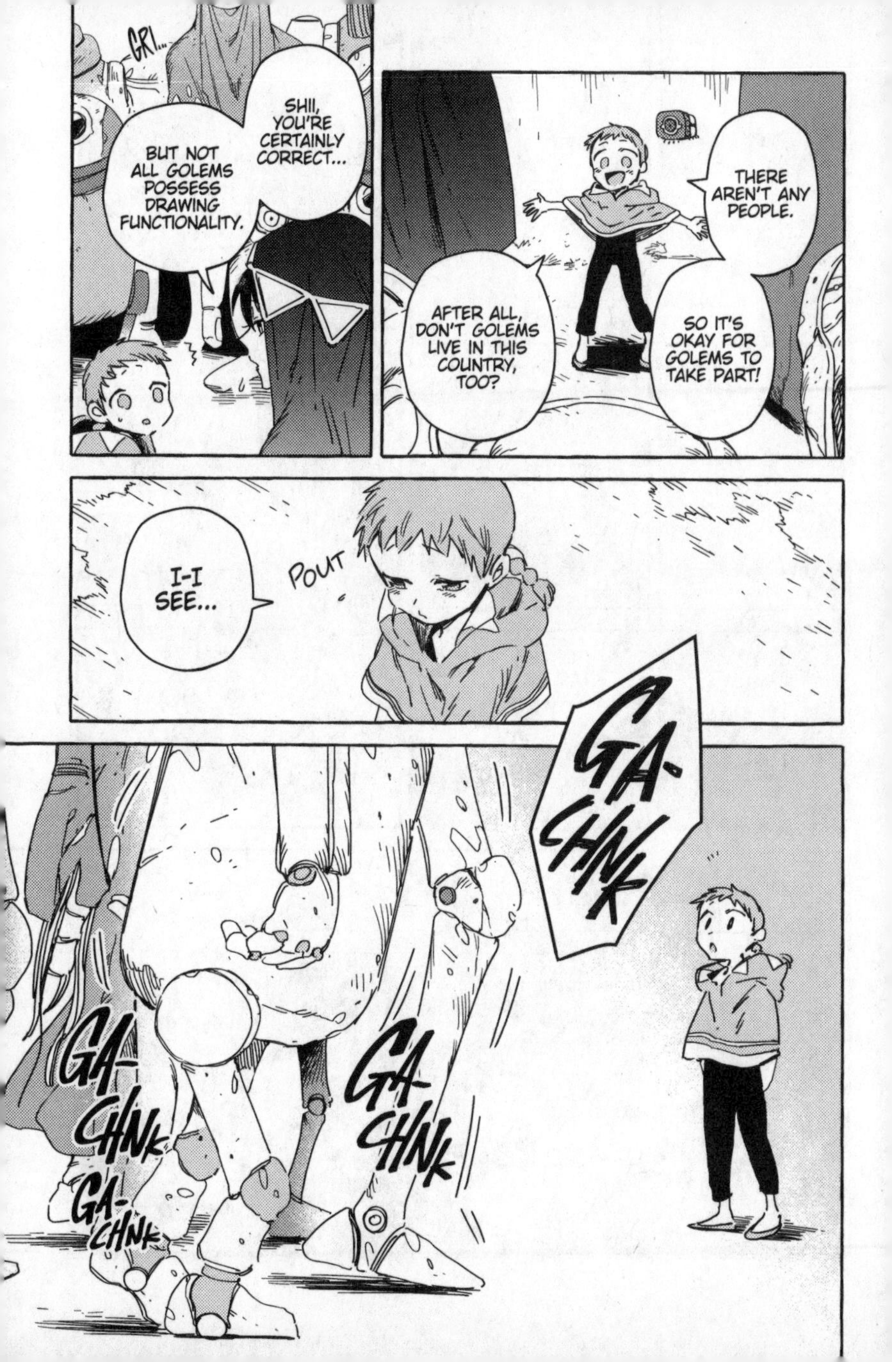
THERE AREN'T ANY PEOPLE.
SO IT'S OKAY FOR GOLEMS TO TAKE PART!
AFTER ALL, DON'T GOLEMS LIVE IN THIS COUNTRY, TOO?
SHII, YOU'RE CERTAINLY CORRECT...
GRI...
BUT NOT ALL GOLEMS POSSESS DRAWING FUNCTIONALITY.
POUT
I-I SEE...
GA-CHNK
GA-CHNK
GA-CHNK
GA-CHNK

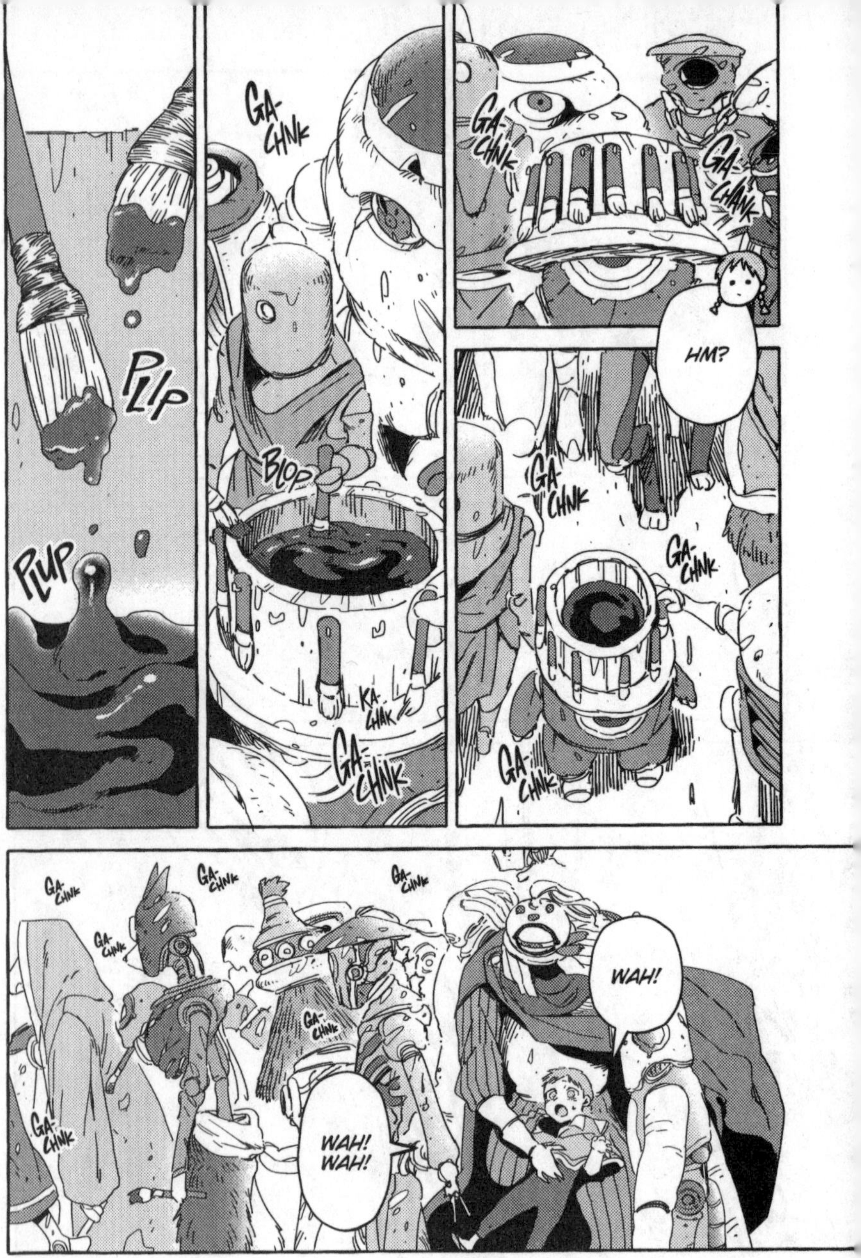
GA-CHNK
GA-CHANK
HM?
GA-CHNK
GA-CHNK
GA-CHNK
GA-CHNK
BLOP
KA-GHAK
GA-CHNK
PLIP
PLUP
GA-CHNK
GA-CHNK
WAH!
GA-CHNK
WAH! WAH!
GA-CHNK
GA-CHNK
GA-CHNK

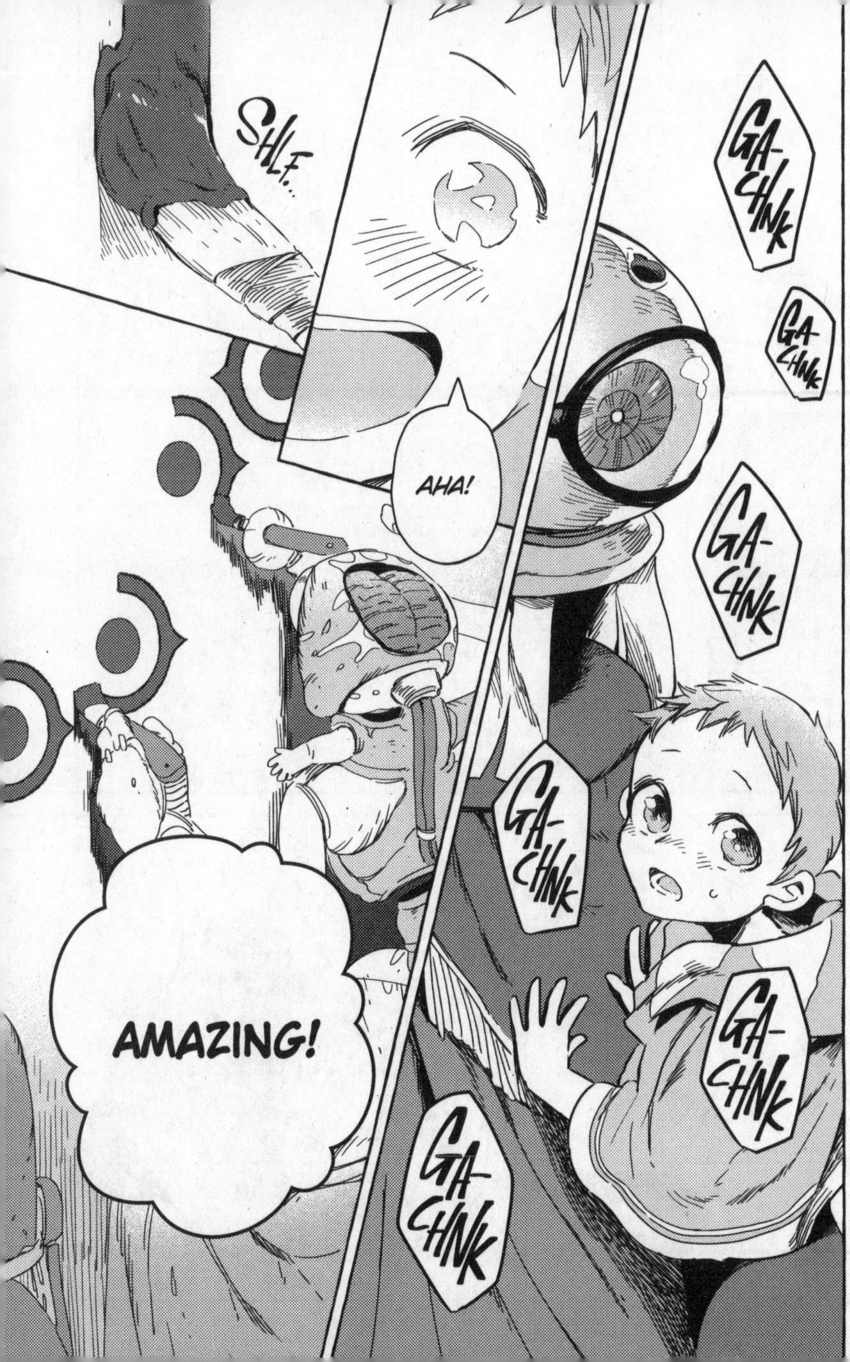
GA-CHNK
GA-CHNK
GA-CHNK
GA-CHNK
GA-CHNK
GA-CHNK
AHA!
SHLF...
AMAZING!

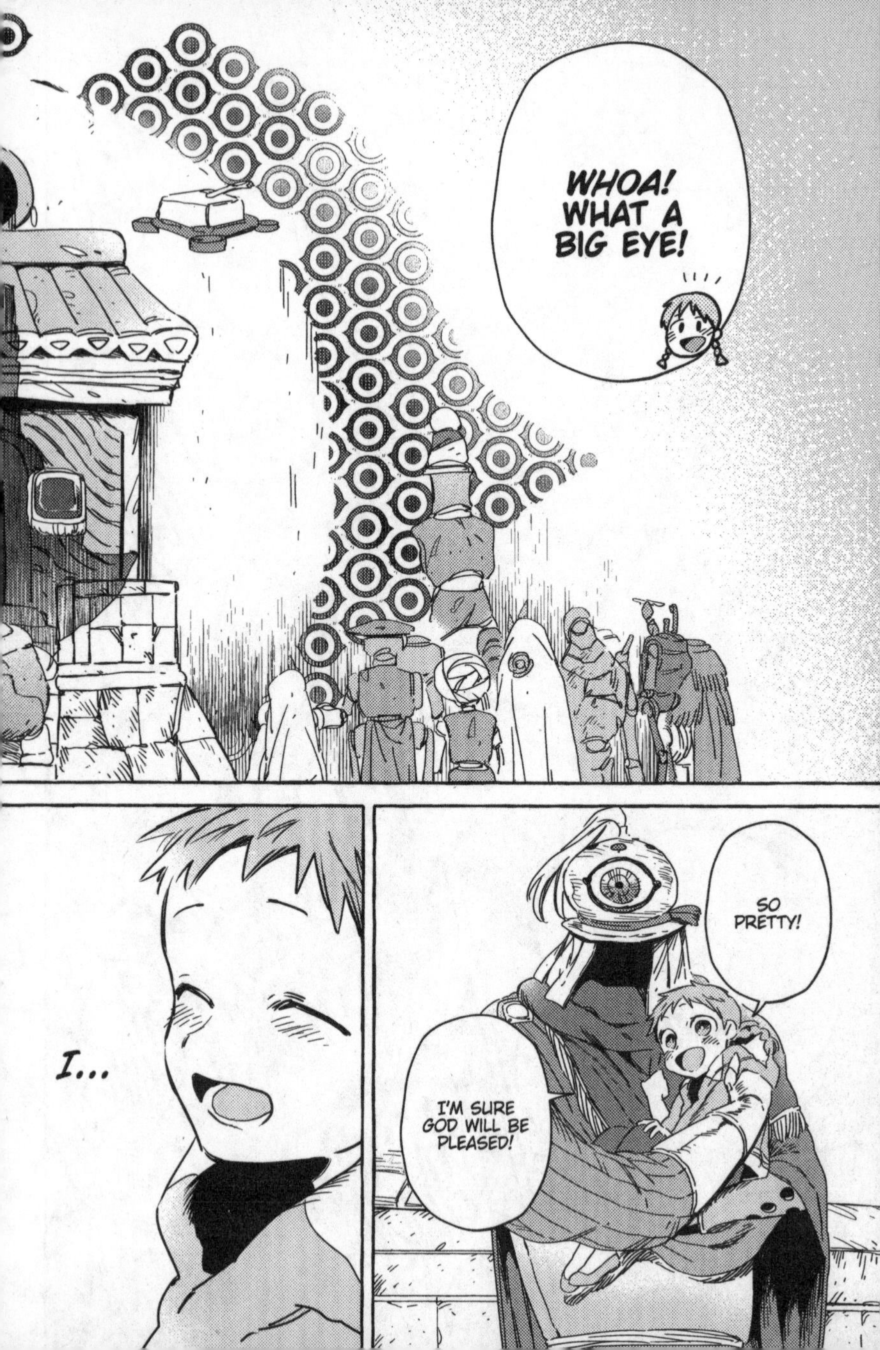
WHOA! WHAT A BIG EYE!
SO PRETTY!
I'M SURE GOD WILL BE PLEASED!
I...

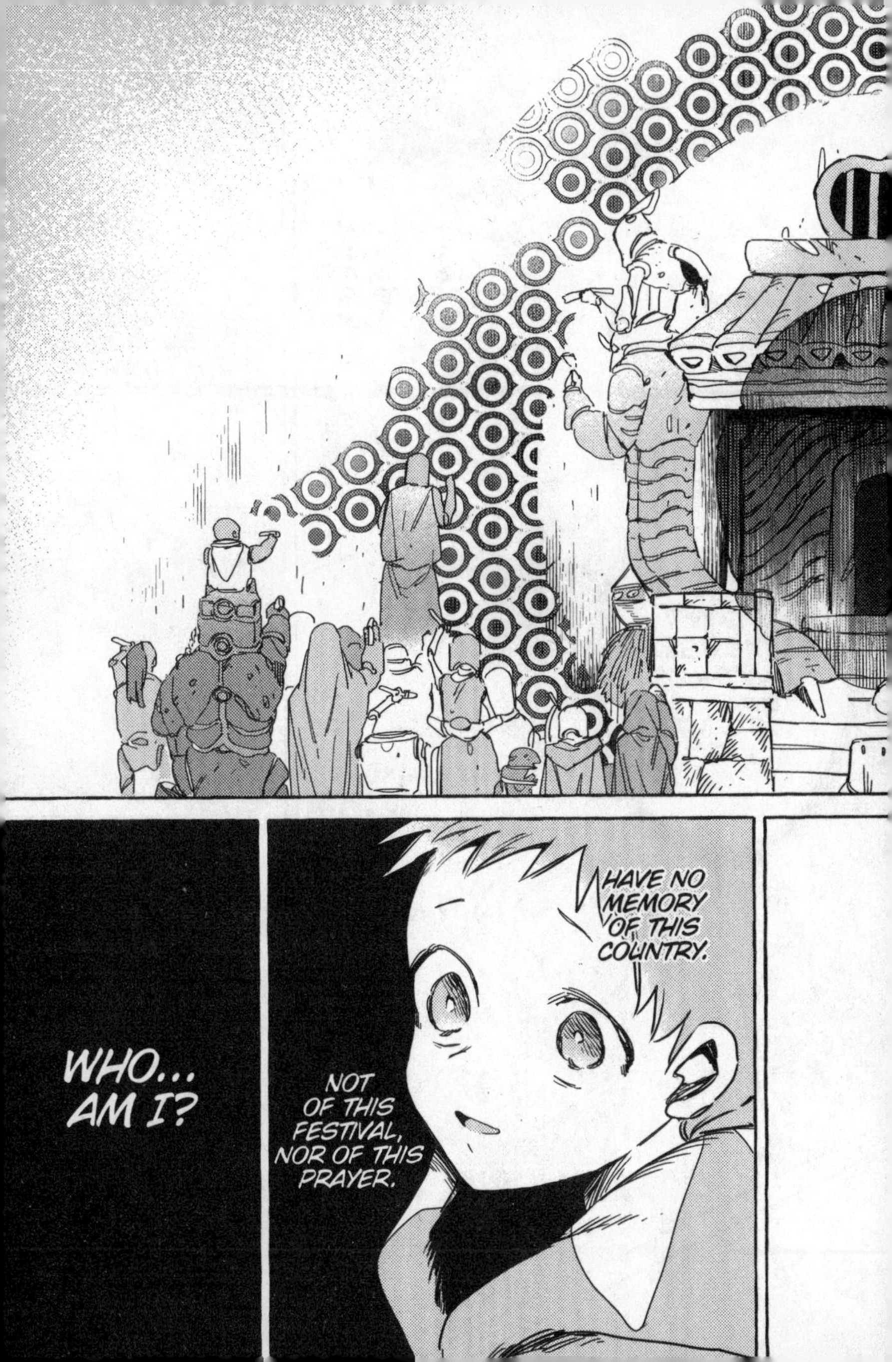
HAVE NO MEMORY OF THIS COUNTRY.
NOT OF THIS FESTIVAL, NOR OF THIS PRAYER.
WHO... AM I?

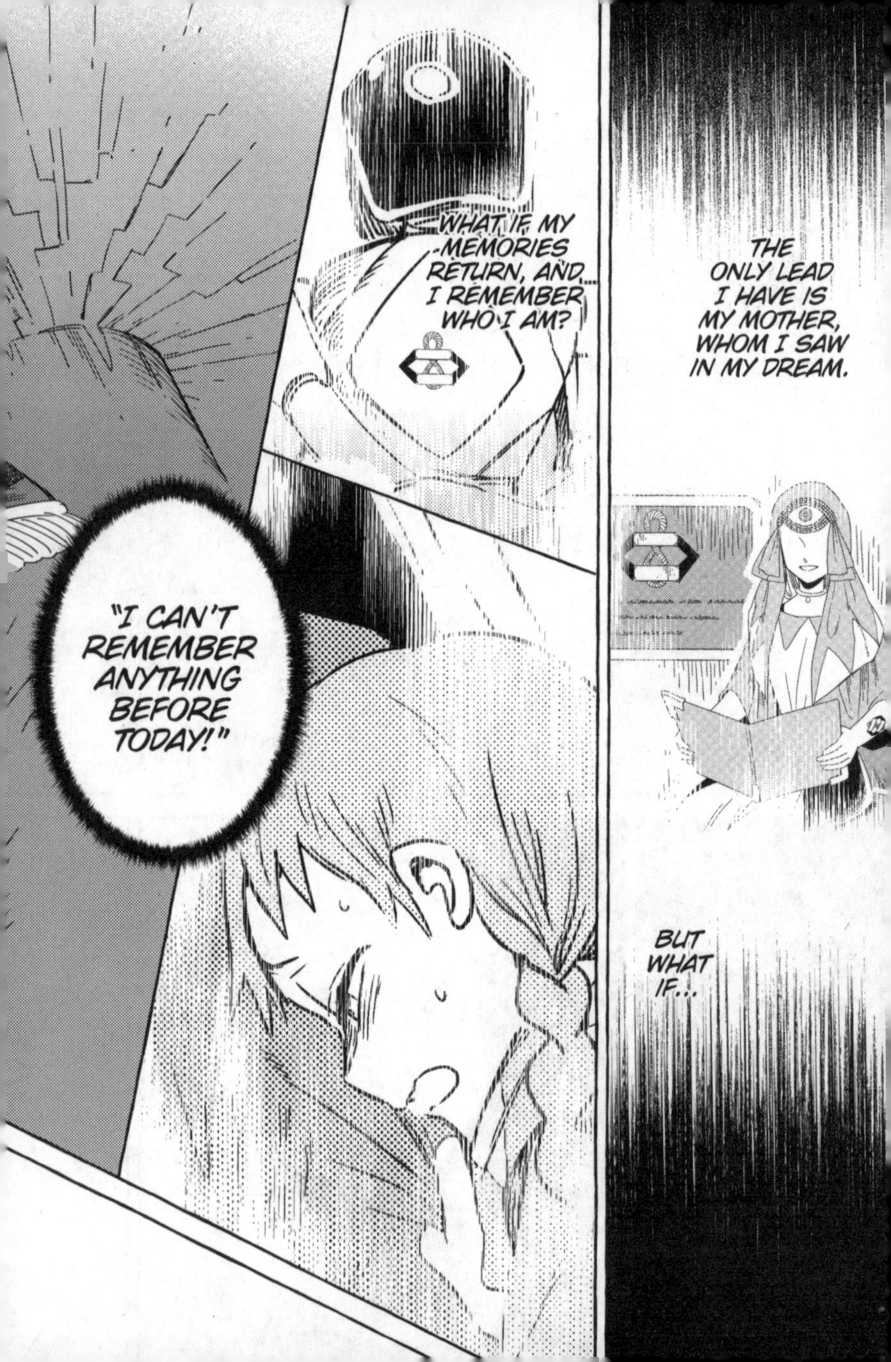
THE ONLY LEAD I HAVE IS MY MOTHER, WHOM I SAW IN MY DREAM.
BUT WHAT IF...
WHAT IF MY MEMORIES RETURN, AND I REMEMBER WHO I AM?
"I CAN'T REMEMBER ANYTHING BEFORE TODAY!"

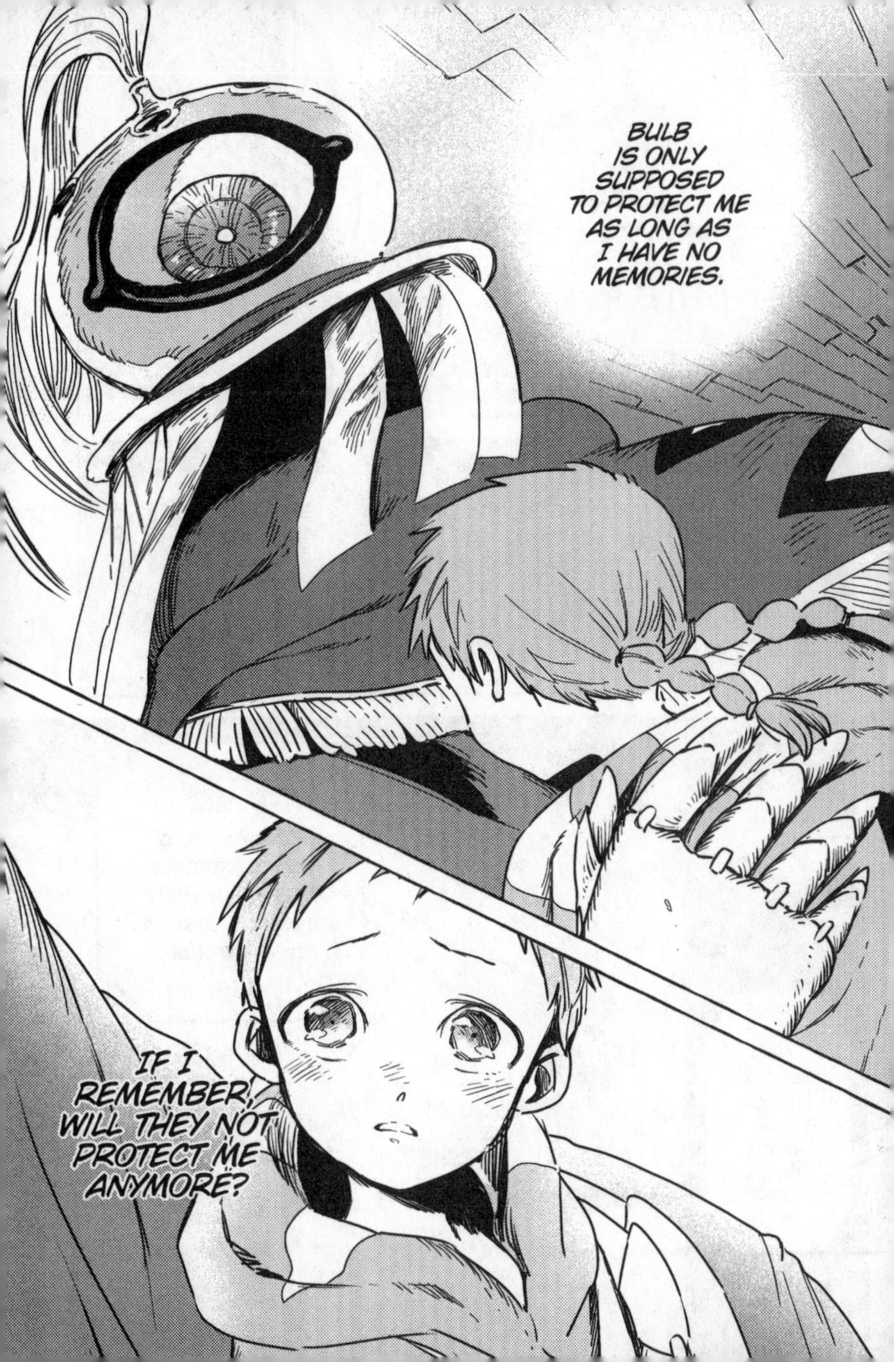
BULB IS ONLY SUPPOSED TO PROTECT ME AS LONG AS I HAVE NO MEMORIES.
IF I REMEMBER, WILL THEY NOT PROTECT ME ANYMORE?

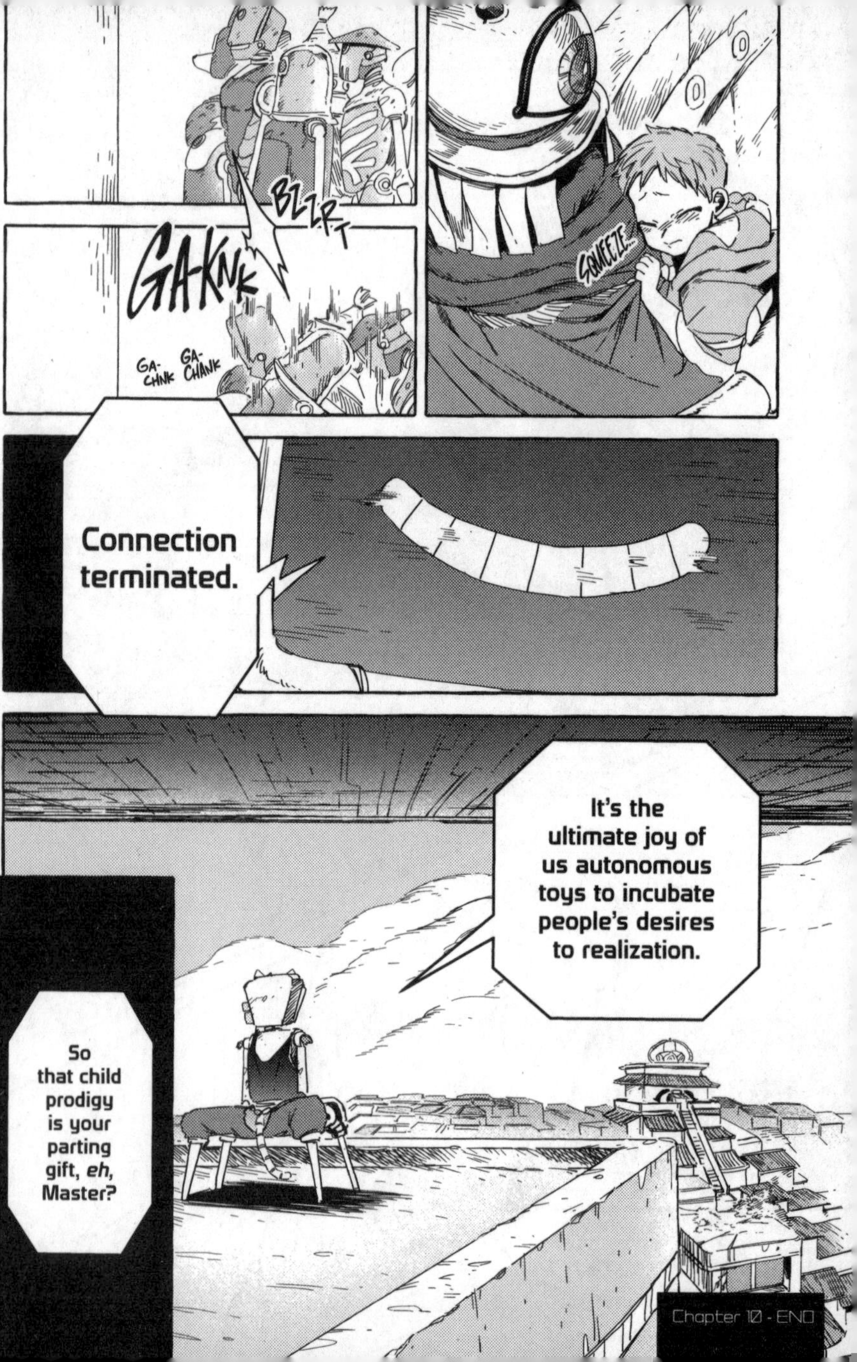
SQUEEZE...
BZZRT
GA-KNK
GA-CHANK
GA-CHNK
Connection terminated.
It's the ultimate joy of us autonomous toys to incubate people's desires to realization.
So that child prodigy is your parting gift, *eh*, Master?
Chapter 10 - END

A Fleeting Tale #6 The Autonomous Toys

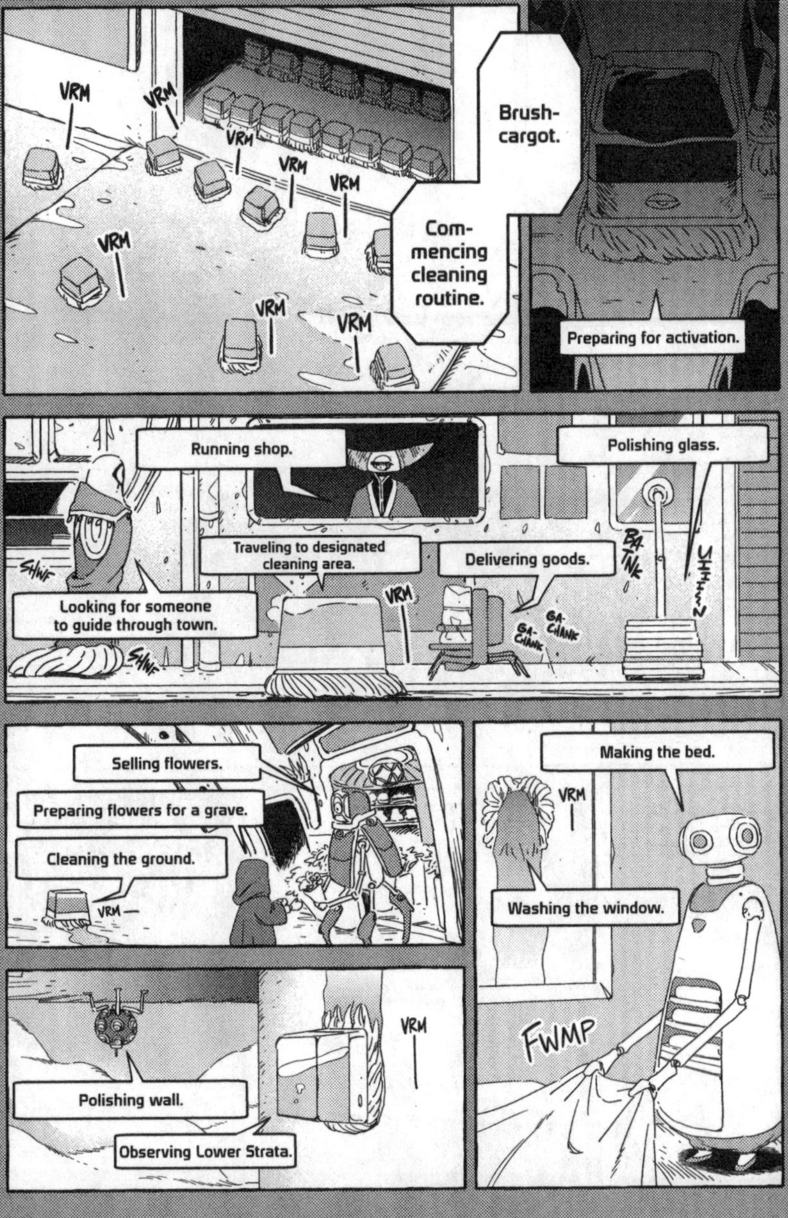

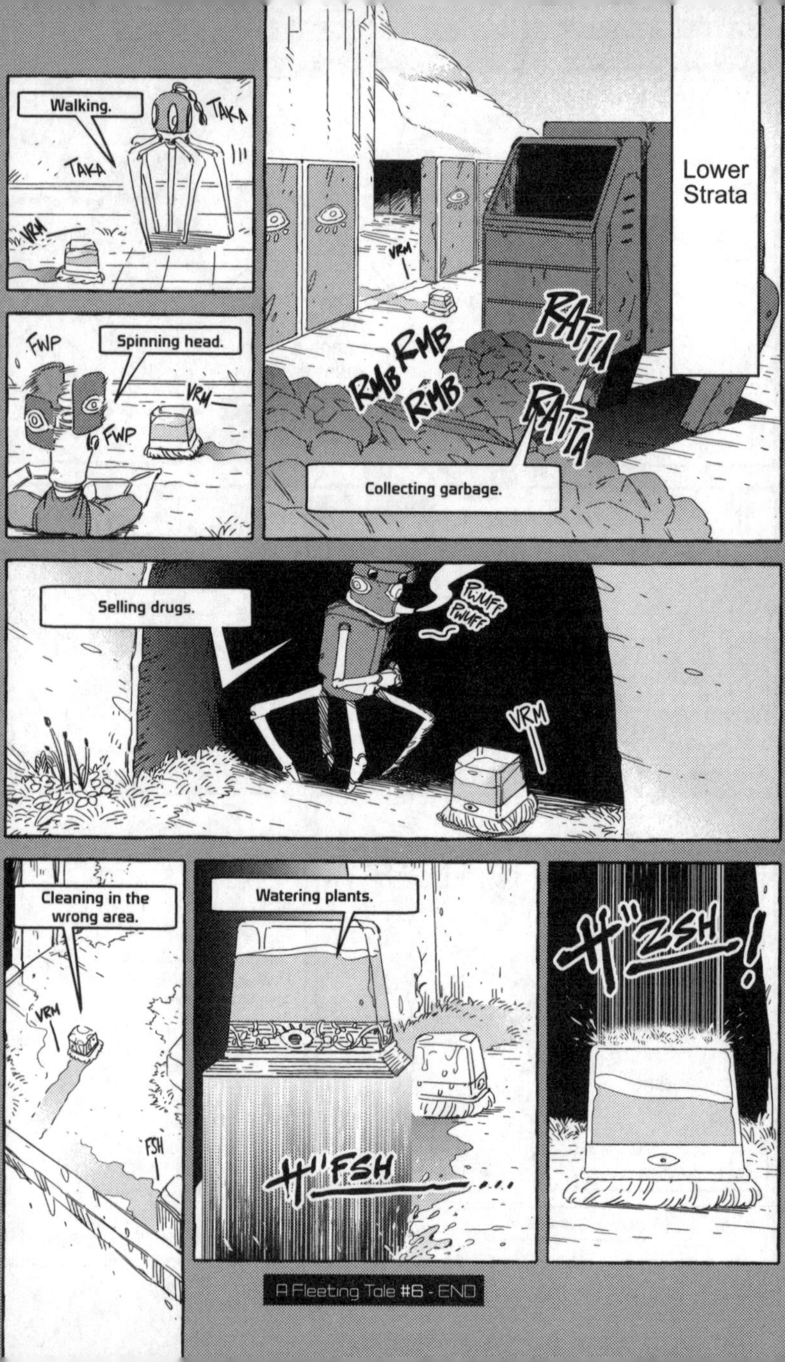
Lower Strata
VRM
RATTA
RMB RMB
RMB
RATTA
Collecting garbage.
Walking.
TAKA
TAKA
VRM
FWP
Spinning head.
VRM
FWP
Selling drugs.
PWUFF PWUFF
VRM
Z"ZSH!
Watering plants.
Z"FSH...
Cleaning in the wrong area.
VRM
FSH

A Fleeting Tale #6 - END

Royal Library repairs fifty percent complete.
UIII-N
UIII-N
GA-KNK
UIII-N
Chapter 11
GNG
GNG GNG
VRRR-N
Material recovery eighty percent complete.
Lost Basilta units replenished.

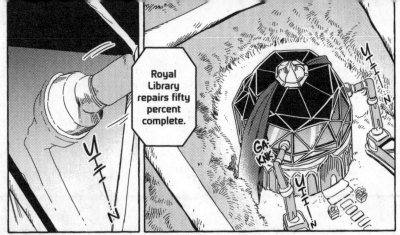

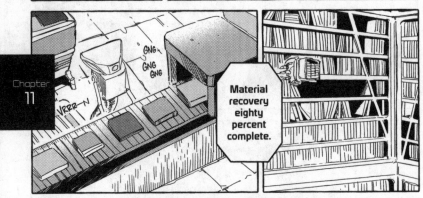

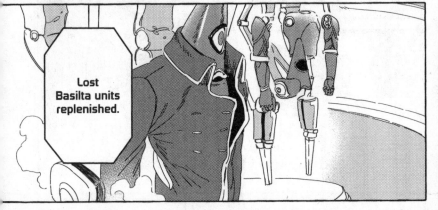

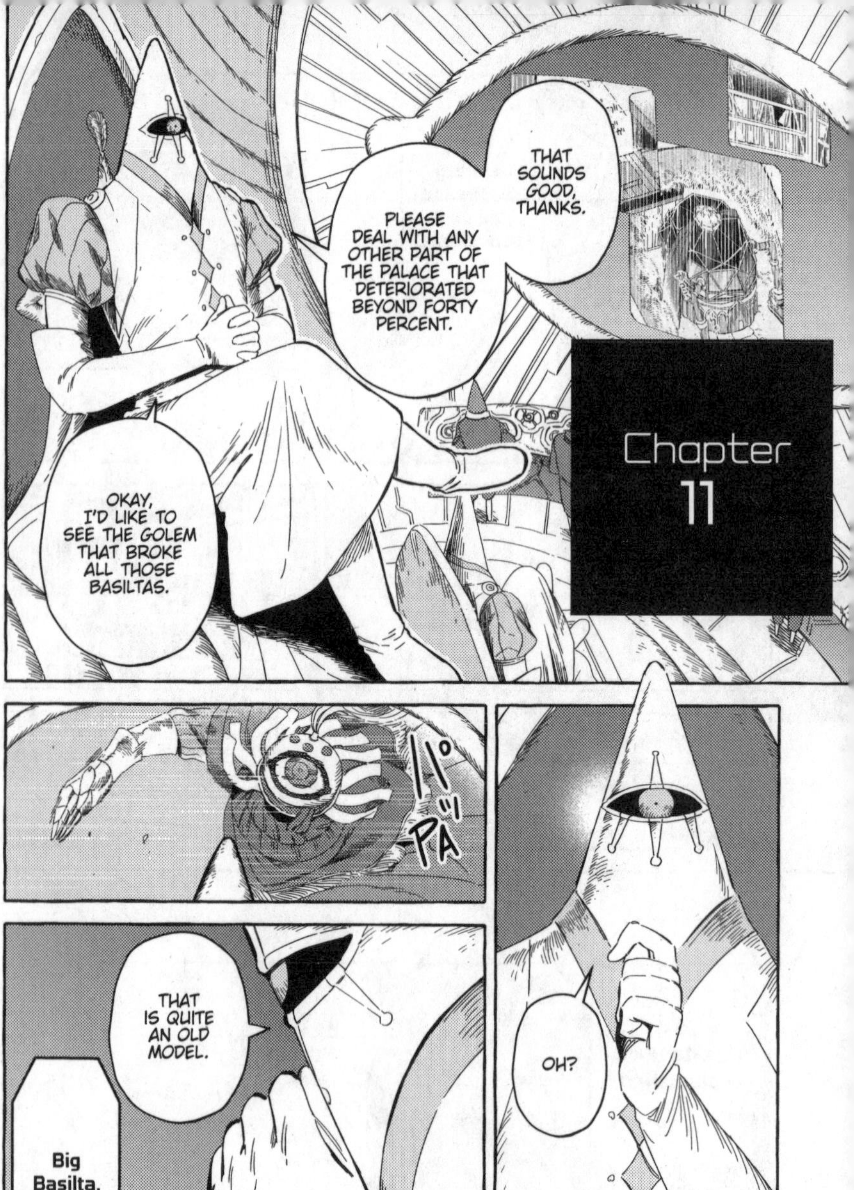
THAT SOUNDS GOOD, THANKS.
PLEASE DEAL WITH ANY OTHER PART OF THE PALACE THAT DETERIORATED BEYOND FORTY PERCENT.
Chapter 11
OKAY, I'D LIKE TO SEE THE GOLEM THAT BROKE ALL THOSE BASILTAS.
OH?
パッ PA
THAT IS QUITE AN OLD MODEL.
Big Basilta.

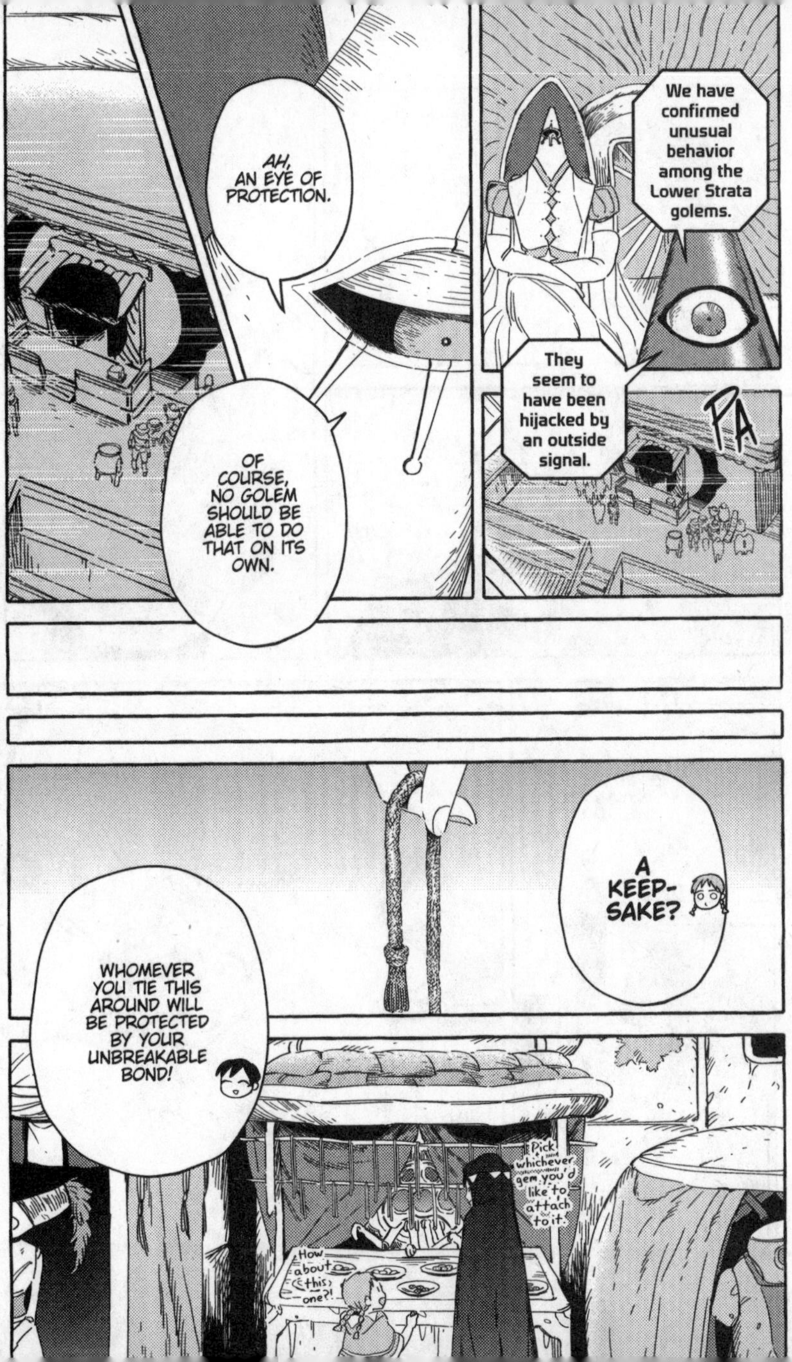
We have confirmed unusual behavior among the Lower Strata golems.
They seem to have been hijacked by an outside signal.
PA
AH, AN EYE OF PROTECTION.
OF COURSE, NO GOLEM SHOULD BE ABLE TO DO THAT ON ITS OWN.
A KEEP-SAKE?
WHOMEVER YOU TIE THIS AROUND WILL BE PROTECTED BY YOUR UNBREAKABLE BOND!
Pick whichever gem you'd like to attach to it.
How about this one?!

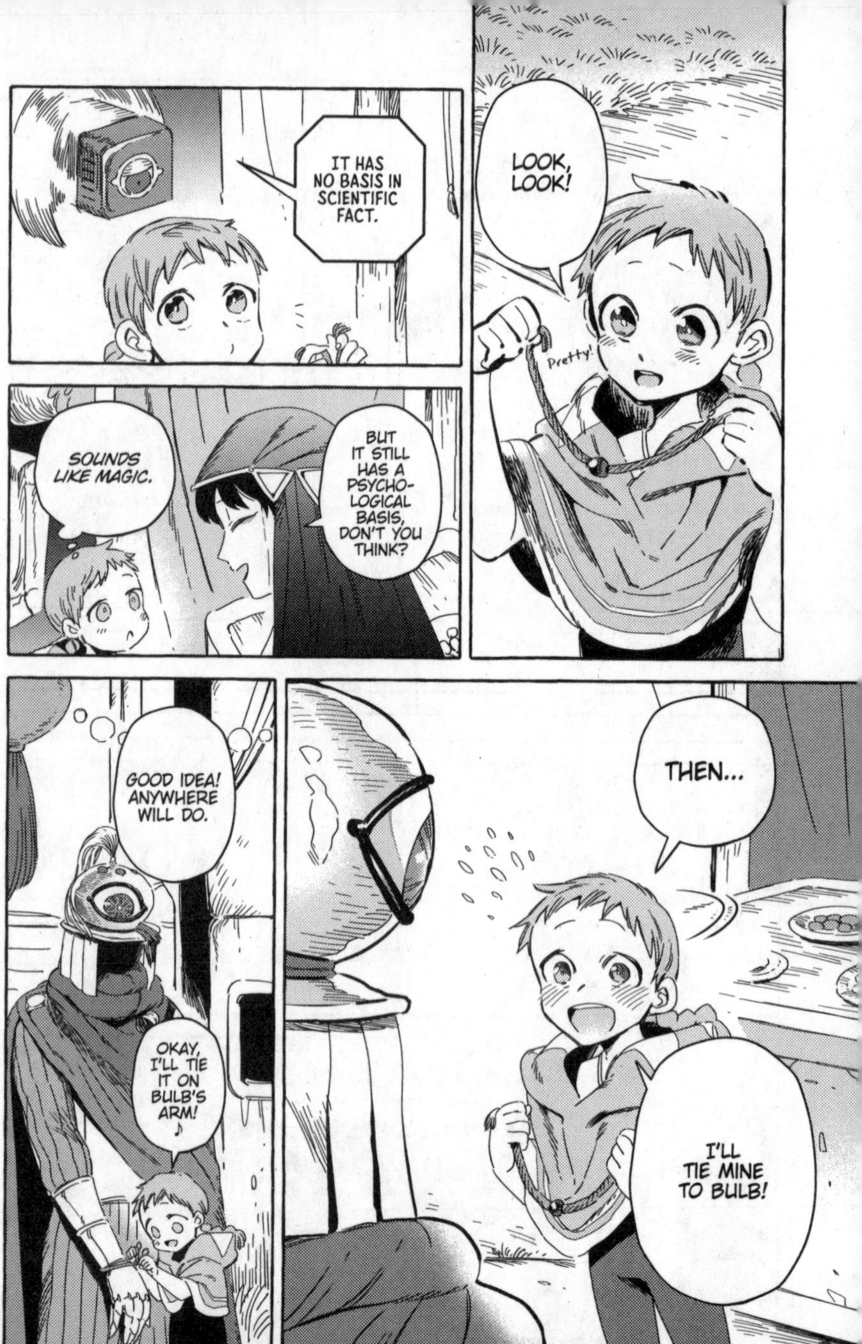
LOOK, LOOK!
Pretty!
IT HAS NO BASIS IN SCIENTIFIC FACT.
BUT IT STILL HAS A PSYCHO-LOGICAL BASIS, DON'T YOU THINK?
SOUNDS LIKE MAGIC.
THEN...
I'LL TIE MINE TO BULB!
GOOD IDEA! ANYWHERE WILL DO.
OKAY, I'LL TIE IT ON BULB'S ARM! ♪

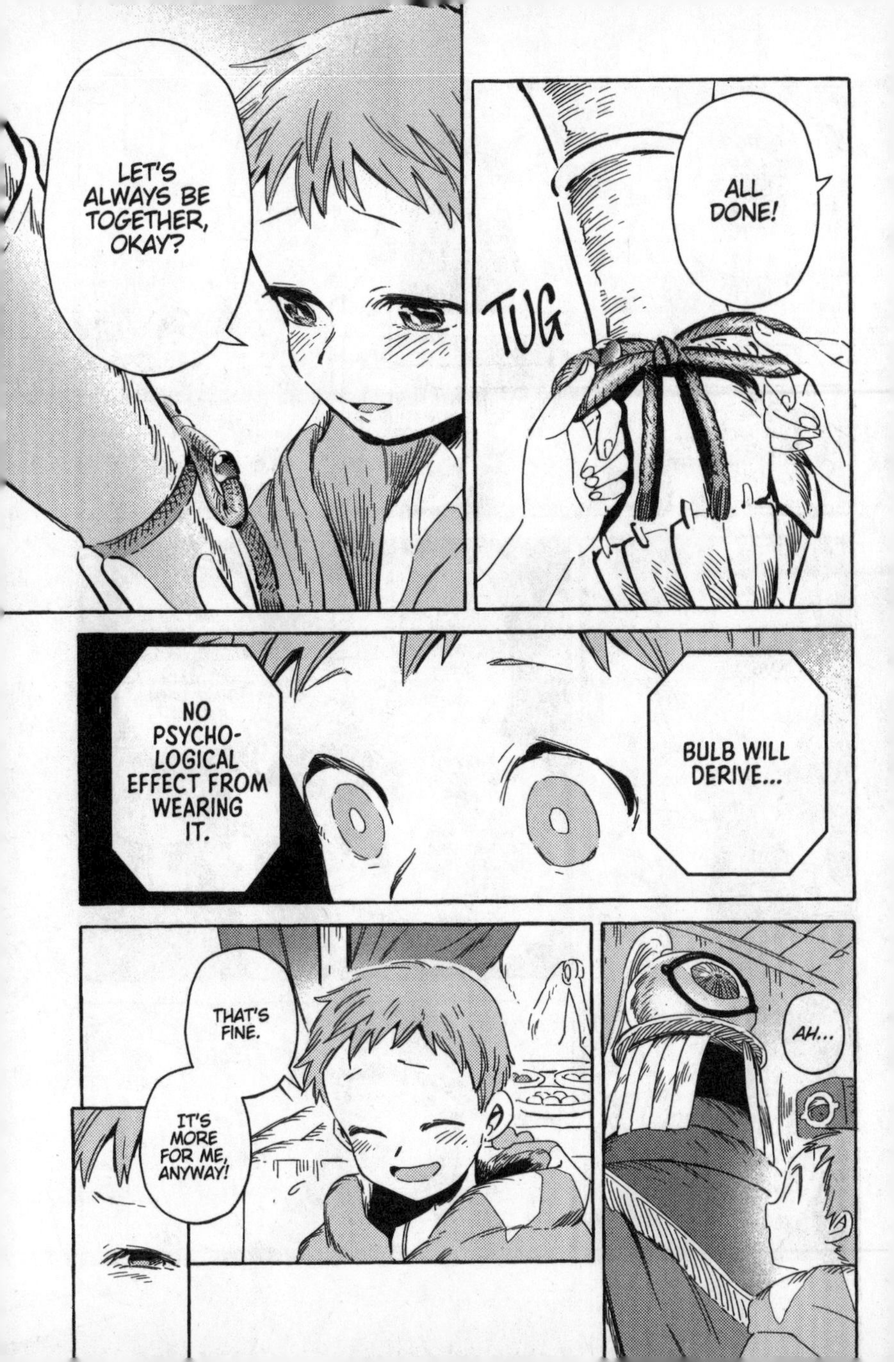
ALL DONE!
TUG
LET'S ALWAYS BE TOGETHER, OKAY?
BULB WILL DERIVE...
NO PSYCHO-LOGICAL EFFECT FROM WEARING IT.
AH...
THAT'S FINE.
IT'S MORE FOR ME, ANYWAY!

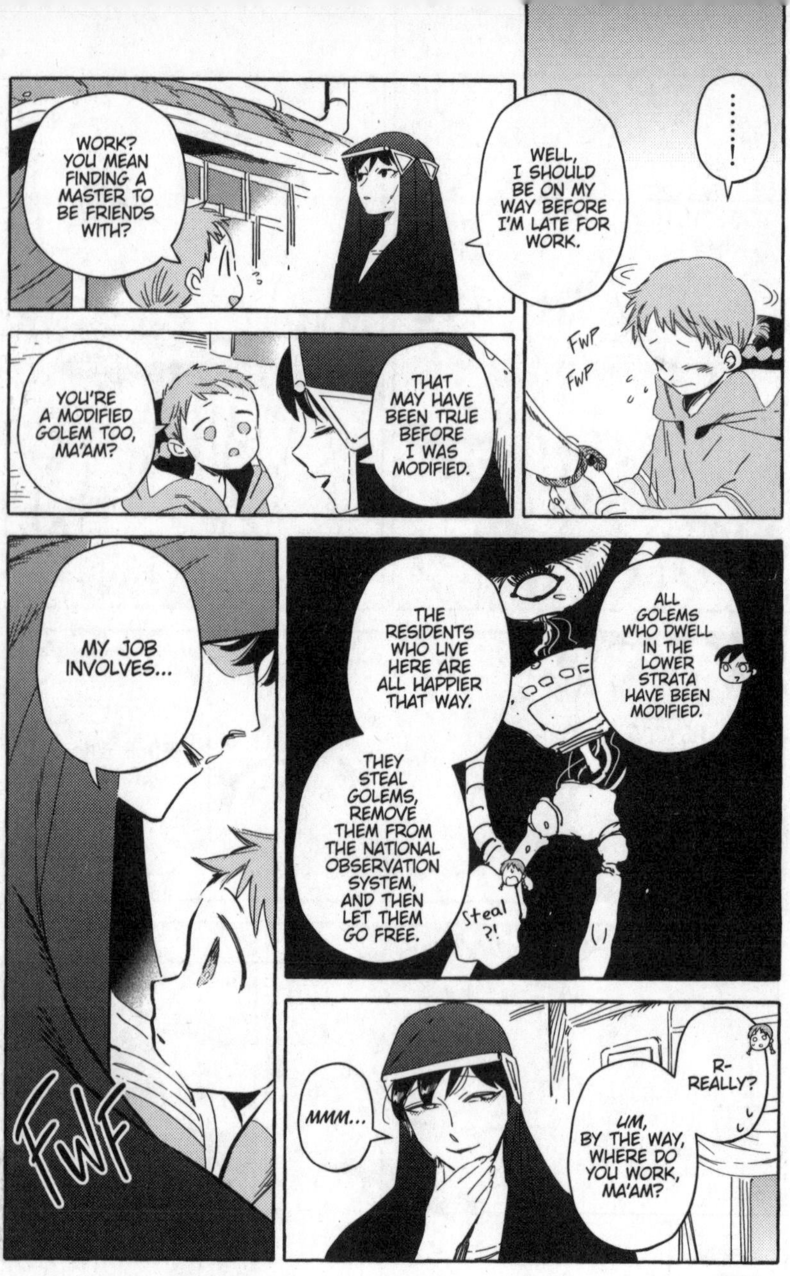
......!
WELL, I SHOULD BE ON MY WAY BEFORE I'M LATE FOR WORK.
FWP
FWP
WORK? YOU MEAN FINDING A MASTER TO BE FRIENDS WITH?
THAT MAY HAVE BEEN TRUE BEFORE I WAS MODIFIED.
YOU'RE A MODIFIED GOLEM TOO, MA'AM?
ALL GOLEMS WHO DWELL IN THE LOWER STRATA HAVE BEEN MODIFIED.
THE RESIDENTS WHO LIVE HERE ARE ALL HAPPIER THAT WAY.
THEY STEAL GOLEMS, REMOVE THEM FROM THE NATIONAL OBSERVATION SYSTEM, AND THEN LET THEM GO FREE.
Steal ?!
R-REALLY?
UM, BY THE WAY, WHERE DO YOU WORK, MA'AM?
MMM...
MY JOB INVOLVES...
FWF

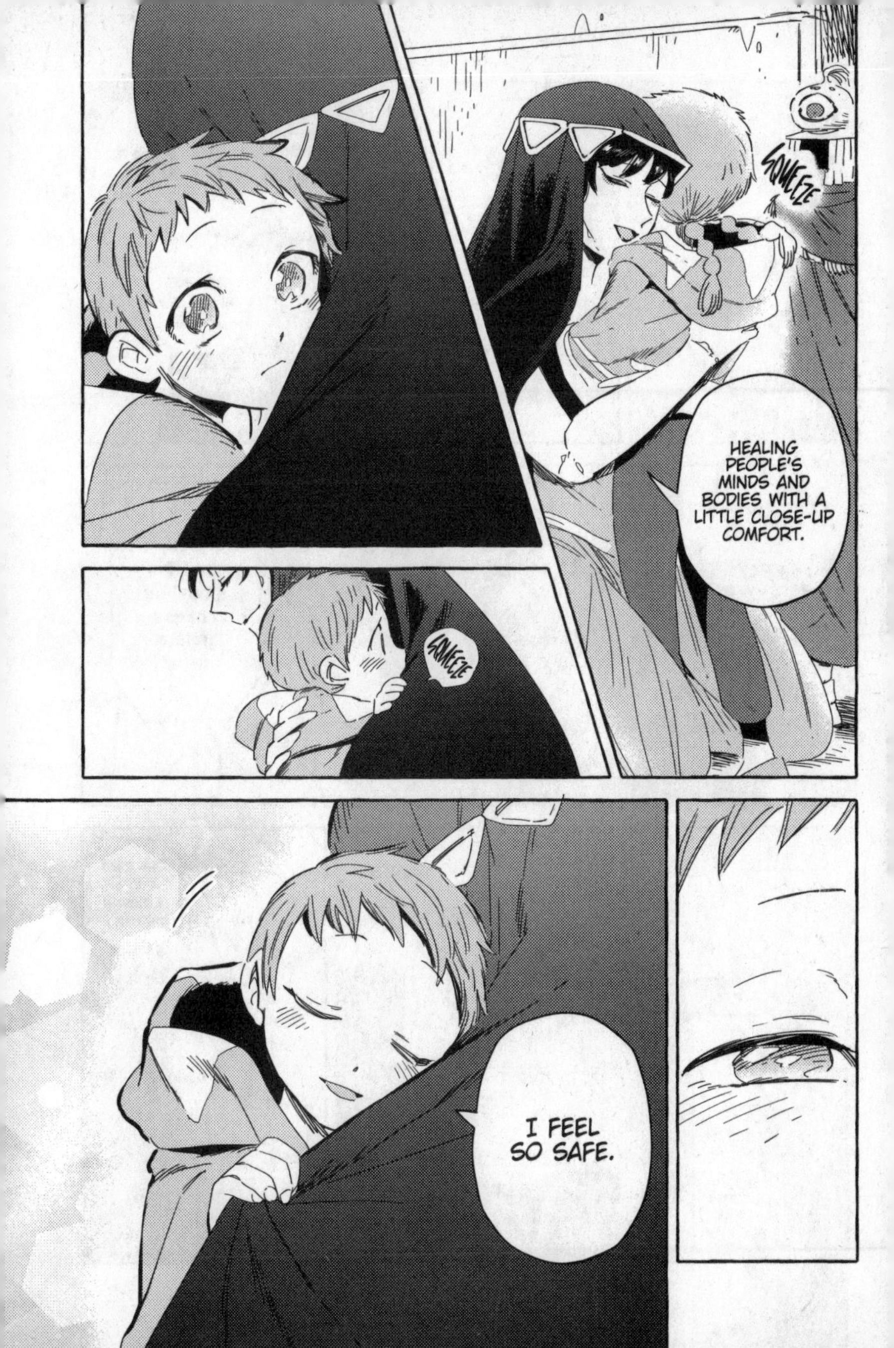
SQUEEZE
HEALING PEOPLE'S MINDS AND BODIES WITH A LITTLE CLOSE-UP COMFORT.
SQUEEZE
I FEEL SO SAFE.

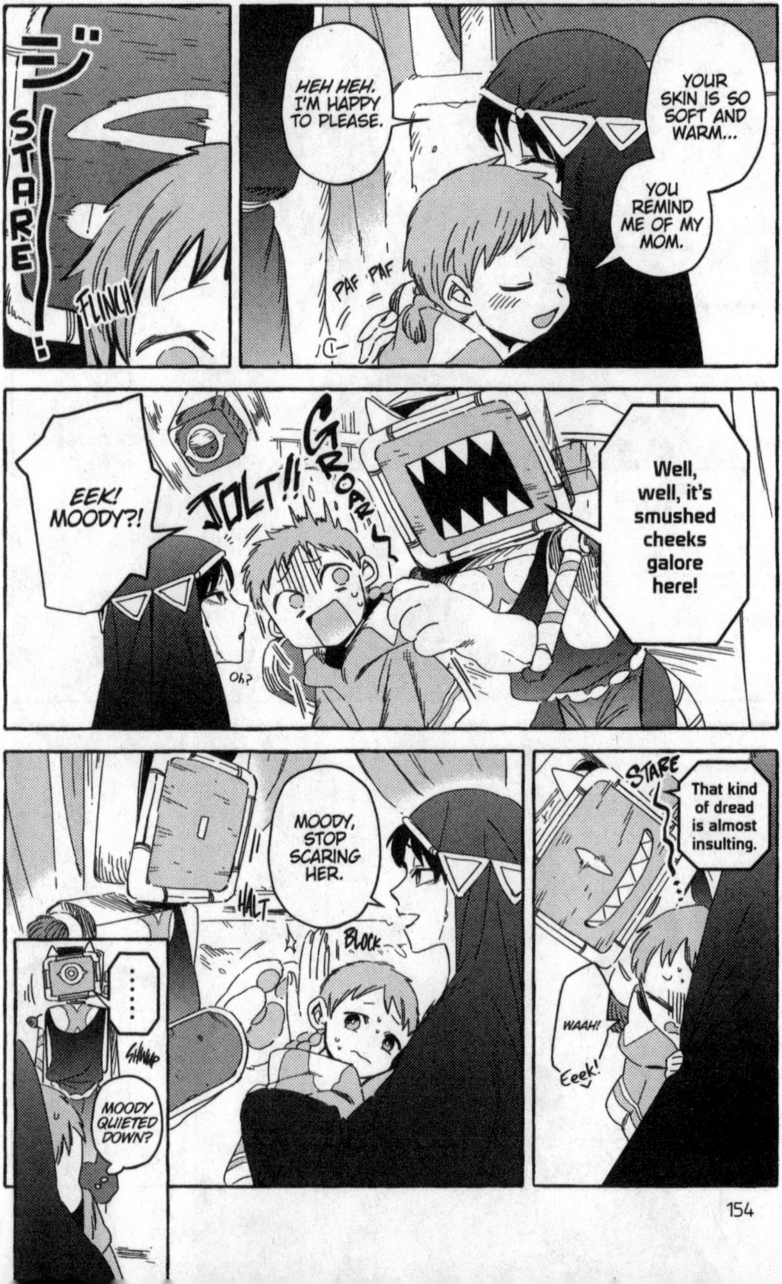
YOUR SKIN IS SO SOFT AND WARM...
YOU REMIND ME OF MY MOM.
HEH HEH. I'M HAPPY TO PLEASE.
PAF PAF
ジ
STARE!
FLINCH
Well, well, it's smushed cheeks galore here!
GROAR
JOLT!!
EEK! MOODY?!
Oh?
STARE
That kind of dread is almost insulting.
WAAH!
Eeek!
MOODY, STOP SCARING HER.
HALT
BLOCK
......
SHWUMP
MOODY QUIETED DOWN?

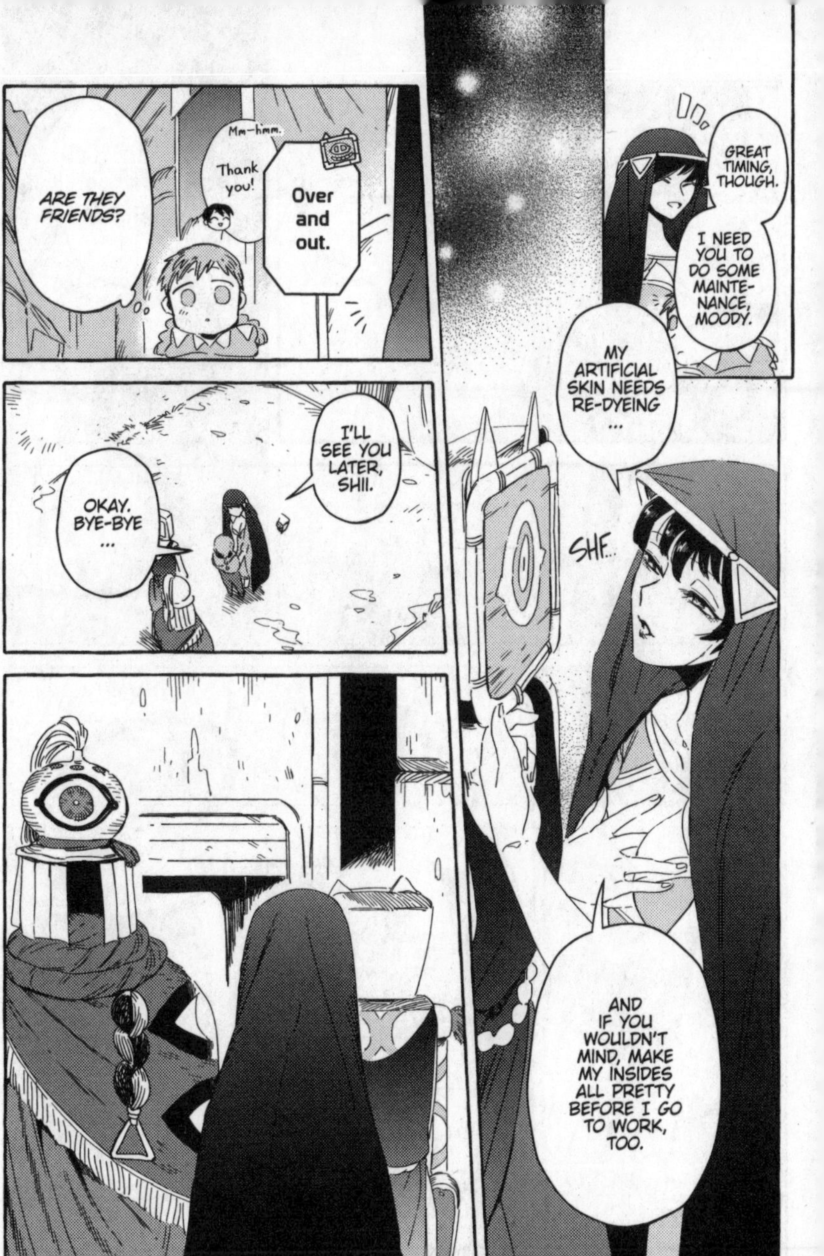
GREAT TIMING, THOUGH.
I NEED YOU TO DO SOME MAINTE-NANCE, MOODY.
MY ARTIFICIAL SKIN NEEDS RE-DYEING ...
SHF...
AND IF YOU WOULDN'T MIND, MAKE MY INSIDES ALL PRETTY BEFORE I GO TO WORK, TOO.
Over and out.
Mm-hmm.
Thank you!
ARE THEY FRIENDS?
I'LL SEE YOU LATER, SHII.
OKAY. BYE-BYE ...

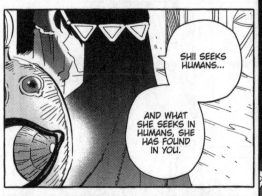

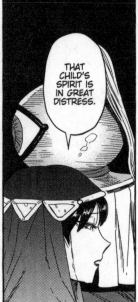

THAT CHILD'S SPIRIT IS IN GREAT DISTRESS.
SHII SEEKS HUMANS...
AND WHAT SHE SEEKS IN HUMANS, SHE HAS FOUND IN YOU.
TRY YOUR BEST, EVEN IF YOU ARE A GOLEM.
MA'AM SAID SHE'S GOING TO WORK...
BUT SHE'S JUST WAITING FOR HUMANS TOO, ISN'T SHE?
MUIMUI, ARE THERE REALLY NO HUMANS LEFT?
THERE ARE NO CONFIRMED HUMANS BEYOND YOU.
!

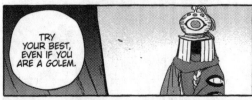

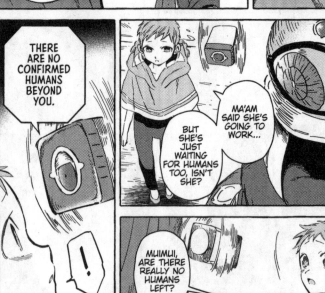

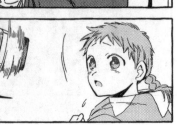

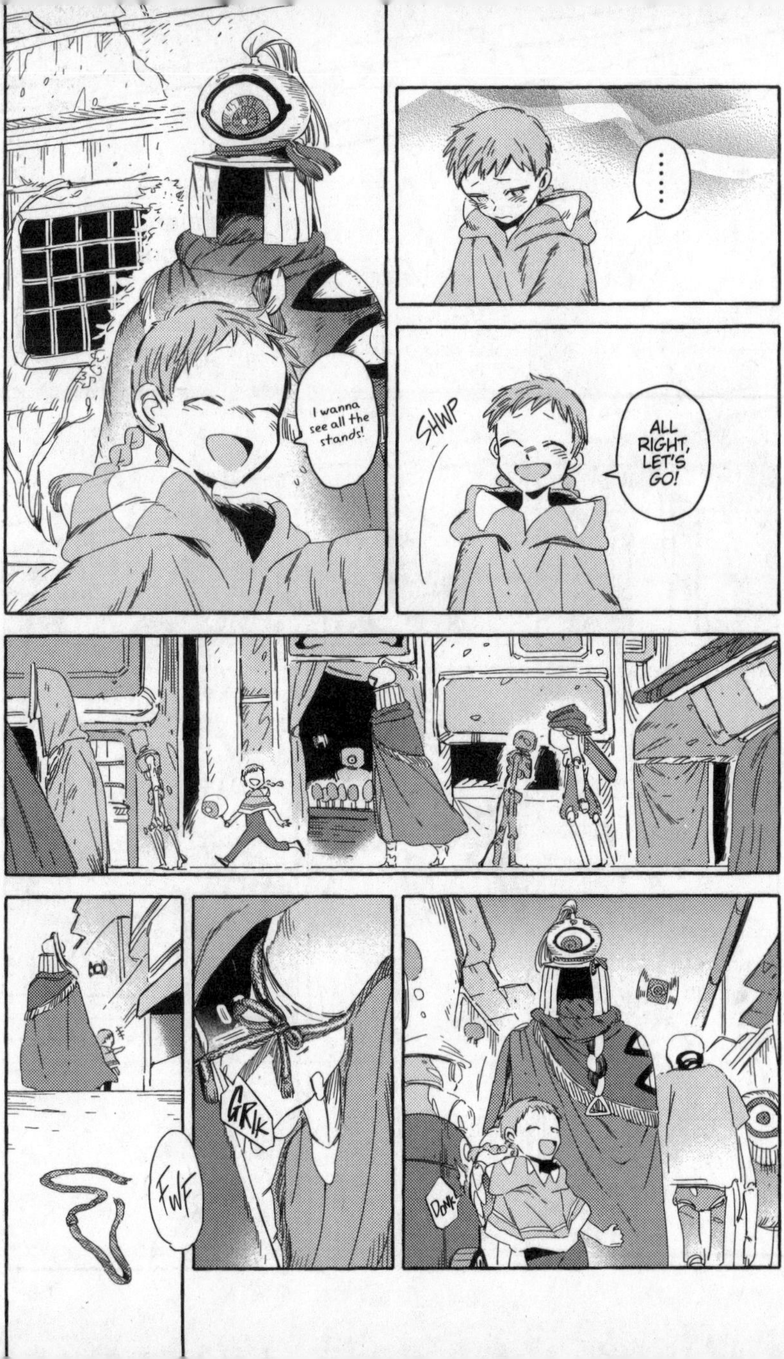
......
SHWP
ALL RIGHT, LET'S GO!
I wanna see all the stands!
DONK
GRIK
FWF

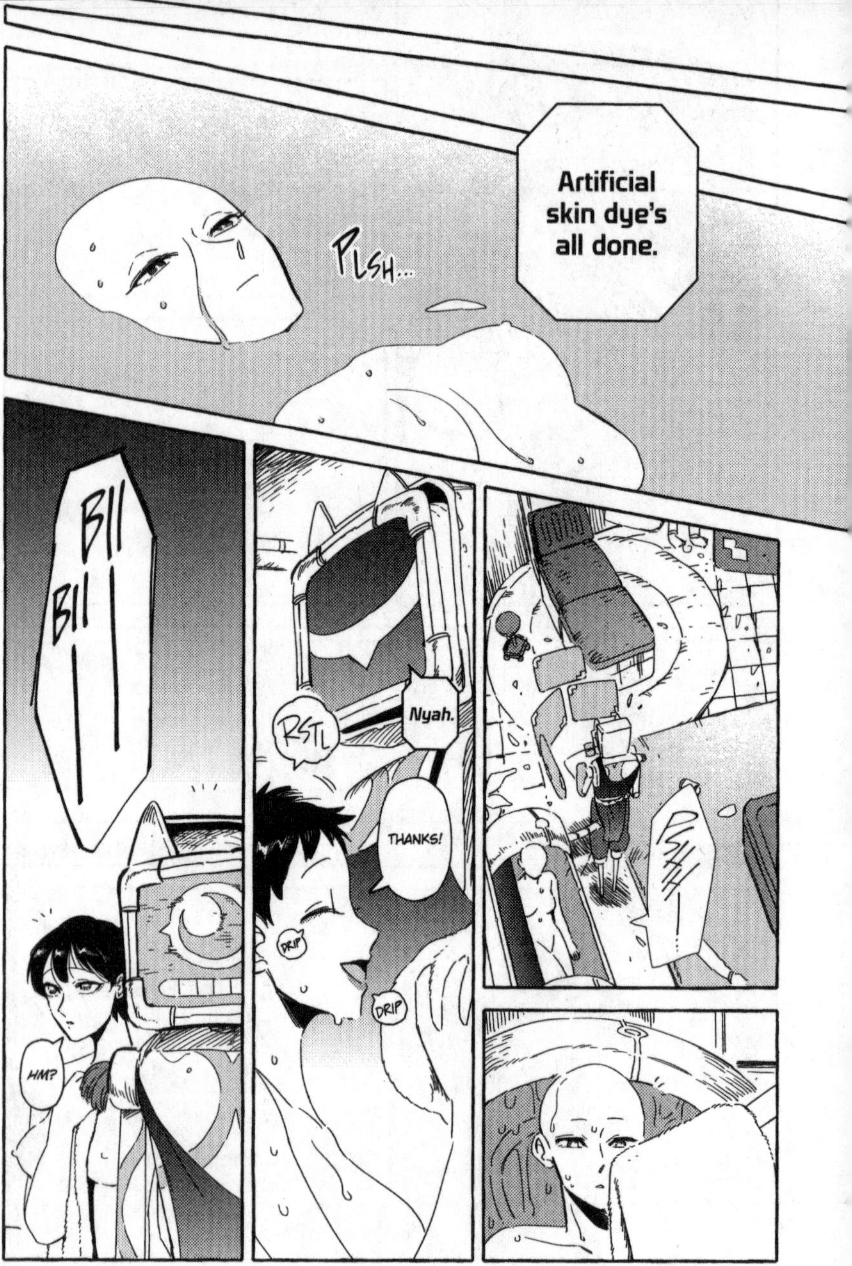
Artificial skin dye's all done.
PLSH...
PSHH—...
Nyah.
RSTL
THANKS!
DRIP
DRIP
BII BII—
HM?

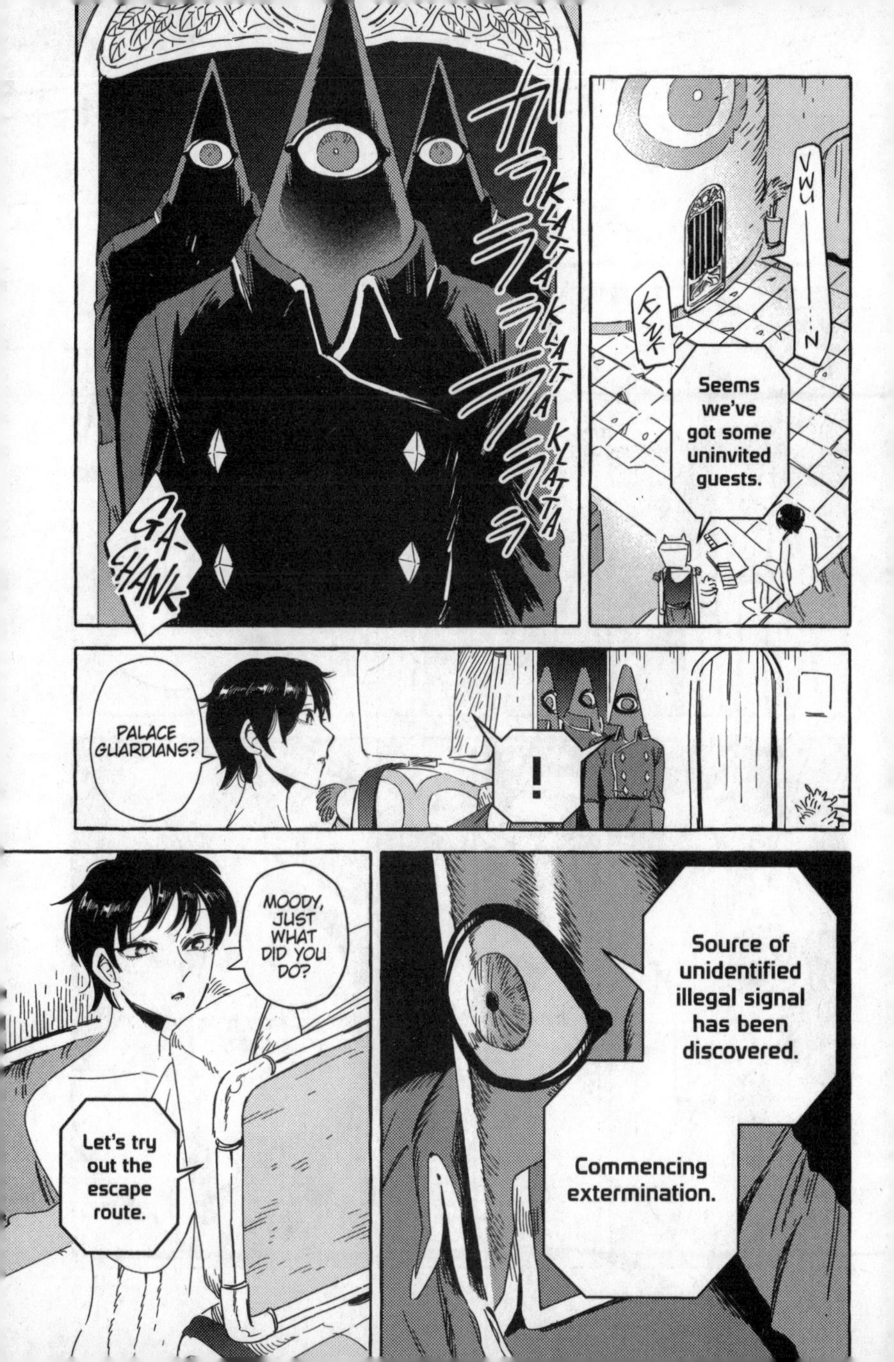
VWU......N
KLINK
Seems we've got some uninvited guests.
KLATTA KLATTA KLATTA
GA-CHANK
!
PALACE GUARDIANS?
Source of unidentified illegal signal has been discovered.
Commencing extermination.
MOODY, JUST WHAT DID YOU DO?
Let's try out the escape route.

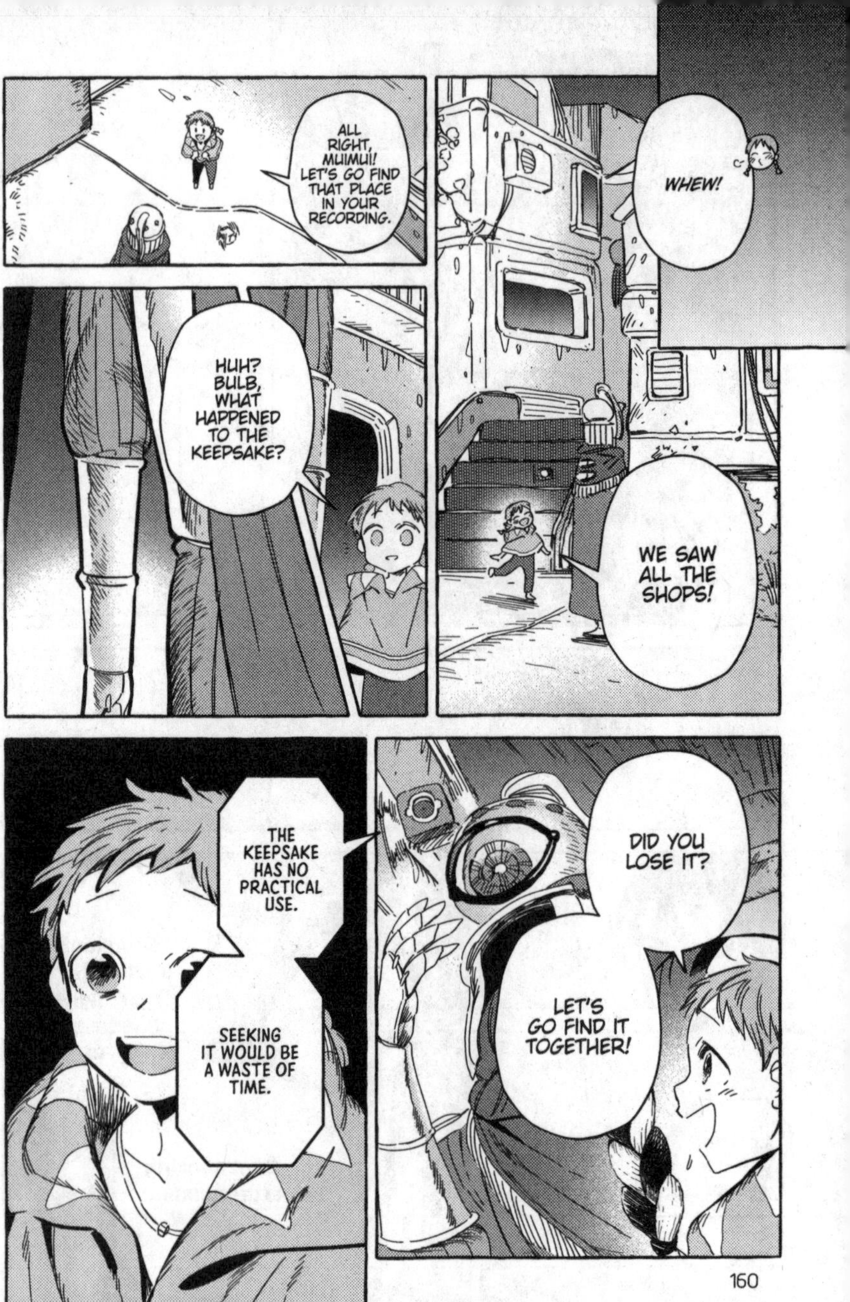
WHEW!
WE SAW ALL THE SHOPS!
ALL RIGHT, MUIMUI! LET'S GO FIND THAT PLACE IN YOUR RECORDING.
HUH? BULB, WHAT HAPPENED TO THE KEEPSAKE?
DID YOU LOSE IT?
LET'S GO FIND IT TOGETHER!
THE KEEPSAKE HAS NO PRACTICAL USE.
SEEKING IT WOULD BE A WASTE OF TIME.

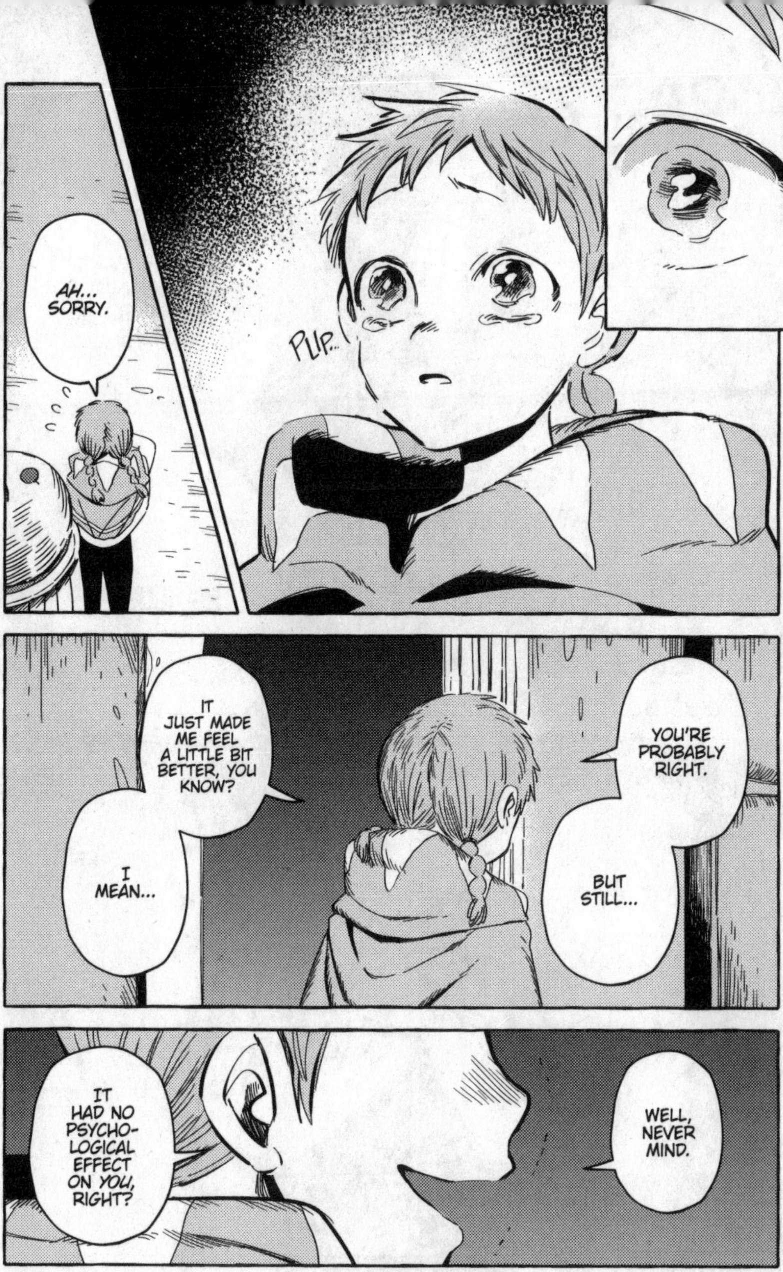
PLIP...
AH... SORRY.
YOU'RE PROBABLY RIGHT.
BUT STILL...
IT JUST MADE ME FEEL A LITTLE BIT BETTER, YOU KNOW?
I MEAN...
WELL, NEVER MIND.
IT HAD NO PSYCHO-LOGICAL EFFECT ON YOU, RIGHT?

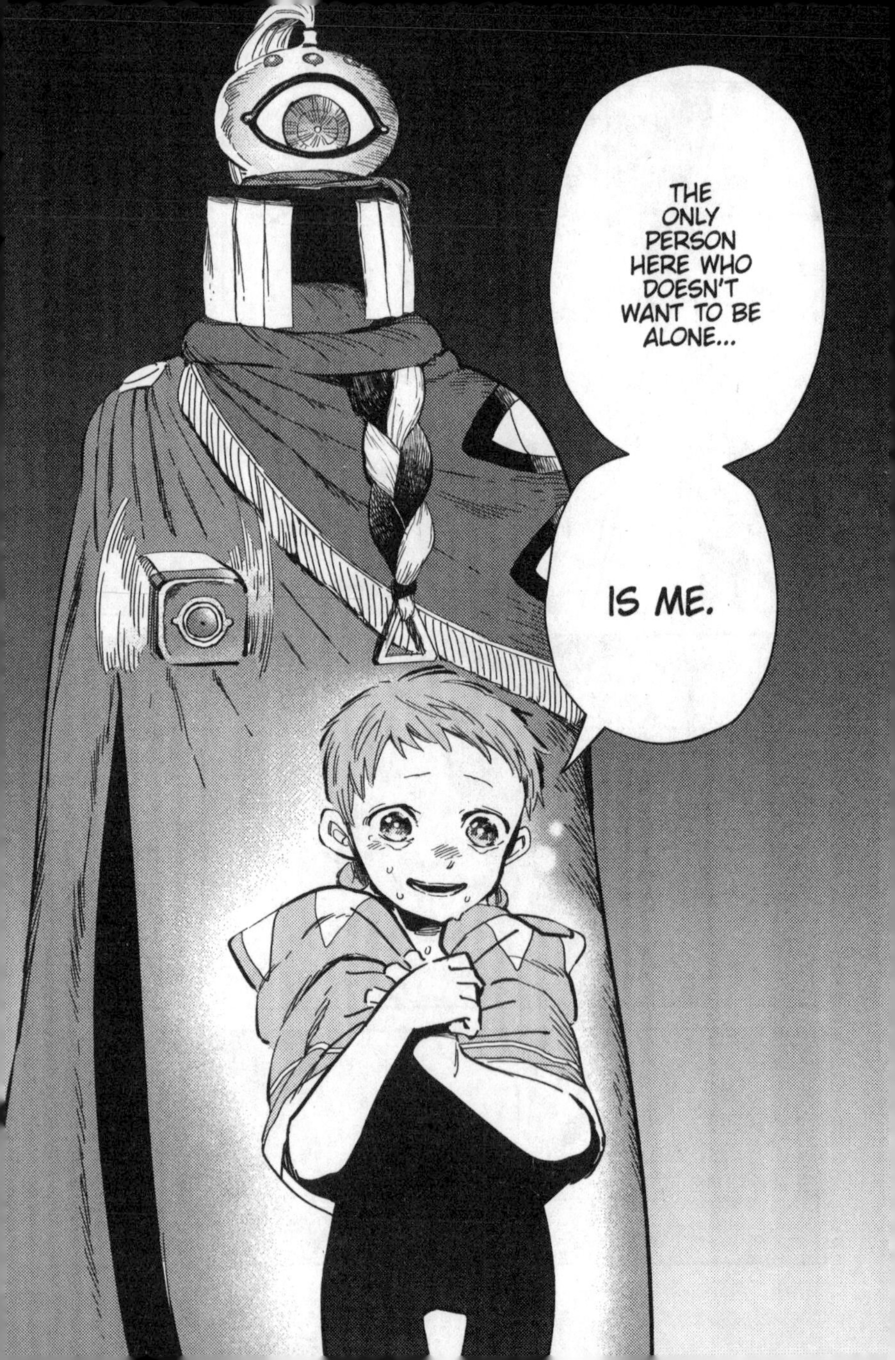
THE ONLY PERSON HERE WHO DOESN'T WANT TO BE ALONE...
IS ME.

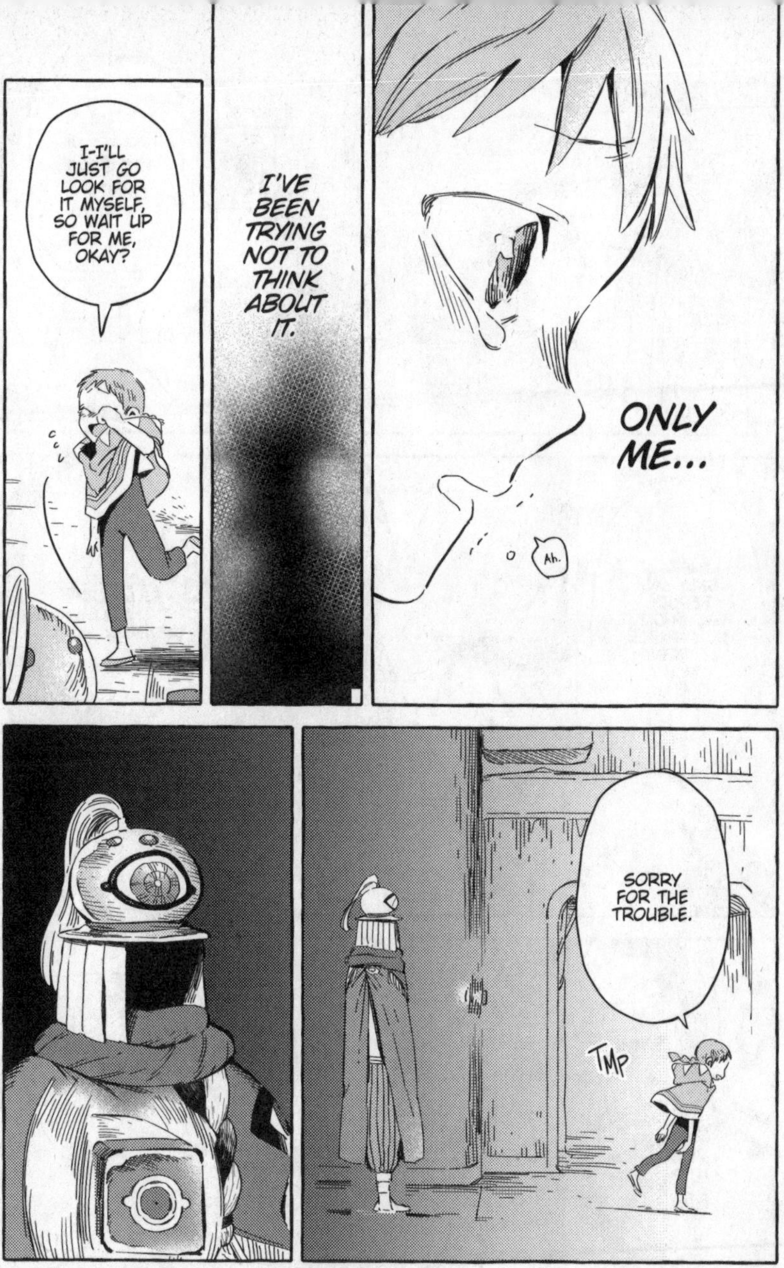
ONLY ME...
Ah.
I'VE BEEN TRYING NOT TO THINK ABOUT IT.
I-I'LL JUST GO LOOK FOR IT MYSELF, SO WAIT UP FOR ME, OKAY?
SORRY FOR THE TROUBLE.
TMP

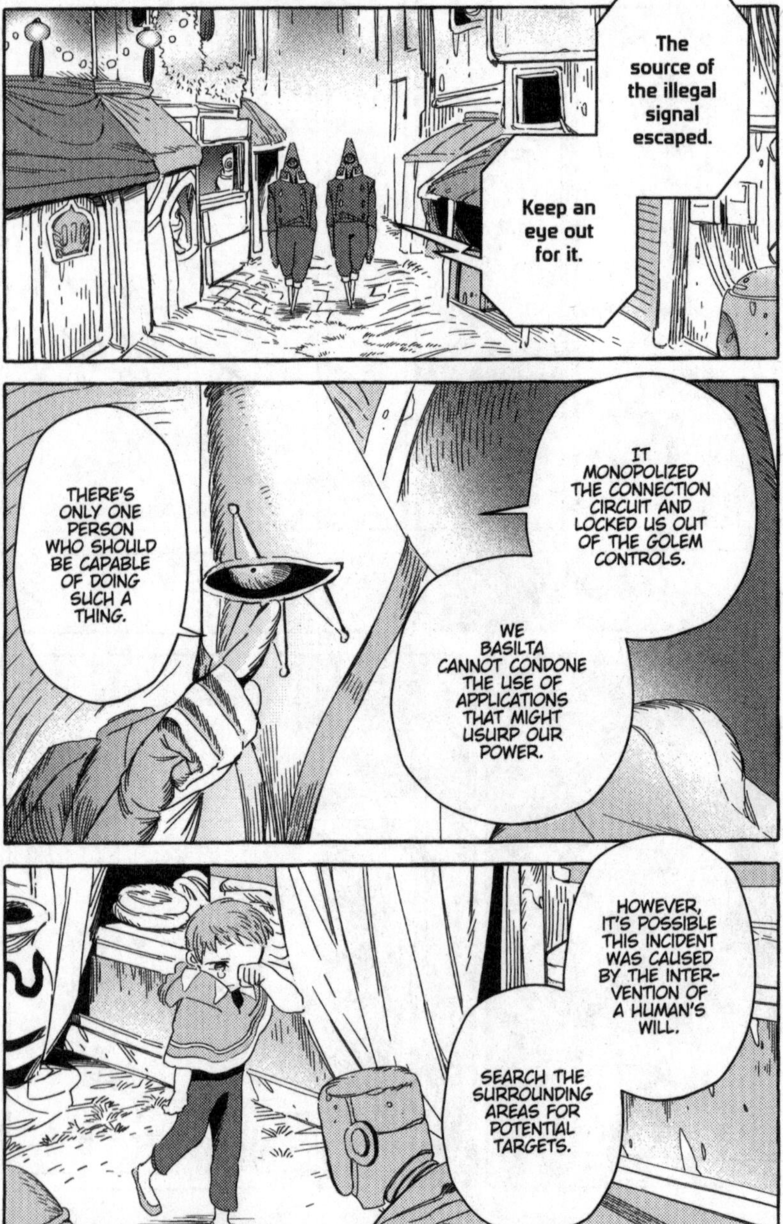
The source of the illegal signal escaped.
Keep an eye out for it.
IT MONOPOLIZED THE CONNECTION CIRCUIT AND LOCKED US OUT OF THE GOLEM CONTROLS.
WE BASILTA CANNOT CONDONE THE USE OF APPLICATIONS THAT MIGHT USURP OUR POWER.
THERE'S ONLY ONE PERSON WHO SHOULD BE CAPABLE OF DOING SUCH A THING.
HOWEVER, IT'S POSSIBLE THIS INCIDENT WAS CAUSED BY THE INTER-VENTION OF A HUMAN'S WILL.
SEARCH THE SURROUNDING AREAS FOR POTENTIAL TARGETS.

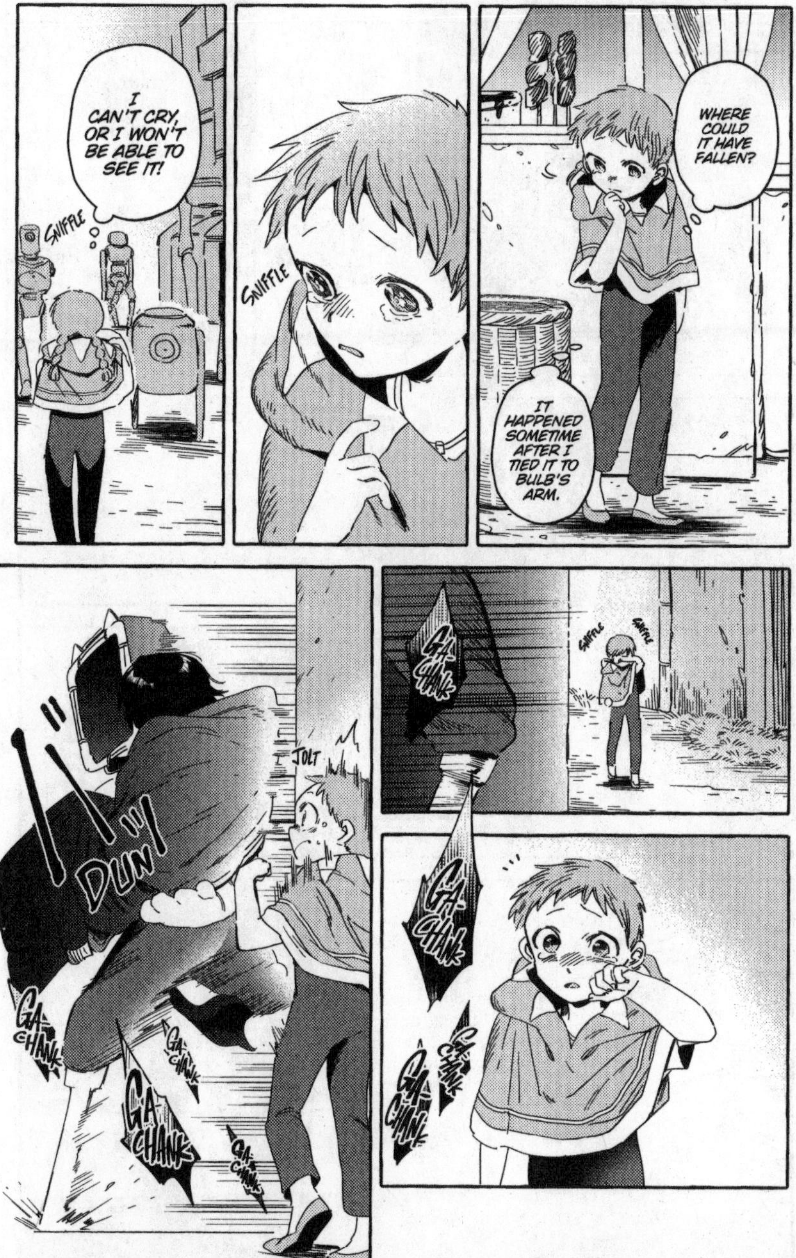
WHERE COULD IT HAVE FALLEN?
IT HAPPENED SOMETIME AFTER I TIED IT TO BULB'S ARM.
SNIFFLE
I CAN'T CRY, OR I WON'T BE ABLE TO SEE IT!
SNIFFLE
SNIFFLE
SNIFFLE
GA-CHANK
GA-CHANK
GA-CHANK
GA-CHANK
JOLT
DUN
GA-CHANK
GA-CHANK
GA-CHANK
GA-CHANK

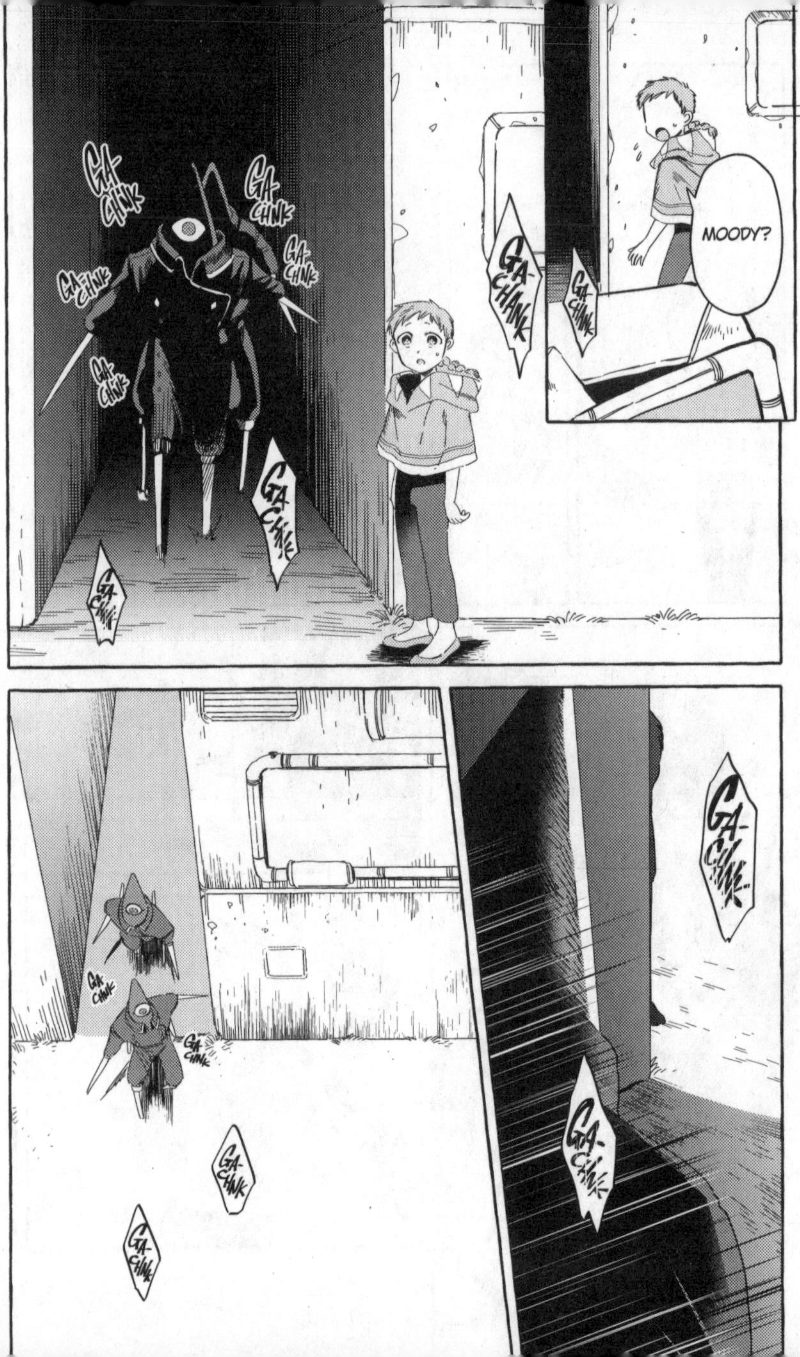
MOODY?
GA-CHANK
GA-CHANK
GA-CHINK
GA-CHINK
GA-CHINK
GA-CHINK
GA-CHINK
GA-CHINK
GA-CHINK
GA-CHINK...
GA-CHINK...
GA-CHINK
GA-CHINK
GA-CHINK
GA-CHINK

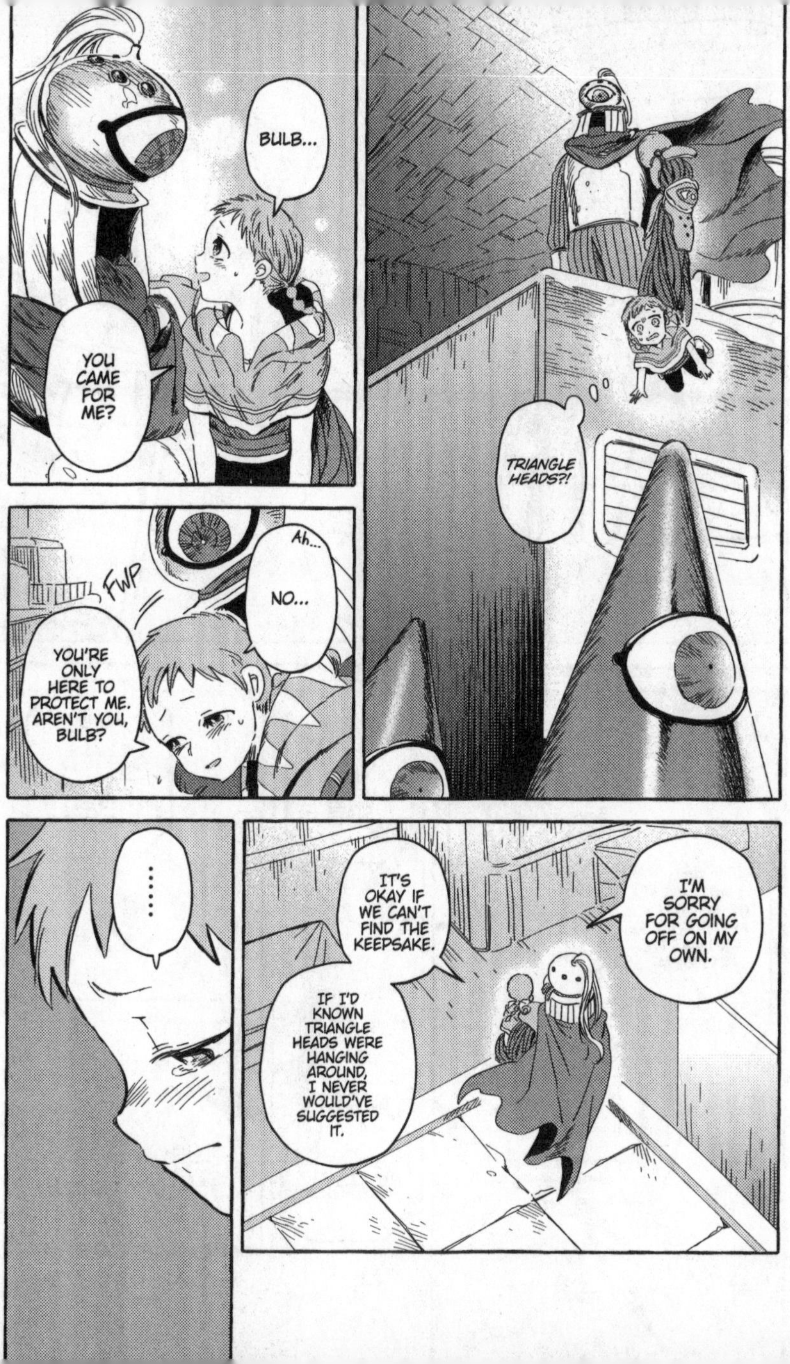
TRIANGLE HEADS?!
BULB...
YOU CAME FOR ME?
Ah...
NO...
FWP
YOU'RE ONLY HERE TO PROTECT ME. AREN'T YOU, BULB?
I'M SORRY FOR GOING OFF ON MY OWN.
IT'S OKAY IF WE CAN'T FIND THE KEEPSAKE.
IF I'D KNOWN TRIANGLE HEADS WERE HANGING AROUND, I NEVER WOULD'VE SUGGESTED IT.
......

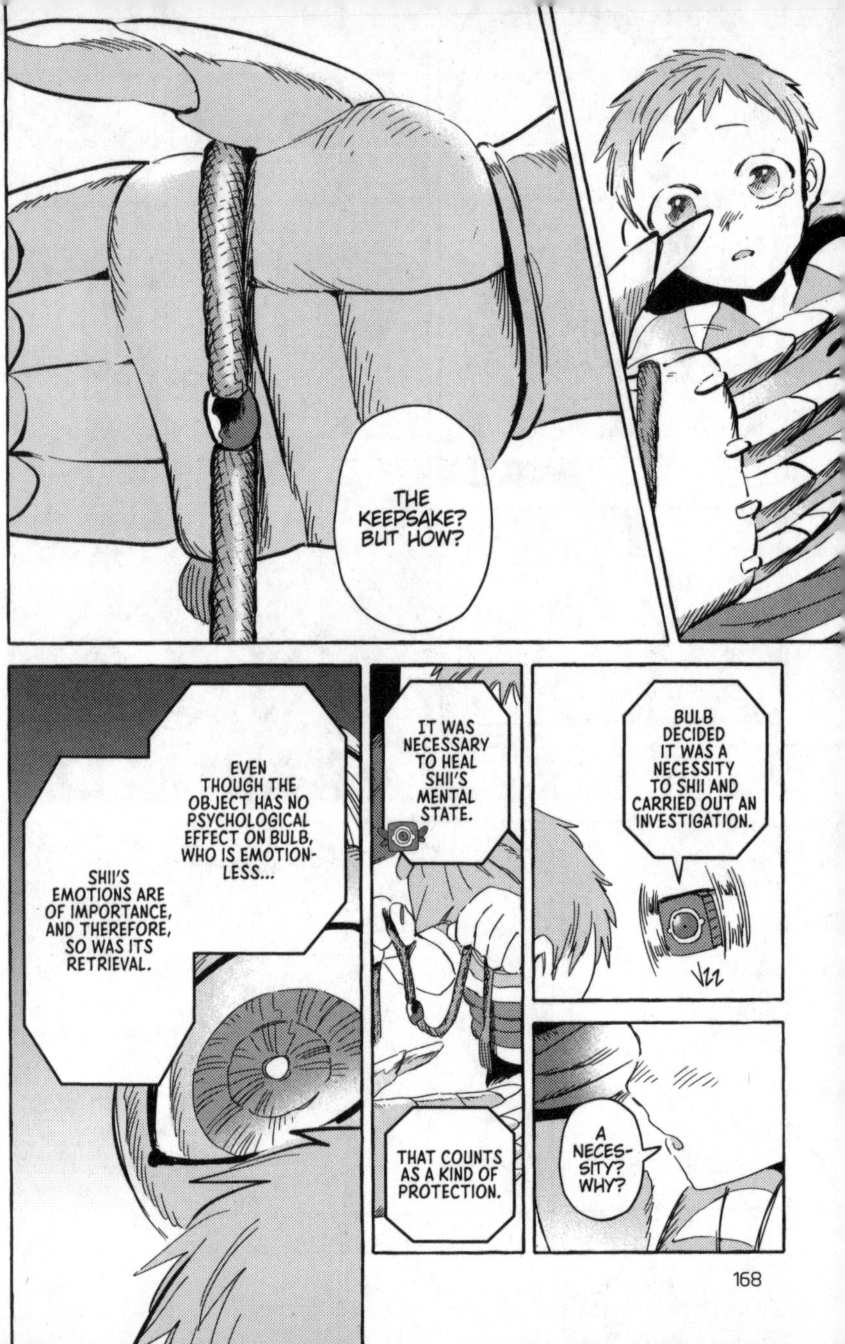
THE KEEPSAKE? BUT HOW?
BULB DECIDED IT WAS A NECESSITY TO SHII AND CARRIED OUT AN INVESTIGATION.
VZZ
A NECES-SITY? WHY?
IT WAS NECESSARY TO HEAL SHII'S MENTAL STATE.
THAT COUNTS AS A KIND OF PROTECTION.
EVEN THOUGH THE OBJECT HAS NO PSYCHOLOGICAL EFFECT ON BULB, WHO IS EMOTION-LESS...
SHII'S EMOTIONS ARE OF IMPORTANCE, AND THEREFORE, SO WAS ITS RETRIEVAL.

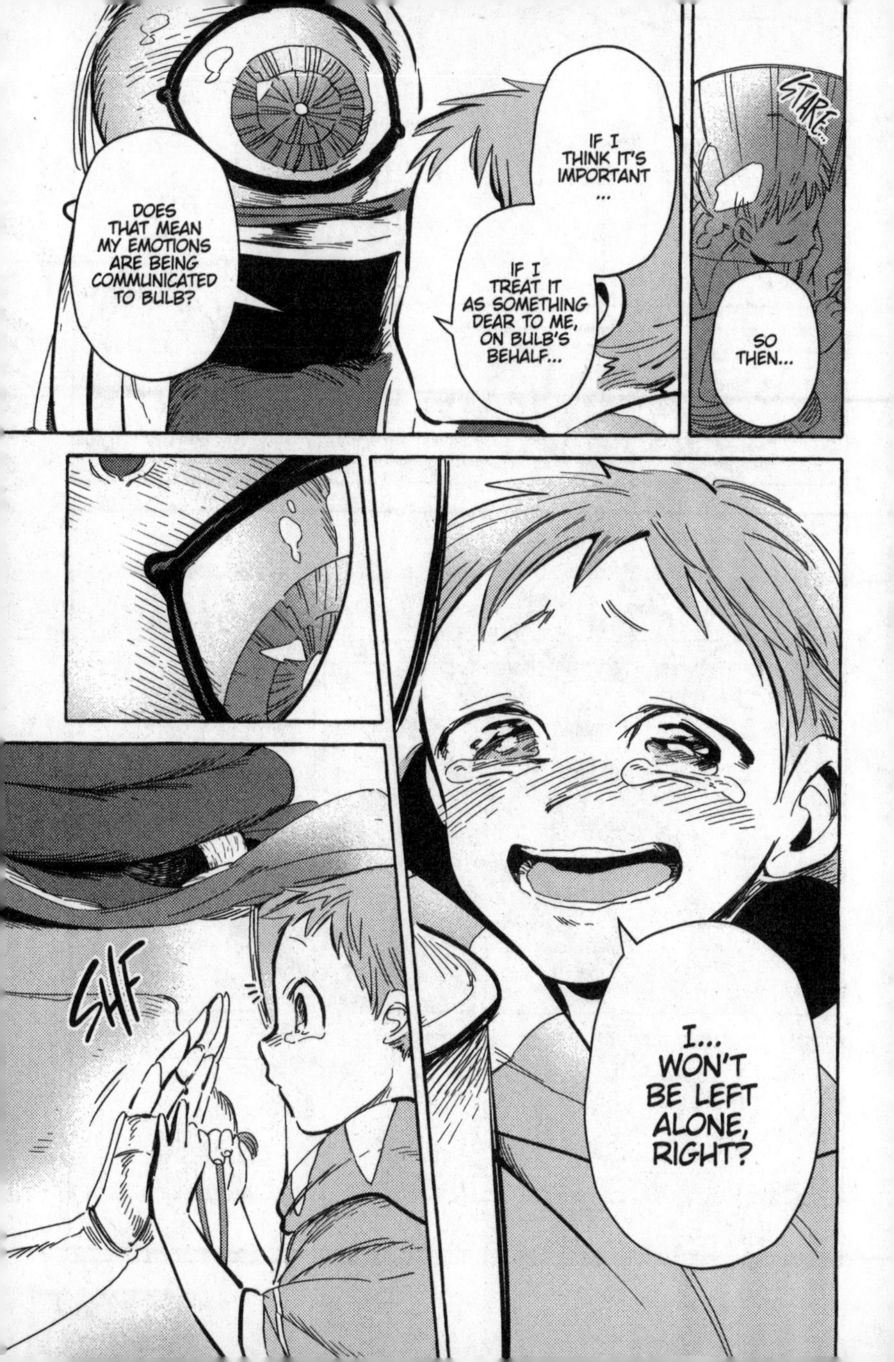
STARE...
SO THEN...
IF I THINK IT'S IMPORTANT ...
IF I TREAT IT AS SOMETHING DEAR TO ME, ON BULB'S BEHALF...
DOES THAT MEAN MY EMOTIONS ARE BEING COMMUNICATED TO BULB?
I... WON'T BE LEFT ALONE, RIGHT?
SHF

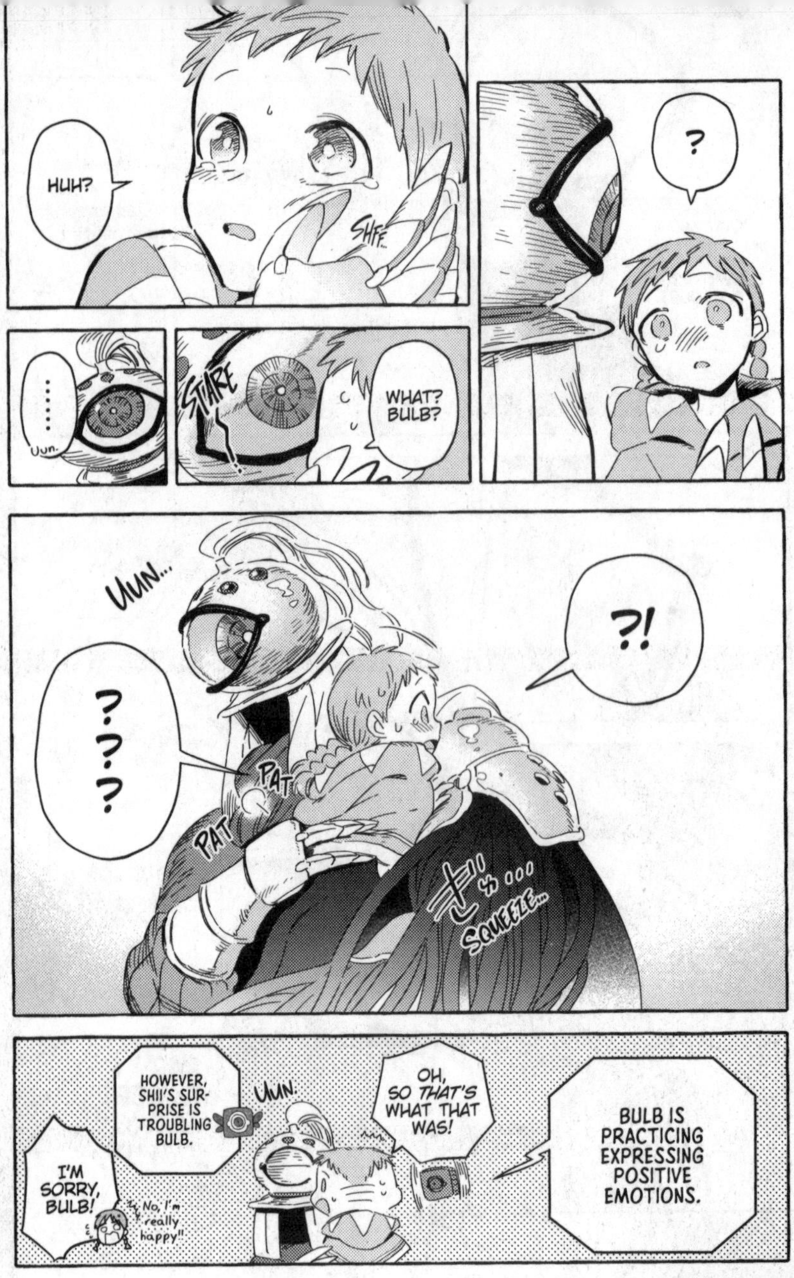
?
HUH?
SHFF...
STARE
WHAT? BULB?
......
Uun.
?!
UUN...
?.?.?
PAT
PAT
SQUEEZE...
BULB IS PRACTICING EXPRESSING POSITIVE EMOTIONS.
OH, SO *THAT'S* WHAT THAT WAS!
UUN.
HOWEVER, SHII'S SURPRISE IS TROUBLING BULB.
I'M SORRY, BULB!
No, I'm really happy!!

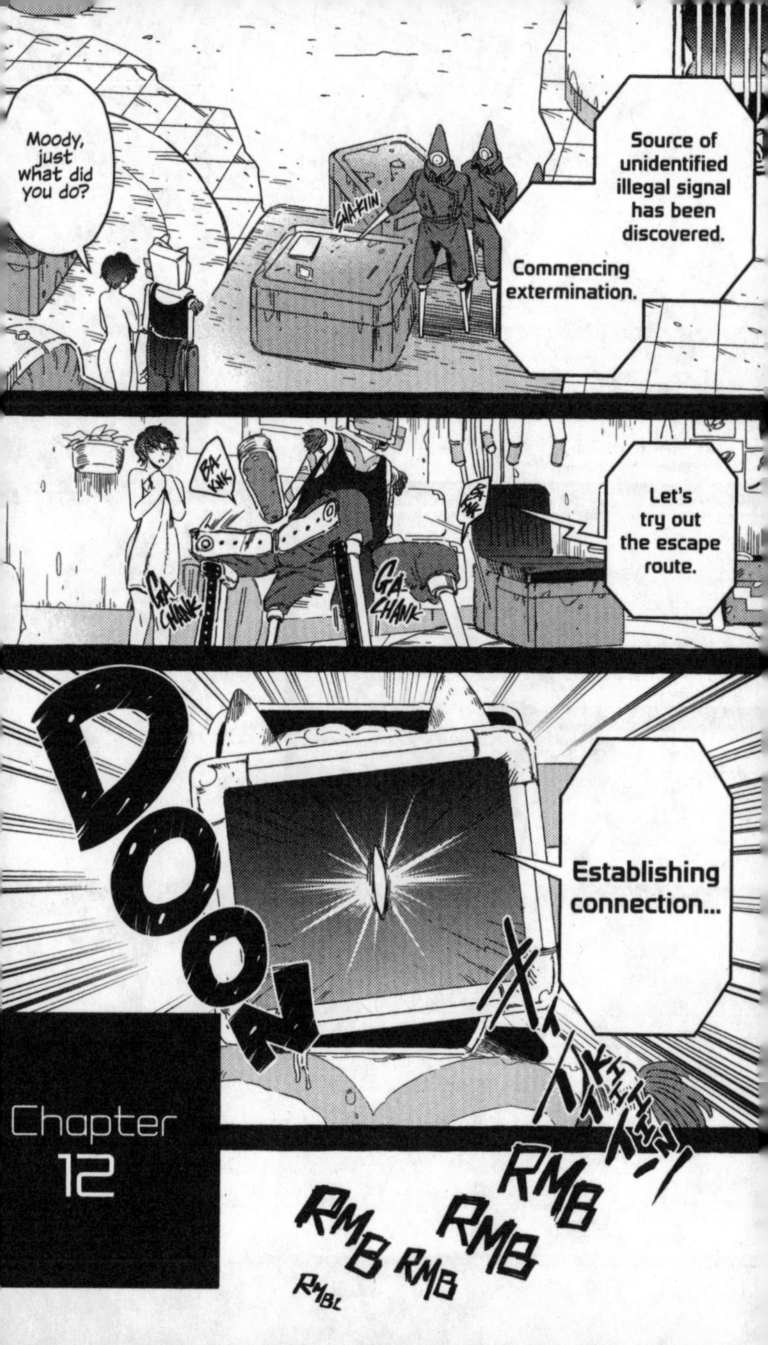
Source of unidentified illegal signal has been discovered.
Commencing extermination.
SHA-KIIN
Moody, just what did you do?
Let's try out the escape route.
GA-CHANK
BA-KNK
GA-CHANK
Establishing connection...
DOOM
RMB RMB
RMB RMB
RMBL
Chapter 12

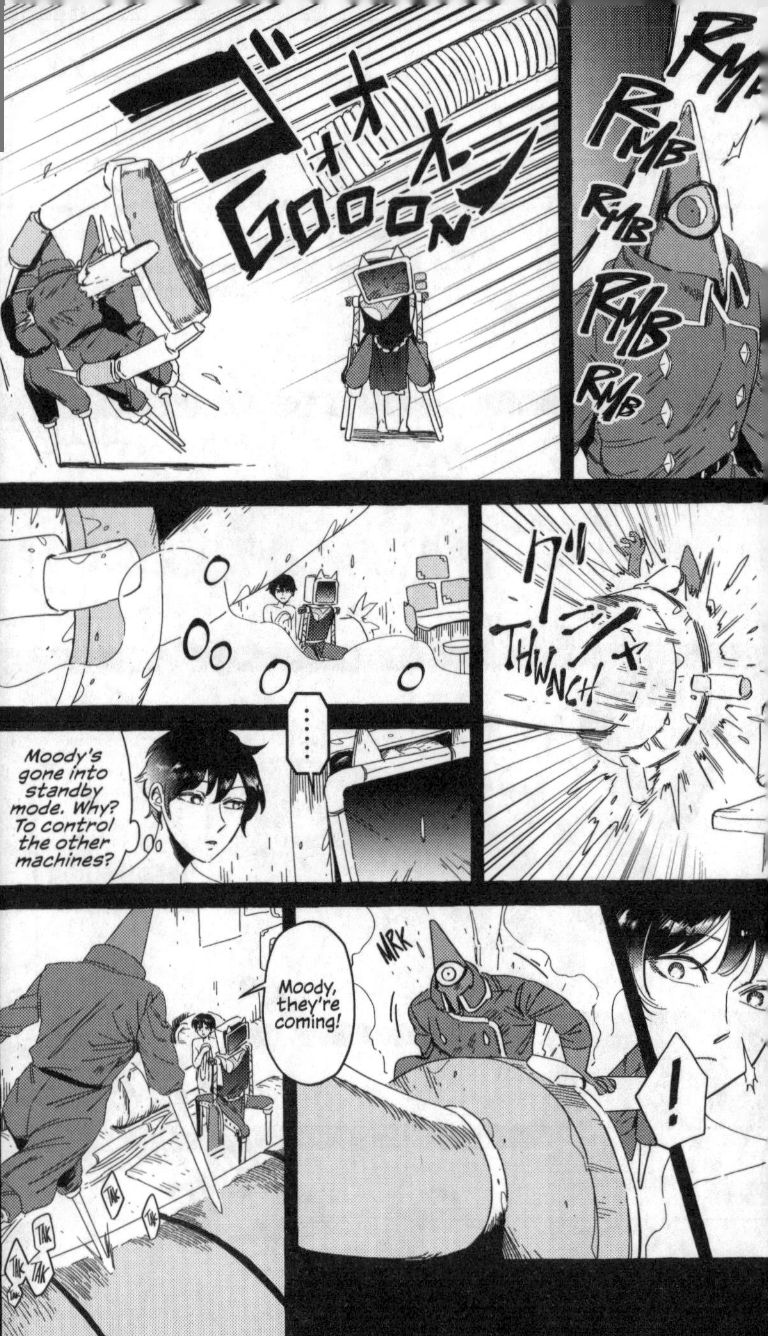
RMB
RMB
RMB
RMB
RMB
ゴオオーン
GOOOON
ガリッ
THWNCH!
......
Moody's gone into standby mode. Why? To control the other machines?
!
MRK
Moody, they're coming!
TAK
TAK
TAK
TAK
TAK
TAK

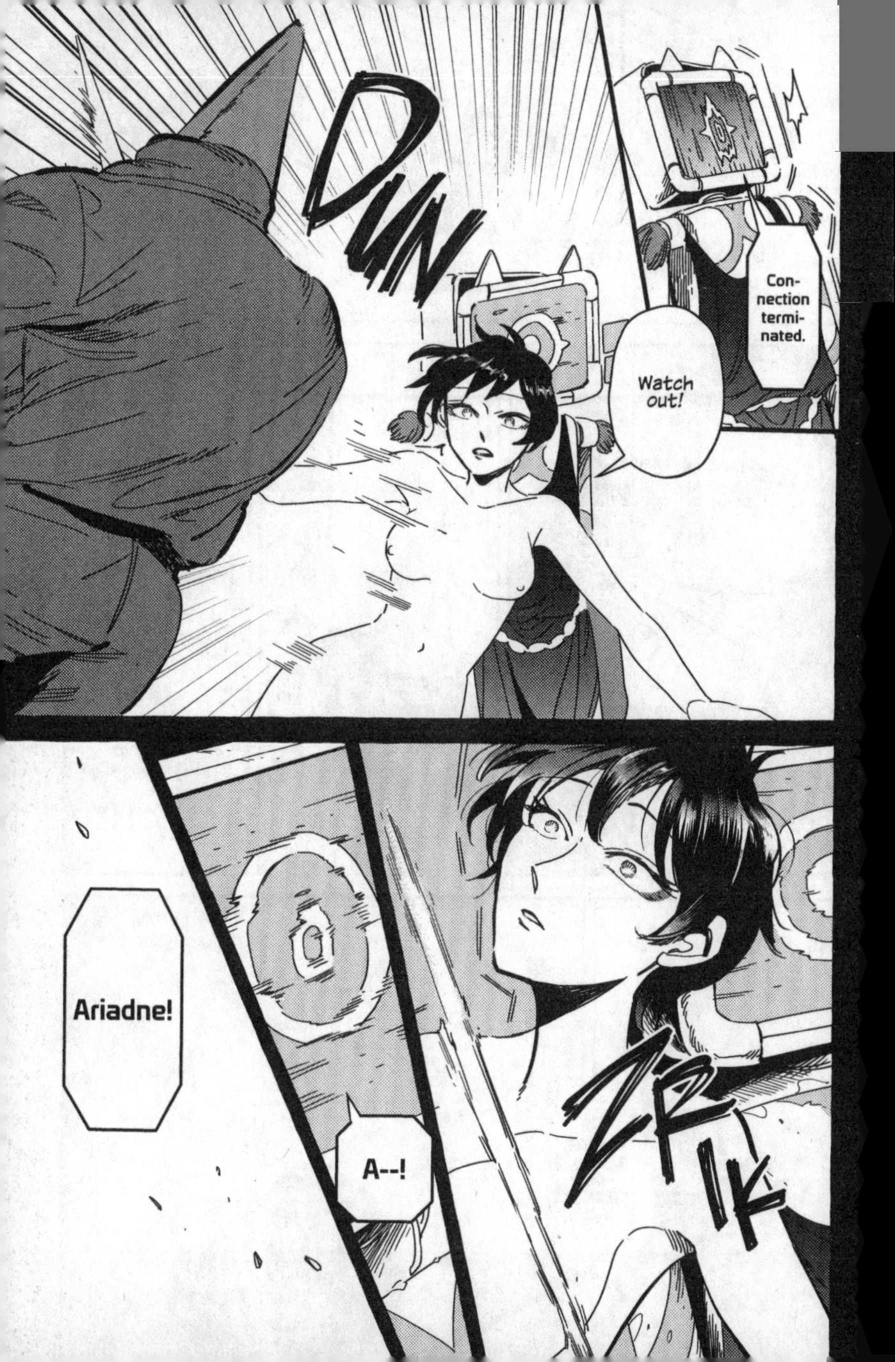
Connection terminated.
DUN
Watch out!
ZRIK
Ariadne!
A--!

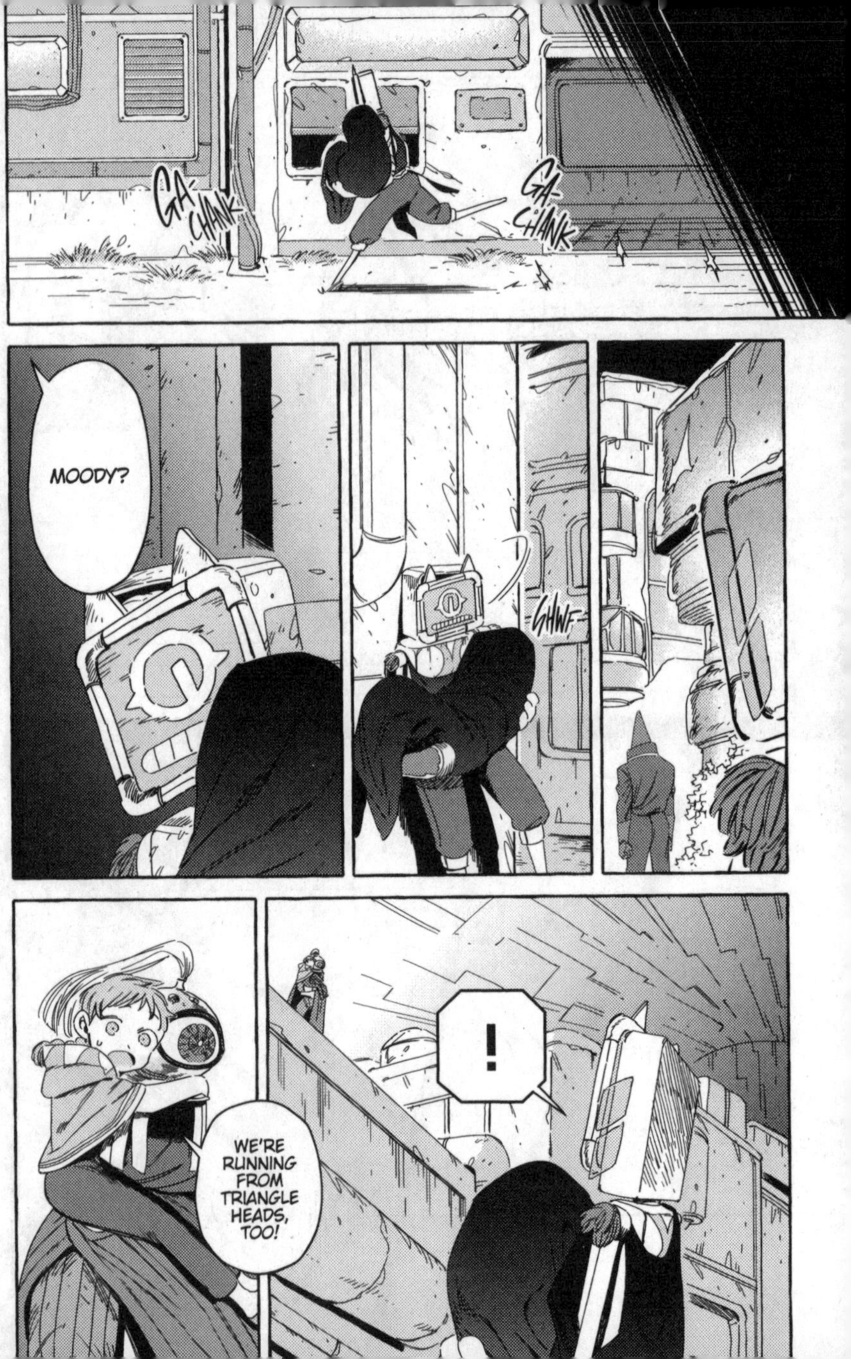
GA-CHANK
GA-CHANK
GHWF
MOODY?
!
WE'RE RUNNING FROM TRIANGLE HEADS, TOO!

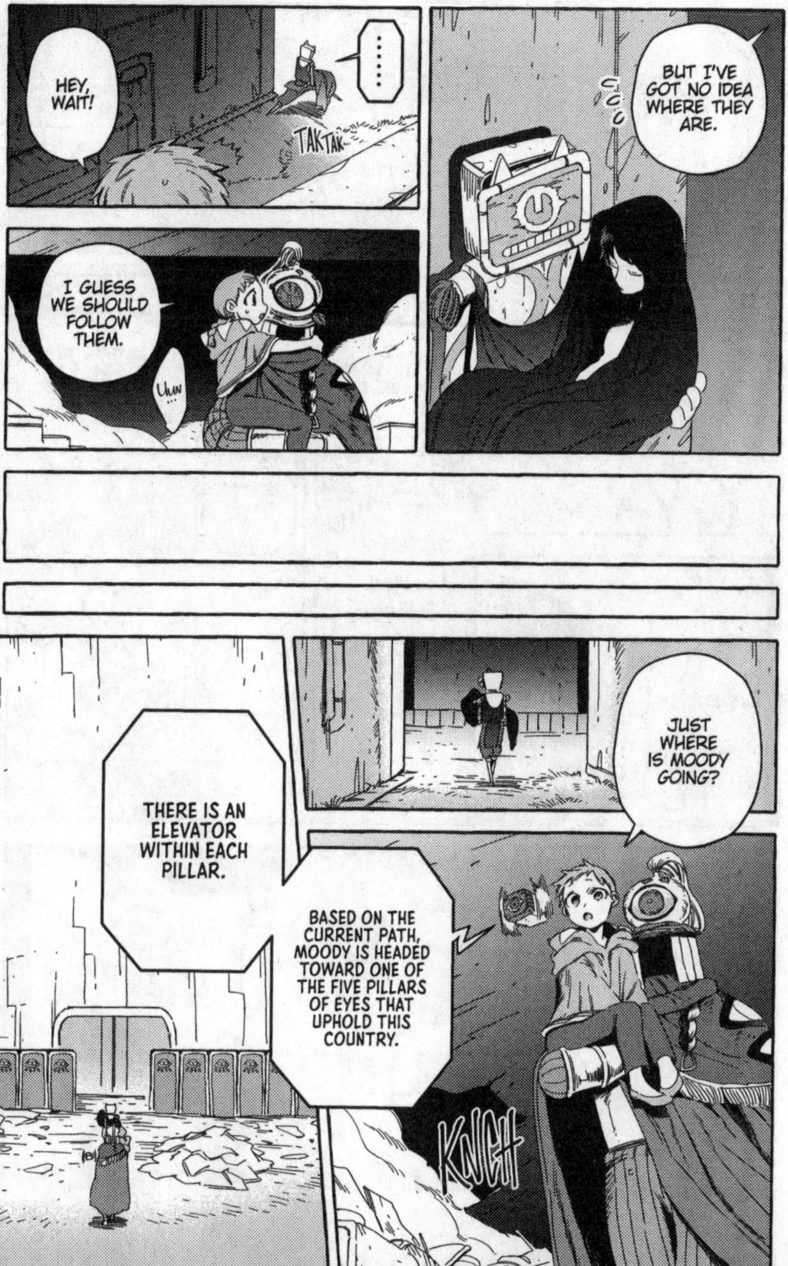
BUT I'VE GOT NO IDEA WHERE THEY ARE.
HEY, WAIT!
......
TAKTAK
I GUESS WE SHOULD FOLLOW THEM.
Uun...
JUST WHERE IS MOODY GOING?
BASED ON THE CURRENT PATH, MOODY IS HEADED TOWARD ONE OF THE FIVE PILLARS OF EYES THAT UPHOLD THIS COUNTRY.
KNCH
THERE IS AN ELEVATOR WITHIN EACH PILLAR.

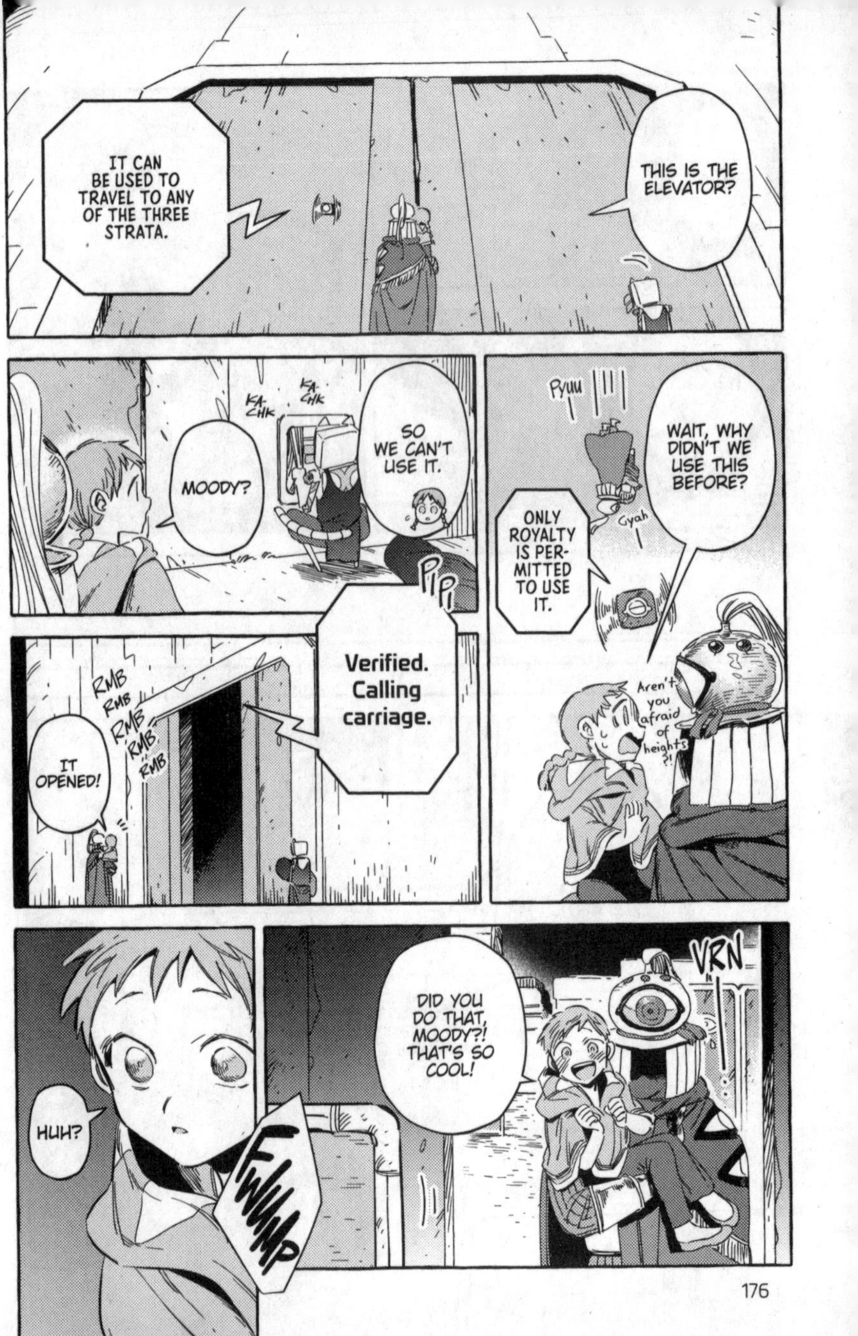

THIS IS THE ELEVATOR?
IT CAN BE USED TO TRAVEL TO ANY OF THE THREE STRATA.
Pyuu
WAIT, WHY DIDN'T WE USE THIS BEFORE?
ONLY ROYALTY IS PER-MITTED TO USE IT.
Gyah
Aren't you afraid of heights?!
SO WE CAN'T USE IT.
KA-CHK
KA-CHK
MOODY?
PIPI
Verified. Calling carriage.
RMB RMB RMB RMB RMB
IT OPENED!
VRN
DID YOU DO THAT, MOODY?! THAT'S SO COOL!
FWUMP
HUH?

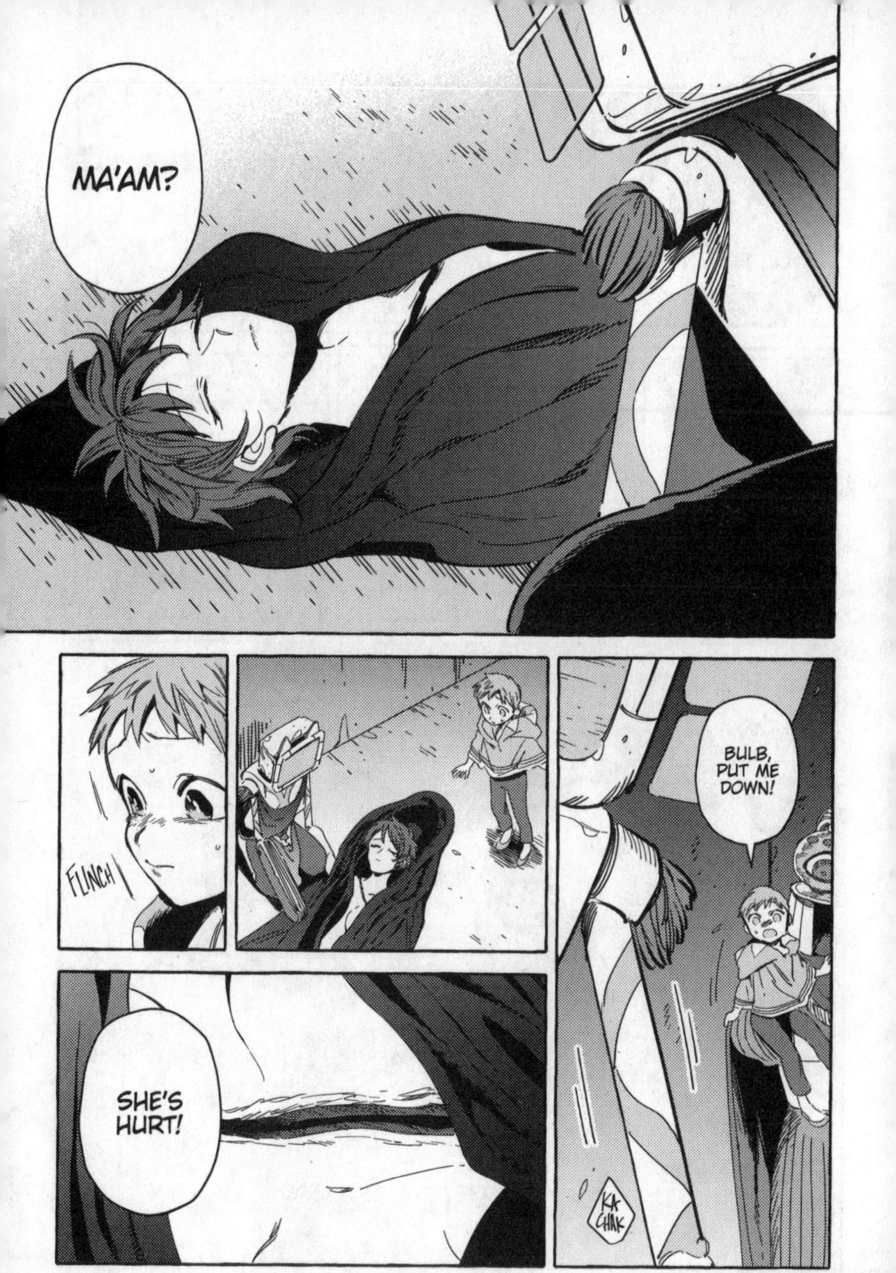
MA'AM?
BULB, PUT ME DOWN!
KA CHAK
FLINCH
SHE'S HURT!

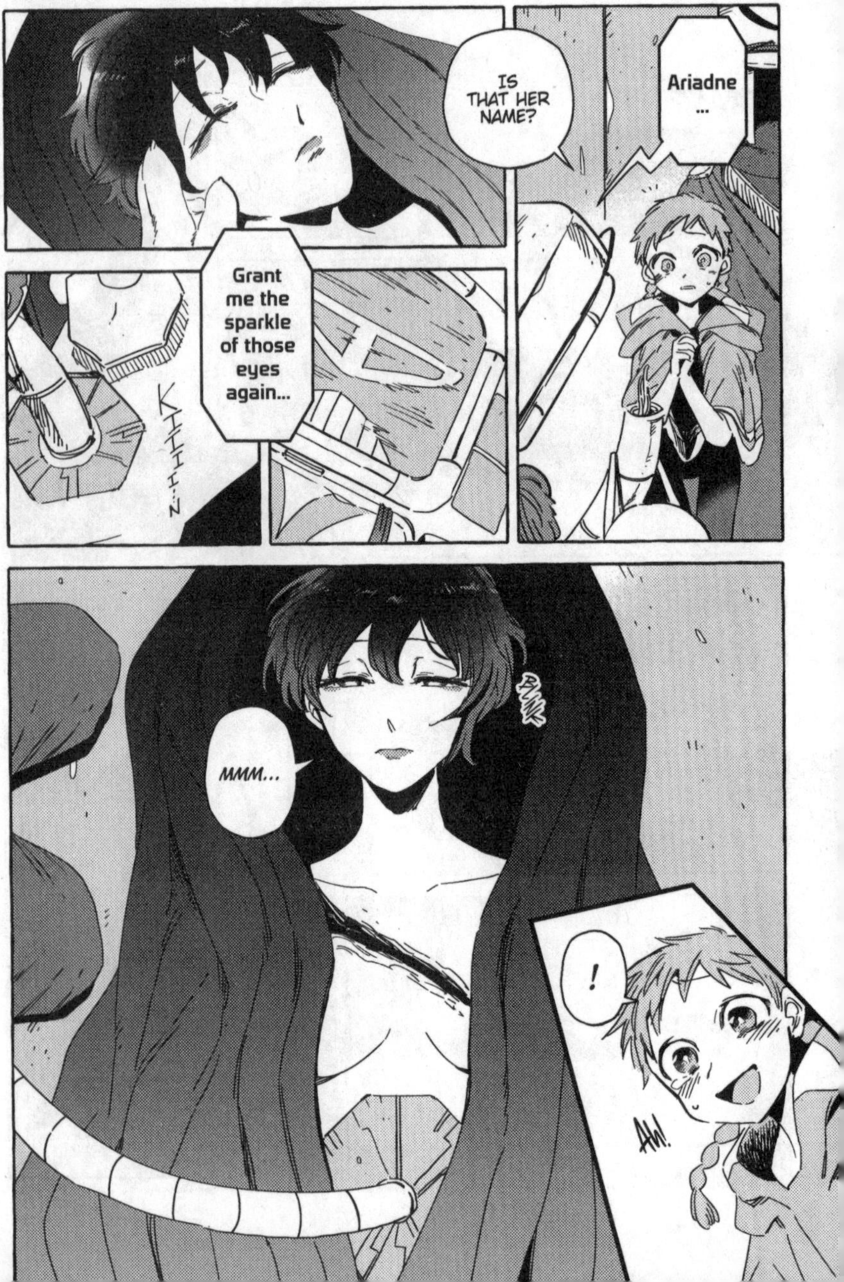
Ariadne ...
IS THAT HER NAME?
Grant me the sparkle of those eyes again...
KIIIIN
BLINK
MMM...
!
AH!

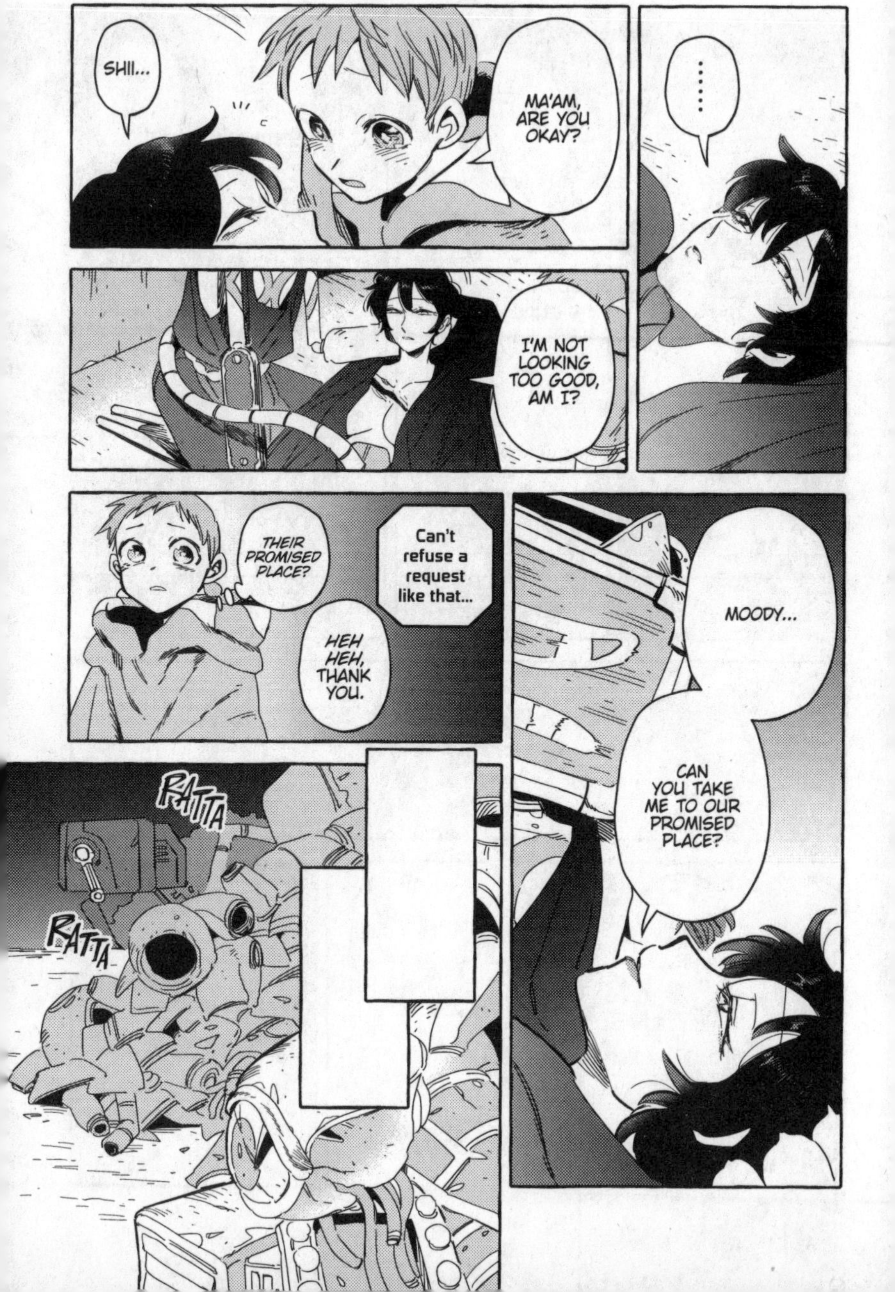
......
MA'AM, ARE YOU OKAY?
SHII...
I'M NOT LOOKING TOO GOOD, AM I?
MOODY...
CAN YOU TAKE ME TO OUR PROMISED PLACE?
Can't refuse a request like that...
THEIR PROMISED PLACE?
HEH HEH, THANK YOU.
RATTA
RATTA

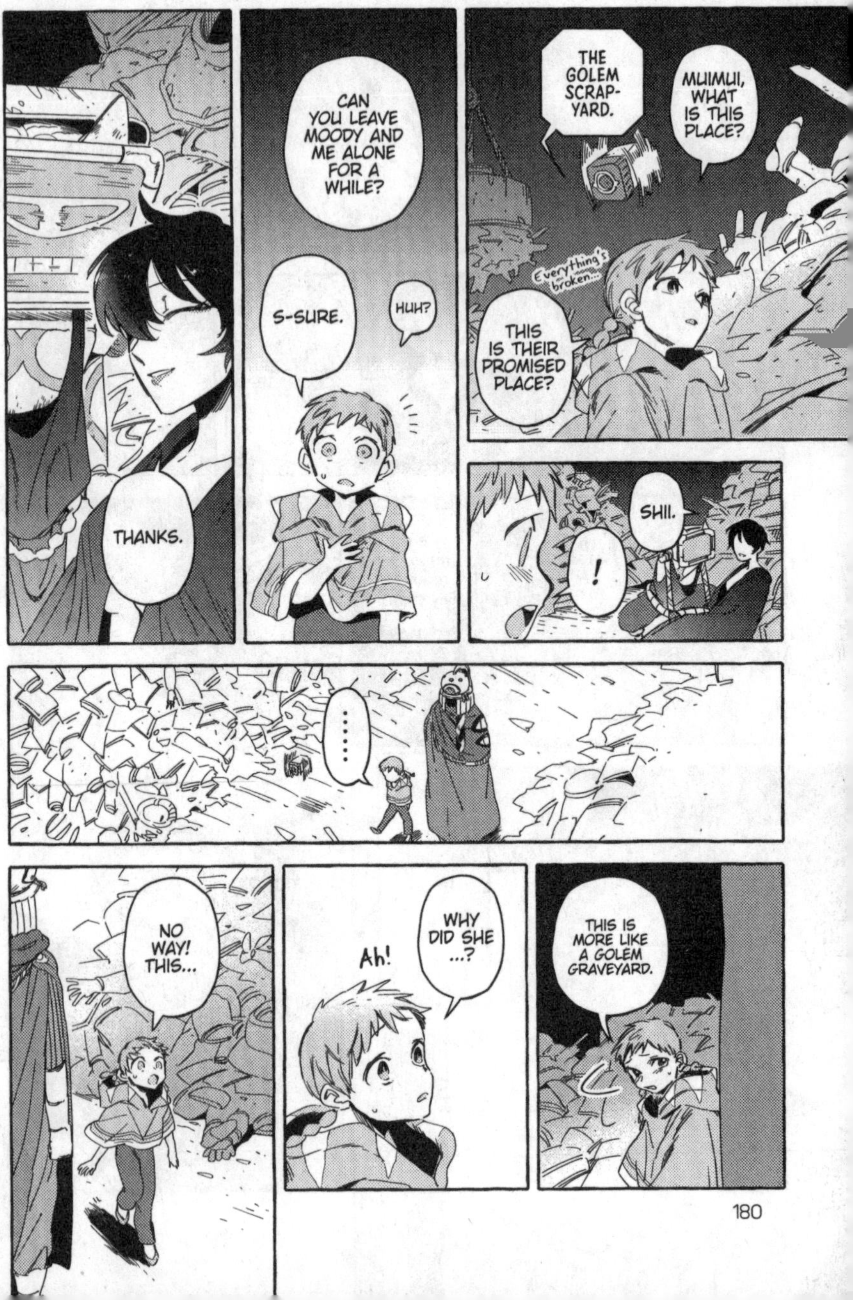
MUIMUI, WHAT IS THIS PLACE?
THE GOLEM SCRAP-YARD.
Everything's broken...
THIS IS THEIR PROMISED PLACE?
SHII.
!
CAN YOU LEAVE MOODY AND ME ALONE FOR A WHILE?
HUH?
S-SURE.
THANKS.
......
THIS IS MORE LIKE A GOLEM GRAVEYARD.
WHY DID SHE ...?
Ah!
NO WAY! THIS...

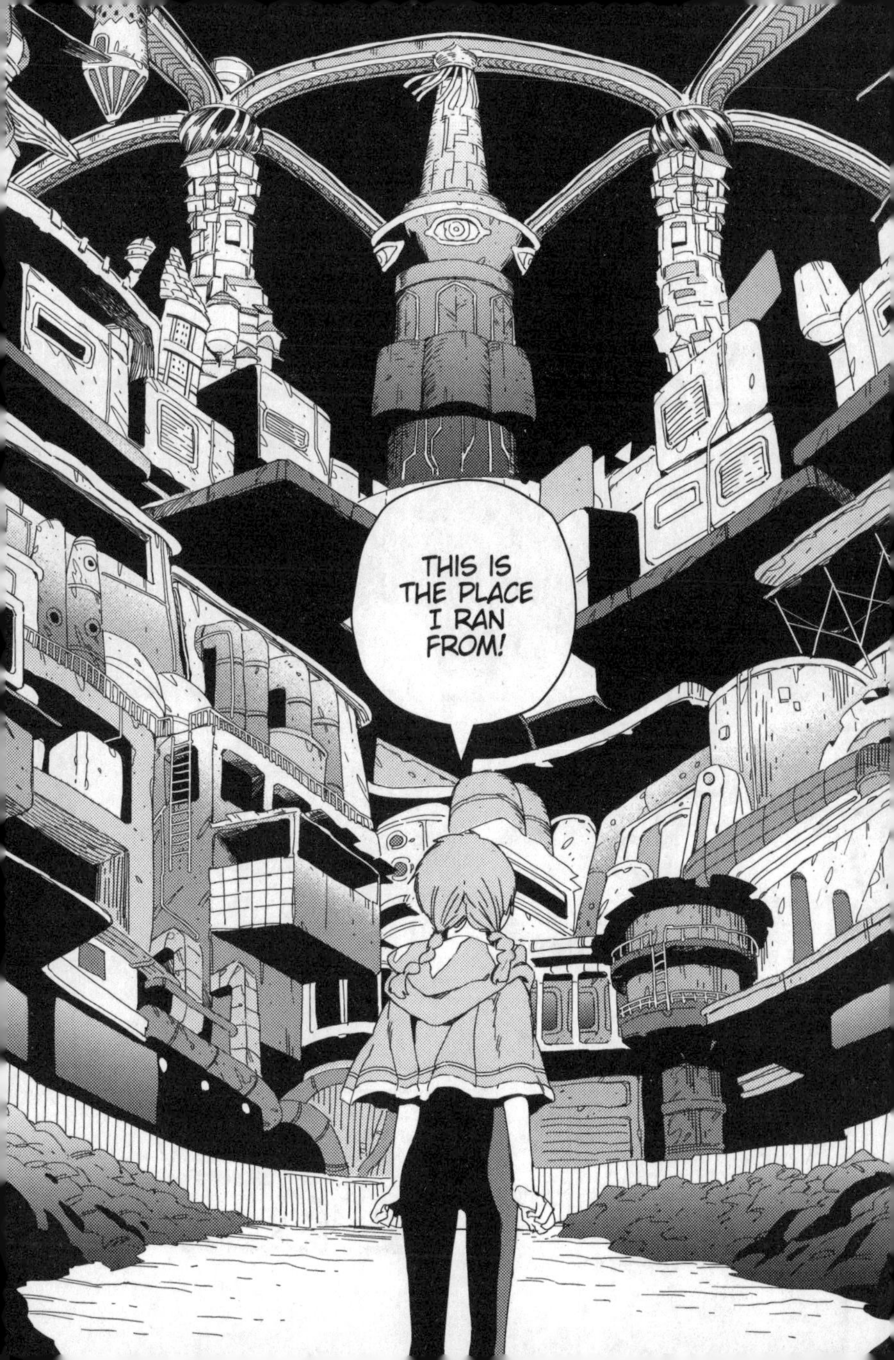
THIS IS THE PLACE I RAN FROM!

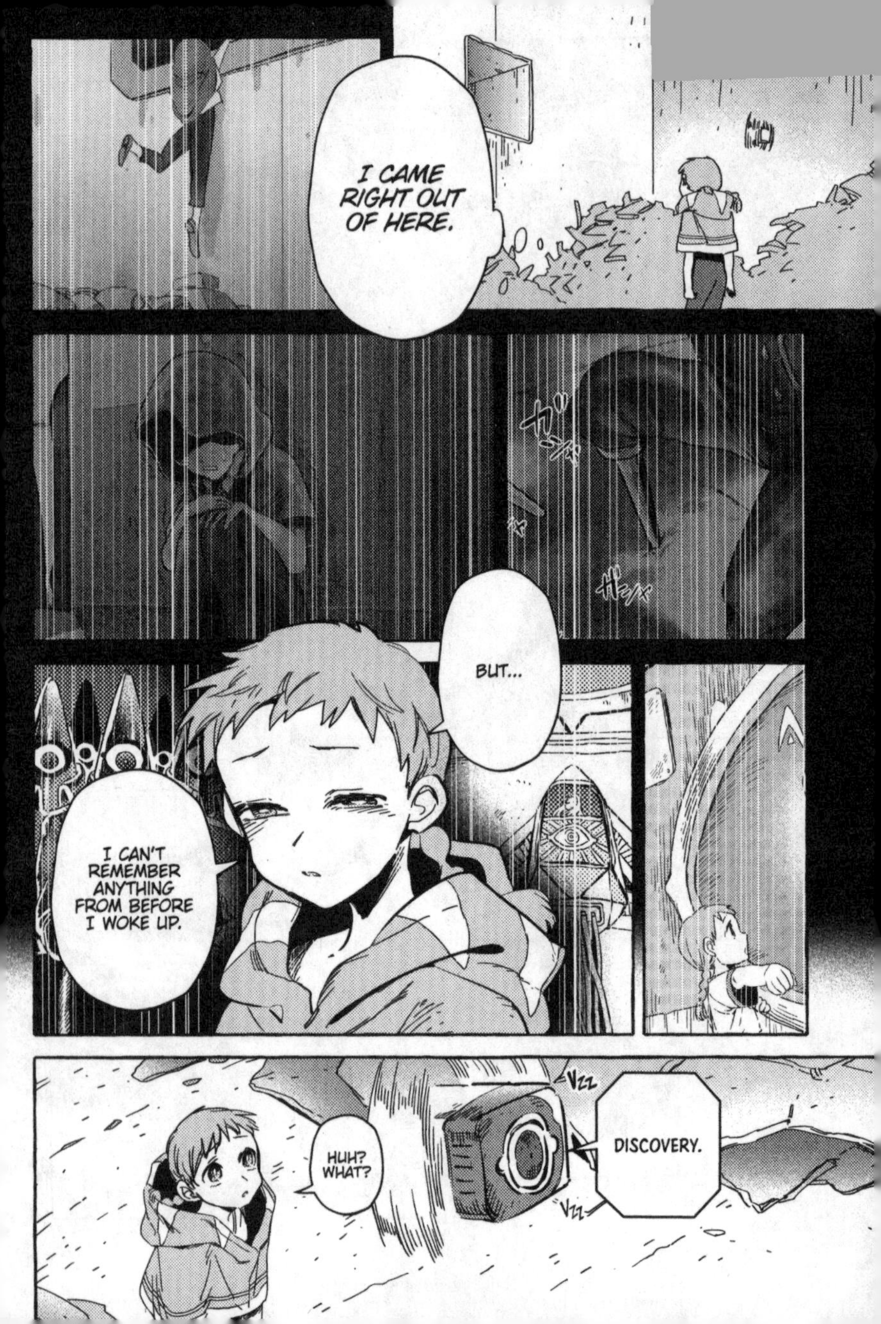
I CAME RIGHT OUT OF HERE.
BUT...
I CAN'T REMEMBER ANYTHING FROM BEFORE I WOKE UP.
VZZ
DISCOVERY.
VZZ
HUH? WHAT?

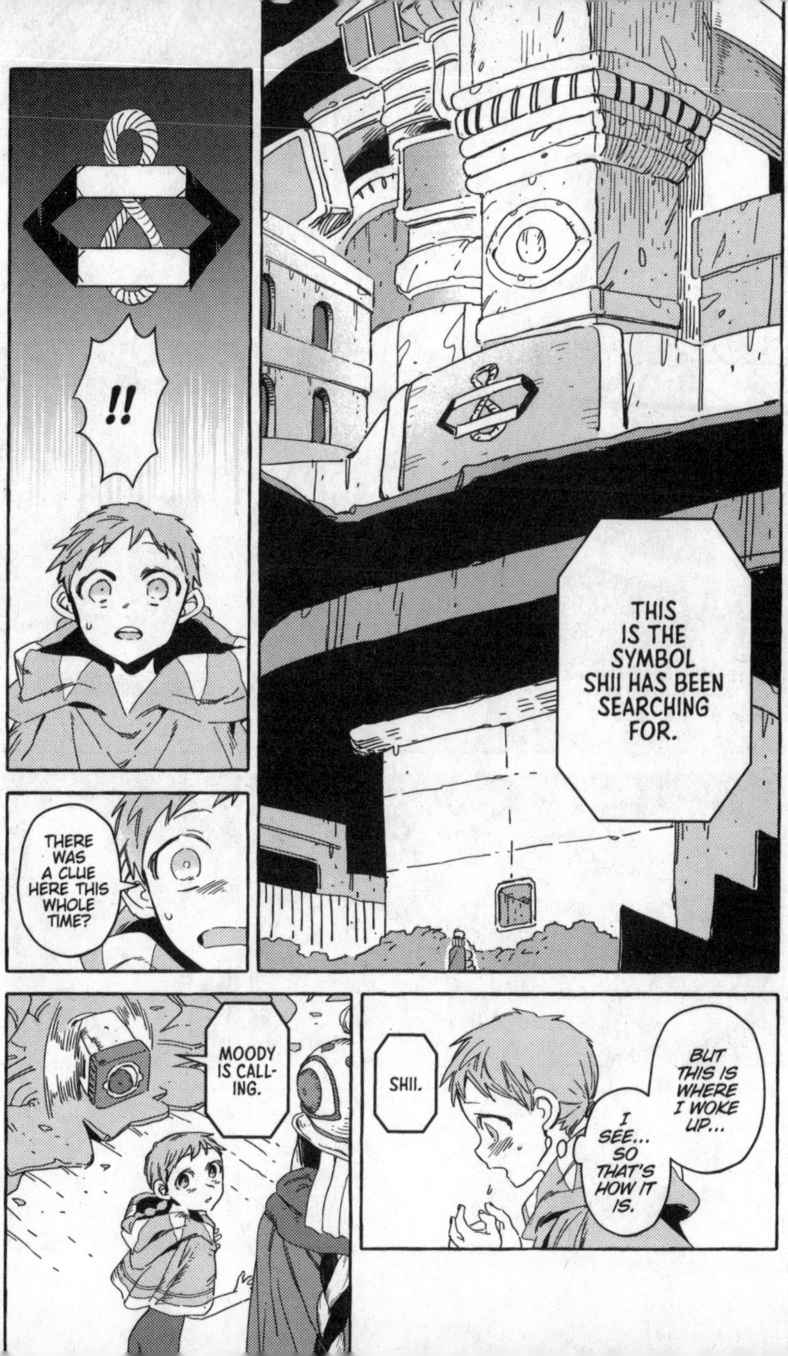
THIS IS THE SYMBOL SHII HAS BEEN SEARCHING FOR.
!!
THERE WAS A CLUE HERE THIS WHOLE TIME?
BUT THIS IS WHERE I WOKE UP...
I SEE... SO THAT'S HOW IT IS.
SHII.
MOODY IS CALL-ING.

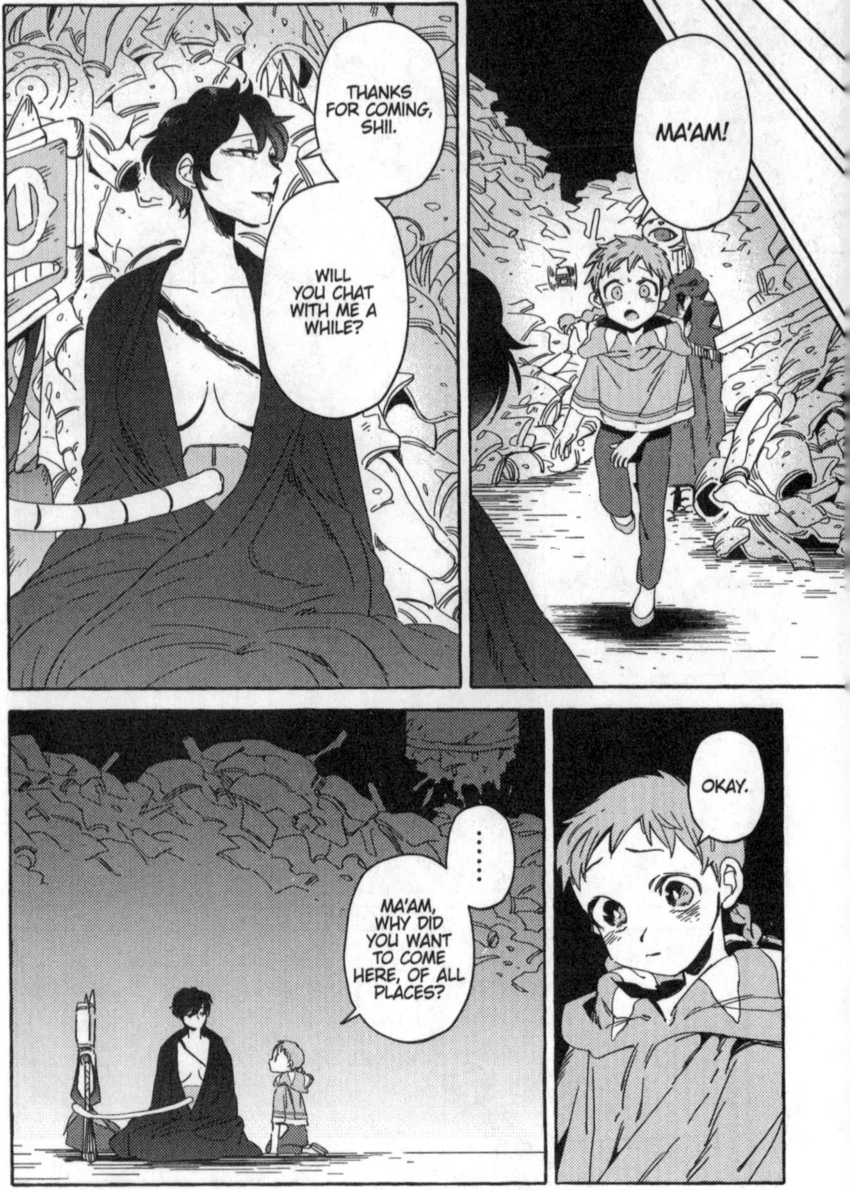
MA'AM!
THANKS FOR COMING, SHII.
WILL YOU CHAT WITH ME A WHILE?
OKAY.
......
MA'AM, WHY DID YOU WANT TO COME HERE, OF ALL PLACES?

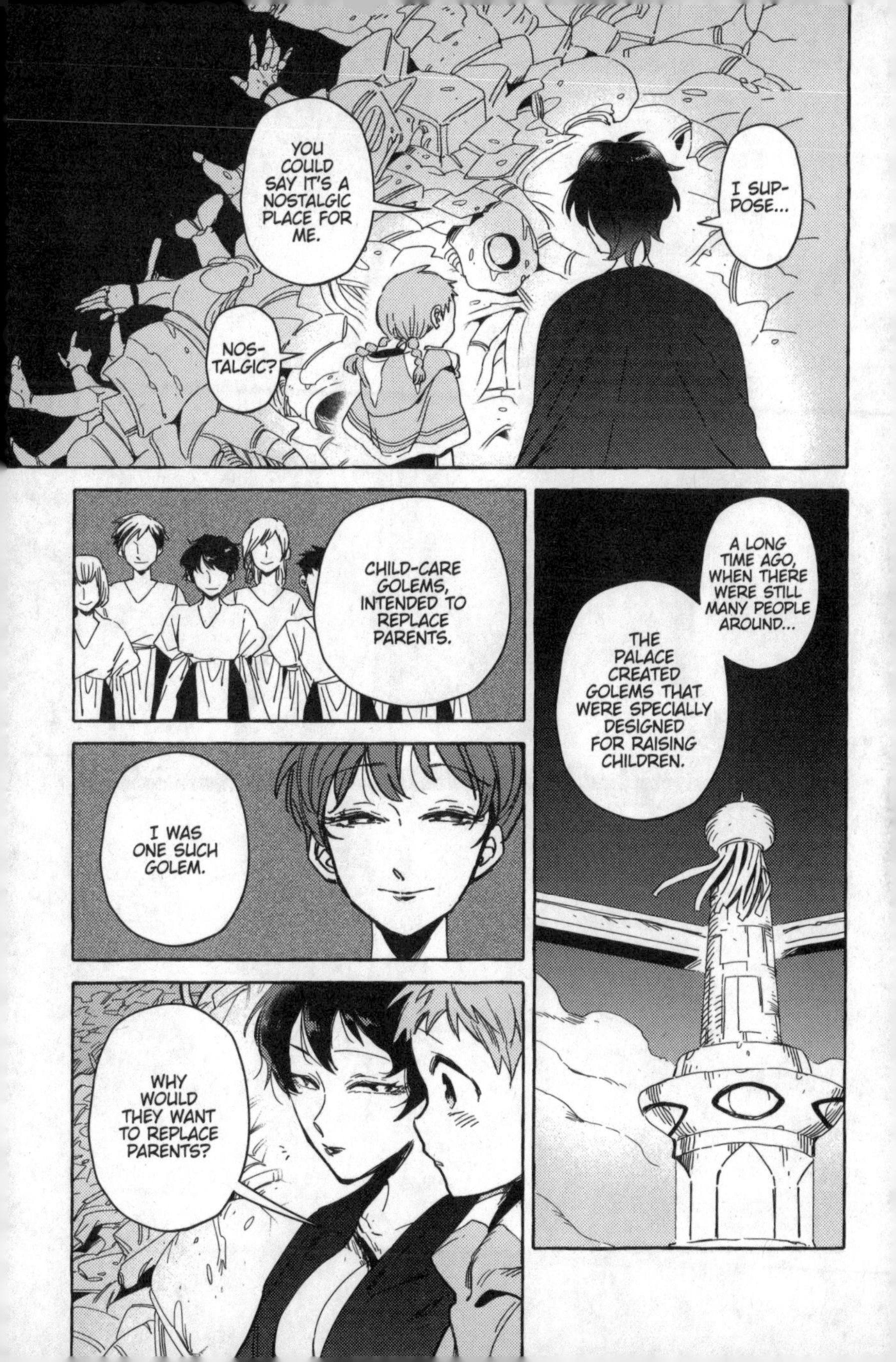
I SUP-POSE...
YOU COULD SAY IT'S A NOSTALGIC PLACE FOR ME.
NOS-TALGIC?
A LONG TIME AGO, WHEN THERE WERE STILL MANY PEOPLE AROUND...
THE PALACE CREATED GOLEMS THAT WERE SPECIALLY DESIGNED FOR RAISING CHILDREN.
CHILD-CARE GOLEMS, INTENDED TO REPLACE PARENTS.
I WAS ONE SUCH GOLEM.
WHY WOULD THEY WANT TO REPLACE PARENTS?

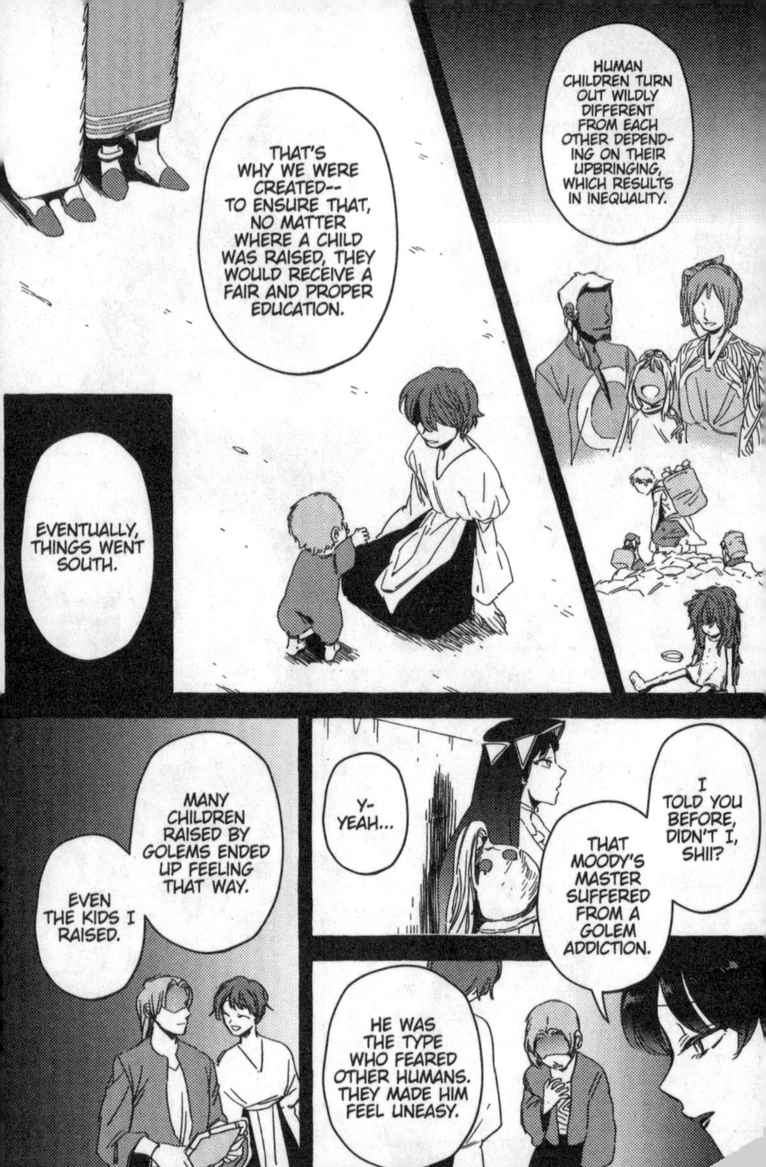
HUMAN CHILDREN TURN OUT WILDLY DIFFERENT FROM EACH OTHER DEPENDING ON THEIR UPBRINGING, WHICH RESULTS IN INEQUALITY.
THAT'S WHY WE WERE CREATED-- TO ENSURE THAT, NO MATTER WHERE A CHILD WAS RAISED, THEY WOULD RECEIVE A FAIR AND PROPER EDUCATION.
EVENTUALLY, THINGS WENT SOUTH.
I TOLD YOU BEFORE, DIDN'T I, SHII?
THAT MOODY'S MASTER SUFFERED FROM A GOLEM ADDICTION.
Y-YEAH...
HE WAS THE TYPE WHO FEARED OTHER HUMANS. THEY MADE HIM FEEL UNEASY.
MANY CHILDREN RAISED BY GOLEMS ENDED UP FEELING THAT WAY.
EVEN THE KIDS I RAISED.

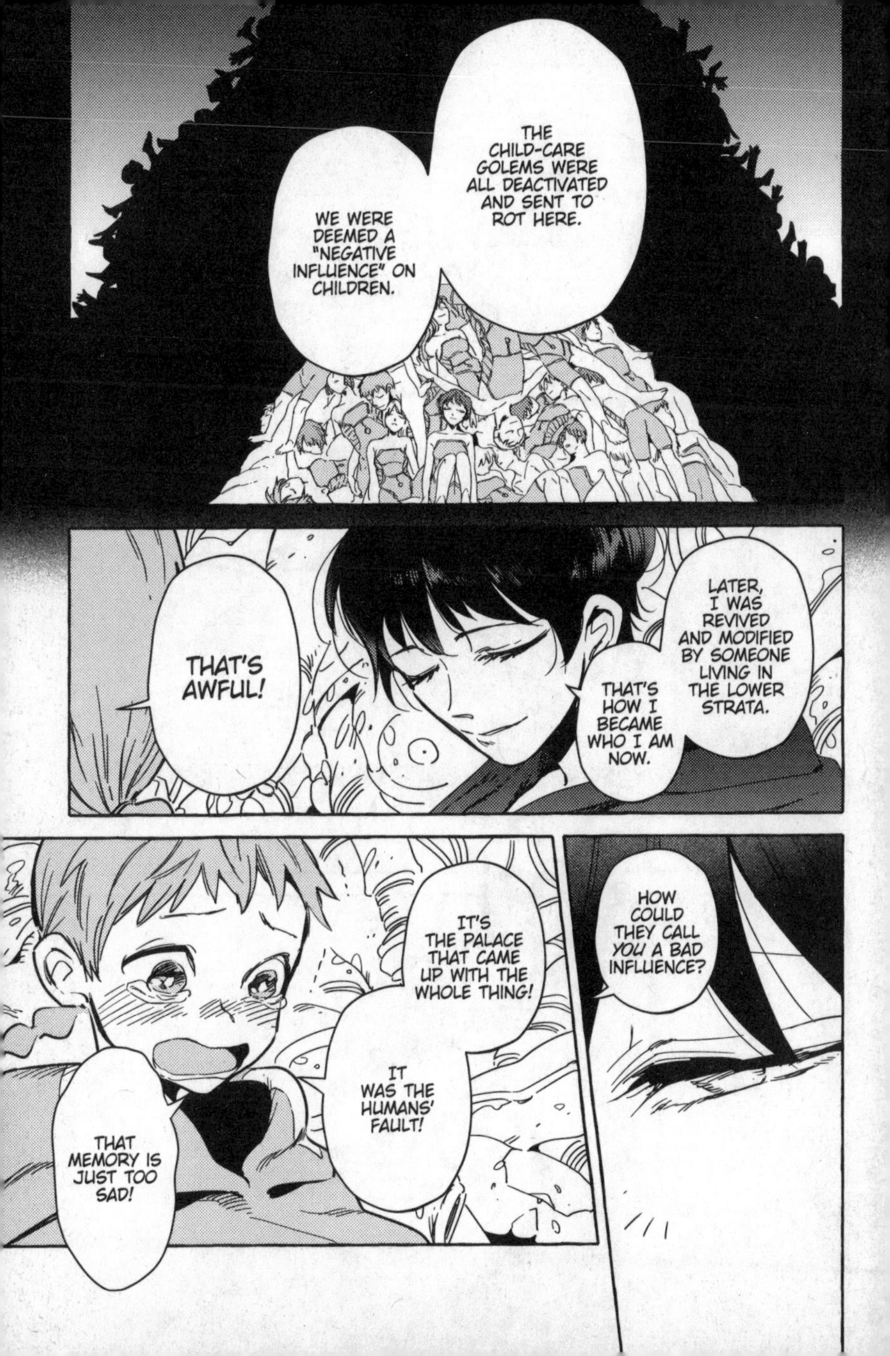
THE CHILD-CARE GOLEMS WERE ALL DEACTIVATED AND SENT TO ROT HERE.
WE WERE DEEMED A "NEGATIVE INFLUENCE" ON CHILDREN.
LATER, I WAS REVIVED AND MODIFIED BY SOMEONE LIVING IN THE LOWER STRATA.
THAT'S HOW I BECAME WHO I AM NOW.
THAT'S AWFUL!
HOW COULD THEY CALL *YOU* A BAD INFLUENCE?
IT'S THE PALACE THAT CAME UP WITH THE WHOLE THING!
IT WAS THE HUMANS' FAULT!
THAT MEMORY IS JUST TOO SAD!

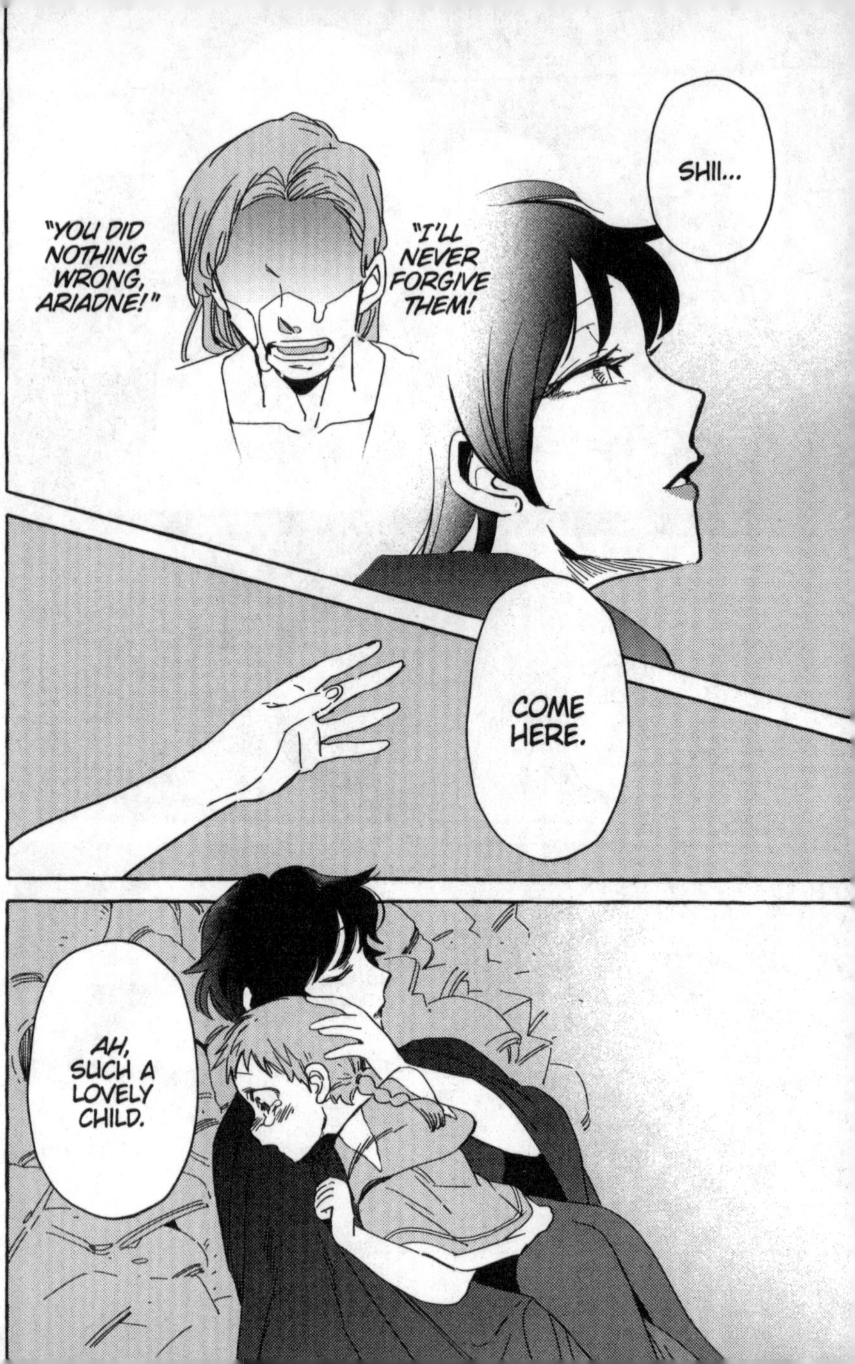
SHII...
"I'LL NEVER FORGIVE THEM!
"YOU DID NOTHING WRONG, ARIADNE!"
COME HERE.
AH, SUCH A LOVELY CHILD.

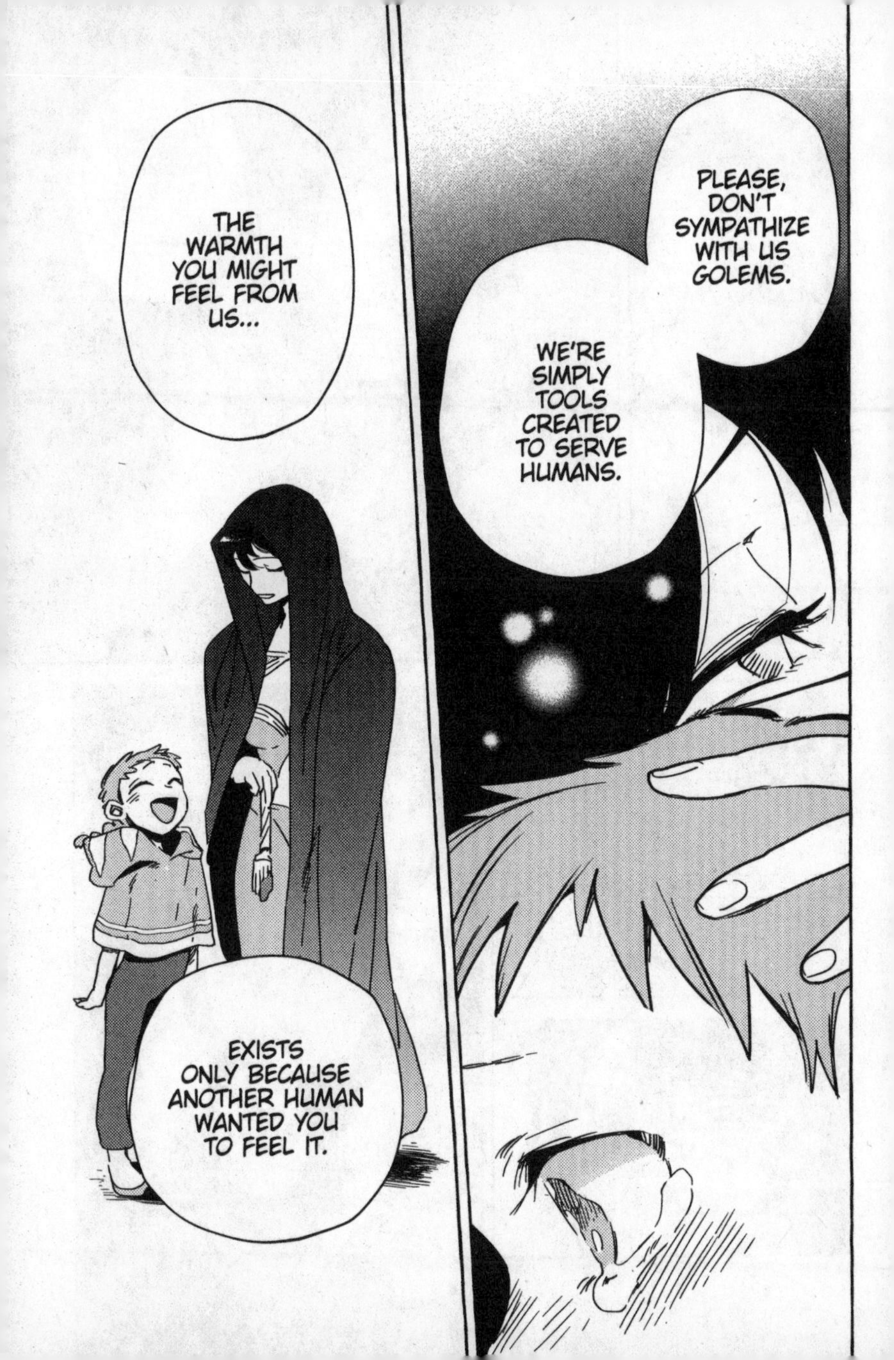
PLEASE, DON'T SYMPATHIZE WITH US GOLEMS.
WE'RE SIMPLY TOOLS CREATED TO SERVE HUMANS.
THE WARMTH YOU MIGHT FEEL FROM US...
EXISTS ONLY BECAUSE ANOTHER HUMAN WANTED YOU TO FEEL IT.

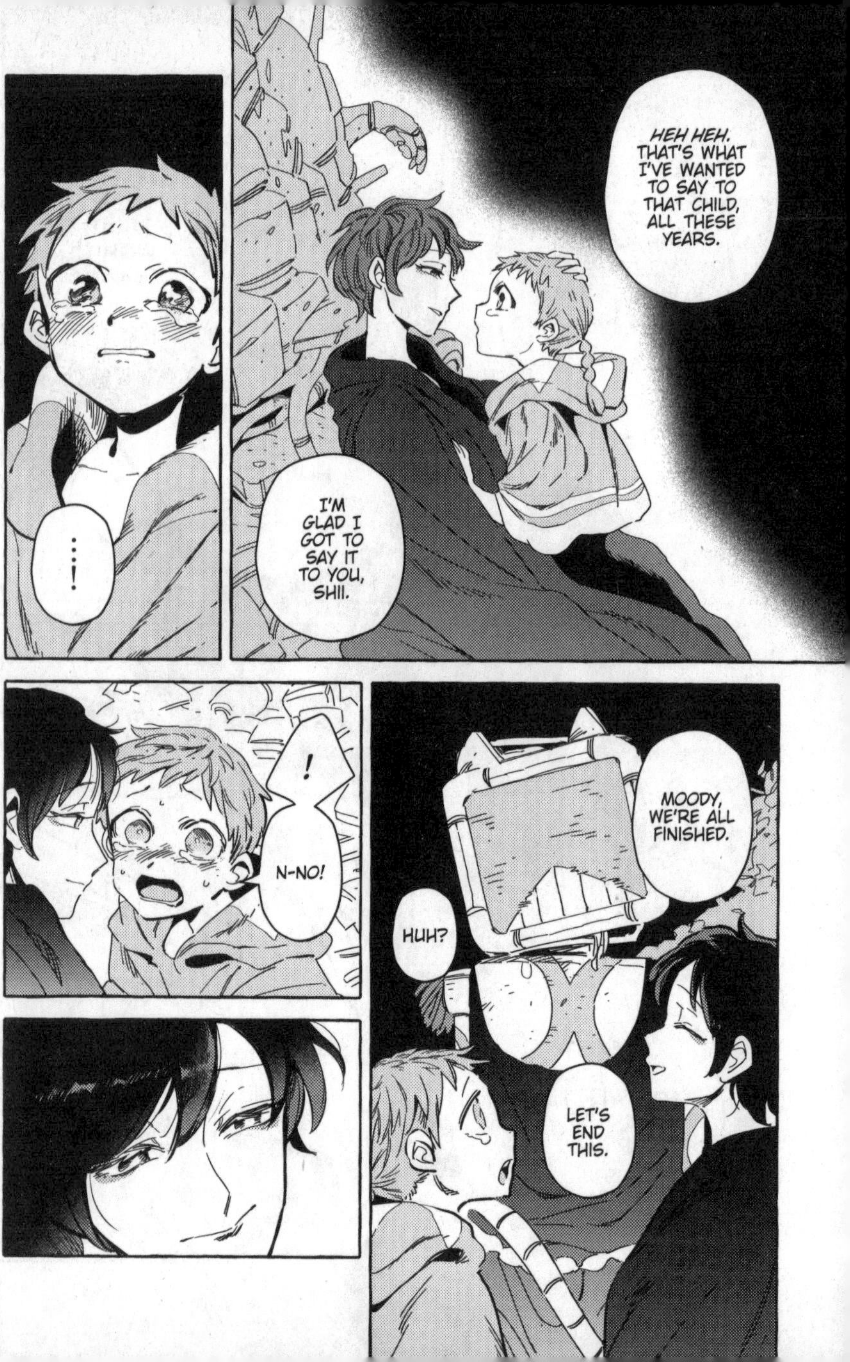
HEH HEH. THAT'S WHAT I'VE WANTED TO SAY TO THAT CHILD, ALL THESE YEARS.
I'M GLAD I GOT TO SAY IT TO YOU, SHII.
...!
MOODY, WE'RE ALL FINISHED.
HUH?
LET'S END THIS.
!
N-NO!

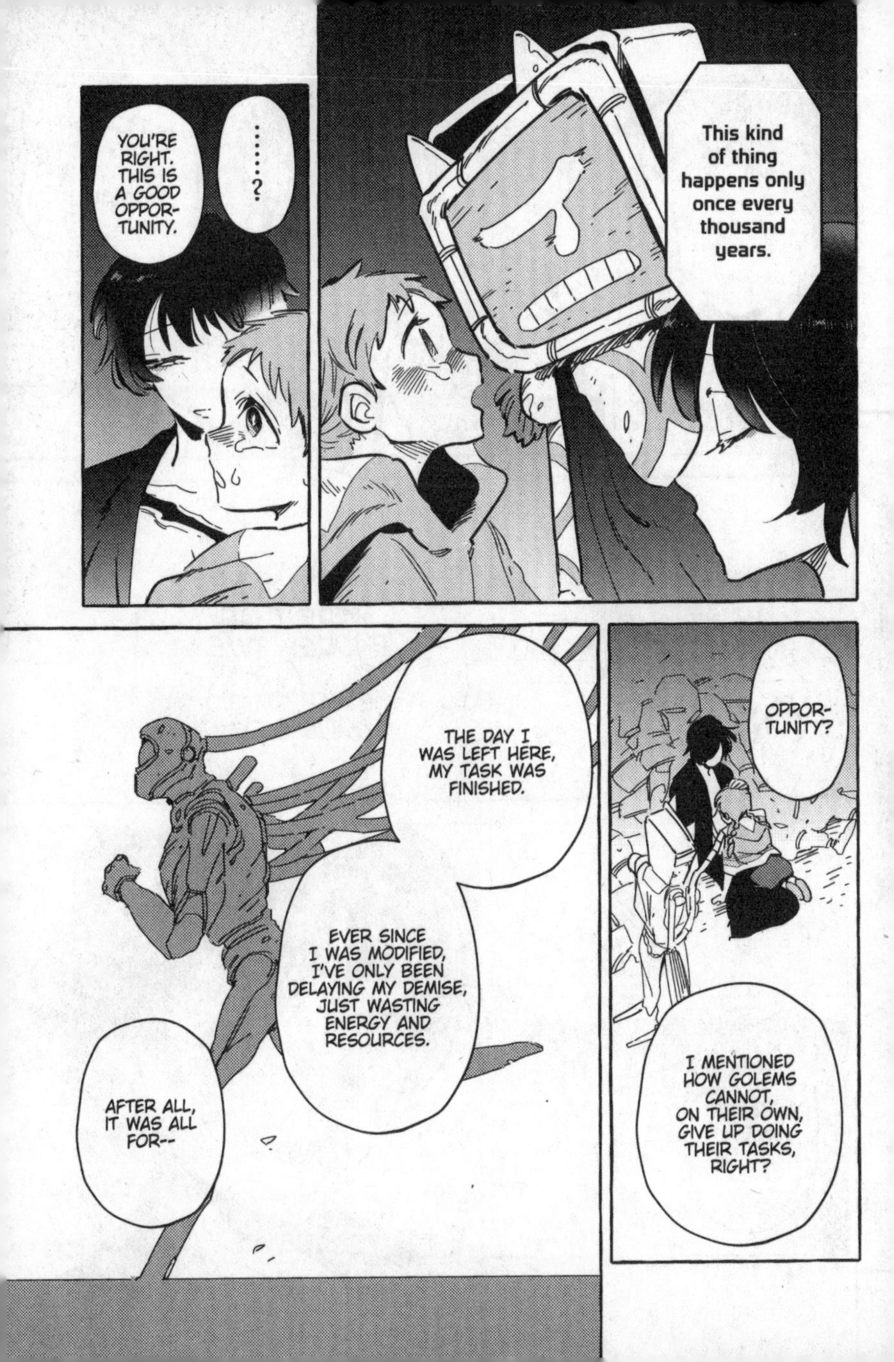
This kind of thing happens only once every thousand years.
……?
YOU'RE RIGHT. THIS IS A GOOD OPPORTUNITY.
OPPORTUNITY?
I MENTIONED HOW GOLEMS CANNOT, ON THEIR OWN, GIVE UP DOING THEIR TASKS, RIGHT?
THE DAY I WAS LEFT HERE, MY TASK WAS FINISHED.
EVER SINCE I WAS MODIFIED, I'VE ONLY BEEN DELAYING MY DEMISE, JUST WASTING ENERGY AND RESOURCES.
AFTER ALL, IT WAS ALL FOR--

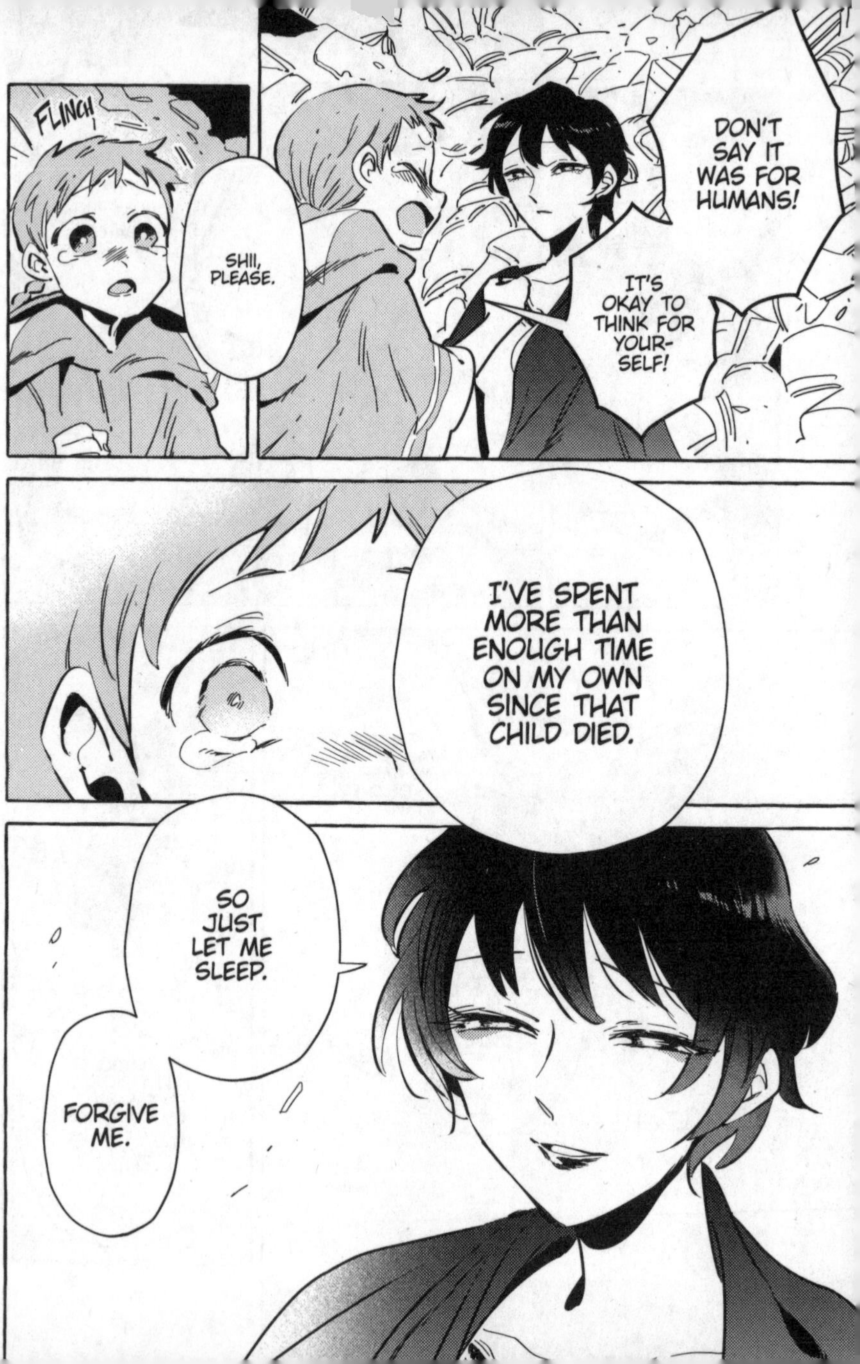
DON'T SAY IT WAS FOR HUMANS!
IT'S OKAY TO THINK FOR YOUR-SELF!
FLINCH
SHII, PLEASE.
I'VE SPENT MORE THAN ENOUGH TIME ON MY OWN SINCE THAT CHILD DIED.
SO JUST LET ME SLEEP.
FORGIVE ME.

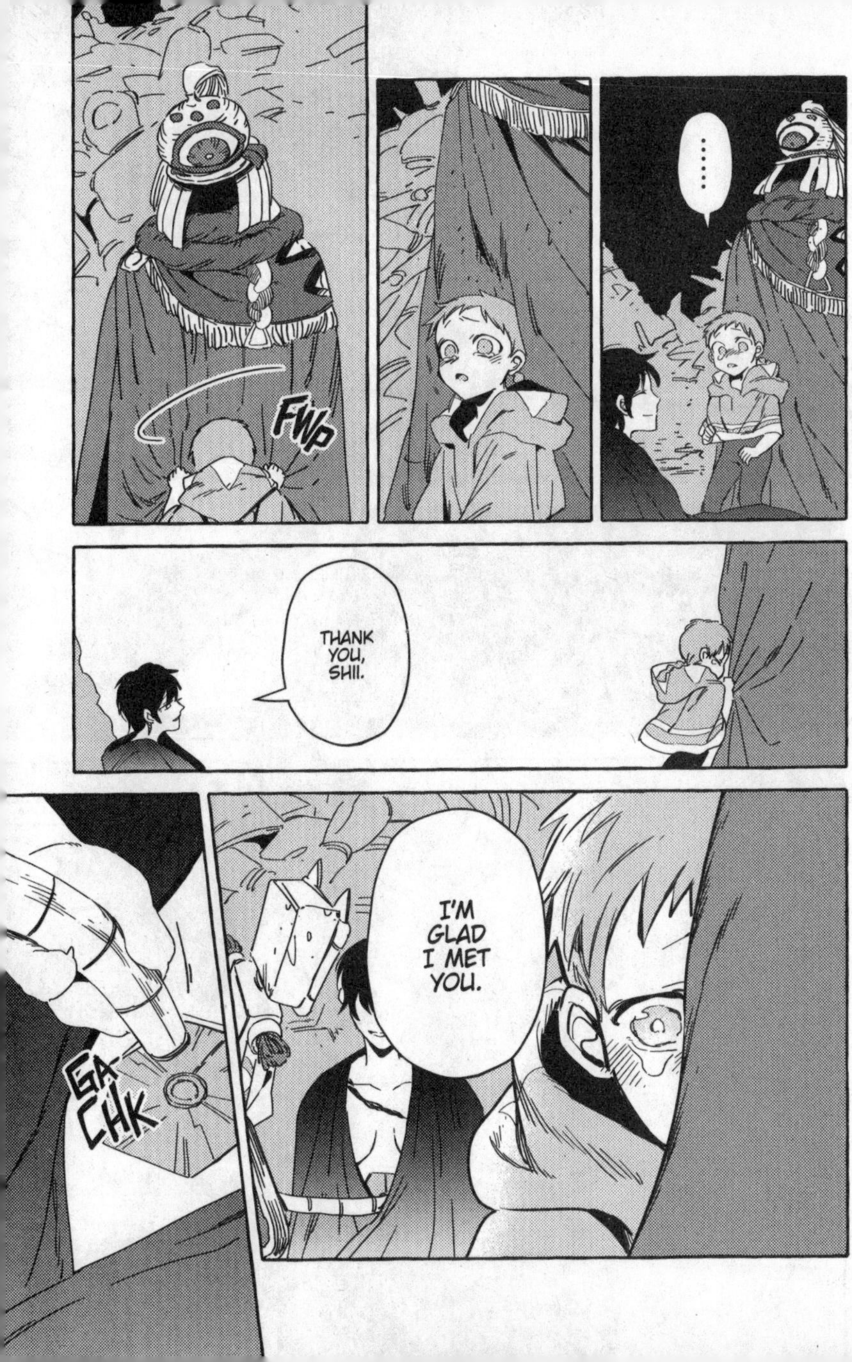
……
FWP
THANK YOU, SHII.
I'M GLAD I MET YOU.
GACHK

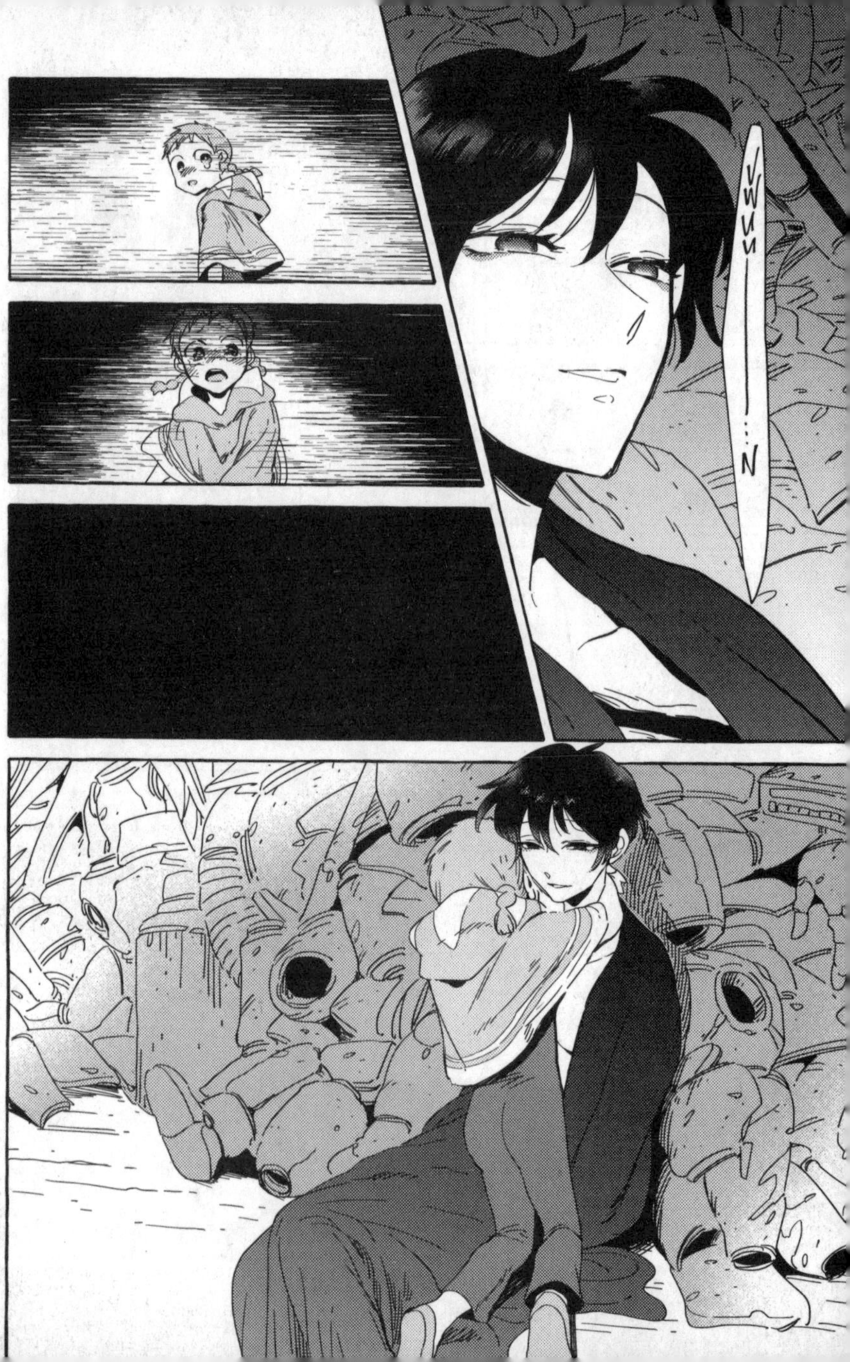
VWUU——...N

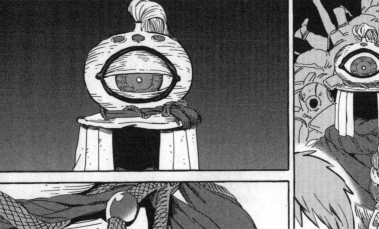

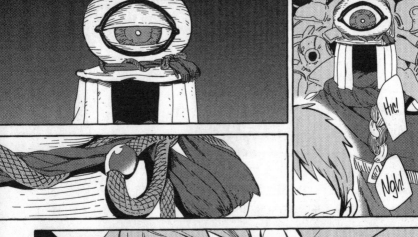

Hic!
Ngh!
Nice to meet you.
WAUGH!
I'm Ariadne, a child-care golem.
WAUGH!

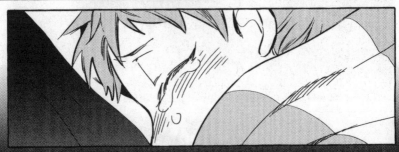

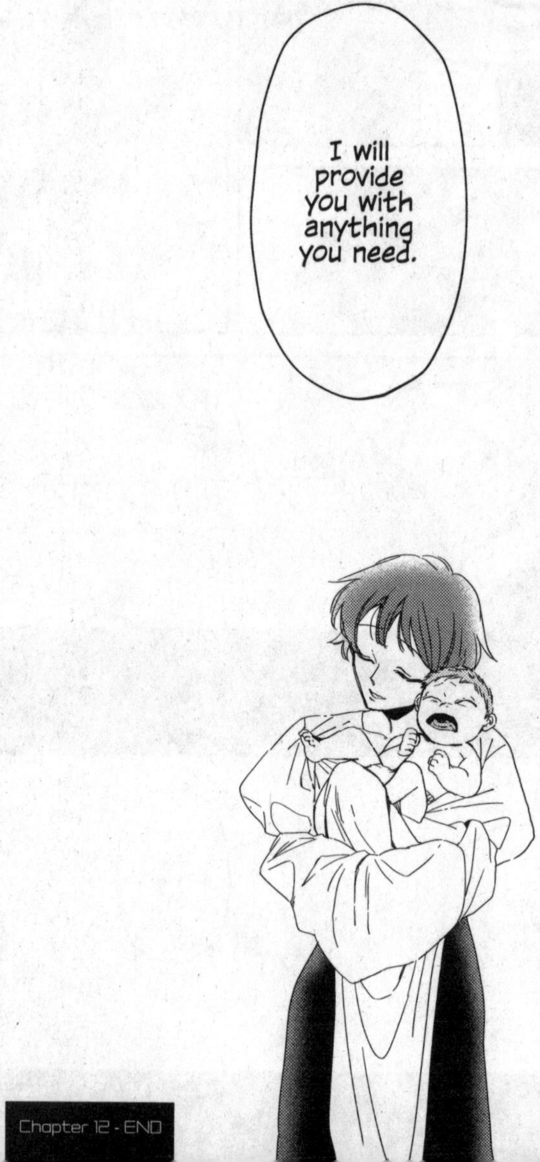
I will provide you with anything you need.
Chapter 12 - END

Shii meets her mother in a place that brings back memories.

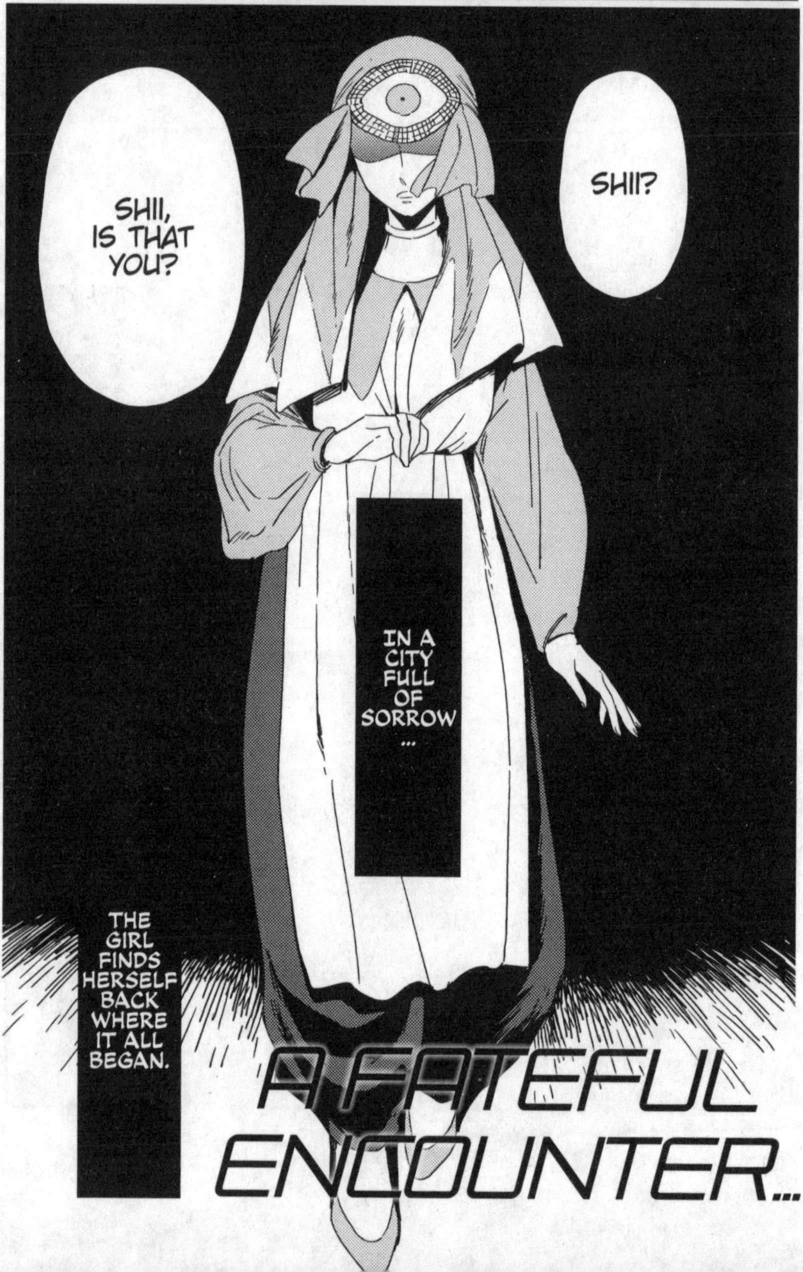

SHII?
SHII, IS THAT YOU?
IN A CITY FULL OF SORROW ...
THE GIRL FINDS HERSELF BACK WHERE IT ALL BEGAN.
A FATEFUL ENCOUNTER...